Y0-EPO-759

SPIRALS

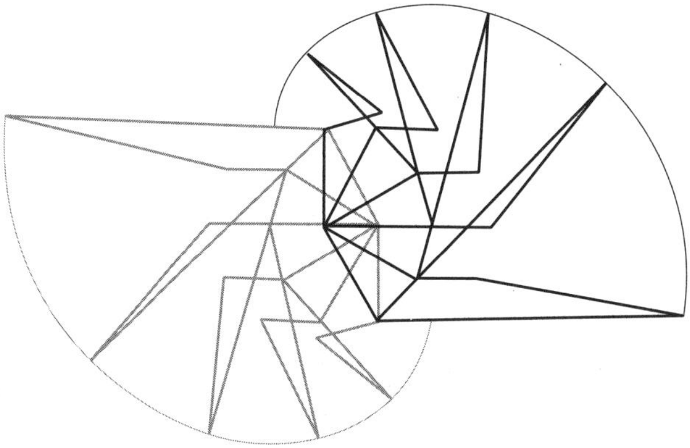

MODERNIST LATITUDES

MODERNIST LATITUDES

JESSICA BERMAN AND PAUL SAINT-AMOUR, EDITORS

Modernist Latitudes aims to capture the energy and ferment of modernist studies by continuing to open up the range of forms, locations, temporalities, and theoretical approaches encompassed by the field. The series celebrates the growing latitude ("scope for freedom of action or thought") that this broadening affords scholars of modernism, whether they are investigating little-known works or revisiting canonical ones. Modernist Latitudes will pay particular attention to the texts and contexts of those latitudes (Africa, Latin America, Australia, Asia, Southern Europe, and even the rural United States) that have long been misrecognized as ancillary to the canonical modernisms of the global North.

Barry McCrea, *In the Company of Strangers: Family and Narrative in Dickens, Conan Doyle, Joyce, and Proust*, 2011

Jessica Berman, *Modernist Commitments: Ethics, Politics, and Transnational Modernism*, 2011

Jennifer Scappettone, *Killing the Moonlight: Modernism in Venice*, 2014

NICO ISRAEL

SPIRALS

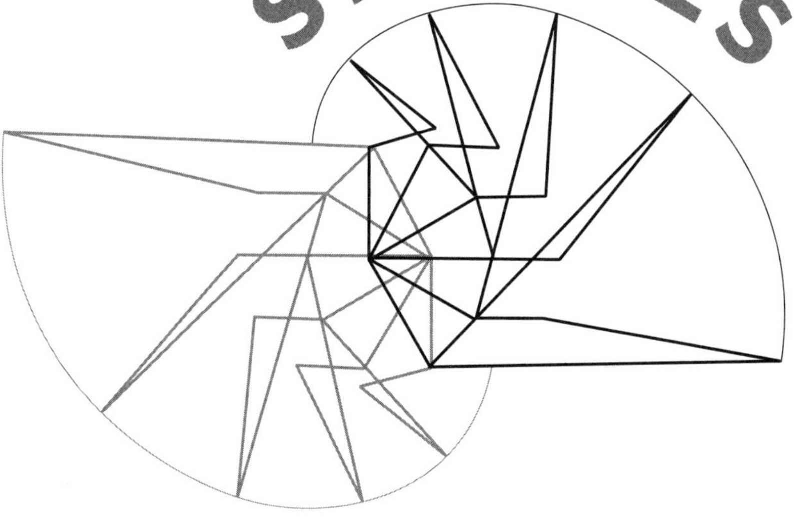

THE WHIRLED IMAGE IN TWENTIETH-CENTURY LITERATURE AND ART

COLUMBIA UNIVERSITY PRESS NEW YORK

Columbia University Press
Publishers Since 1893
New York   Chichester, West Sussex
cup.columbia.edu

Copyright © 2015 Columbia University Press
Paperback edition, 2018
All rights reserved

Library of Congress Cataloging-in-Publication Data
Israel, Nico.
Spirals : the whirled image in twentieth-century literature and art / Nico Israel.
pages cm. — (Modernist latitudes)
Includes bibliographical references and index.
ISBN 978-0-231-15302-7 (cloth : acid-free paper)
ISBN 978-0-231-15303-4 (pbk. : acid-free paper)
ISBN 978-0-231-52668-5 (e-book)
1. Literature, Modern—20th century—History and criticism—Theory, etc. 2. Modernism (Literature) 3. Spirals—symbolic aspects. 4. Spirals in art. I. Title.
PN56.M54187 2015
809'.9112—dc23

2014028478

Columbia University Press books are printed on permanent and durable acid-free paper.
Printed in the United States of America

COVER IMAGE: © Waldemar Cordeiro, *Idéia visível* (*Visible Idea*), 1956, acrylic on plywood.
COVER AND BOOK DESIGN: Lisa Hamm

FOR ESME AND ROMAN

Ihm ist, als ob es tausend Stäbe gäbe
und hinter tausend Stäben keine Welt. . . .

. . . Dann geht ein Bild hinein,
geht durch der Glieder angespannte Stille
und hört im Herzen auf zu sein.

RAINER MARIE RILKE, "DER PANTHER"

CONTENTS

ILLUSTRATIONS

FIGURES

PLATES

SPIRALS

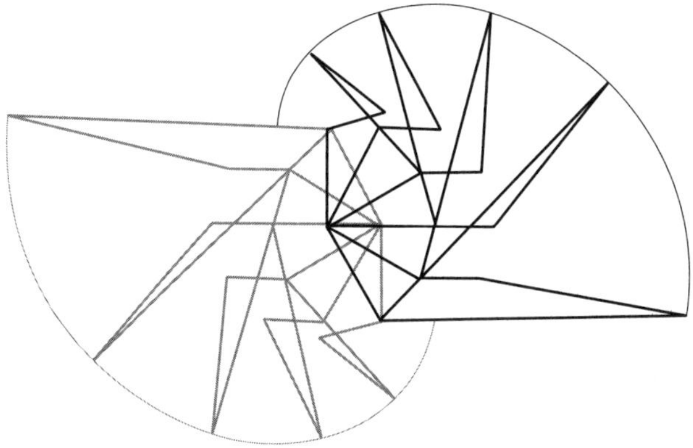

INTRODUCTION

ON SPIRALS

History decays into images, not into stories.

• WALTER BENJAMIN, *THE ARCADES PROJECT*

THE SPIRAL AS IMAGE

Spirals have a curious centrality in some of the best-known and most significant twentieth-century literature and visual art. Consider the writings of W. B. Yeats, whose *Vision* was entranced by a system of widening and narrowing gyres; Ezra Pound and T. S. Eliot, whose poetry traced Dantesque helical journeys into and out of the modern urban inferno; and James Joyce, whose *Ulysses* navigated between the Scylla of Aristotelianism and the Charybdis of Platonism, ultimately casting both into the *Wake* of a thunderous Viconian "gyrotundo." Or think, later in the century, of Samuel Beckett's obsessive circuitry and abortive spiral journeys or of W. G. Sebald, for whom spiral rings signaled the vertiginous emanations of historical trauma. In the field of visual art, picture the work of Italian Futurist Umberto Boccioni, who combined an attraction to speed with a passionate interest in the fourth dimension expressed as bodies in spiraling motion; the Russian Constructivist Vladimir Tatlin, whose proposal for a spiral monument to the Third International that would outstrip the Eiffel Tower sought to give futurist bravado a rational, leftward spin; and the Franco-American proto-conceptualist Marcel Duchamp, whose *Rotoreliefs* and *Anémic Cinéma* added a Surrealist idiom of eroticism to a Dadaist attack on the predominance of the optical sense. Or, in postwar art, recall the work of American earthworks creator and filmmaker Robert Smithson, whose *Spiral Jetty* collided prehistoric past with space-age future, or of South African artist William Kentridge, for whom spiral centers and edges express the inaccessible limits of reconciliation and truth.

Beyond the striking fact that these writers and visual artists draw heavily on spiral forms, what links their diverse projects to one another? Without denying the discursive, generic, and institutional differences between literary and art history, and without arguing, *Laocoön* (or "Newer Laocoön")-like, for the superiority of one medium over the other, how might we see the spiral as a figure that is common to both fields? What might spirals reveal regarding the shifting assumptions about temporality and spatiality, aesthetics and politics in the twentieth century? How do spirals themselves illuminate processes of reading, of interpretation?

Although the path to be followed in answering these questions is necessarily circuitous, the argument of this book can be stated straightforwardly: spirals are a crucial means through which twentieth-century writers and visual artists think about the twentieth century. Approached as *images* in the sense Walter Benjamin gives the term, spirals in literature and art illuminate how conceptions of modernity, history, and geopolitics are mutually involved. Embodying tensions between teleology and cyclicality, repetition and difference, locality and globality, spirals challenge familiar modes of organizing disciplines of study. Spirals not only complicate literary and art history's familiar spatiotemporal coordinates (including those based on nation and period), but also offer a way of reconceiving the "distribution of the sensible" across that century.[1] Put simply, viewed in terms of the spiral, twentieth-century literary and art history—and, indeed, history itself—appear otherwise, are given a different spin.

"Image" is a crucial term in this study. In the *Passagen-Werk*, his unfinished project on the Paris arcades built in the early nineteenth century, Benjamin takes several stabs at defining *Bild*, which he sometimes also refers to as *dialektisches Bild* (dialectical image) or *Denkbild* (thought image). In the set of notes that Benjamin assigned the rubric "Convolute N"—which his editors have subtitled "On the Theory of Knowledge, Theory of Progress"—Benjamin discusses how this conception of "image" can help redefine the relation between the past and the present, terms he prefers to call "what-has-been" (*das Gewesene*) and "now" (*das Jetzt*). "It is not," writes Benjamin, "that what is past casts its light on what is present, or what is present its light on what is past; rather image is that wherein what-has-been comes together in a lightning-flash [*Blitzhaft*] with the now to form a constellation." "In other words," Benjamin continues, "image is dialectics at a standstill. For while the relation of the present to the past is a purely temporal, continuous one, the relation of what-has-been to the now is dialectical: is not progression but image, suddenly emergent [ist nicht Verlauf, sondern Bild, sprunghaft]."[2] It is as "image" in this suddenly springing and flashing sense that I propose to read spirals in twentieth-century literature and art.

In the context of this seminal passage, Benjamin is explicitly elucidating the "constellation" produced by his own earlier and then-current work. Using another photographic metaphor, Benjamin asserts, just a few notes before the preceding excerpt, that "the book on the Baroque"—that is, Benjamin's own study of the German mourning play—"exposed the seventeenth century to the light of the present day. Here," in his then-in-progress book on the arcades, "something analogous must be done for the nineteenth century, but with greater distinctness" (or "with more meaning"; the phrase in the original is *deutlicher*).[3] In both cases, "image" is what results from this projected exposure of "what-has-been" to the "now," an exposure that reconfigures and revises the relation between the two "purely temporal" markers or designations by "giving dates," as Benjamin declares elsewhere in this convolute, "their physiognomy."[4]

While I have little hope of achieving Benjamin's physiognomic distinctness, my ambition in this book is to provide "something analogous" for the twentieth century in the twenty-first—for it is in the twenty-first century that the image of the twentieth-century spiral has, in Benjamin's terms, "attained legibility."[5]

To be sure, I recognize the pitfalls of launching a century-long study, a duration that runs counter to the current penchant for a narrower, more archival brand of historicism predominant in modernist studies in literature, where books focusing on, say, fifteen- or twenty-year chronological slices are now the norm, or to the still-prevalent tendency in early-twenty-first-century art history to concentrate monographically on individual artists or on chronologically circumscribed movements.

And yet, despite the formidable challenge of addressing the now-eclipsed century as a whole—a whole that is not one, but is an amalgam of discrete flashing "images"—the battle over the legacy of that century is of significant political import. In *Le siècle*, French philosopher Alain Badiou asserts the necessity of accounting for the entire hundred years of the twentieth century, and focuses on what he calls "the intimate link that bound art and politics" across that century.[6] For Badiou, what persists in twentieth-century "art"—the kind of literature and visual art that, in Badiou's terms, "thought . . . uninherited, unthinkable thoughts"—is the rhetoric of newness that illustrates, allows for, or hortatorily invokes what Badiou calls "cognitive ruptures," or more simply, the "fidelity to an event."[7] While my elective affinity is decidedly for Benjamin's more nuanced, melancholic, and indeed infidel readings of "image" over Badiou's enthusiastic, more doctrinaire demands for "fidelity," the argument in this book harmonizes with Badiou's claims that, in the twentieth century, literature and art are profoundly connected to political change, and moreover that the century must be approached with a recognition of its endpoint or result—that is, thoroughgoing, though still incomplete, economic and cultural globalization. I contend that spirals in twentieth-century literature and art provide a new way of engaging the histories of our current global modernity—a currency that is itself untimely, unfashionable.

This way is forged by Benjamin in the passage from Convolute N cited earlier, so far ending in "emergent." (It is here that the by-now-familiar critical invocation of the "dialectical image" becomes decidedly less so.) After deploying a connective em-dash, Benjamin concludes the passage by noting that "only dialectical images are genuine (that is, not archaic) images [*echte Bilder*]; and the place [*der Ort*] where one encounters them is language [*die Sprache*]. *Awakening* [*Erwachen*]."[8]

The first half of the conclusion to the passage from this convolute—a rubric that itself nicely evokes a coiling—has been cited often enough. What Benjamin means by "dialectical" (and thus "genuine" or "pure" and not "archaic") has, not surprisingly, led to entirely opposed positions, some (such as that of Susan Buck-Morss) emphasizing Benjamin's connections to European Marxism and others (such as that of Anselm Haverkamp) laying claim to Benjamin's proto-deconstructive impulses, impulses that uproot the very grounds of dialectical thinking.[9] Haverkamp's argument is bolstered by Benjamin's concluding claim here that "the place where one encounters" dialectical images is "language."

But where is this "place"? Is *die Sprache*—language already inherently connected to speech—localizable to writing (or the reading of writing)? Should visual phenomena (including art) be considered in this sense *linguistic*? Benjamin's own elegant readings of visual phenomena, both artistic (by Albrecht Dürer and Paul Klee) and material (shop windows, coffee grounds, a quickly passing black dress), suggest that there is more to "image" than meets the eye.[10] Suffice it to say that my assumption or presumption in the chapters that follow is that the "place [of] language"—the place, perhaps, of "*Awakening*" (or at the very least of language, awakening)[11]—describes neither solely statement nor picture but a terrain between stating and picturing that incorporates both acts. Seen from this vantage, the profanely illuminating image of the spiral, which in the literary and artistic texts to be explored herein often shuttles between the visual and the verbal realms or occupies both simultaneously or in counterpoint, offers an opportunity to reflect, again, on the relationship between what is called "writing" and the kinds of shaping or spacing one finds in visual art.[12] This reflection, which is also necessarily an account of a dialectics that embraces both cursivity and recursivity, need not invest solely in either the "linguistic turn" or the "pictorial turn"; it endorses neither the "formalist turn" (which is, in many ways, a return) nor the torsions of depth-seeking ideological analysis as critiqued in the recent advocacy of "surface" or "distant" reading. In fact, as we shall see, the spiral, in its very nature, evades these culs-de-sac by allegorizing and enacting the relation between depth and surface, closeness and distance, turning and being at a standstill.[13]

METAMORPHOSIS/ES

My interest in spirals was sparked over a dozen years ago during a cross-country road trip from New York City to Rozel Point, at the northern end of the Great Salt Lake in Utah, where a friend and I visited Smithson's earthwork *Spiral Jetty*, which at the time (summer of 2001) was underwater.[14] When we arrived at the jetty site, we saw plenty of evidence of what Smithson, in his essay that accompanied the film version of the earthwork, had called "man-made systems mired in abandoned hopes,"[15] including a dilapidated pier stretching from the shore of the salt lake to some sulfurous oil seeps within the lake, a sort of road created in order to facilitate that oil's extraction.[16] In a delusion possibly brought about by a peculiar combination of the sun, the open sky, our solitude, and our extreme enthusiasm, my friend and I half-convinced ourselves that this road was the miraculously reemerged spiral jetty itself.[17]

Upon returning to New York and reading more about Smithson's project, I would learn that as part of his research for the *Spiral Jetty* film, Smithson had handwritten, under the title "A Metamorphoses [*sic*] of Spirals," a series of quotations of short passages from some twenty-one texts, thereby offering a miniature version of Benjamin's *The Arcades Project* (a book of which Smithson was unaware, but whose strategies of quotation and montage he certainly employed).[18] Where one might have expected to see excerpts from or about such visual artists as Boccioni, Duchamp, Eva Hesse, and Bruce Nauman, each of whom had created and/or written about spirals in a way that clearly influenced Smithson's, one finds instead passages from, or concerning, Yeats, Joyce, Beckett, and Nabokov. Without directly declaring that he was doing so, Smithson, in his notes, which present these figures largely in chronological order from the 1890s to the then-present (1970), traced a metamorphosis (or some metamorphoses) of the spiral from what has come to be called early modernism, through high and late modernism, to the "postmodern turn" associated with such figures as Smithson himself.

In associating spirals with metamorphosis, Smithson was drawing on the figure's long-asserted affiliation with ideas, drawn from nature, about growth and gradual change. As we will explore in chapter 1, throughout their history (which predates ancient Greece and arguably reaches its apogee in European Romanticism, but certainly continued into the twentieth century) spirals have tended to be viewed as emblematic of the organic principle par excellence, an organicism that has frequently lent itself to progressive models of history. And yet, as Smithson himself surely recognized, many of the twentieth-century writers he was quoting firmly opposed an organic or a progressive view of spirals or of history, instead advocating what Smithson himself would call a "dialectical" one, in which spirals often serve as a sort of meta-commentary on the nature of dialectical thinking itself. Indeed, the countermovement contained within the spiral, to which Smithson was so attentive, operates against a progressive view and the anthropomorphic idea of growth that follows from it. (The *Spiral Jetty* film, preoccupied as it is with geologic prehistory and sci-fi futurity, both of which complicate what Smithson called "man-centered" historicism, made this historical perspective crystal clear decades before current discussions about the "anthropocene" emerged.)[19]

There is a comparable tension in this book between *image* and *metamorphosis*. The nature of writing a study of twentieth-century literature and art requires to a certain extent that one tell a "story" about their metamorphosis over that century. After all, presenting a set of spirals largely chronologically invites comparison of later spirals with earlier spirals. Accordingly, I will show that in the early-twentieth-century work of the Italian Futurists, British Vorticists, and Russian Constructivists, the spiral was often associated with modernity, energy, and spatiotemporal expansion, whereas with Joyce and Duchamp spirals began to serve as a sign for an energy-sapping anemia that challenged those early-century associations, and in the later-century work of Beckett and Smithson spirals expressed a recoiling entropy that calls into question the very foundation of the project of modernity and the colonial-imperial project and man-centered histories it subtended. And yet, as the epigraph to this chapter indicates, to do justice to what Benjamin calls *Geschichte* requires viewing those spirals not primarily as telling *stories*, but as *images*, into which history decays or disintegrates (*zerfällt*). Consequently, rather than imagining that through an analysis of these multiple spirals a single, grand meta-spiral can be seen to unfold continuously over time (in the mode of Panofsky-like symbolic form), I encourage the reader to approach this book as a series of snapshots of spirals, each involving or producing the kind of *flash* proposed by Benjamin. To help create the friction required for these images to constellate—to pop out of the implied photo album in the way memories erupt involuntarily—in my central chapters I explore not a single spiral but two, one from a visual-art project and one from a literary text: Yeats and Tatlin, Duchamp and Joyce, Beckett and Smithson. (I explain the rationale for my method more fully later in this introduction and in chapter 1.)

THE INTERVENTION OF SPIRALS

Conceived as image in tension with metamorphosis, spirals in twentieth-century literature and art provide a justification not only for exploring the nature of aesthetic, political, and historical change across the twentieth century, but also for raising, again, the question of the interpretation of interpretation or, at least, for giving it a different twist—a twist that swerves around the closed parameters of the hermeneutic circle.[20] In particular, this book seeks to intervene in the trajectory of literary and visual-art studies by bringing together insights from the new modernist studies (still primarily dominated by literary scholars), the Continental philosophical speculations of comparative literature, and the theoretically inclined art history of the *October* school—three approaches that, although by no means mutually exclusive, have tended to withdraw into separate domains.

Over the past dozen or so years, advocates of the new modernist studies have offered innovative ways of conceiving the connection between twentieth-century literature and ideas of cultural globalization. In her influential book *Cosmopolitan Style*, for example, Rebecca Walkowitz asserts the primacy of what she (drawing on Theodor Adorno) calls "style" as a way of "thinking and feeling beyond the nation."[21] Walkowitz seeks to establish formally experimental twentieth-century English-language narrative as a kind of "critical cosmopolitanism" in which writers at the beginning and end of the century call into question political and ethical norms and rethink the nature of inter- or transnational filiations. Meanwhile, other leading scholars of cosmopolitanism and transnationality in British modernist literature, such as Jessica Berman, Jed Esty, and Laura Doyle, have demonstrated how the geopolitical imaginaries of (the British) Empire's expansions and contractions assert themselves, particularly in the novel.[22]

Accordingly, my contention here is that spiral images are a significant way in which writers and artists across the twentieth century engaged the conceptual space of a world or globe, while also offering a novel mode of interpreting that conceptual space. In the examples explored in this book, spirals in literature and visual art both register and resist ideas about the transnational and the global. Indeed, the centrifugal and centripetal torsions of the spiral I chart over the course of the twentieth century demonstrate transforming conceptions of locality (including both the idea of nationhood and the locality of the body, of *embodiment*) and globality (the extranational political and economic sphere) and the relation between them. In this sense, spirals serve as a way of picturing what sociologist Bruno Latour, in *Reassembling the Social*, calls "connecting sites" linking the local and the global—but the connection reveals itself in sinuous ways, as we shall explore.

In keeping with Walkowitz's emphasis on "feeling beyond the nation" and Bruce Robbins's on "feeling global," it is imperative, when reflecting on the locality as well as the globality of spirals, to recognize their affective dimensions. Consider the fairly recent expressions "spiraling out of control" and "downward spiral," or the still more recent "death spiral," terms encountered daily in the mass media, in relation, for example, to the state of the global economy or a specific aspect of it (stock or mortgage values), or the fortunes of a military or political campaign, or a precipitous mental decline.[23] The feelings frequently associated with the spiral—flying, falling, drowning, or being smothered—are the anxieties of limit, beyond which an entity cannot go. It is precisely these kinds of psychical and perceptual limits that the writers and visual artists whose work I examine seek to reveal and, in some cases, embody.

This embodiment typically involves an amplification of the erotic associations of the spiral, an eroticism that sometimes reiterates but often refuses binary models of gender and desire. In the pages that follow, spirals serve as signs not only of serpentine phallus and potentially penetrable vulva, but also of breasts and anuses, clitorises and ears. The "drives" toward and away from these bodily destinations are rarely reducible to the sensations of private subjects; indeed, they almost always, in the texts explored here, involve consequences for political space. To take one salient example among many, the Italian Futurists, who lauded fast cars with snake-like hoods, fetishized spirals as a way to express the "pure plastic rhythm" of objects whose very nature, the Futurists asserted, was to extend beyond themselves. This outward-bound dynamism applied to the Italian nation itself, which the Futurists sought to prod toward territorial expansion eastward into the Austro-Hungarian Empire and southward into parts of North Africa.

While my project thus embraces the thrust of recent geopolitical critique and affect studies, it seeks to move beyond some of the still-predominant generic, linguistic, and geographic circumscriptions of the new modernist studies by addressing not only novels and poems written in languages other than English, but also theater, painting, sculpture, architecture, and earth and conceptual art across the century.[24]

The analysis of texts produced in different languages and in different national contexts has traditionally been the domain of comparative literature, which, while long grounded in post-structuralist and Continental philosophical approaches, has recently turned its attention toward performance and media studies. Exemplary work in this field has been produced by Samuel Weber, who in *Mass Mediauras* explores the implications of Benjamin's writing for understanding the phenomenon of television and the representation of war.[25] In a lesser-known work, *Targets of Opportunity*, Weber reads the figure of the target across the history of Western metaphysics (from Homer to Freud to the "events" of September 11, 2001), suggesting that targets in literature, mass media, psychoanalysis, and philosophy expose both "the militarization of thinking" and "opportunity" or openness, militarization's opposite.[26] In this Weberian spirit, the spirals under consideration in the chapters that constitute this book might helpfully be conceived as *moving* targets—targets moving across a more narrowly circumscribed field of modernity than Weber's. The idea of "moving target" conveys the dynamism with which spirals, for much of the twentieth century in literature and art, were so often associated.

Over the past decade or so in comparative literary studies, there has also been renewed interest in the idea of "world literature," a field that, according to a number of its advocates, explores works from inside and outside the Euro-American canon that "gain in translation" but, according to some of its detractors, effaces important cultural, historical, and political differences—mistranslations—between zones of production.[27] In analyzing literature and art involving spirals from a number of different national contexts over the course of the entire century, I do not proceed from the presumption that translations, including translations between literary and visual-artistic mediums, have been "successful" or that they add up to a seamless or holistic idea of World. Inspired by the puns of Duchamp and Joyce, to which I will return in chapter 4, I deploy the word "Whirled" in my book's subtitle to put pressure on this politically neutral notion of "World."

My approach to twentieth-century visual arts is indebted throughout to the groundbreaking work of those scholars associated with the journal *October*, who have transformed the field of art history (especially of twentieth- and twenty-first-century art history) by displacing the object-oriented and residually Kantian modernism of Clement Greenberg. In her late-1970s writing, for example, art historian Rosalind Krauss notes the prevalence of the *grid* in visual art beginning in the early part of the century: "Surfacing in pre-War cubist painting and subsequently becoming ever more stringent and manifest, the grid announces, among other things, modern art's will to silence, its hostility to literature, to narrative, to discourse." Krauss continues:

> In the spatial sense, the grid states the autonomy of the realm of art. Flattened, geometricized, ordered, it is antinatural, antimimetic, antireal. It is what art looks like when it turns its back to nature. In the flatness that results from its coordinates, the grid is the means of crowding out the dimensions of the real and replacing them with the lateral result not of imitation, but of aesthetic decree. Insofar as its order is that of pure relationship, the grid is a way of abrogating the claims of natural objects to have an order particular to themselves; the relationships in the aesthetic field are shown by the grid to be in a world apart and, with respect to natural objects, to be both prior and final.[28]

To be sure, spirals, mathematically considered, exist in relation to a grid, as the former can often be measured according the coordinates of the latter. And yet what is undoubtedly true of the grid according to Krauss's persuasive description (which immediately brings to mind work by artists ranging from Piet Mondrian to Agnes Martin) is just as undoubtedly untrue of the spiral, another predominant "structure" (or image) emerging in the early twentieth century and persisting throughout the century, organizing the relationship between art and itself and art and the world. The visual-art spirals I closely examine in this book (Tatlin's, Duchamp's, and Smithson's), though arguably equally "antinatural, antimimetic, [and] antireal," are anything but "flat"—indeed, both affectively and geopolitically they gesture beyond themselves, first, to a "fourth dimension" limning space and time; second, to other cultural forms (architecture, cinema, theater, and especially literature); and finally and most importantly to a "world" becoming ever more "global." In this way, the spiral offers a means of swerving around the spatiotemporal axis of the grid, and of avoiding the schematic periodicity and geopolitical positioning that might be seen as following from it.[29]

(In the conclusion, I discuss at length this grid–spiral relation, and its connection to ideas of economic, political, and cultural globalization, in literary and visual-art texts from the 1990s.)

Pursuing this notion of critical swerving as a way of summarizing my project's intervention: my aim in exploring my archive of twentieth-century spirals is to apprehend the nuances of form without succumbing to a sterile, object-bound formalism; to apprehend the torsions and tensions of history without succumbing to a progressive or schematic historicism; and to apprehend the contours of globality without succumbing to the developmental logic of globalization. To do so it must apprehend spiral apprehension itself.

LIMITED PREVIEW

I have suggested that each chapter of this book should be viewed as a sort of Benjaminian snapshot, involving, or potentially producing, a flash with the now. In order to create such a flash, in each chapter I compare at least two spirals—typically one from a visual-art object and one from a literary text (although as I have already noted, the visual-art objects often involve language and the literary texts, pictures). This method better exposes the nexus of affective, epistemological, historical, and geopolitical issues under consideration than would a set of serial monographs on single texts involving spirals, a mode of analysis that risks leaving in place the very holism that I hope to challenge.

Chapter 1 begins by noting a curious ambivalence or doubleness in the definition of the English word "spiral," a word that defines both a centripetal and a centrifugal motion and that posits a geometric center either inside or outside a structure. Drawing on the *OED*'s examples of uses of the word, I trace a brief history of the spiral back to its arrival in English from French and Italian, and from them back to the ancient Greek geometer Archimedes, through Dante, Leonardo, Athanasius Kircher, and other late medieval and early modern thinkers, and on to the mathematical speculations of Descartes and the botanical-narratological theories of Goethe. Special attention in the chapter is paid to Hegel, Marx, and Nietzsche, each of whom draws on the spiral to articulate a theory of history or of circulation. The last part of this chapter returns to Benjamin, and demonstrates how the twentieth-century philosopher encounters and departs from the speculations of the triumvirate of nineteenth-century thinkers. Specifically, I focus on three generally overlooked *Sinnbilder* (meaning-images) in Benjamin's own writing—*Strudel* (whirlpool or maelstrom), *Kugel* (the sphere or globe), and *Sturm* (storm)—and I demonstrate how each of these meaning-images involves an invitation to think spirally, precisely the approach to history and to geopolitics that I attempt to deploy in the remainder of the book.

Chapter 2 establishes the crucial connection among spirals, vanguardist anti-aesthetic practices, and early-twentieth-century geopolitics, adumbrating a mini-history of the spiral from the year "– 4 of the twentieth century"[30] through to the European artistic climate around the beginning of the Great War. I begin by briefly analyzing Alfred Jarry's play *Ubu Roi* (1896) (whose eponymous obese, puppet-like hero Jarry pictures, in a woodcut for the cover of the published version of the play, with a huge spiral across his chest and belly) and "neo-scientific novel," *The Exploits and Opinions of Doctor Faustroll, Pataphysician,* with its obscene tale of the art machine Clinamen, which spins like a top, ejaculating paint on the ruins of a once-great city. I then focus on how Italian Futurism (which drew heavily on 'pataphysics) and British Vorticism each employ spiral figures to define their movement's relation to particular (art) objects and national and international politics. The Futurists' celebrations of velocity and production are made more nuanced and complicated when one attends to the function of spirals in their art and writing. I examine the interrelated figures of snaking and swerving in Filippo Tomasso Marinetti's Futurist Manifesto and show how these figures function in many early Futurist paintings as well as writings. For Umberto Boccioni, one of the Futurists' prime movers, "spiral architecture" or "dynamism" involves "the creation of a new form that expresses the relativity between weight and expansion, between rotation and revolution."[31] This new form, here described with scientific gravitas, would take its place not only in specific artworks and buildings but, the Futurists hoped, in the geopolitical sphere as well, regenerating the Italian nation and urging it toward territorial expansion. Soon afterward, the Vorticists, who initially sought to distinguish themselves from the Futurists' "automobilism" and perceived effeminacy, defined "their" vortex, in *Blast*, as "the maximum point of energy," a point that could be achieved when the vortex is "stillest." Unlike the putatively profligate Futurists—Futurism was, according to the dismissive Pound, "the disgorging spray of a vortex with no drive behind it, DISPERSAL"—the Vorticists would produce "the most highly energized statement that has not yet SPENT itself it [*sic*] expression, but which is the most capable of expressing."[32] Despite Pound's eventual abandonment of Vorticism, these masculinist maxims would come to describe a hugely influential strand of British-Irish-American literary modernism, one that absorbed many of the territorial and gendered presumptions of Vorticist (and, indeed, Futurist) doctrine. The chapter explores a few of *Blast*'s poems and visual images in which the supposedly stilled spiral vortex approaches "statement," and it ends by tracing the dizzying contours of Henri Gaudier-Brzeska's "Vortex (Letter from the Trenches)," lauding war as "a great remedy."

In chapter 3, I look closely at two spirals produced and frequently revised in the period from 1917 to 1925, both heavily impacted by the First World War: the occult system outlined by Yeats in *A Vision* and Tatlin's never-built *Monument to the Third International*, two of high modernism's most earnestly designed, and most totalizing, towering spiral structures. While it has long been recognized that Yeats's work during this period tended toward fascism, a new look at the system reveals how the metaphors of winding and unwinding gyres, cones, and "perns" in his poetry link spiral-conceived history to spiral thought. In addition to laying out his astrologically defined, communicated-by-Spirits system's moving parts, Yeats, in the first version of *A Vision*, produced an elaborate "Fiction" for the origin of the system, one that gestured geographically both toward the Middle East and toward eastern Europe—the latter zone being where Yeats feared that the then-nascent Russian Revolution would lead to "inevitable murder."

Meanwhile, Tatlin's Tower, as the collectively designed project came to be known, combined Leninist principles of historical development (which development Lenin himself had compared to metamorphic spirals) with planetary and celestial notions of spatiotemporality in order to translate the perceived aims of the international working class. The enormous spiral tower was initially designed to contain a series of glass halls, of different geometric shapes, housing the "Soviet of the People's Commissars of the World" (cube), the Comintern's executive committee (pyramid), and a state-of-the-art information/communication/propaganda department (cylinder, topped by a hemisphere), the shapes of which were designed to rotate yearly, monthly, and daily, respectively. The whole glass-and-steel spiral structure—combining space and time, form and function, and holding in place the other shapes and in turn being informed by them—expressed Tatlin's sense of a new, ultramodern, international society generating energy out of its very core, while also reaching toward and screwing into the earth to anchor its strength. My focus on the question of the translatability of the tower turns (back) to images of the Tower of Babel, which Babelian "confusion" and misapprehension Tatlin's structure itself seeks to encompass and overcome. Yeats's and Tatlin's nearly simultaneous but utterly politically opposed spiral projects, when viewed together, challenge familiar modernist presumptions about the politics of totality and internationalism.

In chapter 4, I bring together Joyce's writing of the early 1920s to the late 1930s with Duchamp's artwork of the same period and examine the entropy embedded in their spirals. Although the word sounds as though it is ancient Greek, "entropy" is a consummately modern neologism, coined in 1865 by German physicist and mathematician Rudolf Clausius, who was pursuing a way to ensure the efficient running of engines (later called "thermodynamics"); Clausius viewed entropy as "closely related" to "energy" (a word coined by Aristotle). Duchamp and Joyce decisively challenge this efficiency with their amplification of what "falls out" of both vision and language. In the case of Duchamp, I focus on the work grouped under the rubric *Precision Optics* (*Rotary Glass*, *Rotary Demispheres*, and *Rotoreliefs*, with particular attention to the film *Anémic Cinéma* [1926], made with the assistance of Man Ray and Marc Allégret). In this work, spirals appear most clearly and reveal the function of spirality in Duchamp's broader project, blending as it does aspects of Dada and Surrealism but eluding aspects of the manifest aims of both groups. In *Precision Optics*, Duchamp explores the relation between vision and language, and tests the limits of carnality, dimensionality, and nonsense. My exploration of *Anémic Cinéma* aligns the film with Duchamp's earlier work on the ready-mades, and asserts its social and political significance, viewing the film as a kind of Freudian tendentious joke. Drawing on this idea of tendentiousness, the second half of the chapter analyzes spirals in Joyce's *Ulysses* and *Finnegans Wake*, especially in the former's "Scylla and Charybdis" episode and in the latter's "Anna Livia Plurabelle" and "Night Lessons" episodes, where spirals are associated with Platonic idealism and vagueness, knowledge and pseudo-knowledge, feminine cursiveness or liquidity, and homosexuality and a fear of drowning. They are also associated, to a great extent, with Yeats, whose ideas Joyce parodies but cannot entirely jettison. My reading of each text demonstrates how Joyce's language and diagrams/drawings both hilariously and deeply naughtily not only address the occult and sexuality and their associated "whirlpools," but also exemplify Joyce's approach to both history and geopolitics—especially the *longue durée* of colonialism and its residues.

Chapter 5 collides Beckett's writing from the later 1940s—particularly the novel *The Unnamable* (*L'Innomable* [1947])—with Smithson's art project *Spiral Jetty*, a title that encompasses the earth artwork (1969), film (1970), and essay (1972). Whereas my earlier central chapters pair works produced around the same time (Yeats's and Tatlin's work of the late 1910s and early 1920s and Joyce's and Duchamp's of the early 1920s through the 1930s)—the Beckett–Smithson collision is less chronologically confined. Moreover, in this case there is a clearer question of "influence," in that Smithson actually quotes from a long passage from *The Unnamable* in the *Spiral Jetty* film and mentions it in a crucial section of "The Spiral Jetty" essay. In fact, in his notes for the film, which as mentioned earlier he calls "A Metamorphoses [*sic*] of Spirals," Smithson also quotes Joyce and Yeats (and Flaubert and Nabokov and many other writers); it is as though these proto-, high-, and late-modernist stylists' spirals are embodied in the earthwork, in Smithson's language, and even in the apparatus of the camera and projector. Yet, already in *The Unnamable*'s tales of botched spiral adventures and homecomings, Beckett gestures toward those precursor figures (most notably Yeats and Joyce) whose spiral writings preceded his own. In part through these repetitions, the spiral, for Beckett and Smithson, becomes a sign of entropy or recoiling in a more fully fledged way than it had in Joyce and Duchamp. My focus in this chapter is on the entropic not only as a sign of the exhaustion of and with philosophical modernity and energetic progress in a general sense, but as a way to grapple with specific geopolitical moments: Beckett refers subtly but unmistakably to the bloodshed of the Second World War and the history of European colonialism, while Smithson refers to American "Manifest Destiny" and the napalm assaults on Vietnam. The inner and outer rings of Beckett's and Smithson's spirals become a way of expressing both an epistemological limit and a geographical border or map linking the near and the far.

"The Spiral and the Grid," the book's concluding chapter, explores literature and visual art produced between 1989 and 2002 in which spirals are centrally featured: South African artist William Kentridge's project *Ubu and the Procession* (1995–1997), Brazilian poet Augusto de Campos's Internet piece *SOS* (1992, 2000), Mexican artists Melanie Smith and Rafael Ortega's video *Spiral City* (2002), and German-born Briton W. G. Sebald's novel *Rings of Saturn* (*Die Ringe des Saturn* [1995]). Each of these multimedia works refers directly to earlier spiral-centered very late-nineteenth- or twentieth-century literature, art, or theory: respectively, Jarry's *Ubu Roi*; Duchamp's *Anémic Cinéma*; Smithson's *Spiral Jetty*, in all its forms, which, as noted, itself already referred directly to earlier modernist literary spirals from Yeats and Joyce to Beckett; and Benjamin's "storm of progress" in the frequently cited aphorisms collected as "Theses on the Concept of History." Yet the contours of this circuit of spiral references do not conform to Fredric Jameson's famous criteria for "postmodernism," those low-affect, pastiche-ridden, high/low–blending examples of the new culturally dominant exemplary of a global consumer society. Indeed, rather than participating in, or smirking at, that cultural dominant, these writers and artists seek, to the extent possible, to resist it in their very (spiral) forms. I argue that these early post–Cold War works' spiralized repetitions-with-a-difference reveal the intimate linkages among spirals, the project of modernity, and extranational or global politics over the course of the century, and I offer spirals as a new way of thinking about modernism after modernism. Throughout the chapter, I engage the work of Italian philosopher Giorgio Agamben, the thinker who, over the past three decades, has done more than any other to extend the political and ethical implications of Benjamin's work, especially on violence, sovereignty, and community. As a sort of postscriptural justification for my entire project, I end with a reconsideration of Dürer's *Melencolia I*, the etching whose meaning-images both Benjamin and Agamben have explored with great sensitivity and nuance.

Perusing this summary of the chapters to come, adumbrating a century-long "story" that leads from Jarry's *Ubu Roi* to Kentridge's *Ubu and the Procession*, the reader may have noticed that many of the texts that I am approaching under the rubric of "visual art" are actually films, but films whose length, form, and intended audience are different from those of traditional narrative cinema—the kind of cinema about which Benjamin wrote in his celebrated essay "The Work of Art in the Age of Its Technical Reproducibility." There is little doubt that this book on spirals might productively have focused more broadly on cinema, a medium whose very display through almost the entire breadth of the twentieth century relied, technologically, on a spiral motion from reel to reel. (Duchamp, Smithson, Kentridge, and Smith and Ortega all clearly recognize this problem of apparatus and respond to it.) Still, neither classical Hollywood nor avant-garde cinema nor even Alfred Hitchcock, whose sinister *Vertigo* (1958) silently informs my study, plays much of a direct role here, and for that I am sorry. It could be argued—and Benjamin does indeed argue thus in "The Work of Art in the Age of Its Technical Reproducibility"—that literature and visual art lose their "social significance" in an age of emerging cinema and other mass media.[33] But my position—and I think it is consonant with Benjamin's own practice—is that amid this loss, something important, a kind of intensity and attention to foundations, is gained, an intensity that, in turn, must be explored for its potential political significances.

However, I want to conclude this introduction by offering an apology in the more affirmative sense, by stressing again the potentiality of spirals, a potentiality that has appealed with astonishing durability to writers and visual artists across the twentieth century. For Jarry, Marinetti, Boccioni, Lewis, Pound, Gaudier-Brzeska, Yeats, Tatlin, Duchamp, Joyce, Beckett, Smithson, Kentridge, de Campos, Smith and Ortega, and Sebald, the curved and recursive contours of the spiral do not simply express a relation to the past, but create an opening for potential newness. It is in the search for the now-ness of the spiral image's newness that my study's own novelty inheres.

ONE

DEFINITIONS

A BRIEF HISTORY OF SPIRALS (AND A WAY OF READING SPIRALLY)

It's no calligraphy for school children. It needs to be studied closely.

• FRANZ KAFKA, "IN THE PENAL COLONY"

THE RESPONSIBILITY OF THE SPIRAL

Spirals are ubiquitous in nature, from plant and insect life, to human hair and fingerprints, to the movement of water and celestial bodies. Spirals have also, and increasingly, been used by corporations and in branding commodities. Innumerable products for children (films and television programs, toys, games) feature spiral shapes, and many companies have spiral logos. Perhaps this is because spirals express both the idea of growth and the pleasures of play. Give a young child a pencil and one of the first things he or she is likely to draw is a spiral. The infantile and youthful pleasures of the spiral, and its association with a kind of *ur*-writing, can certainly be viewed as in some way connected with its preponderance in twentieth-century literature and, especially, visual art. Yet my concern here is not with spirals as playful, ornamental decoration, or contrarily as universal "essence" in the mode of Corbusian architectural theory or Jungian psychoanalysis.[1] Instead, I proceed from the premise that spirals in twentieth-century literature and art express in their very forms a relationship both to history (which is to say, political-economic history) and to novelty and conceptions of the new.

To begin to flesh out this approach, it is imperative to recognize that spirals themselves have a history and to demonstrate how they incorporate that history.

In a short essay on the work of visual artist Bernard Réquichot, which was first published in 1973 and later appeared, in English translation, in the collection *The Responsibility of Forms*, Roland Barthes juxtaposes the contours of the spiral with those of the circle. "The circle," he writes, "is religious, theological; the spiral, like a circle distended to infinity, is dialectical: on the spiral, things recur, but *at another level*: there is a return in difference, not repetition in identity. Thanks to [the spiral], we are not constrained to believe: *everything has been said*, or: *nothing has been said*, but rather: *nothing is first yet everything is new*."[2]

Barthes's subtly emphatic observations provide a productive framework through which to begin to explore more closely the image of the spiral in literature and visual art in the twentieth century. More particularly, they offer a way to conceive the relation of different spirals in literature and visual art to one another across that century. Indeed, Barthes both asserts the inherent historicity of spirals and challenges notions of historical continuity. While his description of "dialectics" is by no means identical with that of Walter Benjamin, explored briefly in the introduction, the possibility that "nothing is first yet everything is new" bears an important resemblance to Benjamin's conception of emergence, for which Benjamin draws on a spiral figuration, as we will shortly see. Moreover, Barthes's notion of the spiral as a "distended" or, better, "deported" circle—Barthes calls it "un cercle déporté à l'infini"—is not only a claim about the relation of the emergent to what-has-been, but a demonstration, on the level of the sentence, of a "profane" spiral effect whose properties this book will pursue.[3]

But before proceeding with an account of this formal profanation, it behooves us to wind back toward the word itself, to seek its definition. The noun "spiral," according to the *OED*, is a term from geometry describing a "continuous curve traced by a point moving round a fixed point . . . while steadily increasing (or diminishing) its distance from this" fixed point. As with many familiar forms—take the classic example of a line—geometry gauges the relation between a fixed or an original point and a point or points in the distance. Unlike many other familiar geometrical forms, however, of crucial importance in and for the spiral is the *movement* that connects those points. The spiral curves or swerves around in such a way as to produce what Barthes calls "levels" of distance from or proximity to the fixed point.

And yet, the *OED*'s definition not only fixes the meaning of the spiral, but, with its unusual parenthetical reversal of direction, reveals an important ambivalence inherent in the geometric form itself, one that confounds attempts to establish origin and distance-from-origin. Does the spiral travel outward from the fixed point, thereby increasing its distance from that point, or curve inward, diminishing that distance? To cite Paul de Man citing *All in the Family*'s Archie Bunker: "What's the difference?"[4] In the former case, the fixed point could be conceived as a kind of center, but one unlike that of a circle, since its circumference stays open. In the latter, the inward, "diminishing" direction implies that the fixed point or origin is in a sense on the outer edge of the structure. Opening or closing, dissipating or concentrating: as we shall see, this ambivalence or bidirectionality inherent to the spiral form is crucial both for the twentieth-century visual artists and writers who embrace the spiral as fundamental to their practice and for a study that seeks to understand or take account of the art and literature involving or revolving around those spirals.

The *OED*'s examples of the usage of "spiral" offer a glimpse of the word's complicated and fascinating history. According to the dictionary, the modern English noun "spiral" was first deployed by Thomas Hobbes in 1656, in his translation of his own *Elementa Philosophica*, and then again by John Dryden in 1697, in his translation of Virgil's *Georgics*, describing the motion of the sun. Not surprisingly, then, the word comes to English via the French and Italian *spirale* from the late medieval Latin *spiralis*, an adjective that the German scientist, philosopher, and theologian Albertus Magnus is noted by the *OED* to have used, in passing, in 1255 when describing the coiling movement of the celestial sphere (notions for which he is said to be indebted to the medieval Andalusian philosophers Averroës and al-Bitruji).[5] The Latin *spiralis* is thus cognate with the Greek σπεῖρα (*speira*), an everyday word describing anything wound, coiled, or wrapped around.

In the classical period, the spiral form was a source of fascination from early on. As Barthes seems to be ventriloquizing, Plato, in *Timaeus*, speculates that there are three fundamental movements of the universe: circular, for the stellar gods; rectilinear, for brute matter; and spiral, for "planetary souls."[6] Accordingly, the earliest geometers, including Euclid, took note of the form, prevalent among planetary dwellers, and made some rudimentary calculations. Yet among the ancient Greeks, the spiral is most closely associated with Archimedes of Syracuse (ca. 287–212 B.C.E.), in whose honor the most familiar representation of the form was eventually named (figure 1).

In a long letter to his fellow geometer Dositheus, thought to have been written around 222 B.C.E., Archimedes set forth twenty-eight increasingly complicated propositions, starting with Euclid's calculations, extending them into a study of the way the form "turns" first once around a center and then turns again, and showing how each of those turns (τρόποι [*tropoi*]) can be measured. (The detailed mathematics of this measurement will not concern us here, but it is worth noting that Archimedes frequently repeats that he seeks to gauge what he calls the "forward" movement of these spiral turns, by which he presumably means "outward.") The understanding of these "tropes" was no abstract exercise for Archimedes, who was not only a geometer but also what today would be called an engineer; it was of enormous practical importance in the Hellenistic period, explaining, for example, the way screws and drills function, and in so doing advancing the science of architecture and the refinement of construction techniques.

Archimedes's letter, along with the manuscript of other work in which it was included, is thought to have been translated into Latin sometime before the late fifteenth century.[7] But that translation, like many Greco-Roman translations, is itself not untendentious: in the Greek original, the text was untitled, but in manuscript editions the chapter accrued the name Περὶ ἑλίκων (Peri helikon; On [*or* About] the Helices), and in fact Archimedes consistently used the noun *helix* and not the adjective *speira*. When the text was given the Latin title *De lineis spiralibus* (*On Spiral Lines*), Archimedes's discussion of a three-dimensional

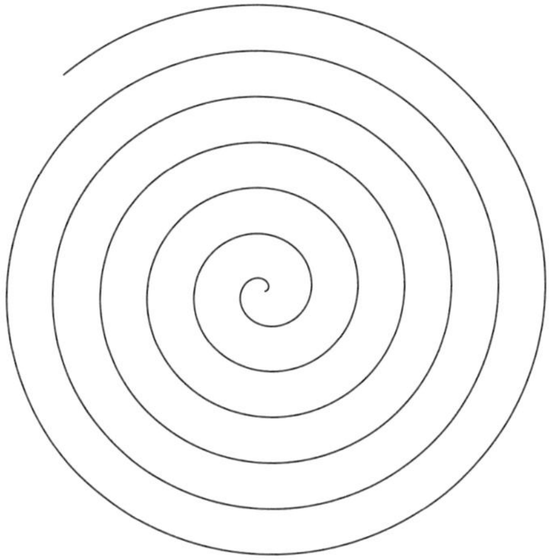

1 Archimedean spiral. (Image courtesy of Marc Edwards)

form (the helix) was in effect, at least titularly, condensed or flattened into a two-dimensional image associated with a "line."[8]

And yet, despite the condensation that takes place in the translation from Greek *helix* to Latin *spiralis,* in the late Middle Ages the spiral form preserved a sense of its helical depth and extensity, drawing on its association in the classical period with the movement of the celestial spheres and of the soul's wandering (Plato) and with zoological ideas about natural life, as in Virgil's *Georgics* or indeed in Lucretius, who, in *De rerum natura*, uses the term *clinamen* to describe the "swerving" movement of atoms.[9] Consider, for example, Dante's *Divine Comedy*, as famously illustrated by Sandro Botticelli, in which the directionalities of the pilgrim's wanderings—which is to say, the architectonics of hell and purgatory—are, respectively, downward and upward spirals; the pilgrim moves, as the Dante scholar John Freccero convincingly demonstrates, *a sinistra*, descending into the funnel of hell, and *a destra*, ascending the Mount of Purgatory (figure 2). These points of reference can make sense, or be cognitively

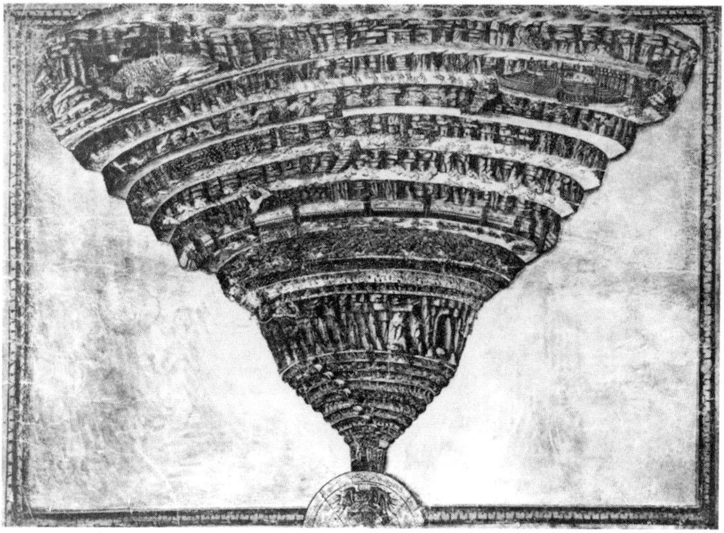

2 Sandro Botticelli (1444–1510), "Map of Hell," ca. 1480, in Dante, *The Divine Comedy*. (The Art Archive at Art Resource, New York)

mapped, only when considered in relation to Dante's broader cosmological world picture, which Freccero argues necessarily involves both spatial and temporal dimensions: "Just as we use a clock in our post-Copernican world for spatial reference when we use the words 'clockwise' and 'counter-clockwise' as well as for measuring time, so celestial movement gives the pilgrim his time references in the poem, and also provides him with a means of telling . . . [his] direction."[10]

If, in the late Middle Ages in Europe, the soul was conceived as capable of either descending to a sinister eternal hell or rightly ascending to an eternal heaven via a "time-filled" spiral journey, it is of little surprise that the form is so frequently found in the architecture of Romanesque and Gothic churches. Consider, for example, the cathedrals of Notre Dame and Chartres and Mont Saint-Michel, with their prevalent narrow spiral staircases and heavenward-pointing spires, not to mention the spiral-like forms in their stained-glass windows; these allegorical forms are as didactic, and sometimes as complicated, as Dante's. (Returning for a moment to the word: curiously, the etymology of the architectural "spire" bears no relation to that of "spiral"; neither does "spirit" or the Latin verb *spirare* [to breathe], though as we shall see these ideas are often viewed as cognate.)

In early modernity, the spiral's late medieval associations with religious aspiration—and indeed, desperation—began to be translated into the dual idioms of scientific utility and aestheticized beauty. In Leonardo da Vinci's illustrations for the *Divina Proportione*, in the architecture (attributed to him) of the Château de Chambord, and especially in his 1493 sketch of his proto-helicopter (a helix that depends on a conical spiral), human beings' propensity for invention and discovery begins to encroach on the realm formerly associated with the gods (figure 3).

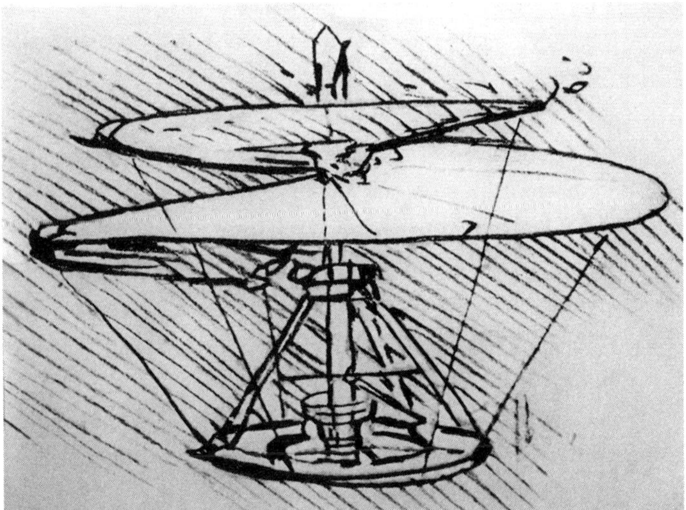

3 Leonardo da Vinci (1452–1519), design for spiral screw enabling vertical flight, ca. 1496. (Gianni Dagli Orti / The Art Archive at Art Resource, New York)

Still, a trace of the sinister, infernal aspect of the spiral, darkly inverting the divinely inspired aspiration, appears in proto-Baroque and Baroque representations of the Tower of Babel, from Pieter Brueghel the Elder to Francesco Borromini to the Jesuit Athanasius Kircher's illustration of the enormous edifice, with its crisscrossing ramps and classical columns (figure 4). In the Torah, the Tower of Babel is never specifically described as *spiral*; it is merely very tall, "with its top [or head] in the heavens [ראשו בשמים]." Yet in several artistic renderings from the seventeenth century, it appears as an up-winding tower. Why this is so invites consideration and speculation. Just as Dante's *Inferno* and *Purgatorio* reveal a broader Greco-Roman/Christian cosmology, reflecting the perceived relation between the human soul and the movement of the celestial spheres, so these proto-Baroque and Baroque representations of the Tower of Babel present, in turn, a nascent world picture. Not only do they disclose anxieties over excessive pride at rapidly achieved material gain in growing European cities, but they express foreboding about linguistic divergence amid the rise of nation-states (and their vernacular forms) and of the international trade and colonial domination that produced a cosmopolitan ethos.

As the philosopher Peter Sloterdijk has shown in his provocative three-volume history of globalization, *Sphären* (*Spheres*), and particularly in volume 2, *Globen* (*Globes*), the emergence of economic and cultural globalization in the twentieth century is in fact globalization's "third wave," the first two arising, respectively, in classical antiquity (in the metaphysical globalization of Greek geometry and cosmology) and in what Sloterdijk calls the "nautical globalization" that began in the fifteenth century in Europe.[11] In fact, viewed together, the images just discussed—Dante's inferno (as rendered by Botticelli), Leonardo's helicopter, and Kircher's tower—exemplify, via their divergent spiral trajectories, their psychical and affective links to different aspects of globalization's "second wave."

This interpenetration among spirals, ideas of beauty, and anxieties over emergent globalization is especially marked at the dawn of philosophical modernity. René Descartes, who was a mathematician and natural scientist as well as a philosopher, is credited with discovering the formula of the equiangular spiral,

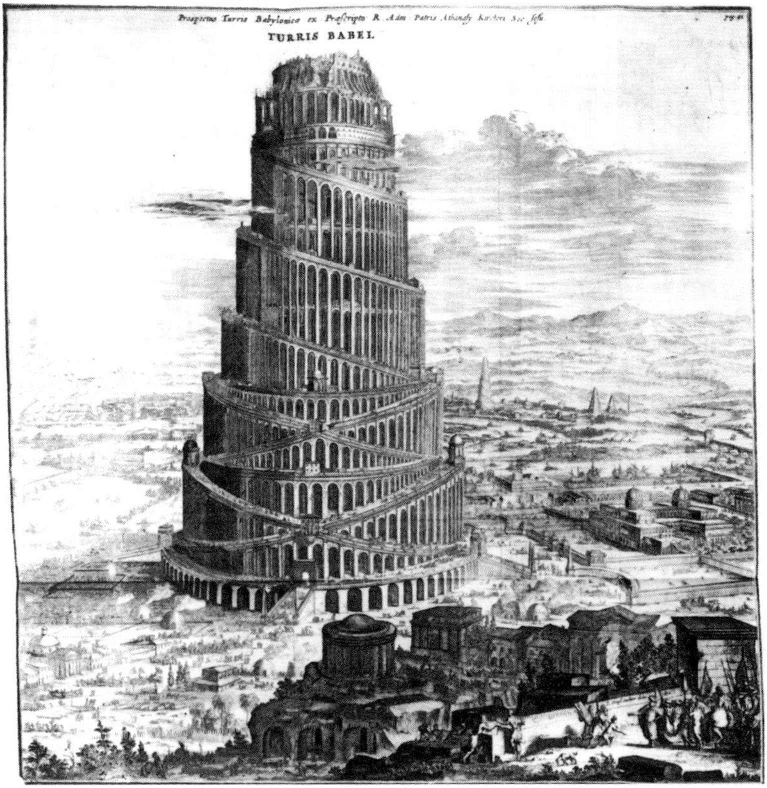

4 Athanasius Kircher (1602–1680), *The Tower of Babel* (engraving), 1679. (Private collection / The Bridgeman Art Library)

associated with both the Fibonacci series and the "golden mean" or "golden cut," in which a straight line is divided into two parts such that the ratio of the whole to the larger part is the same as the ratio of the larger part to the smaller. In geometry, this is considered so beautifully symmetrical as to be positively miraculous; hence the equiangular spiral, with its gracefully widening turns, is sometimes

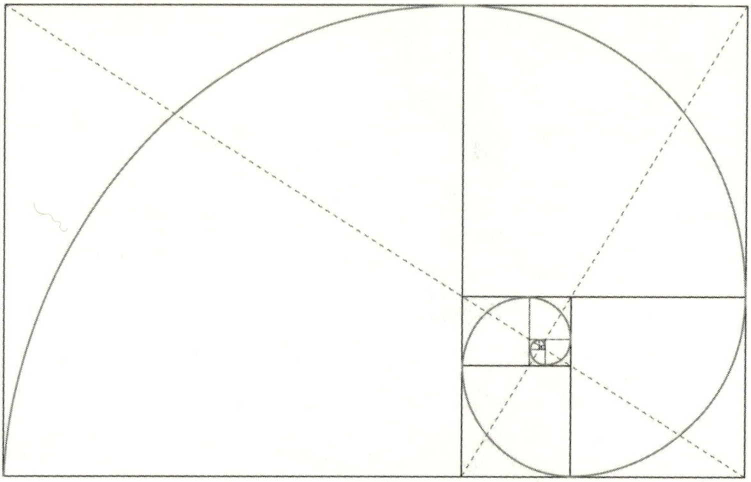

5 Equiangular, or "miracle," spiral. (© beaubelle—Fotolia.com)

called the "miracle spiral" (figure 5).[12] Drawing on his spiral investigations, Descartes, in an excellent example of what Henri Bergson, in *Matter and Memory*, describes as Descartes's linking of matter with "geometrical extensity," further suggested, in *Le monde*, that the origin of the universe could be conceived as cosmic matter rotating around a central axis whose spiral whirl produced the terrestrial system.[13] Analogously, we can recognize that the notion of a fixed or static point (or "eye") around which energy swirls might have influenced Descartes's famous philosophical deduction *cogito ergo sum*, in *Discours de la méthode* (1637), which was written virtually simultaneously with *Le monde*.

It is precisely this eye, or I, that was explicitly challenged by Giambattista Vico in *Scienza nuova* (1725). Vico sought to dispense with Descartes's "geometrical method" and instead offered a novel way of thinking about what he called the "history of civilizations." Yet Vico's attempt to displace Cartesian geometry by addressing the "tortuosities of life" (*tortuosità della vita*) ineluctibly led him back to a spiral-like form. For Vico, history proceeds cyclically through three ages: divine, heroic, and human. After a *ricorso*, or period of reflux, the cycle begins again. In his view, the very emergence of the Cartesian framework signaled the "barbarism of reflection" (*barbarie della reflessione*) and the inevitable spiral "descent" into the divine (a descent that James Joyce, in *Finnegans Wake*, envisions as commencing with a thunderclap, as we shall explore in chapter 5).

ROMANTIC SPIRAL TENDENCIES

If, in setting out some of the key meanings and implications of spirals in the history of the West, we are rushing headlong toward the twentieth century, special consideration must be given to the nineteenth, as perhaps nowhere did the notion of the spiral as an expression of nature, or "life," receive more attention than in Romanticism and its aftermaths. In his essay "Über die Spiraltendenz der Vegetation" (On the Spiral Tendency of Plant Life), Johan Wolfgang von Goethe, who was a botanist as well as a novelist, addresses two "tendencies" in plant life, the vertical and the spiral, the merging of which accounts for what he called "metamorphosis." "There prevails in vegetation a general spiral tendency," he suggests, "whereby, in union with the vertical striving of the whole structure, each formation in the plant is brought about in accordance with the laws of metamorphosis."[14] The spiral is, according to Goethe, a "real producing life-principle, directed to the periphery": that "spiral vessels" in plant organs push their way outward is proof that the spiral tendency dominates the life of plants. This notion of spiral tendencies was so pronounced in Goethe's work that he pursued writing his heavily allegorical novella, almost clinically titled *Novelle*, in an attempt to demonstrate how narrative itself might move spirally, beginning with a striking event (the arrival of a fierce tiger in an unnamed German kingdom) and unfolding as though "organically" in a single day, on its way to "resolving" its "inner and outer conflicts" (the tiger eventually emerging unscathed).[15]

One can easily recognize residues of Goethe's narratological themes, expressed as an organic spiral-shaped striving on the way to resolution, in the work of idealist philosophers such as G. W. F. Hegel, whose dialectics follow a similar course. In fact, in numerous texts, Hegel describes both the Spirit and the totality it expresses as shaped like a *Kreislauf* (circuit or cycle; literally, "circle-run") that manifests a distinctly spiral tendency. In the lectures that comprise his *Introduction to the Philosophy of History*, for example, Hegel declares, "The life of the ever-present Spirit is a *Kreislauf* consisting of steps, in which, looked at from one angle, things seem to exist next to each other, and only when looked at from another point of view appear as past. The elements that Spirit seems to have left behind it, it still possesses in its ever-present profundity."[16] In this latent–manifest model, in which space and time are conjoined, the *Kreislauf* expresses Hegel's notion that the present form of Spirit comprehends, and preserves within it, all earlier ever-present "steps," as on a spiral staircase whose upper flights bear material traces of the lower flights that precede them. To envision the whole course of historical development requires entering into and, as though simultaneously, standing outside the logic of the spiral, which—rather like the picture of the Archimedean spiral discussed earlier (see figure 1)—from one angle appears merely flat and horizontal and from another point of view appears to be a vertically ascending spiral with each step "containing" the steps that came before it. (The civilizational steps are described as *nebeneinander*, a term familiar to readers of *Ulysses*'s "Proteus" episode, in which Stephen Dedalus is walking on the beach and considering both his own footsteps and the movement of history.)

This idea of the spiral-shaped *Kreislauf* had appeared as early in Hegel's career as the *Wissenschaft der Logik*, wherein the philosopher, answering the self-posed question "Womit muss der Anfang der Wissenschaft gemacht werden? [Of what must the beginning of science be comprised?]," writes immediately of the idea of the Whole, which, for him, is equivalent to Truth. As he will later say in a famous maxim, "das Wahre ist das Ganze." Here Hegel, sounding rather like Saint Matthew, suggests that "the Whole itself is in itself a *Kreislauf*, wherein the first becomes the last and the last becomes first [das Ganze derselben ein

Kreislauf in sich selbst ist, worin das Erste auch das Letzte und das Letzte auch das Erste wird]." Hegel's *Kreislauf* of totality, driven by dialectical oppositions, takes a form similar to Goethe's spirally tending plant, with the upwardly spiral movement of history heading or heaving toward its resolution: the realization of perfection.[17]

Karl Marx, despite his materialist recto–verso flipping of Hegelian idealism, still frequently relies on the concept and figure of the *Kreislauf* to describe historical development in general and economic circulation in particular. As early as the *Grundrisse*, in the "Chapter on Capital," Marx writes of the "Kreislauf des Kapitals"; this eventually corresponds to book 1 in volume 2 of *Capital*.[18] And in volume 3 of *Capital*, Marx further describes the falling profit rates during capitalism's inevitable crises as forming a *cercle vicieux*, a term that Friedrich Engels, editing the text, translates into German as *fehlerhafte Kreislauf*—relating "vicious circle" to "faulty circuit" or, to borrow an expression consonant with current economics journalism and discussed in the introduction, "downward spiral." The figure of the spiral would later, with Vladimir Lenin, become associated with Marxist dialectics itself: Lenin described the Marxist version of Hegelian dialectics as a "development that repeats, as it were, stages that have already been passed, but repeats them in a different way[—]a development, so to speak, that proceeds in spirals, not a straight line."[19] Indeed, the image of the spiral became so pervasive in Leninism—one could claim (as Vladimir Tatlin does, following Lenin) that the spiral embodies the very idea of "revolution"—that by the middle of the twentieth century, Ralph Ellison, in his Cold War novel *Invisible Man*, would have his Marxism-weary protagonist warn: "Beware of those who speak of the spiral of history. [T]hey are preparing a boomerang. Keep a steel helmet handy."[20]

That historical "development" could be viewed both organically and mechanistically as taking the shape of a spiral is addressed and problematized by the self-proclaimed "philosopher with a hammer," Friedrich Nietzsche, later in the nineteenth century, in his evocation of eternal recurrence (*ewige Wiederkehr*). In the famous "thought experiment" in *Gaya Scienza*, Nietzsche posits the hypothetical situation of a demon approaching a man and challenging the very foundation of his chronologically based notion of existence:

> What if some day or night a demon were to steal after you into your loneliest loneliness and say to you: "This life as you now live it and have lived it, you will have to live once more and innumerable times more; and there will be nothing new in it, but every pain and every joy and every thought and sigh and everything unutterably small or great in your life will have to return to you, all in the same succession and sequence . . . even this moment and I myself[?]"[21]

This crushing hypothetical proposition concludes with two questions: "Would you not throw yourself down and gnash your teeth and curse the demon who spoke thus? Or have you once experienced a tremendous moment when you would have answered him: 'You are a god and never have I heard anything more divine'[?]" As Pierre Klossowski asserts in his brilliant analysis, *Nietzsche and the Vicious Circle*, Nietzsche in the *Gaya Scienza* presents thought itself as caught in an "inconceivable spiral." For Klossowski, this vicious circle or spiral is the sign of the vertigo produced by recognition of the possibility of eternal return, the sign of "*an event that stands for everything that can ever happen*, for everything that has ever happened, for everything that could ever happen in the world—and indeed, in thought itself."[22]

Nietzsche's inconceivably spiral "vicious circle" challenges the foundations and limits of both Hegelian and Marxist-Leninist notions of history in that it suggests that there is no "outside" from which to observe the vaunted historical "steps"—a critique that extends to the entire Western metaphysical tradition we have thus far been exploring in terms of the spiral.[23] This critique, which in an important sense brings us back around to our opening engagement with the definition of the spiral and its "fixed point" and "distance," could be said to inaugurate twentieth-century ideas in which spirals, as markers of repetition and potential difference, begin to express a new entwinement of space and time—and, indeed, of politics.

SPIRALS AND THE EXTREME CENTURY

Is the more than two millennia history of spirals we have explored so far in this chapter merely a *story* in the sense Benjamin denigrates in the epigraph to the introduction? Insofar as the spiral has not yet coalesced into the kind of *image* that can constellate "what-has-been" with "the now," yes. Yet even a hasty adumbration of the appearance of spirals in the history of the West, from classical antiquity through the nineteenth century—one that by necessity has had to "deport" consideration of a number of other important thinkers on or evokers of spirals (Fermat, Leibniz, Blake, Coleridge)—has served to demonstrate that the spiral is more than simply a recurrent theme, form, or motif that one finds in the arts. Indeed, spirals traverse now-distinct areas of inquiry: geometry, physics, astronomy, celestial mechanics, botany, natural history, economics, and architecture, as well as philosophy, literature, and visual art. Aside from this disciplinary transversality, the spiral, throughout much of its history a figure of metamorphosis, has itself undergone a number of metamorphoses: it has represented or allegorized ideas concerning cosmology, temporality, historicity, politics, and, indeed, growth and life itself. Clearly, many of these spiral imaginings extend into the twentieth century, but in that century they are again transformed. It will be the rest of this book's task to show how and why this is the case.

There is another history of the spiral that must be acknowledged—that of the non-West (and one immediately recognizes the faultiness of this heuristic nomenclature). Think, for example, of the Hindu or Buddhist mandalas of East Asia or the pre-Columbian (Mayan, Hopi) architecture in the Americas, each of which materially engages with questions of time and temporality, often through spirals or labyrinths. To this category we might add ancient or "prehistoric" spirals such as those found in Aegean wall paintings and at the megalithic Newgrange (Sí an Bhrú) tomb in Ireland, with its multiple spiral forms (figure 6). Imagining these cultural products together, one might be tempted to conceive an alternative history (or "story") of the spiral, juxtaposing non-Western (or Eastern, or archaic) ones with more modern (or explicitly modernist) Western ones;

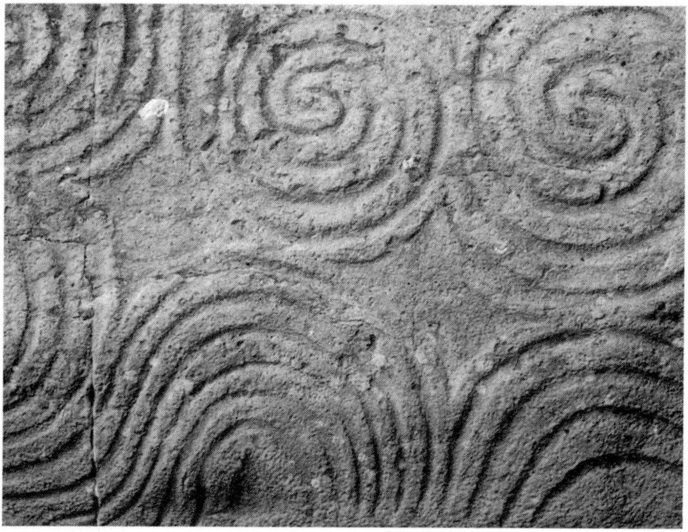

6 Tri-spiral from Newgrange (Sí an Bhrú) tomb in Boyne Valley, Ireland, ca. 3200 B.C.E. (© Alessandro Bonini—Fotolia.com)

or, contrarily, to universalize the spiral and lay claim to its special mystical, life-giving powers across cultures and histories—an idiom one finds in much New Age rhetoric, but not only there, as we shall see. Although these are no doubt interesting approaches, they are not the ones to be pursued in this book, focused as it is primarily on the spatialities and temporalities of twentieth-century Western literature and art.[24]

What is, however, important to recognize is how these non-Western, aboriginal, or archaic forms and idioms became embedded, embodied, in Western literature and art, especially in the twentieth century. In part, this embodiment owes something to the proximity of early modernist aesthetics (and anti-aesthetics) and such social or "human" sciences as anthropology and archaeology, which a generation of literature and art scholars has theorized.[25] In part, it owes to the fascination of figures like Yeats and Tatlin with different strands of spiritualism, the one (Yeats) blending Irish nationalism and "visionary" Spenglerian ideas of civilizations, and the other (Tatlin) conflating ideas of Russianness with idioms of Communist internationalism. (The Yeats–Tatlin connection will be addressed more fully in chapter 3.)

While it may readily be acceded that literary and visual-art spirals are linked to the social sciences in the twentieth century, spiral forms are pervasive across the "long" century in the physical or "hard" sciences as well. Consider discoveries in epidemiology (the detection of spirochete bacteria that, for example, caused syphilis and the massive influenza of the First World War), astrophysics (Edwin Hubble's 1920 observations of the Milky Way, or the 1960s revelations of orbits around black holes), genetics (James Watson and Francis Crick's double helix), and speculative mathematics (Benoit Mandelbrot's fractals), each of which significantly altered—blasted apart—prior conceptions of space, time, or matter. In fact, bearing in mind the technical reproduction of these images and ideas in photographs and films, as well as their treatment in literature and visual art, one can confidently assert that in no earlier era did spirals or spiral-like shapes appear in such disparate fields of knowledge with such frequency and force.

Still, the crucial question remains: *How is one to read* or apprehend the twentieth-century literary and visual-art spirals that I am claiming are both singular in their irreducible specificity and representative in that they constellate as *images* of that century (a century in which art and politics were, as Alain Badiou notes, "inextricably bound")? To respond to this question, I propose following the example of Benjamin himself, a thinker who was certainly well aware of, and in fact responding to, the work of the triumvirate of thinkers discussed earlier: Hegel, Marx, and (arguably especially) Nietzsche.[26]

Benjamin's work is geared away from generic, systemic boundaries and instead pursues what he termed "the necessary tendency towards the extreme [die notwendige Richtung aufs Extreme]."[27] To describe this extreme tendency or direction, Benjamin turns and returns to spiral and spiral-like figures. As early in his writing as the preface to the *Ursprung des deutschen Trauerspiels* (*Origin of the German Mourning Play* [ca. 1925, published 1928]), Benjamin, complicating the familiar idea of "origin" as fixed starting point for (a) history, draws on the idea of the "spring" embedded in *der Ursprung*, and suggests that "origin stands in the flow of becoming as a whirlpool [*Strudel*] that tears the stuff of emergence into its rhythm [Der Ursprung steht im Fluß des Werdens als Strudel und reißt in seine Rhythmik das Enstehungsmaterial hinein]."[28] For Benjamin, clearly echoing Nietzsche here, origin does not *precede* or stand outside history's becoming but is already pulled into its ever-swirling flow. The *Strudel* (whirlpool, maelstrom, vortex) is Benjamin's figure for the kind of flow that "tears" into its rhythm the very material of formation or emergence.[29]

In this figure, Benjamin may have intended something akin to a moment in Stéphane Mallarmé's unfinished prose poem "Igitur," published in fragmentary form in 1925 (the same year as *Trauerspiels* was submitted as a postdoctoral dissertation and, incidentally, also the year of the publication of Yeats's *A Vision*), in which the speaker describes taking the shape of a bird and flying in a "dizzy spiral," a flight that would have gone on indefinitely "if some progressive oppression . . . had not implied the certain escape in an interval, the cessation [in which] oppression and escape were mixed."[30] For Benjamin, as for Mallarmé (and Yeats), a spiral implies a dual directionality or tendency, with both "extremes" exerting a pull on the image. Image reveals itself in and as a cessation or "caesura in the movement of thought. . . . It is to be found where the tension between opposites is greatest."[31]

This idea is clarified and amplified in the body of *Trauerspiels*. Here, when describing Albrecht Dürer's early-sixteenth-century engraving *Melencolia I*, Benjamin focuses on three "allegorical emblems" or, better, "meaning-images" (*Sinnbilder*): the dog, the stone, and the sphere, each located on the left side of the famous etching, in the contemplative, melancholy angel's foreground (figure 7). Of these, the sphere (*Kugel*) is of particular importance, and it is, according to Benjamin, linked both to the blunt fact of "cold, dry earth" and to the then-emerging idea of "globe." The sphere's very gravity represents, and indeed in the angel *produces*, "acedia," what Benjamin calls a "dullness of the heart, or sloth,"

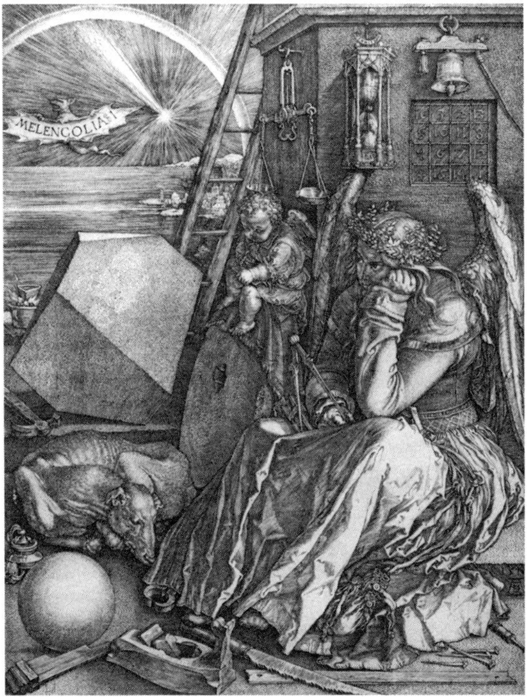

7 Albrecht Dürer (1471–1528), *Melencolia I* (engraving), 1514.
(The Art Archive at Art Resource, New York)

a perhaps-inevitable response to recognizing how earth is in the process of becoming globe.[32] (The angel, surrounded by tools of measurement, is powerless to stop this process, a powerlessness that deepens his melancholy.) What is especially noteworthy is how Benjamin reads this apparently perfectly round sphere as though it were an inward-moving spiral; in describing it, he repeatedly invokes a notion of downward pressure or "concentration"—both in terms of how the sphere's very weight pulls it downward gravitationally, and in the angel's saturnine response to thinking. Benjamin writes of the tropological "sequence of analogies which embrace thought: concentration–earth–Melancholy [*Gall*],"[33] such *Konzentration* linking the act of cogitation to a form of centering without reaching a center.[34] In a signal turn for Benjamin, the concentrating, galled angel is seen as embracing the apparently lifeless objects that surround him precisely "in order to redeem them."[35] It is this quasi-theological notion of redemption that links the ideas of "image" and "now-ness" to the act of reading.

Lest *Strudel* and *Kugel* seem unpalatably exotic to those seeking direct access to Benjamin's "historical materialism," let us turn to a passage from the late "Theses on the Concept of History," which is much more likely to be familiar. Here Benjamin writes, concerning Paul Klee's watercolor *Angelus Novus*, of a "storm blowing out from paradise" that is "so strong" it will not allow the angel of history to close his wings. This storm, which propels the angel into the future, toward which his back is turned, is, in Benjamin's formulation, "what we call progress" (*Fortschritt*), implying the still-pervasive history-as-improvement model of historicism, which ought instead to be recognized as *catastrophe*, blowing the redemptive angel ever farther away from its destination. The task of the "historical materialist" is precisely to brush against the grain, or, more literally, against the stroke (*gegen den Strich bürsten*), which reminds us of the tactility of the painting and accords better with the force of the storm.[36] This reading technique, oriented toward the extremes, would apply whether that directionality is apparently inward, as in the whirlpool or sphere, or outward, as in the storm.[37]

These three Benjaminian figures, offered as "allegorical emblems" for the mode of reading I aspire to pursue in the rest of this book, do not simply reiterate the by-now-familiar critique of modern progress or temporality. Indeed, they offer a way to think more generally about the imbrication of the temporal and the geopolitical. In my view, Benjamin's conception of image (*Bild*), which in *Trauerspiels* he calls "image of the world" (*Bild der Welt*), in which "world" is irresistibly in the process of becoming "globe," offers a necessary philosophical counterpart not only to the critique of cosmopolitanism and "world literature" prevalent in recent work in modernist literary criticism, but to many social science approaches to globalization as well.

@ @ @

To read twentieth-century spirals in literature and visual art as *images* thus involves what Shoshana Felman once called "turning the screw of interpretation"[38]—turning it both in toward itself to observe its own torsions *and* out to the "globe" to try to take stock of how specific spirals, in their makers' desire to combine language *and* visual media, assert their relation to the geopolitical. To trace this double movement, and to see what it produces, is the rest of this book's responsibility.

TWO

ENTERING THE WHIRLPOOL

'PATAPHYSICS, FUTURISM, VORTICISM

> We have abolished pyramidal architecture to arrive at spiral architecture. A body in movement, therefore, is not simply an immobile body subsequently set in motion, but a *truly mobile object*.
>
> • UMBERTO BOCCIONI, "PLASTIC DYNAMISM"

> [The vortex is] the most highly energized statement that has not yet SPENT itself it [*sic*] expression, but which is the most capable of expressing.
>
> • EZRA POUND, "VORTEX"

THE LIFE OF CURVES

Perhaps no other scholar of spirals has ever evinced more enthusiasm for his topic than has Theodore Andrea Cook. In 1914, Cook, a London art critic and well-known former editor of *The Field*, an illustrated magazine appealing to gentlemen sportsmen, completed more than a dozen years of research into spiral forms of all kinds.[1] In his sprawling (and sprawlingly subtitled) book *The Curves of Life: Being an Account of Spiral Formations and Their Application to Growth in Nature, to Science, and to Art; With Special Reference to the Manuscripts of Leonardo da Vinci*, Cook offers a detailed description of insect and conch shells, plant life, animal horns, various parts of the human body (thigh bone, umbilical cord, ear canal, hair), and spiral nebulae, often drawing on mathematical formulas to demonstrate what he views as the perfect proportion of his specimens. Cook, whose decided preference is for the miraculous logarithmic spiral (which he calls the "curve of life" and "essence of beauty"), then goes on to analyze examples from Renaissance and Baroque architecture, sculpture, and painting and, in addition to exploring spiral staircases, columns, and volutes, shows how both Leonardo's pursuit of aesthetic perfection and Albrecht Dürer's vaunted advances in the idea of perspective rely on spiral and helical formations. According to Cook's preface, dated March 28, 1914, "Spirality (if the word may be allowed) is a generalization of far-reaching importance," and to make the case for this generalized importance, *The Curves of Life* is "profusely illustrated" with 415 illustrations and 11 plates. One of these illustrations happens to be "The Lucky Swastika," which, according to Cook, is "one of the most ancient and widespread of all symbols,"[2] connected both to the orientation of the sun and to the growth of the lotus flower, the latter itself, according to Cook, considered a "sacred" spiral form (figure 8).

Within a few short months of the publication of *The Curves of Life*, much of Europe would be at war—the Great War, of course, which preceded the world war emblematized by the swastika—by the end of which few devotees of the arts would unequivocally espouse universal, triumphant notions of beauty such as Cook's (whose next publication, not incidentally, concerned the Olympic Games). But these vitalist, unabashedly aesthetic notions had, of course, already been exposed to examination and attack for some time. Indeed, just as Cook's ideas were coalescing, vanguardist European artists of diverse and even antagonistic allegiances had begun to draw on the figure of the spiral not to express "the profound significance . . . of mankind" as eternal beauty, but precisely as absurdity and hideousness.[3]

This chapter traces the spiral's crucial role in articulating the foundations of Italian Futurism and the London-based literary and visual-art movement known as Vorticism. Its focus is on the way spirals shed their organicist, residually Euclidian, nineteenth-century associations of "life" and "growth" (Goethe and Hegel), and began to express a new kind of creative potentiality—one that explicitly

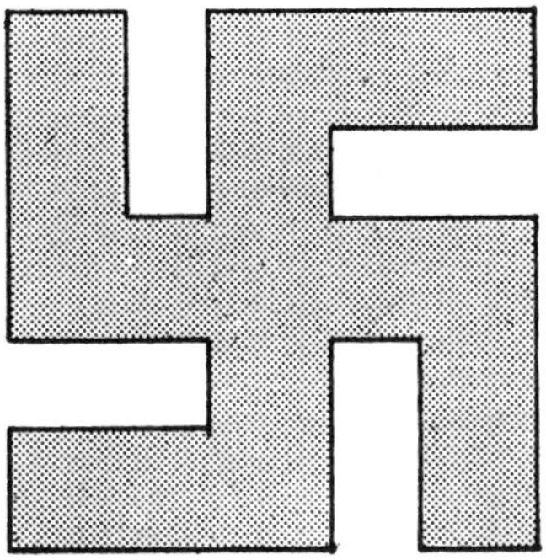

8 "The Lucky Swastika," in Theodore Andrea Cook, *The Curves of Life* (1914). (Courtesy Dover Publications)

embraces a destructiveness that is itself contrarily viewed as life-affirming. The chapter begins by briefly encountering Alfred Jarry's terroristic theater and narrative: specifically the play *Ubu Roi* and the novel *The Exploits and Opinions of Doctor Faustroll, Pataphysician*, both of which prominently feature spirals of this new, destructive type, and both of which were acknowledged by Italian Futurists as important precursors. My focus then turns to some of the key writings and visual art of Futurism, in which spirals occupy a powerful position in articulating both speed and potentiality—ideas that for the Futurists are by no means to be confined to the aesthetic sphere but are by their very nature imbricated in the political sphere. The last part of the chapter explores how some of the prime movers of Vorticism—Wyndham Lewis, Ezra Pound, and Henri Gaudier-Brzeska—explain the vortices of Vorticism, itself ostensibly set firmly against the perceived effeminacy of Italian Futurism, and how spirals play a role in articulating some of the masculinist and racist presumptions of the movement. Throughout the chapter, we will be attentive to the ways the spiral image negotiates ideas of the vanguard, (anti-)aesthetics, and early-twentieth-century conceptions of history and the geopolitical.

UBU AND THE "UNFORESEEN BEAST"

In Alfred Jarry's raucous play *Ubu Roi* (1896), the title character is depicted as a nonchalantly rapacious monster insatiably seeking food, land, money, and blood, destroying and absorbing everything and everyone he encounters. This cyclonic, destructive absorption is emphasized by Jarry's own irreverent treatment of precursors, including Rabelais and, especially, Shakespeare, whose Macbeth is obviously a model for Ubu's bloody power grab. When Jarry designed a woodcut of his "grotesque anti-bourgeois" hero, he depicted Père Ubu as a rotund, hooded dummy with an oddly blank, feline facial expression; thin arms under which he is pinning a kind of stick (that could be his oft-mentioned "green candle"); stubby little legs; and, most noticeably, a large Archimedean spiral splayed across his torso, emanating from, or perhaps ending at, his navel (figure 9). Although the rationale for portraying Ubu in this manner is never directly explained in the play—and has not been pursued by scholars—a glance at Jarry's offhand articulations of "'pataphysics" provides an important clue.

In the book 2 of his "neo-scientific novel" *The Exploits and Opinions of Doctor Faustroll, Pataphysician*, written in 1898 but not published until 1911, four years after Jarry's death at age thirty-four, the author of *Ubu* declares 'pataphysique to be "the science of that which is super-added to [*se surajoute à*] metaphysics, whether within or beyond the limits of metaphysics."[4] If metaphysics ostensibly studies that which is beyond the physical, 'pataphysics (whose little recoiling spiral apostrophe, Jarry claims, is used "to avoid a simple pun")[5] extends "as far beyond metaphysics as the latter extends beyond physics."[6] Yet despite this ostensibly long reach, 'pataphysics is turned not toward the universal, but toward the particular and, especially, the "accidental." Accordingly, it "examine[s] . . . the laws that govern exceptions [les lois qui régissent les exceptions],"[7] as will, eventually, the rather less facetious approaches to the question of exception taken by Carl Schmitt and Walter Benjamin.[8]

As if to set out such an "examination," Jarry launches into a raunchy story of his Circassian-born hero, Faustroll, whose name seems to be an amalgamation

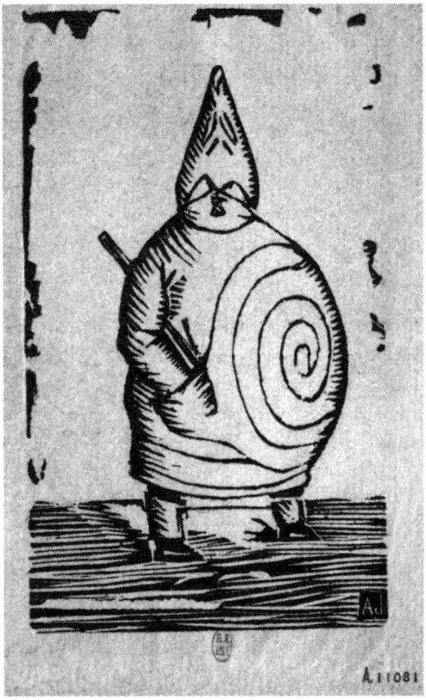

9 Alfred Jarry (1873–1907), *Père Ubu* (woodcut), hero of *Ubu Roi* (1896). (Numbered edition, Bibliotèque Nationale, France. CCI / The Art Archive at Art Resource, New York)

of Goethe's soul-selling Faust and the deflating "troll."[9] Chapter 33 of Faustroll's saga is called "Concernant les termes" (Concerning the Termes)—*termes* in French referring not only to "terms" in a legal, contractual sense but to termites or "woodworms," spiral-shaped and destructive. Here, Faustroll has met a woman curiously named Visité (Visited), a "bishop's daughter" (!) who has a bed made out of elaborately hand-carved wood. On the wall over this bed, itself obviously a parody of Penelope's Odysseus-carved bed in Homer's *Odyssey*, is found a "spiral-painted tapestry," under which Visité "desired to discover" whether Faustroll had a heart "capable of pumping out with its open and closed fist the projection of circling blood."[10] The potent and destructive eroticism of this set of spirals is made even clearer when, after at least two hours of what one hesitates to call "lovemaking," Visité is unable to "survive the frequency of Priapus."[11] This multiply spiral motif (woodworms, tapestry, circulating blood, trajectory of seminal fluid) is then immediately extended in the following brief chapter, "Clinamen," which, as we have noted, is what Lucretius called the unpredictable swerve of atoms. In Jarry's text, one finds an astonishing description of a "Painting Machine" amid a "Palace of Machines" that is "the only monument left standing" in a deserted and razed Paris of the not-so-distant future. The machine, itself named Clinamen, dashed itself "like a spinning top" against the pillars and "followed its own whim blowing onto the walls' canvas a succession of primary colors,"[12] rather like a mobile automatic painting of the type that Damien Hirst employed a century later.

Faustroll's little parable concludes, charmingly, "the unforeseen beast Clinamen ejaculated onto the walls of its universe."[13] In Jarry's text, written (to paraphrase Jarry himself) in "the year – 2" of the twentieth century, spiral forms are thus associated with sexuality and power, sexuality-as-power. This power would allow "'pataphysical" contemporary art-of-the-future to "dash itself" against the architecture of the decaying old and, unforeseen, "ejaculate against the walls" with its destructively primal, primary, priapic/pudendic colors. In this explosively violent vision, body limns machine: indeed, body is a kind of sex- and art-making machine.

It is far from incidental that the parable of Clinamen unfolds in a burned- or bombed-out Paris. Jarry's aim, like that a generation of 'pataphysicians and 'pataphysical fellow travelers after him (including, as we shall see, Marcel Duchamp) was not merely to mock the presumptions of aestheticians and belle-lettrists, but to buzz energetically in the field of the political rather like Clinamen's spinning top. This aim is apparent when one returns to Jarry's play, which is subtitled *ou, les Polonais*. The action of *Ubu Roi* is said to take place in Poland, "c'est-à-dire, nulle part" (that is to say, nowhere): by the time of the writing and performance of the play, the nation had effectively been wiped off the geopolitical map after a century-long series of partitions by its more powerful imperial neighbors Prussia, Austria, and Russia. Of course, this notion of national extinction is rendered hyperbolically and absurdly in the play. Yet in giving incidental characters the names Jan Sobieski and Stanislas Leczinski, kings of Poland right before partition began, Jarry suggests that the Polish setting is far from insignificant; indeed, the trajectory of *Ubu*'s long, obscene, windy (in both senses) voyage is precisely from Poland to France—thus reversing the Napoleonic invasion of the early nineteenth century that Poles mistakenly believed would free them from fealty to their stronger neighbors, especially Russia.[14] Accordingly, it could be suggested that spiral-fronted Ubu, like Clinamen, spins like a battling top from Poland "back" to France in anticipation of the destruction to come. And if one thinks ahead for a moment to the midcentury period emblematized by the not-so-"Lucky Swastika," it is precisely Poland's status as "nulle part," or zone of exception beyond the pale, that allowed it to be the primary extermination arena of the Second World War.

ACCIDENTAL TOURISTS: ITALIAN FUTURISTS AND THE SPEEDING SPIRAL

Jarry's 'pataphysics, thriving on the accidental, thus offers both spirally armored Ubu and spinning, ejaculating Clinamen as exceptionally exemplary models for destructive production. The Italian Futurists responded, in part to Jarry's provocation, with a call to "wreck the cities pitilessly," to torch libraries and museums, and to embrace the hard sleekness of the machine.[15] First published in 1909 in Italy and France, and swiftly translated into numerous other languages (including Russian and Japanese),[16] Filippo Tomasso Marinetti's "Foundation and Manifesto of Futurism" begins with a prefatory, indeed foundational, description of an erotic-cum-anti-aesthetic absurdist reverie, one punctuated with spiral images. Marinetti describes an exhorting exclamation he makes to unnamed insomniac "friends": "Let us break out of the hideous shell of Wisdom and hurl ourselves like pride-spiced fruit into the wide, contorted mouth of the wind! Let's give ourselves completely to the Unknown, not in desperation but only to replenish the deep reservoirs of the Absurd!"[17] Just as in Jarry, where the "unforeseen beast Clinamen ejaculated onto the walls of its universe," here, the erotic nature of Marinetti's justly famous exhortation is evident: breaking out of a "hideous shell"—*gangue* can also be translated as "matrix"—"we" should "enter" (*entrons*) the wide and contorted mouth (the adjective *torse* also invoking the noun form for "torso") of the wind. The prosthetic vehicle through which this eroticized entry will take place is the racing automobile, which is later described, with phallic verve, as having "a hood that glistens with large pipes resembling a serpent with explosive breath [orné de gros tuyaux tels des serpents à l'haleine explosive]."[18] The coiled destructiveness crucial to the Italian Futurists' hyper-masculinized rhetoric is emblematized by this muscle-car's serpentine hood, which stands in clear contradistinction to the feminized "hideous shell."

Marinetti's exhortation to hop in is almost immediately followed in the preface by a sudden swerve—a stylized description of the minor accident in which Marinetti claims to have steered his car into a ditch to avoid two bicyclists.[19] The description begins, immediately after the *torse*/torso exhortation, with Marinetti's macho out-skidding:

> The words were scarcely out of my mouth when I spun my car around with the frenzy of a dog trying to bite its tail, and there, suddenly, were two disapproving cyclists coming towards me, shaking their fists, wobbling like two equally convincing but nevertheless contradictory arguments. Their stupid undulation [Italian, *dilemma*; French, *ondoiement*] was blocking my way—How boring! Auff! I stopped short—and in disgust rolled over into a ditch with my wheels in the air.[20]

The notion of speedily "swerving" to avoid two contradictory modes of reasoning—modes that would "disapprove" of the speeding automobilist (*deux cyclistes me désapprouvèrent*)—is crucial to Marinetti's description not only of thinking, but of art practice, as it will be to the British Vorticists. Marinetti's response to this "dilemma"—to skid out and then roll over into a ditch, wheels up—thereby implies an oxymoronically violent submission and a return to the canine metaphor of the previous sentence, in which a dog is portrayed chasing his tail.

Submission entails rebirth: describing how the accident threw him into a pit of dark industrial muck, Marinetti continues his prefatory outburst with a series of metaphors that again evoke the (possibly but not certainly feminine) sexualized body, connecting it through spirals with a specifically North African orientalism already invoked in the preface's opening line (where the "friends" are introduced as standing "under mosque lamps" from the Marinetti family's collection of knickknacks from Alexandria): "O maternal ditch, almost full of muddy water! Fair factory drain! I gulped down your nourishing sludge; and I remembered the blessed black breast of my Sudanese nurse!"[21]

The set of associations informing Marinetti's oral-to-anal-to-oral reverie—mouth–ditch–sludge–mother–mud–wet nurse—catapults this primal scene of modernism from being one of speed to one of domesticity, and then to the colonial framework and toward the erotic, albeit erotic in a decidedly infantile sense: the Egyptian-born Marinetti's dream of "hurling" into a breast is, post-crash, transmogrified and personalized into "la sainte mamelle noire de ma nourrice soudanaise."

The specificity and miniaturization of Marinetti's post-crash sucking dream does not by any means diminish the potential explosivity of spirals, which in the list of eleven manifesto "announcements" appear in the form of automobiles, planes, and trains, the last of which are portrayed (positively) as "smoke-plumed serpents" devoured by "famished railway stations [gares gloutonnés avaleuses de serpents qui fument]."[22] The controlling force of the railway station links Marinetti's loudly self-advertised "aggressive character" of art and "scorn for woman" together in a classically Freudian topos.

Spirals—as sign for "fire, hatred and speed," for "spasms of action and creation," and for the moment of exception—are found not only in the manifesto, but, frequently, in Marinetti's drawings, including "SCRABrrRrraaNNG" (also called "In the Evening, Lying on Her Bed, She Reread the Letter from Her Artilleryman at the Front") (figure 10), through whose multiple serpentine swerves—and especially those that surround the onomatopoetic bomb dropping (or scream of agony) "GRAAAAO"—one may easily picture the Marinettian skid-out. Indeed, this near-obsession with spiral forms spans the entirety of the Italian Futurist project, from Giacomo Balla's *Speed of a Motorcycle* (1913), in which the movement of a practically invisible motorcycle is rendered as sequential spiral

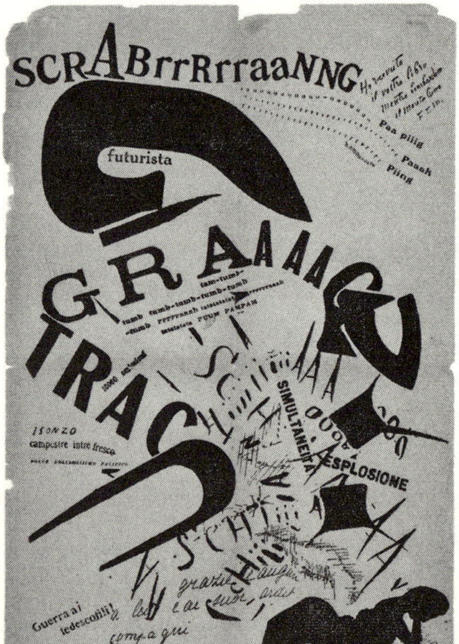

10 Filippo Tommaso Marinetti (1876–1944), "In the Evening, Lying on Her Bed, She Reread the Letter from Her Artilleryman at the Front," 1919. (© 2013 Artists Rights Society [ARS], New York / SIAE, Rome. Digital image © The Museum of Modern Art / Licensed by SCALA / Art Resource, New York)

swirls (figure 11);[23] to the same artist's *Mercury Passing Before the Sun* (1914), which depicts the eclipse-like planetary transit as though it were swept up in a spiral cosmopolis (figure 12);[24] and on to the later Futurist Vitorio Corona's *Dinamismo di elica e mare* (1922), which connects the spiral motion of the sea to the power of machines. Yet among the Futurists, the most patient and elaborate articulation of the group's approach to spirality is found in the writing and artwork of an early member of the Milan Futurist circle, Umberto Boccioni.

Like Marinetti, Boccioni sought to liberate Italian art from its fealty to past civilizational achievements; the past for him, as for Marinetti, is viewed as an inhibiting, constraining force. Yet, unlike the violent, spasmodic break with which Marinetti usually associated the spiral swerve, Boccioni found in spirals the form best able to express what he called "dynamic continuity." In *Pittura e scultura Futuriste: Dinamismo plastico* (1914), Boccioni, using quasi-Einsteinian jargon, declares that "plastic dynamism is the simultaneous action of the motion characteristic of an object (its absolute motion), mixed with the transformation which the object undergoes in relation to its mobile and immobile environment (its relative motion)."[25] Summarizing this claim of simultaneous action with the mathematical formula "environment + object," Boccioni asserts that dynamism describes "the creation of a new form which expresses the relativity between weight and expansion, between rotation and revolution."[26] The new form, which he will go on to call "spiral architecture" (*architettura spiralica*) is "life itself caught in a form which life has created in its *infinite succession of events*."[27] This "caught" form, a form of life created by life, thus contains both a spatial (architectural) and a temporal (arrested succession) component, and the two components are as inextricable as energy, speed, and mass.

Sharply juxtaposing this project with that of the Cubists, whom he does not directly name—"this succession is not to be found in the repetition of legs, arms and faces, as many people have idiotically believed"[28]—Boccioni asserts the need of art to embody four dimensions: height, width, depth, and the kind of unfolding time that intersects with space: "dynamic continuity." "We are not necessarily

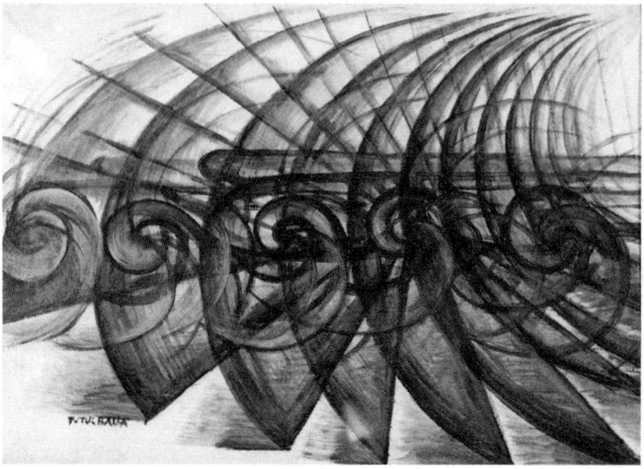

11 Giacomo Balla (1871–1958), *Speed of a Motorcycle*, 1913. (© 2013 Artists Rights Society [ARS], New York / SIAE, Rome. Image courtesy of the owners of the painting)

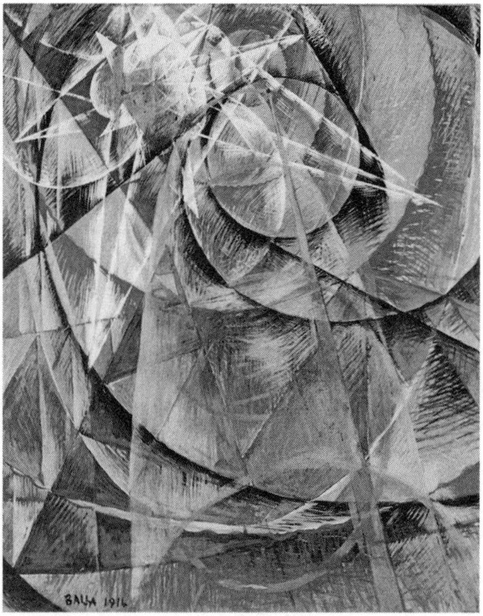

12 Giacomo Balla, *Mercury Passing Before the Sun*, 1914. (The Solomon R. Guggenheim Foundation, Peggy Guggenheim Collection, Venice, Italy. © 2013 Artists Rights Society [ARS], New York / SIAE, Rome. Erich Lessing / Art Resource, New York)

looking for *pure form*," clarifies Boccioni, emphatically, in another jab at Cubism, "but for *pure plastic rhythm*, not the construction of an object, but the construction of an object's action. We have abolished pyramidal architecture to arrive at spiral architecture. A body in movement, therefore, is not simply an immobile body subsequently set in motion, but a *truly mobile object*."[29] If pyramidal architecture, which must be "abolished," implies both the static and the hierarchical, "spiral architecture," which for Boccioni is also the foundation for painting, embodies movement and, through its rhythm, opposes the hierarchical with the fluid.

In 1913, Boccioni made several series of paintings expressing this quest for mobility, including *Dynamism of a Human Body*, *Plastic Dynamism of Horse and Apartment Block*, and a number of *Spiral Constructions*, including the one shown in figure 13. Here Boccioni's painterly spiral architecture sets a purple humanoid (probably male) body, pictured headless, against what appear to be houseplants. The antipathy to Cubism is visually evident, primarily in the bright colors and softened contours in the form, which give a more organic impression than that of the clinical (and, for the Futurists, excessively Euclidian) geometry of Cubist painting. In the middle of the canvas appears a large hand/giant phallus, camouflaged by its similarity in color to what appear to be the houseplants' pots. And yet, despite Boccioni's theorization of bodily movement, and possible depiction of propelling phallus, the figure appears as though sitting and thus oddly static.

It is in Boccioni's sculptures of this year that the principles of "dynamic continuity" are expressed most forcefully. In *Spiral Expansion of Speeding Muscles* and *Unique Forms of Continuity in Space* (figure 14), which appears to be a more finished version of *Speeding Muscles*, a body is depicted as if moving through space—"as if" because access to actual movement must remain imaginary and only notionally generational. Given Boccioni's Marinettiesque extolling of newness and movement, it seems odd that his sculpture should appear at first so freighted with classical allusions (helmeted head, armored shoulders, Mercury-like winged feet) and so bulky. Yet the small, cyborg-like head; large, muscularly torsioned legs; "flaming" appearance; and square block feet manage to convey a

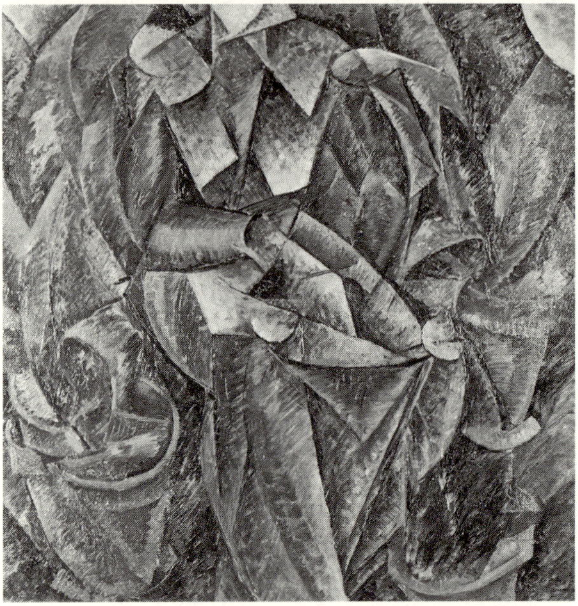

13 Umberto Boccioni (1882–1916), *Spiral Construction*, 1913–1914. (Galeria Arte Moderno, Milan, Italy. Album / Art Resource, New York)

spiralized tension between weight and expansion, between what Boccioni calls, with a clear nod to politics, "rotation and revolution."

While Christina Poggi, laying out her thesis of the Futurists' "artificial optimism," identifies a potential source in Nietzsche—as did Wyndham Lewis in the Vorticist Manifesto, as we shall see[30]—other art historians have recognized that much of Boccioni's vocabulary in *Dinamismo plastico* is actually drawn from the very different philosophy of Henri Bergson. Indeed, swaths of the Futurists' writing on spiral architecture appear directly to quote from Bergson's *Matter and Memory* and *Creative Evolution*, particularly their invocation of "extensity," "vital energy" (*élan vital*), and the experience of time as "duration" as understood

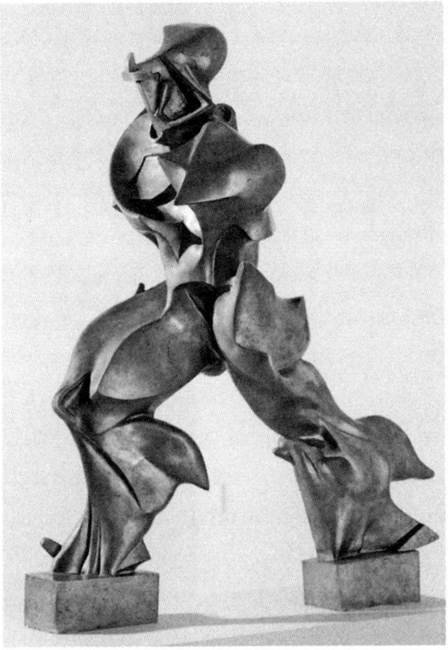

14 Umberto Boccioni, *Unique Forms of Continuity in Space*, 1913. (Museo del Novecento, Milan, Italy. SCALA / Art Resource, New York)

through creative intuition, as opposed to mere intellection. In *L'évolution créatrice* (*Creative Evolution* [1907]), Bergson writes, "La vie en général est la mobilité même," and goes on to compare "the living [*les vivants*]" to "vortices of dust [*tourbillons de poussière*] carried aloft by the wind": like these vortices, the "living turn on themselves suspended by the grand breath [or blast] of life [suspendus au grand souffle de la vie]."[31] The spiral vortex, for Boccioni—and one can apprehend this in *Unique Forms of Continuity in Space*—tangibly represents these Bergsonian terms.

Yet by no means are these spiral effects (and affects) restricted to the philosophical, aesthetic, or quasi-scientific realms. Indeed, as art historian Mark Antliff has shown, Boccioni's spirally mobile, striding "architecture" projects itself into space and can readily be seen as fusing with the loudly trumpeted Futurist program of national regeneration and imperialist expansion that reached its apotheosis in Mussolinism. "The Futurist correlation of the fourth dimension with a Bergsonian spatial-temporal flux made up of 'force forms' and 'force lines,' unfettered by the limitations of three-dimensional space or measured 'clock' time," writes Antliff, "fused with a political program premised on intuition and an anti-materialist call for national regeneration and imperialist expansion."[32] Indeed, the very first page of *Plastic Dynamism* extols the "campaign to transform the consciousness of the Italian citizenry and inaugurate a political revolt against Italy's democratic institutions," institutions the Futurists believed to be slow, inefficient, and in thrall to bourgeois notions of individuality.[33]

The deep connections among spirality, creativity, and territorial expansion are especially evident in Carlo Carrà's multilingual, multimedia collage, *Patriotic Celebration* (also called *Demonstration for Intervention in the War* [1914]), in which *linee-forza* (an expression later associated with Gilles Deleuze and Félix Guattari in their "lines of flight") travel in and shoot through a spiral form (figure 15). Said to have been inspired by the helical spinning of leaflets dropped from an airplane over Milan's Piazza del Duomo, Carrà's work, published in the Futurist magazine *Lacerba*, passionately sought to press Italy into a war with Austria-Hungary over disputed territory, including Trento and Trieste.[34] Along with text taken from Marinetti's *Zang Tumb Tumb*—in Carrà's painting, it is called "Zang Tumb Tuuum"—and invocations of the speed of airplanes ("aviatore," "ITALIA, battere il record," and, especially interestingly, "eliche perforanti" [perforating propellers or helixes]), there are numerous Italian flags and as-if-vocalized declarations of "EVVIVAAA L'ESERCITO" (LO-ONG LIVE THE ARMY).[35]

The barrage of evidence thus clearly demonstrates that the spiral image allowed many of the most important Italian Futurists a means of expressing

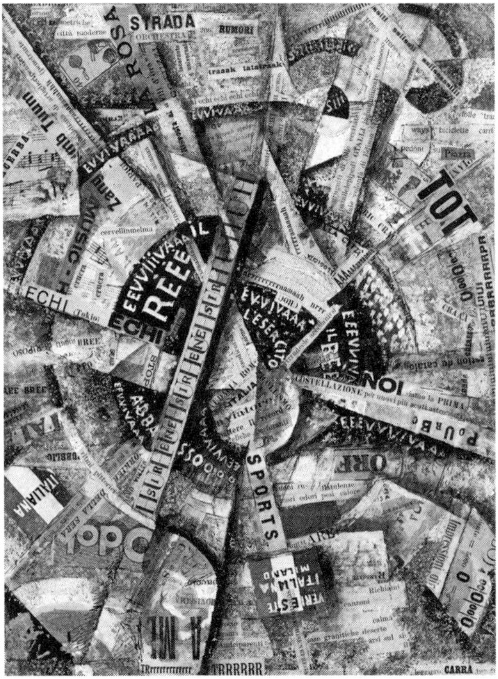

15 Carlo Carrà (1881–1966), *Patriotic Celebration, Free Word Painting*, 1914. (© 2013 Artists Rights Society [ARS], New York / SIAE, Rome)

a belligerence intimately linked to creativity, a belligerent creativity that leads ineluctably from the very form of an object to an expression of temporality and historicity, to a willed outcome in the geopolitical realm—including Italy's occupation and/or annexation of the former Austro-Hungarian–controlled areas of what is now eastern Italy and the former Ottoman-controlled areas of Ethiopia/Eritrea, Somalia, Libya, and parts of what are now Albania, Croatia, and Greece.

LAUGHING LIKE A BOMB: BRITISH VORTICISM AND THE EXPLOSIVE SPIRAL

The Futurists' artistic production and, to an even greater extent, their widely broadcast swaggering pronouncements were to have almost immediate influence throughout vanguardist European literature and visual art. Futurist ideas of spiral movement and emanation gave both a name and a directionality to a would-be revolutionary literary and artistic British group, the Vorticists, who, in their organ *Blast* (1914–1915), railed against the perceived effeminacy and "automobilism" of the Marinetti circle but deployed many of their precursors' central motifs and tactics.[36] It is hardly surprising that a movement named Vorticism—from *vortex*, Latin for "whirling motion," a term used by Descartes in his description of the origin of matter—should be concerned with spirality. But in the pages of *Blast*, the frequency with which spiral vortices serve as a figure for a specific kind of twisting, sucking, recoiling explosiveness is remarkable.

In "Great Preliminary Vortex," the preface to the two "manifestos" of Vorticism, Wyndham Lewis, speaking for the collective of London-based artists, notoriously and hilariously "blasts" phenomena from "bourgeois Victorian vistas" to French "poodle temper" to the English climate (also cursing, with an "expletive of whirlwind," British aesthetes) and then calmly and benevolently "blesses" English ships, ports, and hairdressers (for their "mercenary" war on "wildness"), ultimately asserting as the first principle of the manifesto, "Beyond action and reaction we would establish ourselves."[37] Here, with notable similarity to Marinetti's swerving around two, or beyond two, bi-cyclic modes of thought, Vorticism will "set up" the "violent structure of adolescent clearness between two extremes."[38]

In the pages of *Blast*, the primary means of expressing this elusive, conditionally posited adolescent "beyond" or "between"—a zone also reminiscent of the "'pata" in Jarry's 'pataphysics—is through spiral images, both linguistic and visual. In *Group*, Cuthbert Hamilton depicts geometrically rigid and curved spaces with attention to, and a tension between, explosiveness and collapse. *Radiation*, by

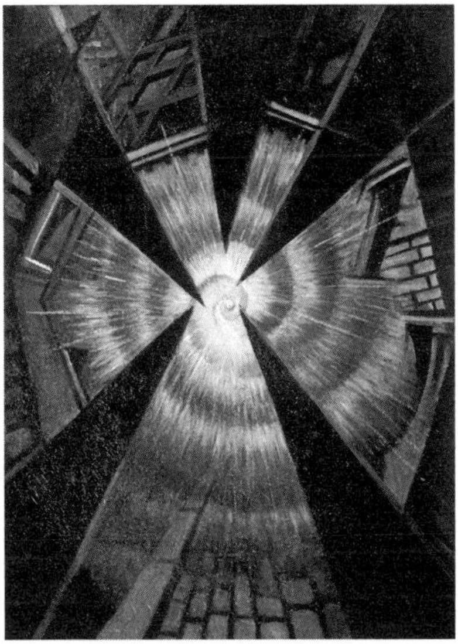

16 Christopher R. W. Nevinson (1889–1946), *A Bursting Shell*, 1915.
(© Copyright Tate Gallery, London. Tate, London / Art Resource, New York)

Edward Wadsworth, who elsewhere in the same issue of *Blast* favorably reviews Kandinsky's *On the Spiritual in Art* (wherein the latter advocates "the abstract element" in art), conveys a frenzied sense of illumination with its multiple sources of incandescence, some machine-generated. And, although it did not appear in *Blast*, Vorticist fellow traveler Christopher R. W. Nevinson's painting *A Bursting Shell* similarly emblematizes the Vorticist attachment to spiral incandescence, linking it to explosive destruction (figure 16).[39]

Lewis's own sketch, in *Blast*, for a sculpture (figure 17) sharing the same title as his utterly radical play *The Enemy of the Stars*, looks like a slimmed-down version of the cyborg's leg and head from Boccioni's dynamically continuous *Unique Forms of Continuity in Space*. *The Enemy of the Stars*, whose name clearly draws

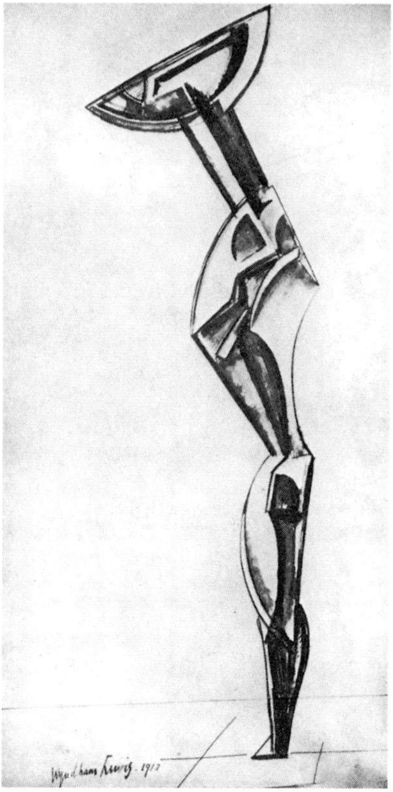

17 Wyndham Lewis (1882–1957), *The Enemy of the Stars*, 1914. (© Bridgeman Art Library for the Wyndham Lewis Trust)

on the Futurist Manifesto's concluding "insolent challenge to the stars," conveys a sense of drilling downward and broadcasting outward—two central motifs from Lewis's manifesto. In his analysis of this image, art historian Hal Foster writes of two hardenings that "seem to converge: on the one hand, with a head like a receiver, the figure appears reified from without, its skin turned into a shield; on the other hand, stripped of organs and arms, it appears reified from within, its ossature turned into 'a few abstract mechanical relations'" (the embedded quotation is from T. E. Hulme, an early translator of Bergson). "In either case," Foster concludes, "it looks the part of an 'enemy of the stars.'"[40] Yet, bearing in mind Boccioni's notion of dynamism, it is possible to view this sculpture less as "ossified" psychoanalytically or politically and more as an attempt to drive down, as though with a spiral screw, and to extend.

This alternative interpretation would put the sculpture more in line with Lewis's writing in *Blast*, which everywhere draws on the figure of the spiral to express both concentration and extension. In the incantatory poem "Our Vortex," which concludes the long section "Vortices and Notes," in which Lewis writes of phenomena ranging from a recent exhibition of German woodcuts to his understanding of the "just so"-ness of Chinese *feng shui*, Lewis lays out the fundamental principles of the Vorticist movement. On behalf of the collective, Lewis begins with a setting of the temporal contours of "their" vortex:

> Our vortex is not afraid of the Past: it has forgotten it's [*sic*] existence.[41]
> Our vortex regards the Future as as [*sic*] sentimental as the Past.
> The Future is distant, like the Past, and therefore sentimental.
> . . .
> The new vortex plunges to the heart of the Present.[42]

If avoiding bathetic sentimentality is paramount, then, as Nietzsche suggests in "On the Use and Abuse of History for Life," the Past must be actively forgotten so as not to be a hindrance to action. Meanwhile the Future, because it is no more tangible or proximate (or less "sentimental") than the Past, is likewise not to be fetishized, as Lewis insinuates it is among Marinetti's circle. According to Vorticist logic, only the Present, into whose "heart" the "new vortex" assertively "plunges," as though either knowing carnally or killing anti-vampirically, can be the proper home for artistic production. Put succinctly: "Life is the Past and the Future. / The Present is Art."[43]

The "Present" of "Art" in this sense is antithetical to "Life," the sentimental embrace of which Lewis associates both with a residual Romanticism and with the aestheticism of a humanist critic like Cook, with whom we began this chapter. Lewis himself had already emphatically dispensed with "Life" along with "Nature" in the sarcastically titled "'Life is the Important Thing!'" an entry that appeared earlier in the "Vortices and Notes":

> NATURE IS NO MORE INEXHAUSTIBLE, FRESH, WELLING UP WITH INVENTION, ETC., THAN LIFE IS TO THE AVERAGE MAN OF FORTY, WITH HIS GROOVE, HIS DISILLUSION, AND HIS LITTLE ROUND OF HABITUAL DISTRACTIONS.[44]

Romantically conceived "NATURE," like "LIFE" for the habit-bound man of forty, is not to be viewed as a wellspring or source of invention. Consequently, the "new vortex," notwithstanding its vital energy, is not to be confused with Life itself or Nature. Rather, this new vortex is that force that is able to escape the "groove"—avoiding the kind of mechanized repetition associated with the record player (cue Eliot and Duchamp)—and to "plunge" into the heart of the not-Life of Art in the "Present." The Vorticist is thus conceived as an active plunger toward a "heart," art, but the plunging always results in a casting or spinning out.

The oft-cited definition of Vorticism as the "maximum point of energy," coined by Pound in 1913, appears in the very next section of "Our Vortex," where Lewis returns to the figures of the Past, the Future, and Nature. But the explicitly libidinal nature of this pointed energy is made clearer when one looks at the actual line in its first appearance in poetic context:

> The Past and Future are the prostitutes Nature has provided.
> Art is periodic [*sic*] escapes from this Brothel.
> Artists put as much vitality and delight into this saintliness, and escape
> out, as
> most men do their escapes into similar places from respectable existence.
> The Vorticist is at his maximum point of energy when stillest.[45]

Whereas "most men," presumably the grooved men-of-forty, "escape out," inventively, to the "Brothels" of "the Past and Future," the singularly saintly Vorticist, steadfastly avoiding sentimentality, periodically embraces the perpetually novel energy of the now. This "maximum point of energy," a source of vitality and delight, is contrarily accessed when the Vorticist is "stillest."

While Lewis was the most public spokesperson of the "group," and its most vociferous advocate, the tension between compression and bursting up, "plunging" and remaining still also appears frequently in the Vorticist writings of Pound. One of the first poems in *Blast* is the surprisingly tender-seeming "Before Sleep," which describes a liminal state of somnolence, in which a speaker imagines or envisions himself "caressed" by "lateral vibrations," the source of which is not at first described:

> The lateral vibrations caress me,
> They leap and caress me,
> They work pathetically in my favour.[46]

It eventually becomes clearer that these "lateral vibrations," which at once leap and caress and work "pathetically"—Pound had already drawn on this kind of Latinate residue in the "apparition" of the Imagist "In a Station of the Métro"—owe to the intervention of "the gods of the underworld," whose "realm is the lateral courses."[47] So the poem features an emanation coming from below, an emanation that necessarily precedes a journey out. The second half of the two-part poem reads, in part:

> Light!
> I am up to follow thee, Pallas.
> Up and out of their caresses.
> You were gone up as a rocket,
> Bending your passages from right to left and from left to right
> In the flat projection of a spiral.[48]

"Falling" asleep, which usually takes place in the dark, is here associated with light and is conceived as a kind of flight "up" on a rocket, a vehicle of transportation that in the context of the era in which the poem was written was associated not with space exploration but with potential destruction and "brilliant visual display."[49] The speaker in the poem claims to be "up" to follow Pallas. Whether this Pallas is the titan of warcraft and husband of Styx or, far less likely, the goddess of wisdom and protectress of Odysseus, is not clarified. In either case, Pound conceives pursuing Pallas's rocket-like flight out of "the underworld" (the zone of dead souls that, elsewhere, Pound associates with backwater America or with the British or European poetic status quo) as taking place in the "projection of a spiral." This flat projection, its "bending" but penetrating "passages" mimicked by the suddenly expanding and then contracting line-lengths in the stanza, links the shape of superhuman power, the power to escape, to the act of writing, a fundamentally "flat" act that nevertheless here is portrayed as lifting up and out.

Toward the end of the inaugural volume of *Blast*, Pound offers a quasi-poem, almost redundantly called "VORTEX," that is less lyrical and more manifesto-like, less cursive and more incantatory. Working himself into a kind of rhetorical lather, Pound returns once again to Lewis's stilled whirlpool figure:

> The vorticist relies on this alone; on the primary pigment of his art, nothing else.
>
> Every conception, every emotion presents itself to the vivid consciousness in some primary form.
>
> It is the picture that means a hundred poems, the music that means a hundred pictures, the most highly energized statement that has not yet SPENT itself it [*sic*] expression, but which is the most capable of expressing.[50]

The sheer potentiality of the Vorticist "statement" swamps mere poem, picture, or musical composition, artistic modes ordered in quasi-Nietzschean hierarchy of their expressivity. Amplifying the earlier "maximum point of energy when stillest" formulation, Pound here sexualizes the statement, or rather portrays it in erotic terms and desexualizes it in the mode of tantric or Kantian proscriptions against the expenditure of semen: the most highly energized statement is that which "has not yet SPENT itself" in "expression." (A moment later, Pound juxtaposes this "Anglo-Saxon" form of manly withholding from Italian profligacy, making clear the links between Jarry and Futurism discussed earlier: "Futurism is the disgorging spray of a vortex with no drive behind it, / DISPERSAL.")[51]

MANLY WITHHOLDING AND THE VORTEX OF WAR

Given that Pound goes on to call the "primary pigment in poetry" "IMAGE," and given that Pound's and Lewis's 1914 notions of "maximum energy" and "stillness" share structural similarities with Benjamin's "dialectics at a standstill" (probably first articulated around 1927 and itself offered as a sort of definition of Benjamin's conception of "image," one that guides this book's argument), it behooves us to address for a moment key distinctions between the "whirlpool"-like thinking of the men. Whereas Pound, Lewis, and Benjamin each suggest the potentially redemptive dimension of stilled dialectics of the "now," Lewis advocates a Nietzschean active forgetting of the past, while Pound's conception of the accessible past consists largely of architecture, art, and poetry—including what Eliot, in his famous and clearly Pound-influenced essay "Tradition and the Individual Talent" will call "great poetry" or "the greatest poetry."[52] For Benjamin, who is of course also passionately invested in the idea of cultural continuity, which he asserts is impossible under massified modernity, such notions of tradition are always inflected with the remnant of the *Namenlosen*, unnamed and unnamable people trampled in history's narrative of progress. This remnant informs Benjamin's terse but poignant quasi-Brechtian statement in thesis 7 of "Theses on the Concept of History": "There is no document of civilization which is not at the same time a document of barbarism."[53]

Pound's intriguing figure for the "highly energized statement that has not yet SPENT / itself it [*sic*] expression" can further be usefully compared with Benjamin's own juxtaposition of "historicism" and "historical materialism" in thesis 16. For Benjamin, "Historicism offers the 'eternal' image of the past; historical materialism supplies a unique experience with the past. The historical materialist leaves it to others to be drained by the whore called 'Once upon a time' in historicism's bordello. He remains in control of his powers—man enough to blast open the continuum of history."[54] Benjamin's oddly macho version of the "man enough" "historical materialist" may seem out of character when considered against the lasting impression of the melancholic Berliner, hand on anguished-but-ever-thinking forehead, but it has to be acknowledged and reckoned with. Indeed, note that the verb with which Benjamin associates what ought to happen to historical continuity is *aufzusprengen* (to blow out or explode), which translator Edmund Jephcott rightly renders as "blast."

Yet the distinction between Pound's and Benjamin's priapic versions of stasis and potentiality emerges more clearly in Pound's "THE TURBINE," which follows immediately after "the most capable of expressing," as if an enjambment:

> THE TURBINE
>
> All experience rushes into this vortex. All the energized past, all the past that is living and worthy to live. All MOMENTUM, which is the past bearing upon us, RACE, RACE-MEMORY, instinct charging the PLACID, NON-ENERGIZED FUTURE.[55]

Pound distinguishes between a passé simple and an "energized past," one "living and worthy to live"—the latter apparently overlooked by the Futurists. This kind of past, depicted as a voracious hunter, "bears upon" and "charges" the inert, feminized future. Clearly, for Pound, though not for Benjamin, the idea of the past is inherently linked to emphatic ideas of "RACE" and

"RACE-MEMORY," ideas that, for Pound, make life "worthy to live." Benjamin's investment in the past is precisely the redemption of what advocates of race and race-memory consider bare or mere life (on which they act, endlessly hunting). Thus, notwithstanding its structural similarities to Benjamin's mode of a stilled, stormy dialectics, Pound's momentous, totalizing turbine is headed in a quite different direction.

Pound's direction will reveal itself clearly enough in the *Cantos* of the following decade, especially those cantos that, like the proclamations of Italian Futurists whose ideas he had excoriated, extol the leadership of Mussolini. But the militarism implicit in Pound's previously rather abstractly Vorticist claims, and their direct connection to the geopolitical field, are amply evident in the *Blast* writing of Henri Gaudier-Brzeska. In the concluding entry to *Blast*'s first volume, Gaudier-Brzeska offers still another "Vortex," this one consisting of a series of vortices, through which he traces, à la Oswald Spengler, but over the course of a scant few pages, the whole history of civilizations understood in part through their conceptions of sculpture. Beginning with the "Paleolithic Vortex," in which man's "manhood was strained to the highest potential," Gaudier-Brzeska considers the "Hamite Vortex" of Egypt, where the "use of the vertical" inspires awe.[56] The Hamites, according to Gaudier-Brzeska, in turn influenced "the fair Greek"[57] and, through the Greek, the "Indians," who "felt the hamitie [*sic*] influence through Greek spectacles."[58] Here sculpture was produced "without new form perception," the result being a "Vortex of Blackness and Silence."[59] Following then-current ethnographic and proto-eugenic notions that the German race descended from these wandering, conquering Aryans, Gaudier-Brzeska asserts, "The Germanic barbarians were verily whirled by the mysterious need of acquiring new arable lands."[60] Against their veritable whirling stood the "Semitic Vortex," where "the lust of war" flourished; sculpturally, these Semites contrarily "elevated the sphere in a splendid squatness and created the HORIZONTAL."[61]

Once this Vorticist classical-civilizational racist genealogy is established, Gaudier-Brzeska, an eager student at Pound's self-styled "Ezuversity," shifts his attention to China, land where "THE VORTEX WAS INTENSE MATURITY," until the arrival of the "Neo-Mongols," with their "VORTEX OF DESTRUCTION."[62] Meanwhile, in contrast to art of the "highly developed peoples," there are the quickly surveyed inhabitants of Africa and Oceania, where the "VORTEX OF FECUNDITY" can be found.[63] Here the one great cultural gift of these "inhabitants" is offered: those "masterpieces . . . knowns [*sic*] as love charms."[64]

Ultimately, harnessing the energy of all these different geographical vortices are the "moderns": Gaudier-Brzeska ranks himself alongside Jacob Epstein, Constantin Brancusi, Aleksandr Archipenko, Xawery Dunikowski, and Amedeo Modigliani—half of whom, surprisingly, might be traced, via Poundian race-memory at least, to the "Semitic Vortex"—who, with "the knowledge of our civilisation," have "mastered the elements." These six "moderns" have "made a combination of all the possible shaped masses—concentrating them to express our abstract thoughts of conscious superiority. / Will and consciousness are our / VORTEX."[65]

Reaching the bold vortex of "will and consciousness"—"will" understood in more Nietzschean than Schopenhauerian terms and "consciousness" in more Hegelian than Nietzschean terms—Gaudier-Brzeska's cavalcade of vortices abruptly cuts off. "Their" vortex represents the consummation of the vortices, the "VORTEX OF THE VORTEX" that Gaudier-Brzeska trumpets elsewhere in the short essay-cum-sculptural manifesto. "Will and consciousness are our / Vortex" constitutes the essay's terminus, apotheosis, or ne plus ultra.

And yet this was not Gaudier-Brzeska's final word on the matter. The second volume of *Blast*, the "War Volume," featured Gaudier-Brzeska's letter from the battlefields of the Great War, where he was fighting with the French army, in which he had enlisted (and been decorated for bravery), and where he would die, giving his final words even more resonance. This missive was also titled "Vortex," though subtitled "(Written from the Trenches)," and in it Gaudier-Brzeska, after two months of fierce fighting, still shockingly asserts with Futurist verve that "THIS WAR IS A GREAT REMEDY," though remedy for precisely what ailment—civilizational malaise?—is left unstated.[66] He stubbornly concludes by affirming, "Nothing has changed. . . . MY VIEWS ON SCULPTURE REMAIN ABSOLUTELY THE SAME. IT IS THE VORTEX OF WILL, OF DECISION, THAT BEGINS."[67] This "vortex," in which will and decision are paramount because generative—what this vortex "begins" Gaudier-Brzeska again does not say—repeats with a difference Gaudier-Brzeska's own earlier demand for "will and consciousness"; "will and decision" would presumably excise the vagaries and undecidability generated by consciousness. In a spiral, what appears to be "THE SAME" is never quite the same.

While the amateur sportsman Theodore Andrea Cook—whose enthusiastic study of spirals, published in 1914, was addressed at the beginning of this chapter—stressed the connection between spiral curves and "life," it is clear that Gaudier-Brzeska's vortex of "decision," coming "from the trenches" the following year, points deathward, dragging with it untold numbers of bodies, including his own. Yet it is a kind of death that Gaudier-Brzeska insists would be generative.[68] Indeed, while the issue of *Blast* in which his missive appears effectively marked the death of the Vorticist project, "their" blasting vortex, a result of the impulses generated over a trajectory leading from Jarry through the Italian Futurists, would send aftershocks in (at least) two opposed directions, each with a distinct historical and geopolitical sensibility. On one hand, in one land, was W. B. Yeats's grandiose, mystical-civilizational "vision" and, on and in another, Vladimir Tatlin's equally grandiose scientific socialism. The next chapter will trace these opposed spiral directionalities and attempt to harness their energies into a productive constellation.

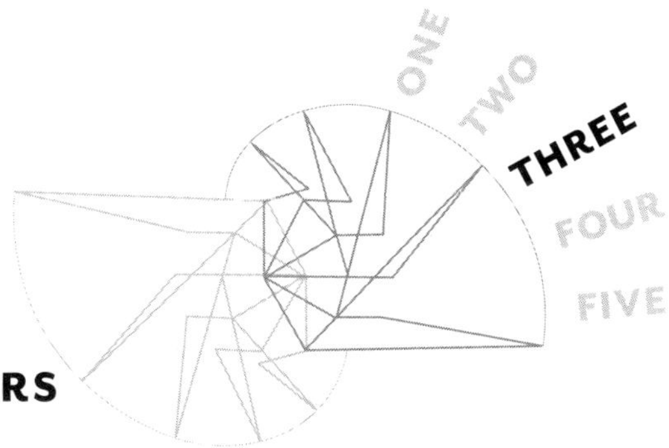

TWINNED TOWERS

YEATS, TATLIN, AND THE UNFASHIONABLE PERFORMANCE OF INTERNATIONALISM

[T]he limit itself has become a new dimension.

- W. B. YEATS, *A VISION*

I am waiting for well-equipped artistic "depots" where an artist's psychic machine might be repaired as necessary.

- VLADIMIR YEVGRAFOVICH TATLIN, "MY ANSWER TO 'LETTER TO THE [RUSSIAN] FUTURISTS'"

RE-ENVISIONING TWO SYSTEMS

William Butler Yeats's best-known poem, "The Second Coming"—with its widening gyre, falconless falconer, "things" falling apart, and correspondingly monstrous rough beast slouching toward Bethlehem to be born—presents in condensed verse some of the central insights of the text that would eventually be called *A Vision*, his all-encompassing occult system explaining in detail how both an individual life and human history move ineluctably in and through time. In the same year that "The Second Coming" was written, 1919, Russian artist and would-be architect Vladimir Yevgrafovich Tatlin conceived his *Monument to the Third International*, an enormous, transparent double-spiral iron-and-glass structure that would exceed the height of the Eiffel Tower and straddle Saint Petersburg's one-third-mile-wide Neva River, reflecting the historical struggles of the working class and gesturing proudly toward the Bolshevik Revolution's triumphant futurity. Tatlin's Tower, as the never-built structure has come to be known, was presented in model form in Saint Petersburg in 1920, the year Yeats's poem first appeared, and exhibited in revised form in Paris in 1925, the year *A Vision* was published.

A central couplet in a draft of the opening stanza of "A Second Coming" initially had less to do with a general historical malaise and more with then-current events: "The Germans are now to Russia come . . . / though every day some innocent has died."[1] "The Germans" to whom Yeats refers formed the proto-fascist paramilitary Freikorps supporting the anti-Bolshevik White Russian forces, who invaded post-revolutionary Russia before eventually being repelled by the Red Army; their "coming" would seem to indicate a momentary quelling of what for Yeats was a disaster. In any case, the "though" indicates clearly enough Yeats's anxiety about and antipathy toward the then-nascent Soviet revolution. Indeed, the Bolshevik victory and Marxism in general signaled for the self-proclaimed aristocrat Yeats not the beginning of the end of history envisioned by Marx and Hegel but the death of innocents and, indeed, "inevitable murder."[2] While "the Germans" were eventually replaced in the poem's published version with the classically Yeatsian hyphenic-adjectival "blood-dimmed tide" that, as if without agent, "is loosed," and while the "drowning" of the deliberately archaic-sounding "ceremony of innocence" occurs not in the Soviet Union but "everywhere," the published version of the poem preserves, as if a palimpsest, a trace of its specific, gyrational history, a history and a vision of history—red trampling white—that Tatlin's Tower simultaneously aims to celebrate and to monumentalize.

Yeats, the son and brother of visual artists, and himself trained as a painter, knew a good deal about then-contemporary art;[3] likewise, Tatlin was well acquainted with contemporary poetry—particularly that of Russian Futurists Vladimir Mayakovsky and Velimir Khlebnikov, both of whom wrote about Tatlin's art and incipient architecture. Yet no evidence exists that Yeats and Tatlin knew of each other's work.[4] Still, despite their lack of mutual influence; utterly distinct notions of "artistry"; and apparently diametrically opposed spiral visions of history, contemporaneity, and futurity—Yeats's famously occult and anti-rational and Tatlin's explicitly "transparent" and dialectically materialist—the two artists share the highest of high modern characteristics: a totalizing systematicity and the ambition of transforming the actual through art. Moreover, there is a profoundly theatrical dimension in each of their projects, one that is perhaps less surprising when it is recalled that both Yeats and Tatlin worked throughout the first two decades of the twentieth century on stage productions: Yeats was a playwright and manager for Dublin's Abbey Theatre, and Tatlin was a director and set designer for more than a dozen productions in Saint Petersburg, Moscow, and elsewhere. In this chapter, I focus on the central period of Yeats's spiral-gyric *Vision*—from the moment in early November 1917 when Yeats began to divine the early contours of his occult system from the late-Symbolist, proto-Surrealist "automatic writing" of his newlywed wife, George, to mid-1925, when the first version of *A Vision* (usually called *A Vision A*) was published—which is also the period of the "Great October Socialist Revolution" (early November 1917 in the Gregorian calendar) and, soon afterward, of Tatlin's work on the monumental tower.[5] I explore the spiral tendencies of Yeats's and Tatlin's work—poetry, literary criticism, *Vision*, sculpture, architecture, and theater—and accordingly demonstrate that these two towering figures of high modernism, despite their apparently opposite political views, share a sense of the structure of history, one that connects the local and the global, the past and the future, all in a spiral form.

Specifically, the two men, working both alone and in their particular collectives, including the collective of government itself—Yeats in 1922 became a senator in the Irish Free State, and Tatlin was a major figure in the National Arts Council (IZO) in post-revolutionary Russia—draw on concentric, conical double spirals[6] to illuminate connections between knowledge and power, a relation that Yeats interrogates in the closing couplet of his second-best-known gyre-system poem, "Leda and the Swan" (1924). The "putting on" of "knowledge" and "power"—crucial for any genealogy—requires a standpoint, and it is no accident that the latter word in this duo in "Leda" rhymes with "tower." Accordingly,

Yeats's and Tatlin's towering spirals entail a further, potentially vertiginous question: How is it possible to survey a history or a system in which one is living or, quite literally, embodying? Acknowledging the tensions between surveying and embodying in Yeats's and Tatlin's spirals will require a new approach to the idea of theatricality.

ROUGH BEAST: YEATS'S WHIRLED PICTURE

Spirals, cones, and spools pervade Yeats's poetry and plays of the years 1917 to 1925, from the allegorical golden king and silver lady in "Under the Round Tower"

> Bellowing up and bellowing round . . .
> Prancing round and prancing up
> Until they pranced upon the top

to the description of thought in "All Soul's Night" as winding "[a]s mummies in the mummy-cloth are wound," and from the Shepherd and Goatherd's dialogue in *The Wild Swans at Coole*:

> He unpacks the loaded pern
> Of all 'twas pain or joy to learn,
> Of all that he had made. . . .
> Knowledge he shall unwind
> Through victories of the mind

to, implicitly, the inevitable death spiral of the proud but conflicted pilot in "An Irish Airman Foresees His Death."[7] Yet it is in the rarely performed Noh-influenced play *The Only Jealousy of Emer* (1917–1918) that the playwright first discloses the complexity and the profound implications of his and his wife's occultly divined, theosophically inspired "system." The Musician's song concludes with a signature Yeatsian question:

> How many centuries spent
> The sedentary soul
> In toils of measurement
> Beyond eagle or mole,
> Beyond hearing or seeing,
> Or Archimedes' guess,
> To raise into being
> That loveliness?[8]

The soul's "centuries" of sedentariness, of course, anticipates the twenty centuries of stony sleep described in "The Second Coming." But here the result of the centuries spent in "toils of measurement," a conflation of the long uncoiling of history and a figure for the lonely soul's thinking of that history, is a "loveliness" that evades the verticality of the soaring eagle or boring mole and even displaces "Archimedes' guess." It is a spiral geometry whose contours evade the chief theorizer of the spiral in geometry.

Unwinding Yeats's elaborate "pern" (Sligo-ese for a kind of spool) requires pursuing the highly theatrical self-reflexivity of *A Vision A*. The text relies on a complicated rhetoric that at once disperses (via a set of refractions, fictionalizations, and dialogues) the disclosures of the, for Yeats, very "real" spirits and asserts the deep import of the image of the gyres for grasping the shape of history and futurity. As Clare Nally notes, "the project [that] emerged as *A Vision* [is] emphatically a partnership,"[9] in which the complicated explanation of the gyres was imparted to Yeats beginning in late 1917 by spirits called "Instructors" (and sometimes "Communicators" or "Guides," and occasionally "Daimons"), who communicated through the automatic writing of his numerologically inclined wife, George, and through her utterances during sleep; Yeats would pose questions to these Instructors and receive sometimes-elaborate answers, which he then dutifully recorded in notebooks.[10] The results of these question-and-answer sessions provide the raw data for the rest of *A Vision A*.

But Yeats, whose propensity for self-disclosure led his wife to call him "William Tell," would, supposedly out of deference to George's wishes, not unveil this odd-enough story of the inception of his spiritual access until the second, much-revised edition of *A Vision* (*A Vision B*). Instead, in *A Vision A* he substituted for the spiritual dramatis personae an arguably even odder blend of characters, some of whom were resuscitated from his earlier theatrical work and poetry, while others were reconstituted from standard-issue Victorian imperial-era travel literature. *A Vision A*'s subtitle was *An Explanation of Life founded upon the Writings of Giraldus and upon Certain Doctrines Attributed to Kusta ben Luka*, supposedly edited by Yeats's sometime–alter ego Michael Robartes, a once-lascivious spiritual wanderer.

At the beginning of *A Vision A*, the pious Catholic and more temperamentally conservative Owen Aherne (another Yeatsian alter ego) relates the story of how his one-time friend Robartes came to his house and asked him to arrange an interview with their mutual friend, the famous poet Yeats, from whom Robartes had been estranged. When asked, "What have you to say to Yeats?" Robartes immediately launches into a fantastical tale, claiming that twenty years previously he had gone to Cracow, partly because of his interest in printing (for which then-German-dominated Poland was famous) and partly because of his interest in alchemy. Upon arriving, he took up with "a fiery handsome girl of the poorer classes," rented a couple of rooms in "a tumble down house," and discovered an early, incomplete copy of a certain Giraldus's *Speculum Angelorum et Hominum* (1594) propping up the leg of the ramshackle bed.[11] After arguing with this "beggar maid," in part because of her jealousy over his growing obsession with Giraldus's book, Robartes, who had begun to translate the text from Latin, decides to abandon "all sensual pleasure" and flees to the Holy Land. While in Damascus, he sees some markings in the sand by a nomadic tribe that correspond to a diagram in the *Speculum*, and "plung[es] into the desert in pursuit."[12] Here he meets an old wise man from the "tribe of Judwalis"—the made-up name is not actually Arabic but vaguely Hindi (with the Semitic-related *Jud*, German for

"Jew," thrown in for good measure)—with whom he decides to wander for several years. The Judwalis, according to Robartes, are "known among the Arabs for the violent contrast of character amongst them, for their licentiousness and their sanctity,"[13] a description that applied to Robartes (as well as to Yeats's vision of himself). The old Arab eventually trusts Robartes enough to show him a book by the tribe's onetime leader, "Kusta ben Luka, the Christian philosopher and man of science at the court of Harun al-Rashid."[14] After prolonged study of the Giraldus and Kusta texts, both of which abound with images of wheels and whorls, Robartes reports that he is convinced that both are drawn "from a lost Syriac [Syrian Christian] original."[15]

This initial, highly elaborate explanation of *A Vision*'s genealogy would have the reader believe that the diagrams to be interpreted traveled from the deserts of the Middle East (think *Arabian Nights* in the era of a rapidly declining Ottoman Empire) to Middle Europe (itself, during the Great War years, a contested geopolitical zone, as the draft first stanza of "The Second Coming" already indicates), before eventually arriving with Robartes at the Bloomsbury lodgings of an Irish poet. The geographical and chronological admixture of this far-flung tale—which, it must be emphasized, is an elaborate "cover" for Yeats's collaboration with his wife, George—is emblematized in the frontispiece for this narrative, where "Robartes" places a portrait of Giraldus from the *Speculum Angelorum et Hominum* (figure 18).

In the drawing, made by the French-born British artist Edmund Dulac but unattributed in *A Vision A*, the old man has a good head of hair, a full but groomed beard, and a rather aristocratic mien. He sports a kind of turban. Yet, considering his association with the desert, it seems odd that he also wears a rather elaborate and heavy coat and a shirt with a starched collar. His eyes look off to the side as though into the sun, so that one of them appears to be squinting and the other almost winking—perhaps an appropriate gesture considering the elaborateness of the origin-fictions. His large, Semitic-looking nose features prominently along the vertical central axis of the picture, as do the three elaborate fish-eye buttons of his coat (the fish shapes, along with Giraldus's beard, recall familiar Christian

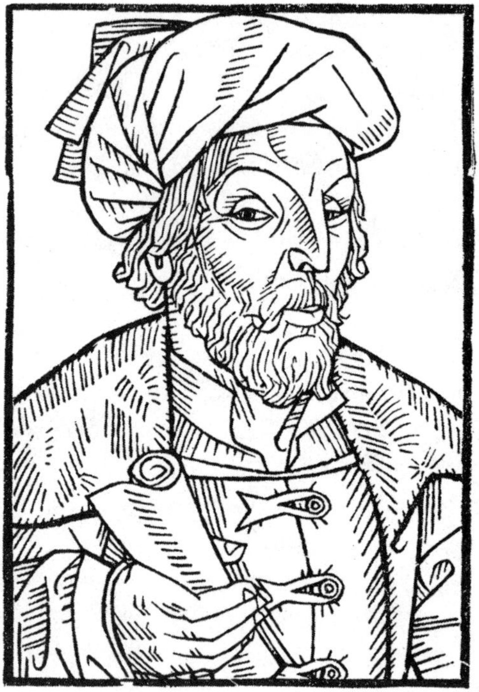

18 Edmund Dulac (1882–1953), portrait of Giraldus, in W. B. Yeats, *A Vision* (1937). (Reprinted with the permission of Scribner Publishing Group. Copyright © 1937 by W. B. Yeats; copyright renewed © 1965 by Bertha Georgie Yeats and Anne Butler Yeats. All rights reserved)

iconography). In his right hand, Giraldus holds a parchment that is, appropriately, coiled; this parchment apparently contains the image of the "great wheel." His eyebrow forms another large spiral with his nose. In his right ear is a hooped earring; whether this is a sign for a sailor, a Semite, or a former decadent pleasure-seeker is not explained. In these ways, Giraldus's portrait mirrors features one might associate with "Kusta ben Luka," Michael Robartes, and indeed Yeats himself, who, according to Richard Ellmann, had "a complexion so dark that he looked foreign; [p]eople would often think he came from India."[16] The semiotic admixture of the portrait reflects a theosophy-like blending of East and West, ancient and modern.

The erotic exoticism, gothic gnosticism, and occulted history of what Yeats would later call the "Fictions" (in *A Vision B*'s "Packet for Ezra Pound") were apparently intended to mirror the "desert geometry" of the gyrational Vision that the multiply dialogic, embedded narratives introduce. In fact, the dialogic dimension of the tales continues in *A Vision A*'s next section, Book I, "What the Caliph Partly Learned," which begins with a dialogue in verse in which Aherne and Robartes, while walking and sounding rather like characters in a Noh play, speak of Robartes's discoveries:

AHERNE:

Sing out the song; sing to the end, and sing
The strange award of all that discipline.

ROBARTES:

All thought becomes an image and the soul
Becomes a body: that body and that soul
Too perfect at the full to lie in a cradle,
Too lonely for the traffic of the world:
Body and soul cast out and cast away
Beyond the visible world.[17]

As the Musician in *The Only Jealousy of Emer* sings of how the sedentary soul struggles with "toils of measurement"—eventually, through that labor, raising into being a "loveliness"—here Robartes, singing the "strange award of all that discipline," the discipline of his long study of the Great Wheel, describes thought becoming image and soul becoming body, both body and soul eventually cast into an invisible, occulted realm.

Robartes then immediately complicates the ghostly consubstantiation and disappearance by alluding to the "full" phase of the twenty-eight-day cycle of the moon, which not only affects individual lives but corresponds to a broader historical pattern in which civilizations (defined largely by their artistic production) rise and fall, wax and wane: the "fullness" of phase 15 is too perfect, and is thus exiled from human understanding. The reference to the cradle recalls "The Second Coming"'s returning gyre and the latter's eclipse of the historical present's modality; the dialogue is thus another poem anticipating a "Coming," defined always as a "coming again," a gyrational return.

A more complete zodiacal description of the commingling of body, soul, fullness, and invisibility comes in the lengthy description in "What the Caliph Partly Learned" of the diagram of the Great Wheel, which relates how a life is governed by occult forces.[18] More pertinent for this study, focused on the spirality of Yeats's gyres, is Book II, "What the Caliph Refused to Learn," which begins with a poem about Harun's "Desert Geometry"; as it goes on, however, Yeats increasingly lets drop the dialogic form as well as the Middle Eastern and eastern European stage design and dramatis personae. In their place suddenly appear the precursor thinkers of the gyrational system: Flaubert, Blake, and Swedenborg.

Yeats (through a now largely invisible Robartes) claims that "Flaubert talked much of writing a story called 'La Spirale' and died before he began it."[19] The story, according to Yeats, would have "concerned a man whose dreams during sleep grew in magnificence as his life became more and more unlucky."[20] To the arch literary realist, stylist, and patron saint of early modernism—Pound's Mauberley's "true Penelope," after all, was Flaubert—Yeats juxtaposes Swedenborg, the eighteenth-century mystic who believed that he could visit heaven and hell and talk with angels and demons; like Yeats, Swedenborg was given the gift of spiritual vision in his fifties, though the elder man's was more direct. According to Yeats/Robartes, "Swedenborg wrote occasionally of gyrations, especially in his 'Spiritual Diary,' and in 'The Principia' where the physical universe is described as built up by the spiral movement of points."[21]

Of Blake, the writer (along with Shelley) whose writing Yeats knew best, and whose influence, benign and anxious, Yeats criticism has most often visited and revisited, Yeats writes simply and rather hastily that "in the 'Mental Traveller,' [Blake] describes a struggle . . . perpetually repeated between a man and a woman, and as the one ages the other grows young."[22] Each of the acknowledged spiral-obsessed precursors is thus invoked primarily for its assertion of the interpenetration of opposites, which in *A Vision A* is visualized by means of two interlinked cones, each of which, it is eventually explained in a series of diagrams, contains a gyre. Yeats names the compass points to the cones "Destiny" and "Will," and "Mind" and "Fate" (figure 19), the four "faculties" that he shortly afterward renames more precisely, respectively, "Mask" and "Will," and "Creative Mind" and "Body of Fate," in order to promote a sense of human agency within the faculties. According to this system of belief, these interpenetrating gyres contain the pattern followed by all life, by all movements of "soul" and "civilization"—terms with crucial significance in almost all of Yeats's poetry and thought.

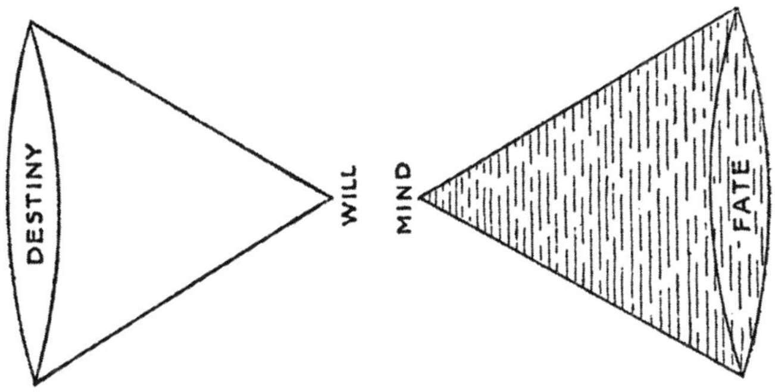

19 Gyres of "Destiny and Will" and "Mind and Fate," in W. B. Yeats, *A Vision* (1937). (Reprinted with the permission of Scribner Publishing Group. Copyright © 1937 by W. B. Yeats; copyright renewed © 1965 by Bertha Georgie Yeats and Anne Butler Yeats. All rights reserved)

What Yeats generally "refuses" to discuss in his (or Robartes's) brief nod to various precursors in "What the Caliph Partly Learned" is the profound effect of Friedrich Nietzsche on his *Vision*. As early as 1902, Yeats had written to Lady Gregory of the philosopher he calls "that strong enchanter": "I have read him so much that I have made my eyes bad again."[23] It is significant that Yeats associates Nietzsche with poor vision; in fact, in the grand civilizational survey later in *A Vision A*, which we will discuss shortly, Yeats is enchanted with eyes and with different civilizations' representations of eyes: "The Greeks painted the eyes of marble statues and made out of enamel or glass or precious stones those of their bronze statues, but the Roman was the first to drill a round hole to represent the pupil."[24] He goes on in this vein to write, "When I think of Rome I see always those heads with their world-considering eyes . . . and compare in my imagination vague Grecian eyes gazing at nothing, Byzantine eyes of drilled ivory staring upon a vision, and those eyelids of China and of India, those veiled or half-veiled eyes weary of world and vision alike."[25] Yeats is clearly drawn to the "drilled" pupil, which he later claims "reveals so much."[26] Here he seems to prefer not the Roman eye "considering the world," but the Byzantine one "staring upon a vision," and the imagined world of cultural perfection, of East meeting West (or, in Yeats's systemic vocabulary, "primary" meeting "antithetical") that that vision represents. But the challenge to Yeats's thinking of Nietzsche (who also heavily draws on and runs with an image of the East) was the latter's presentation of the untimeliness of history, an untimeliness that troubles historical vision and makes the gyres "unfashionable" in several senses.[27]

In his letter to Lady Gregory, Yeats goes on to assert, using a Poundian arboreal metaphor, that "Nietzsche completes Blake and has the same roots."[28] As Yeats well knew, but refrained from writing about directly in *A Vision*, William Blake, in texts ranging from *The Four Zoas* through *Milton* to "Jerusalem," repeatedly evokes the image of the vortex, which tends in Blake (as in Yeats) to represent "mental processes" themselves and which often appears as dangerous whirlpool or abyss. Urizen, Blake's law-creating and -obeying man, for example, is described as trapped within the vortex of his own creation:

> For when he came to where a Vortex ceasd to operate
> Nor down nor up remaind then if he turnd & lookd back
> From whence he came twas upward all. & if he turnd and viewd
> The unpassd void upward was still his mighty wandring[.][29]

For Urizen, and indeed for Nietzsche, the vortex of thought does not "ceas[e] to operate," and even if it did cease, Urizen could not adequately map his position, as his coiling path appears both abyssal and vertiginous. Perhaps this is why Yeats offers, in *A Vision A*, a disavowal of the most far-reaching implications of Nietzsche's "thought experiment" of the eternal return: "It seems that ancient men except the Persian and the Jew who looked to an upward progression, held Nietzsche's doctrine [*sic*] of the eternal return, but if religion and mathematics are right, and time an illusion, it makes no difference except in the moral effect."[30]

WHITE RUSH: THE HISTORICAL CONES

This rather offhand leveling of "upward progression" of the Persians and Jews and the eternal return of the other ancients, by means of a conditional embrace of "religion and mathematics" and a bracketing of "moral effect," is sustained and elaborated on in the third and most famous book of *A Vision A*, "Dove and Swan," in which Yeats tries to steer a course between a teleological-organic vertical spiral view of civilizational history (Goethe, Hegel, Spengler) and a recursively spiral one (Vico, Blake, Nietzsche).[31] This third book was originally to be titled simply "History"; the rubric was changed as *A Vision A* went to press, "Dove" and "Swan" representing two different annunciations and

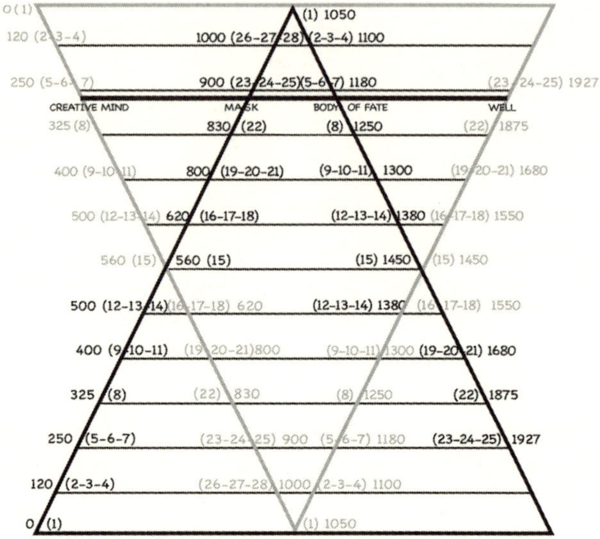

20 "The Historical Cones," in W. B. Yeats, *A Vision* (1937). (Reprinted with the permission of Scribner Publishing Group. Copyright © 1937 by W. B. Yeats; copyright renewed © 1965 by Bertha Georgie Yeats and Anne Butler Yeats. All rights reserved)

conceptions—Jesus and Helen of Troy, respectively standing for the Christian and classical eras.

Here Yeats (or if the theatricalized fiction is still in operation, Robartes) begins by presenting a new diagram called "The Historical Cones," in which appear two interpenetrating cones, the red and the black (figure 20). Each cone is marked with dates from 0 to 1050 and from 1050 to 1927 along its two vertical sides, so that the cones inversely correspond. Taken together, they map out the eras in which the four faculties are predominant. For Yeats, the diagram's significance lies in not "the movement only from the beginning to the end of [each] historical cone, but the gyres that touch its sides, the horizontal movement."[32] In the gyres, which embody both the vertical and the horizontal, one finds "a continual oscillation" produced by opposites, "each age unwind[ing] the thread another age has wound."[33] The oscillating thread metaphor, which we have seen before in the "pern" and which here refers obliquely to Penelope's patient weaving to ward off her suitors in the *Odyssey*, aptly conveys the notion of the widening and contracting gyrations that drive the system.

After inserting "Leda and the Swan" under its original rubric, "Leda," as a sort of epigraph (which, titularly at least, emphasizes the position of historical rape victim), Yeats presents, in the twenty-five or so pages of Book III that follow, a sweeping theory of the relation between literary and art history (about which he modestly claims to know "but little"), understood through works of its most famous producers, and History, understood as the history of rising and falling civilizations, about which he could at that time fairly claim to have only a sketchy idea.[34] In the "Stray Thoughts" that commence his historical reflections, Yeats defines "civilization" as "a struggle to keep self-control,"[35] and one could say that the system's very systematicity consists of an ongoing tension between history unwinding and winding up, a form of self-control ever on the verge of spinning out of control.

Yeats's presentation of "capitalized History" proceeds in three parts: from 2000 B.C.E. to 1 C.E., from 1 to 1050, and—the area of Yeats's clearest envisioning—from 1050 to the present.[36] The presentation of the first two sections is necessarily rapid-fire. In each historical era, as in each individual life, one of the tinctures predominates. In *A Vision A*, Yeats tends to associate the Primary with masculinity and the Antithetical with femininity; at times, these are loosely associated with geographical East and West, respectively. At crucial phases, the Antithetical West comes together with the Primary East, introducing a newness that produces utter change. Some of Yeats's speculations regarding this commingling are far-reaching and phantasmagoric: concerning the second century B.C.E., when Rome began to displace Greece, he observes, "One knows not into how great extravagance Asia, accustomed to abase itself, may have carried what soon sent Grecians and Romans to stand naked in a Mithraic pit, moving their bodies as under a shower-bath that those bodies might receive the blood of the bull even to the last drop."[37] Others draw from literature in translation conclusions about civilizational intermingling: Yeats identifies in the *Arabian Nights* the Caliph's recognition of a beauty-in-itself that Yeats calls "sanctity"; he then deduces that this sanctity, "come back from the first Crusade or up from Arabian Spain or half Asiatic Provence and Sicily," around the eleventh century C.E., "created romance"[38]—by which he means Provençal poetry.

According to Yeats's scheme, each gyre "corresponds" to a period two millennia earlier, such that "the period from 1005 [*sic*] to 1180," with its "Arthurian Tales and Romanesque architecture," repeats the historical and artistic conditions of "the Homeric period some two thousand years before," and by this logic Yeats's then-historical-present was on the verge of reiterating the dual annunciations of Helen and Christ.

Consequently, the period from the fifteenth century onward, where "Body of Fate" and "Will" predominate and the Church loses power, are of particular interest to Yeats's historical vision; as he approaches his then-historical-present, each phase is described in greater detail. One of the most salient of these phases is the gyre corresponding to phases 19, 20, and 21 of the Historical Cones and lasting from 1680 to 1875. This is effectively the gyre of philosophical modernity, early capitalism, urbanization, and imperialism—though Yeats does not use any of these terms. Here, in Yeats's vocabulary, "personality" (a term he uses admiringly) has come under the sway of "Will" and "is everywhere spreading out its fingers in vain, or grasping with an always more convulsive grasp a world where the predominance of physical science, of finance and economics in all their forms, of democratic politics, of vast populations, of architecture where styles jostle one another, of newspapers where all is heterogeneous, show that mechanical force will in a moment become supreme."[39] This furiously listed etiology, in which jostling architectural styles and "democratic politics" are symptoms of the same grand malaise of "grasping" under the sign of objectivity—which thinkers of a different political persuasion (or bent) diagnosed as "reification"—encompasses literary production as well, and Yeats indulges in a bit of literary criticism, dispensing in a searing sentence with Austenian sentimentality: the grasping gyre "makes the heroines of Jane Austen seek, not as their grandfathers and grandmothers would have done, theological or political truth, but simply good breeding."[40] Not only literary technique, but narrative subject matter itself, runs on the gyres.

Given that it corresponds to Yeats's lifetime, the Communicators' (or Kusta ben Luka's) phase 22—the phase that lasts, or will last, from 1875 to 1927—is of crucial importance in the gyrational schema. Like that from 1250 to 1300 (phase 8), it was, according to Yeats, "preceded by the great popularisers of physical science and economic science, and will be followed by social movements and applied science."[41] But phase 8 was also the gyre of Dante, who serves as a model for Yeats in that "in the Divine Comedy [he] imposes his own personality upon a system and a phantasmagoria hitherto impersonal"[42]—clearly something that Yeats envisions of *A Vision*.

In the middle of his description of phase 22, Yeats, almost as an afterthought, inserts a very short paragraph about war: "It is said"—presumably by the Instructors, but the passive voice is telling—"that at Phase 8 there is always civil war, and at Phase 22 always war, and as this war is always a defeat for those who have conquered, we have repeated the wars of Alexander."[43] These, along with the hasty mention of "social movements," are among the only references in *A Vision A*'s description of the course of history to the Great War and the liberation and decolonization struggles of the years 1917 to 1925, and the references are decidedly indirect. (Another, albeit also indirect, reference is discussed shortly.) In fact, the "drilled eyeballs" of sculpture merit far more mention in *A Vision* than do the then-just-completed world war or attempted or then-just-completed revolutions. As we have shown, the news of the October Revolution aroused revulsion in Yeats, and he praised the major colonial powers' intervention on the side of the White Russians; meanwhile, and not entirely consistently, Yeats opposed the British-supported Black and Tan incursions to suppress revolution in Ireland. In the early years of the Great War, Yeats, rather like the Italian Futurists, had embraced the potentially cleansing effects of battle, later viewing with alarm the mounting carnage as increasingly symptomatic of the inevitably turning gyre.

Yet the description of the Historical Cones in *A Vision A* largely follows the recommendation of silence that Yeats had advocated in "On Being Asked for a War Poem":

> I think it better that in times like these
> A poet keep his mouth shut, for in truth
> We have no gift to set a statesman right.[44]

"The gift" that a poet, or a playwright, did have was to condemn, Dante-like, the work of those artists who were his contemporaries. Part of what Yeats recognized to be a "personal phantasmagoria," coming again at the end of phase 22 and the newly stirring phase of the impending gyre that only the visionary can perceive, involves the careful placement of contemporaries in their allotted architectonic neighborhoods. In this new phase, Yeats places those "writers, poets and sculptors" (but does not mention painters), some of whom are Yeats's "friends," "who have a form of strong love and hate hitherto unknown in the arts"—one may recollect immediately the "blasts" and "blessings" of the Vorticist Manifesto—and are "absorbed in some technical research to the entire exclusion of the personal dream."[45] Yeats mentions Wyndham Lewis by name here, as well as Constantin Brancusi, "who has gone further than . . . Lewis from recognizable subject matter and so from personality."[46] In these artists' ostensibly "objective" work, Yeats curiously sees a "hatred of the abstract," and Pound, Eliot, and Joyce stand accused of "eliminat[ing] from metaphor the poet's phantasy and substitut[ing] a strangeness discovered by historical or contemporary research or [of] break[ing] up the logical process of thought by flooding them with associated ideas or words that seem to drift into the mind by chance."[47] Thus the solid, concrete objectivity of the high modernist American-born poets is one with the flowing consciousnesses of the high modernist Irish-born novelist; in all, according to Yeats's phantasmagoric schema, Myth "gropes its way out of the mind's dark but will shortly pursue and terrify."[48]

It is remarkable that, as early as 1925, Yeats reflected on the very writers whose works (along with his own of this early-1920s period) would eventually be considered to form the hard, irreducible core of "British" modernism. While Yeats gestures toward this incipient canon, he clearly aims to set himself apart from these figures, primarily on the basis of "personality," a personality that rejects scientific objectivity and embraces "metaphor." Yeats's reference to "the mind's dark," where Myth dwells and whence it will escape, combines nineteenth-century German idealist notions of *Geist* with slightly later notions of psychoanalytic eruption.

As for Yeats's signature "pursue and terrify"—as indicated by the blank spaces in the bottom right and top right of Dove's or Swan's Historical Cones, extending to two years past the (initially) then-present year of 1925[49]—the system cannot predict exactly when the impending phase 28, signaling the final turnings of this double gyre, will emerge or what it will entail. It can only gesture, theatrically, in that direction, as "The Second Coming" does with its concluding question, thoroughly rhetorical, which neither grammatically nor logically follows the assertion of the knowledge ("now I know") it confidently offered.

And yet Yeats was profoundly invested not only in occult knowledge of the past—the kind offered in theosophy, Golden Dawn, and spiritualism, with their potential connections with the dead—but specifically in a clairvoyance that could expose the impending future.[50] In a letter written in 1921, Yeats mentions Eugénie Strong's *Apotheosis and After Life*, and notes, "I read many books of this kind now, searching out signs of the whirling gyres of the historical cone as we see it & hoping that by their study I may see deeper into what is to come."[51] Accordingly, in *A Vision A*, Yeats claims to foresee a period in the near future in which the domination of "applied science" will accompany "the elimination of intellect." Beyond this almost Frankfurt school–like diagnosis, there are hints, for Yeats, of "the adoration of force." Finally, well after Y2K, the triumph of (the?) Will might lead to the emergence of a "tribal genius," of "covens of physical or intellectual kin melted out of the frozen mass." "I imagine," writes Yeats, "new races, as it were, seeking domination"—why, one wonders, the hedging "as it were"?—"history grown symbolic, the biography changed into a myth. Above all I imagine everywhere the opposites, no mere alternation between nothing and something . . . but true opposites, each living the other's death, dying the other's life."[52] In galley proofs, this last sentence, its concluding phrase (often reiterated in *A Vision*) echoing Heraclitus, was substituted for an even stronger sentence: "Victory bringing control of the world's surface must come to those who have made life a preparation for war and so established life in the terror and sweetness of solitude that every act of war is an act of creation and the solitude of each the tribal solitude."[53] This double gyre will produce "kindreds [who] must obey irrational force and so create hitherto unknown experience." It is a gestation that some await and from which others recoil.[54]

In a far more charming, local vein, Yeats once wrote that "the place that has really influenced my life the most is Sligo. There used to be two dogs there—one smooth-haired, one curly-haired—I used to follow them all day long. I knew all their occupations, when they hunted for rats and when they went to the rabbit warren. They taught me to dream, maybe. Since then I follow my thoughts as I then followed the two dogs—the smooth and the curly—wherever they lead me."[55] Yeats's curly thoughts, aided by the "discipline" that produced *A Vision*, eventually lead him to contemplate the "world" 's gyrations, from "turning" to "com[ing] round," in turn registering geopolitical anxieties and ambitions, folding them theatrically into the apparent assurance of a System—a systematicity subject, like an individual or a civilization, to losing control, falling apart.

TATLIN'S TOWER OF POWER AND THE STRIDE OF MODERNITY

In early 1921, the Russian-Soviet writer Victor Shklovsky, who would later gain an international reputation for his involvement with the Russian Formalist school of literary criticism, published a short essay, in the journal *Life of Art*, responding to his first glimpse of Vladimir Tatlin's model of the *Monument to*

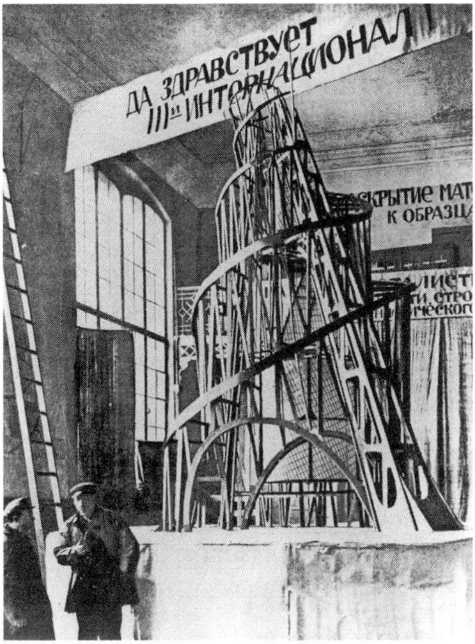

21 Vladimir Tatlin (1885–1953), model of the *Monument to the Third International*, 1919–1920. (Reprinted by permission of the Museum of Modern Art. Art Resource, New York)

the Third International, which had been exhibited publicly in Saint Petersburg a few months earlier (figure 21). In the essay, Shklovsky compares the meanings generated by the monument with those generated by poetry: "The word in poetry is not just a word, it produces dozens, indeed thousands, of associations. A literary work is permeated with them, as Petersburg's air is permeated with snow in a blizzard. The painter or counter-relief artist is not free to bar the way to this blizzard of associations, leading through the canvas of the painting or out through the rods of the iron spiral. These works of art have their own semantics [семантика]."[56]

Shklovsky's evocative appraisal offers an affirmation by way of an oddly doubled negative: the visual artist—Tatlin's career up to that point had included painting, then "counter-relief" sculptural assemblages, then architecture (as well as theatrical design)—is "not free to bar the way to" poetic associations, any more than someone could arrest the snowflakes in a blizzard in Saint Petersburg, a city known for its massive snowfall (and also the location where the monument was to be erected). Shklovsky, who plays throughout his essay with spiral motifs—вьюга, or "blizzard," for example, also implies "whirlwind"—imagines meaning traveling "out through" the iron rods of the tower, rods that connect matter-bound earth to ethereal, snowy sky, and in which the other rotating geometric shapes (cube, pyramid, cylinder), each housing a different quasi-governmental body and moving at a different speed, are suspended.[57] Concluding the essay, Shklovsky at once literalizes the fundamental material, spatial, and temporal components of Tatlin's proposed tower, "The monument is made of iron, glass and revolution," and articulates some of its most foregrounded sculptural "semantics"—support, striding, heft, and speed—in the sloganistic rhetoric of the era: "The Revolution must . . . be supported; and we have to stride forward in order to promote its weight and speed."[58]

Only a few months earlier, before the first model of the monument had even been completed, the emerging art critic Nikolai Punin—who would become chief curator at the Hermitage Museum, common-law husband of poet Anna Akhmatova, and (still later) imprisoned suspected anti-Stalinist dissident—published his own enthusiastic endorsement.[59] Most likely ventriloquizing Tatlin, his colleague in the post-revolutionary Free State Artistic Studios (SVOMAS), Punin proclaimed the project an "international event in the world of art."[60] Such a Badiouian "event" occurred because Tatlin, "the best artist of the Russia of workers and peasants," and the other members of Tatlin's "creative collective"[61] managed to unite a "utilitarian form" and a "pure artistic form," thereby creating an architecturally based monument that corresponds to "the modern understanding of history," one, he claimed, entirely distinct from classical and Renaissance ideas of memorialization and of art. Traditional (or "bourgeois") monuments feature "contemplators on granite pedestals" developed in "the reign of loggias, mule transport and stone cannon balls," and these can easily be ignored in the bustle and noise of the vast modern city. "A wartime telephone wire," claims Punin, "is more conspicuous than the memorial of an [individual] hero."[62] In contrast, Tatlin's resolutely modern form, according to Punin, "express[es] the mental and emotional tension of the collective"; it "strives to overcome material and the force of gravity," although "the force of resistance is great and massive." The structural means of achieving this collectively heroic "overcoming" is through "the most resilient and dynamic lines that the world knows—spirals."[63]

Without explicitly saying so, Punin reads Tatlin's proposed spiral monument as emblematizing the tension of dialectics. "The form rests on two axes," writes Punin, "engaged in a permanent conflict with each other."[64] In 1914, Lenin had described the Marxist version of Hegelian dialectics as a "development that repeats, as it were, stages that have already been passed, but repeats them in a different way[—]a development, so to speak, that proceeds in spirals, not a straight line."[65] The proposed tower's spiraling axes would seem, "as it were" and "so to speak," to metaphorize the coiled power of this dialectic (figure 22). According to Punin, the axes cause the tower to seem to "oscillate" or "slither" (колебаться also means to "be of two minds") "like a steel snake . . . ris[ing] above the ground."[66]

What Punin calls the "concentrated movement" of spirals situates the Bergsonian idiom of potentiality of the work of the Italian Futurists, who themselves (as we have seen) compared spirals to poised-to-strike snakes, within a more ironclad Marxist-Leninist framework.[67] According to Punin, spirals "are full of movement, striving, speed," but, lest the connection to labor be missed, "they are as taut . . . as a flexed arm-muscle . . . holding a hammer."[68] Punin, who in another essay on Tatlin inveighed against what he viewed as the faux-scientism of Cubism, called Tatlin's proto-Constructivist project "a major breakthrough . . . in the vicious circle of the overripe decadent art of our time"—implicitly juxtaposing the "vicious circle" (which Marx, as noted in chapter 2, associated with tendencies in capitalist economics) with the dialectical spiral. Summing up Tatlin's vicious circle–breaking spiral achievement, Punin declared "the present project

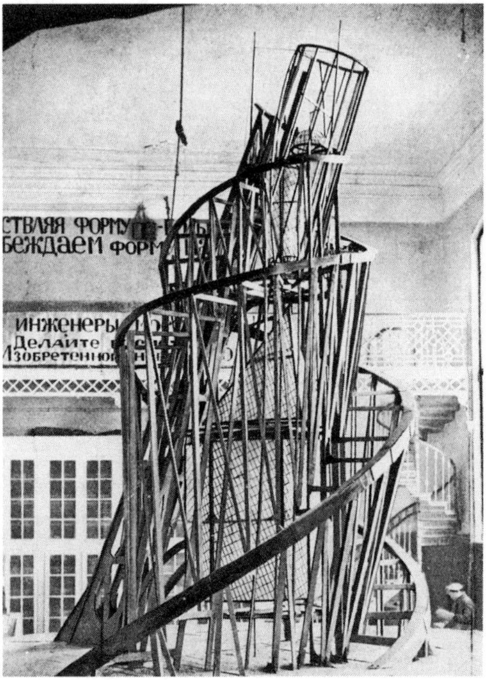

22 Vladimir Tatlin, model of the *Monument to the Third International*, 1920. (The Museum of Modern Art, New York. Digital image © The Museum of Modern Art / Licensed by SCALA / Art Resource, New York)

[to be] the first work of revolutionary art that we can send—and do so—to Europe."[69]

Shklovsky's and Punin's early, enthusiastic appraisals, heralding the tower's poetically muscular modernity and snake- or whirlwind-like dialecticality, paved the way for much of the art-historical scholarship on Tatlin that has followed in the near-century since the plans for the tower first emerged. Art historians have compared the proposed tower's size with that of the Eiffel Tower; its shape and grandeur with those of Leonardo's staircase in the Château de Chambord, Francesco Borromini's Sant'Ivo alla Sapienza, and Auguste Rodin's *Tower of Labor*; its "whiplash curves" with Jugendstil artist Hermann Obrist's whimsical models for sculptures and monuments; and its "emphatic leaning strut" with that of both the Tower of Pisa and Umberto Boccioni's *Unique Forms of Continuity in Space* (see figure 14) and *Development of a Bottle in Space* (1912). (It is unclear whether Tatlin was aware of many of these precursor works.) The cumulative effect of these studies has effectively been to endorse Punin's claim that Tatlin's proposed tower belongs in, and contributes to, the European artistic and architectural "tradition"—the very tradition that, according to Punin himself, it sought to revise, indeed revolutionize. Other art historians have stressed the tower's distinctly "Russian" qualities, and Tatlin's project and his other work have been likened to Russian Orthodox church design (especially its projection of a "dominating silhouette"), church frescoes, icon painting, and "folk" idioms.[70]

One image with which Tatlin's proposed tower has repeatedly drawn comparison, by both art historians and other artists,[71] is that of the Tower of Babel, particularly in Pieter Breughel the Elder's and Athanasius Kircher's renditions of it (figure 23). In his comprehensive study of Tatlin's Tower, for example, Norbert Lynton offers a quasi-theological reading of the proposed project, suggesting that the implicit divine warning against excessive collective human endeavor in Kircher's *Turris Babel* becomes, in Tatlin's version, an emblem of the future possibility of *overcoming* God. Lynton suggests that in the early post-revolutionary period, this overcoming necessitated a kind of state-promoted "god building" of the state itself, and he points to the influence on Tatlin of the writer Maxim Gorky; of Anatoly Lunacharsky, Tatlin's later patron as head of the Soviet Commissariat of Enlightenment; and, especially, of the polymath and science-fiction writer Alexander Bogdanov.[72]

Lynton, noting that Tatlin and Kircher were themselves both researchers and craftsmen, emphasizes the alchemical rhetoric of both tower projects—and, indeed, of all of Tatlin's work, including *Letatlin*, his post-tower flying machine. In elevating this alchemical aspect of Tatlin's work and downplaying the tower's

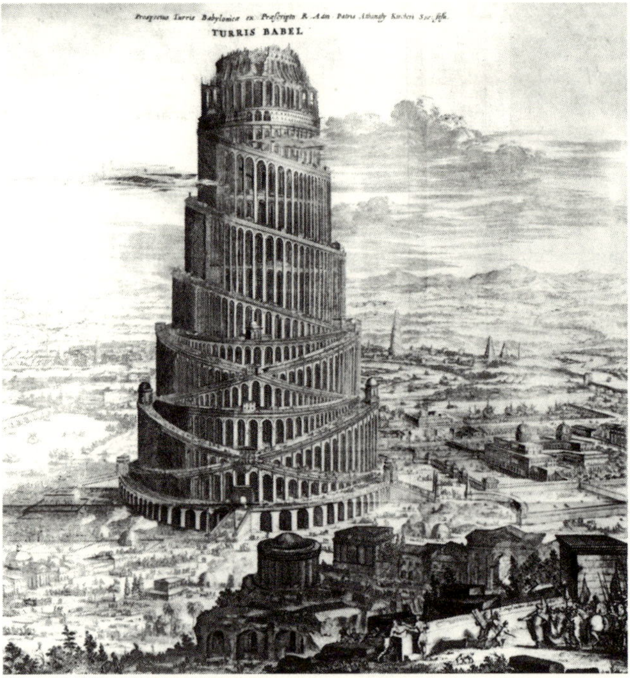

23 Athanasius Kircher (1602–1680), *The Tower of Babel* (engraving), 1679. (Private collection / The Bridgeman Art Library)

overt connections to Leninism, Lynton effectively refashions Tatlin's tower for the post–Cold War historical era, in which the utopian aspirations of the early revolutionary years are rescued from, and elevated above, their tainted association with the final sixty-five years of the Soviet Union.

There is indeed much to be gained from comparing Tatlin's proposed tower with Kircher's etching of the giant spiral tower, which the former undoubtedly resembles. Yet to undertake such a comparison requires that the comparer recognize not only the relation to liturgical doctrine requiring submission to a divine authority, as Lynton does, but also the crucial link between the figure of the spiral and the emergence of anxieties and aspirations concerning the very idea of the "globe." As noted in chapter 2, images of the Tower of Babel *as spiral* (including Kircher's and Brueghel's) began to appear in the proto-Baroque and Baroque, during an era of vastly increased international trade and nascent modern colonial domination—the period that Peter Sloterdijk associates with the "second wave" of globalization. Not only do these spiral images register a rejoinder to excessive pride at rapidly achieved material gain in growing European cities (which is to say, early international capitalism), but they reveal anxieties about encountering linguistic divergence amid increasingly mobile, cosmopolitan societies.

First proposed some 240 years after Kircher's etching of the Tower of Babel was completed, Tatlin's initial outline of the tower addresses these concerns and anxieties not from the perspective of their nascence, as the Jesuit Kircher did, but from that of capitalism's supposed fullest fledging, what Lenin prematurely called its final stage, during which its dialectical opponent, the working class, had already emerged and putatively begun to defeat it. One of the central ambitions of the Marxist movement was to unite the dispersed, mutually uncomprehending peoples of the world under the banner of the redeeming Internationale, which would "be the human race." Yet what kind of internationalism, what kind of post-Babel ingathering, would Tatlin's Tower broadcast?

As we have seen, Punin's account of some of what Shklovsky called the more prominent "poetic" meanings of the monument emphasizes the tower's (and the revolution's) *exportability*, during a period when workers' revolutions were perceived as inevitable (and yet when, it bears stressing, the civil war in Russia against the various, foreign-supported White forces was ongoing). In 1918, Tatlin was chief of "monumental propaganda" in Moscow—the two words themselves reveal a tension between memorialization and propagation, weight and lightness—and he oversaw the proposals for other similarly daring, and radically "new," monuments, such as Nikolai Kolli's temporary monument, *The Red Wedge Cleaving the White Block*, which was exhibited in Moscow in November 1918

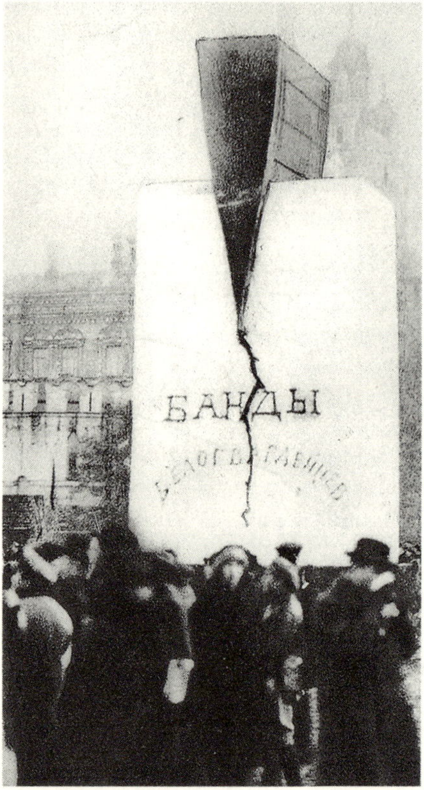

24 Nikolai Dzhemsovich Kolli (1894–1966), *The Red Wedge Cleaving the White Block*, 1918.

(figure 24).[73] Yet unlike Kolli's sculpture, which represented smashing, Tatlin's Tower would evoke uniting, in the manner of the aspirants of Babel. In its earliest conception, the tower was intended to commemorate the less-than-two-year-old October Revolution with the original name "Monument to the Liberation of Humanity." Yet while initial "research" was in progress—the rhetoric of scientific discovery pervades Tatlin's own writing as well as Punin's—its memorial source soon became the Communist, or "Third," International.

In early 1919, shortly after the deaths of German leftist revolutionaries Rosa Luxemburg and Karl Liebknecht and the failure of left-wing uprisings in Germany, Lenin called a meeting of far-left political groups and "workers associations" from all over Europe, with delegates also appearing from the United States, Japan, and Korea. The group was christened the Third International in honor of the first and second such international Marxist- and Syndicalist-led gatherings, which began in the 1860s and late 1880s, respectively.[74] The importance of the Third International's inaugural gathering is evident when one considers that it was attended by all the prime movers of the October Revolution—Lenin, Leon Trotsky, Grigori Zinoviev, Josef Stalin, and Mikhail Bukharin.

The Comintern, its acronymic rubric itself highly redolent of an international modernity, would ostensibly coordinate Communist political activity both inside and outside Russia. In his address to the gathered delegates, Trotsky juxtaposed two kinds of internationalism: the bourgeois version and the working-class version. The former, according to Trotsky, inevitably led to the Great War and survived after the war in the League of Nations. "Today when Europe is covered with debris and smoking ruins," Trotsky asked,

> [i]s all toiling mankind to become the bond slaves of victorious world cliques who, under the firm-name of the League of Nations and aided by an "international" army and "international" navy, will here plunder and strangle some peoples and there cast crumbs to others, while everywhere and always shackling the proletariat—with the sole object of maintaining their own rule?[75]

"Or," Trotsky continued, offering the other possible outcome to this incorporated future, "shall the working class of Europe and of the advanced countries in other parts of the world take in hand the disrupted and ruined economy in order to assure its regeneration upon socialist principles?"[76] Trotsky, invoking the tone of the *Communist Manifesto*, does nod to the victims of European colonialism:

"Colonial slaves of Africa and Asia! The hour of proletarian dictatorship in Europe will strike for you as the hour of your own emancipation!"[77] His emphasis, however, in line with Marx's own and that of early-twentieth-century Marxism, is on the "working class of Europe and the advanced countries in other parts of the world," since this region is where Marxists of this era fully expected the next workers' revolutions to take place.

In this sense it is surely significant that—of the four geometrically shaped, rotating, Comintern-serving structures housed in a double-spiral iron encasement, each shape progressively smaller as one ascends—the shape at the very top of Tatlin's Babel-overcoming tower was to be a *hemisphere* (figure 25). This hemisphere is not regularly mentioned in the early critical treatments: Shklovsky refers to a cylinder that takes a year to turn, a pyramid moving once a month, and a sphere rotating once a day; Punin describes a cube making a yearly revolution, a pyramid moving once a month, and an "upper cylinder" rotating once a day. Perhaps this is because two critics viewed the design at different times in 1919 and 1920; perhaps the superstructural hemisphere was in some way to be connected to the cylinder, which it is perched above. The cylinder was designed to hold the Comintern's information and propaganda department, in which newspapers were to be published and there was to be a radio station "of global reach," as well as a huge bank of telephone and telegraphic equipment.[78] From here—presumably from the hemisphere—films were to be projected onto large screens, and there were even plans for a garage out of which motorcycles and cars would descend the spiral frame to distribute "appeals, proclamations and publications."[79] Punin mentions daily messages being emitted from the top of the spiral, in a kind of architectural skywriting. Shklovsky claims that the propagandistic apparatuses "on the very top of the spiral perpetuate the monument in the air."[80]

The notion of extension beyond an individual art object or a single, monumental building is crucially connected both to Tatlin's art practice and to Russian revolutionary political ideals in the pre- and early revolutionary period. Tatlin's counter-relief assemblages of the mid-1910s, for example, were both held in place and extended by visible tension wires. While drawing on the religious tradition

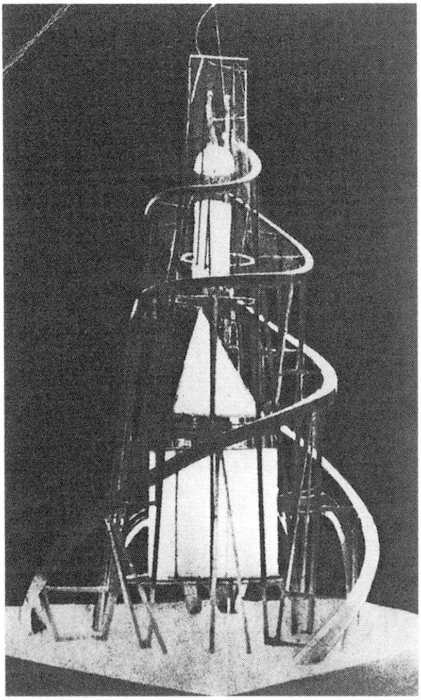

25 Vladimir Tatlin, model of the *Monument to the Third International*, 1920.

of Russian icons, which also typically occupied upper wall corners, they extended their machine-made and human-assembled "aura" and simultaneously responded to, and *countered*, the perceived limitations of Church orthodoxy.[81]

This notion of countering and extending while nonetheless holding in place and unifying was also critical to early revolutionary rhetoric. In his collection of essays gathered under the title *Lenin* (1925), written in part to emphasize his own connections to the recently deceased Russian leader, Trotsky notes that in 1917, between the February and October Revolutions, Lenin wrote an essay called "A Stranger's Letter" (sometimes translated "Letter from Afar"), published in the new Communist Party organ, *Pravda*. This essay, according to Trotsky, reveals Lenin "in his whole collective strength."[82] Drawing on Lenin's own spiral figures, Trotsky claims that the argument in "A Stranger's Letter" resembles "a powerful steel spiral, surrounded by a strong band, which in the future will expand, spread out and embrace ideologically the entire meaning of revolution."[83] Tatlin, both in his design for the tower in general and specifically in the ideological hemisphere encompassed by it, similarly intended to extend this very local monument—it would have straddled the Neva River in the city that would soon come to be called Leningrad—through such an international "embrace" of "strangers."[84] According to Tatlin's main ideological promoters of the era, the spiral tower would thereby do for the Russian Revolution what Jacques-Louis David's history painting did for the French, and would serve as a socialist counterpoint to the "bourgeois" (and decidedly un-spiral) Eiffel Tower and its comparatively limited notion of internationality (figure 26).

THE BABBLE OF TRANSLATABILITY

While Tatlin's Tower's post-Babel spirality calls to be analyzed in relation to historically specific Leninist principles of spiral development and internationalism, which principles the tower's design seeks to translate into the global sphere, or hemisphere,[85] it also necessitates a theoretical consideration of the question of *translatability* itself, which, as we have seen, is crucial to the possibility of "overcoming" Babel's plight by addressing the international working class—at the very least that of "Europe and the advanced countries in other parts of the world."

In his essay "Des tours de Babel" (1985), Jacques Derrida notes a cleavage in the very origin of "Babel," a word that signifies both "City [or gate] of God" in the ancient Babylonian language and, in Hebrew via the kind of pun one finds frequently in the Torah, "confusion."[86] Similarly, although he does not directly draw attention to it, Derrida's essay's title, "Des tours de Babel," gestures to the confused filiations between "towering" and "touring," as *des tours* in French

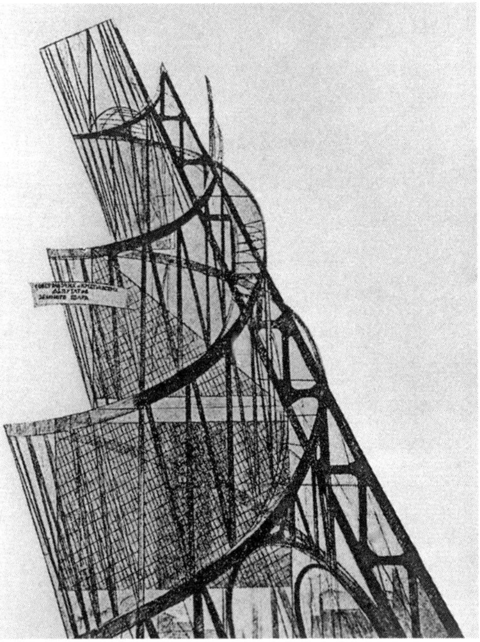

26 Vladimir Tatlin, hand-drawn model of the *Monument to the Third International*, 1920.

suggests both "on [or of] towers" and "some tours"—the latter "tours" implying both a visit (by a stranger) and a circling or spiraling around: revolution.[87] This spiraling-around the question of Babel suggests, for Derrida, "an impossibility of completing" a translation: "The 'tower of Babel' does not figure merely the irreducible multiplicity of tongues; it exhibits an incompletion, the impossibility of finishing, of totalizing, of saturating, of completing something on the order of edification, architectural construction, system and architectonics."[88] A translation, like an "edifying" architectural construction, cannot be completed in part because the desire to unify, to make "one tongue," is always already subject to destruction. To make this point, Derrida draws on not one but two different French translations of Genesis 11, emphasizing the tower builders' pre-destruction desire to "make a name" so as not to be "scattered," the tension between "naming" and "scattering" informing their post-destruction fate as well.

For Derrida, who in "Des tours de Babel" is effectively translating while revising Walter Benjamin's argument in "The Task of the Translator" (as well as grappling with Benjamin's earlier essay, "On Language as Such and on the Language of Man"), concerning the relation between the original and the copy and the possibility of a "sacred" translation, the tower episode is the archetypal example of a sacred text about the possibility of translation, which itself requires and demands translation, but which, once translated, loses its distinctive quality, its status as *naming* in the Adamic sense. And yet, despite the impossibility of completing a translation, of accessing sacredness, the singularity of any translation itself, according to Derrida, produces, *performs*. "No theorization"—even Derrida's own or, for that matter, that of God, whose Latin name is invoked—"will be able to *dominate* the Babelian performance."[89] As such, the "tour de Babel" reveals both the impossibility of translation and its absolute necessity.

Derrida's tours of Babel offer a new perspective, or spin, on questions concerning the constructability of Tatlin's Tower, designed first in the name of the liberation of humanity and then in the name of the Third International. Art and architectural historians typically claim that the project was unbuildable not only because of Soviet-era shortages in raw materials (especially steel) and the later-1920s shift toward socialist realism, but also because its engineering ideas were unrealizable.[90] Yet if the translations of the Tower of Babel that Tatlin proposed are viewed as a Derridean *necessary incompletion*, it might be germane to think of the failed tower project less as an unbuildable building and more as a "performance." This would be an especially fruitful avenue to pursue if one also considers Tatlin's work as a set and costume designer, beginning in the early 1910s (precisely the time Yeats was working with the Abbey Theatre) and flowering in 1923 in his production of his recently deceased poet friend Velimir Khlebnikov's *Zangezi*, which he also directed and produced, and in which he acted.[91] *Zangezi* was a radically vanguardist play that Tatlin himself called a fusion, "in the form of a supernarrative," of Khlebnikov's "work on language and the study of laws of time."[92] These laws of time, which Khlebnikov called будетлянство, were a kind of future-orientation that Khlebnikov described as "the study of the influence of the future on the past." According to art historian John Milner, "Khlebnikov considered time to be a spatial phenomenon, permitting an investigation of its rhythms and structure across history."[93] Clearly, this spatialization of time and rhythmic history informed Tatlin's Tower as well.

For his theatrical adaptation of the poem, Tatlin constructed a set of block-like boxes and placed them toward the rear of the stage; in front of them, leaning at about a seventy-five-degree angle from stage right toward center stage, was a large tower to be ascended by the hero (played by Tatlin himself). Punin called the poem "one of the most synthetic plotless mysteries of our age, a marvelous stupendous shawl, a cloth hanging over our century," but he lamented the audience's "incomprehension" of the performance of Khlebnikov's rational "irrationalism." Nevertheless, as he did with Tatlin's Tower, he called the production of *Zangezi* at the Museum of Artistic Culture "an event."[94]

Of course, Derrida's invocation of the Tower of Babel's indomitable *performativity*, a term that appears in his work even before his essays "Signature Event Context" (1971), on J. L. Austin, and "Limited Inc a b c . . ." (1977), on John Searle, is not identical with or simply translatable to a theatrical performance on stage. Yet it must be recognized that there is a theatrically performative quality in almost all of Tatlin's work (as well as in much of that of Yeats, as we have explored). As Samuel Weber notes in *Theatricality as Medium*, theater might productively be "considered as a medium in which conflicted forces strive to secure the perimeter of a place in dispute."[95] In this nod to theater's military sense, Weber, drawing on both Benjamin and Heidegger, asserts that theatricality is "a process of placing, framing, situating rather than . . . a process of representation."[96] It is this sense of theatricality *as medium* (in every sense of that term) that infuses Tatlin's and Yeats's rhetoric of theater despite the entirely opposite political and artistic convictions they espouse.

There is yet another Tower of Babel/Babylon that has appeared frequently in Tatlin criticism, usually in passing—and it, like "theatricality," links Tatlin to

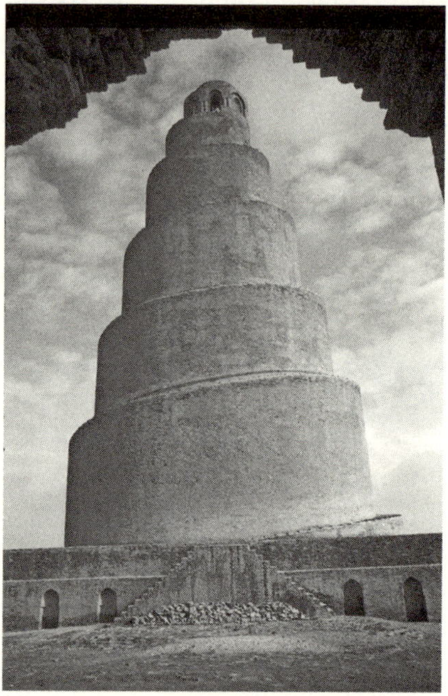

27 Spiral minaret of the Great Mosque, Samarra, Iraq, ca. 850.
(© World Religions Photo Library / The Bridgeman Art Library)

Yeats. It has been suggested, by Lynton, Anatoly Strigalev, and others, that during his travels abroad as a seaman during his twenties, Tatlin may have visited the Great Mosque of Samarra, Iraq, with its Malwiya (Arabic for "twisted" or "snail shell") minaret (figure 27); in the early twentieth century, this region was still part of the rapidly shrinking Ottoman Empire.[97]

Whether or not he personally saw this enormous minaret, with its ascending conical spiral reaching some 170 feet into the sky, it seems almost certain that he had come across images of it, and many Russians considered the sandstone construction to be the actual tower of Babel.[98] This fact, when considered along with the inner pyramidal shape incorporated into the design for Tatlin's Tower, might inflect the Eurocentric internationalism of Lenin, Trotsky, and the Third International in new way: built into the tower, with its glass and steel a testament to Western modernity, is a gesturing toward the geographical Near East, as a source both of civilization and of indomitable confusion. As we have seen, this region proved mesmerizing to Yeats's vision, with its "Syriac" codes, which Yeats was careful to associate with early Christianity, not Islam. (As if to emphasize Weber's linking of theatricality as medium with the "theater" of war: on April 1, 2005, the top of the Malwiya minaret was damaged by a bomb. Insurgents reportedly attacked the tower because occupying U.S. troops had been using it as a lookout position and had placed snipers there.)

A third and final aspect to consider when imagining—or imaging—Yeats's and Tatlin's iconic yet unfashionable towers together, is the question of "failure": in Yeats's case, a failure to convince anyone about the validity of the Communicators' system, and in Tatlin's, not just a failure to be built, but a failure to *translate*. Concerning the latter, as early as 1920, European Dada artists George Grosz and John Heartfield, attempting to draw on the energies emanating from the Russian Revolution, misconstrued Tatlin's project as "machine art" (see especially their work *Elektro-mechan. Tatlin-Plastik*). A few years later, in 1923, the Berlin-based Russian émigré El Lissitzky made a photomontage/watercolor/drawing that showed Tatlin working on the *Monument to the Third International*, a set of mathematical symbols including a spiral graph and the sign for infinity by his feet. El Lissitzky's drawn image of Tatlin was extracted from the 1920 photograph of the latter in workingman's clothes appearing with his collaborators in front of a model of the tower (see figure 21); in El Lissitzky's rendering, Tatlin appears alone, with a protractor jutting out of his eye, as though the collectively inclined socialist artist were a kind of modern Ptolemy.[99] While Tatlin surely looked to the sky—and in fact may, like Yeats, have been interested in astrology[100]—one of his central aims in the tower project was, in fact, to bring the stars down to earth.

Meanwhile, back in the USSR (in fact as early as 1922, before the declaration of the Soviet Union), Tatlin wrote a letter to Mayakovsky complaining that he had learned that, instead of the first model of the *Monument to the Third International*, the House of the Unions (Дом союзов) had decided to exhibit a samovar. This displacement, or replacement, represented the very beginning of a process that would eventually lead, in 1933, to the exhibition "Artists of Russia" in which Tatlin's artworks, in a gesture not unlike that of the notorious "Degenerate Art" exhibition in Germany, were relegated to a small hall dedicated to "Formalist excesses," and state-sponsored art critics derided him as "no artist whatsoever."[101] Tatlin—who, after building the model of the tower, worked for several years on *Letatlin*, the individualized aerial bicycle that he hoped could be mass produced—ended up not soaring to the sky like Dedalus (or, for that matter, Leonardo), but, mostly unappreciated, painting portraits and still-lives of flowers, with nary a spiral in sight. Meanwhile Yeats, in the last decade of his life, still clung to his vision of gyres "running on," yet increasingly scorned the sort of artist or poet "now growing up . . . all out of shape from toe to top," and retreated to the solidity of localized native stone, singing, at times bitterly, of human unsuccess.

Their inevitable "failures" aside—the word "fail" is etymologically related not only to "lacking" but also to "falling"—Tatlin's and Yeats's twinned spiral towers of the early post–Great War period amply demonstrate the durability of their makers' grand and totalizing ambitions, ambitions that include not only ways of making art (with or without "Personality") but also ways of activating history and theatrically giving shape to the future. Although spirals later in the twentieth century never again achieved quite the earnest, energetic grandiosity with which they were associated in Yeats's and Tatlin's work, and although that grandiosity would, in fact, itself come to be derided, the spiral *ambition* itself still must be admired, wondered at.

Next we explore two equally wonderful forms of spiraling, though ones associated less with energy than with *entropy*: those of James Joyce, who of course had his own interest in flying, Dedalus-like, and that of Marcel Duchamp, who had his own notions of spirals "running on."

FOUR

L'HABITE EN SPIRALE

DUCHAMP, JOYCE, AND THE INELUCTABLE VISIBILITY OF ENTROPY

Language is just no damn good—I use it because I have to, but I don't put any trust in it.

- MARCEL DUCHAMP, IN CALVIN TOMPKINS, *THE BRIDE AND THE BACHELORS*

Anemic a little. . . .Your head it simply swirls

- JAMES JOYCE, *ULYSSES*

PORTRAIT OF THE ARTIST AS A THRUSTING SPIRAL

In 1929, the editors of the newly formed, Paris-based English-language publishing house Black Sun Press commissioned a drawing of James Joyce from the Romanian sculptor Constantin Brancusi for a limited edition of fragments of the ongoing *Work in Progress* that they planned to publish later that year.[1] Brancusi produced two drawings that certainly resembled Joyce but did not have the modern signature style sought by the editors, so the editors asked the artist to try again. This time, Brancusi created a far more abstract work, titled *Symbole de Joyce*, consisting of three vertical, straight lines of varying lengths spaced at intervals along the paper and, on the right half of the drawing, a large Archimedean spiral (figure 28). Brancusi later commented that this portrait captured *le sens du pousser* (the sense of pushing or thrusting) he thought to be his model's

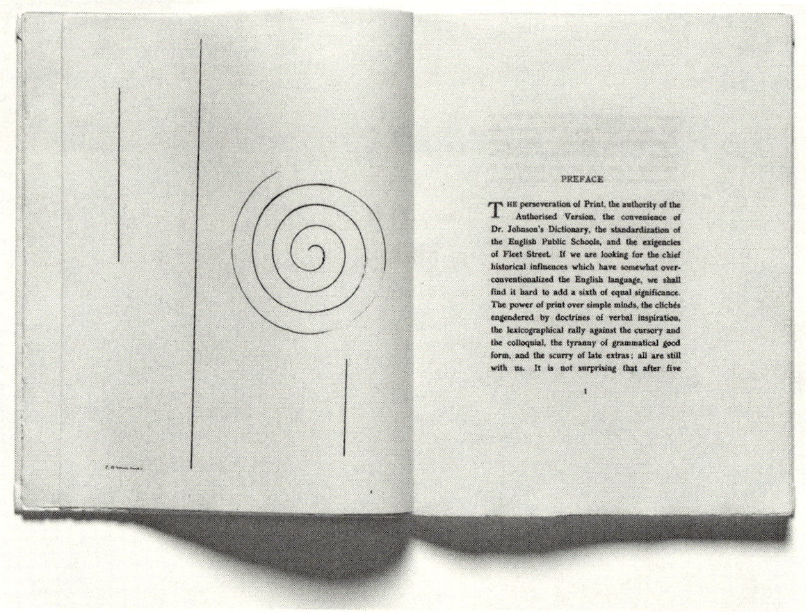

28 Constantin Brancusi (1876–1957), *Symbole de Joyce*, in James Joyce, *Tales Told of Shem and Shaun: Three Fragments from Work in Progress* (1929). (Digital image © Museum of Modern Art / Licensed by SCALA / Art Resource, New York. © 2013 Artists Rights Society [ARS], New York / ADAGP, Paris)

principal characteristic. Joyce's biographer Richard Ellmann claims that when Brancusi's drawing was eventually shown to Joyce's father, who had not seen his self-exiled son in many years, the elder Joyce wryly remarked, "The boy seems to have changed a good deal."[2]

What Brancusi saw as the "symbol" of one of the key features of Joyce's personality is borne out in noteworthy ways in the latter's early fiction, from the narrative emphasis on the "missing corkscrew" in *Dubliners*'s "Clay" to the "whirl of scrimmage bodies" that defines Stephen Dedalus's first moments at school in the opening pages of *Portrait of the Artist as a Young Man*. But it is in *Ulysses* and in

Finnegans Wake that spirals are ubiquitous, most notably in the former's "Scylla and Charybdis" episode (whose rock and whirlpool seem embedded in Brancusi's *Symbole de Joyce*) and in the latter's "Anna Livia Plurabelle" (whose riverlike coursings expand fractally) and "Night Lessons" episodes; in the *Finnegans Wake* episodes, spirals are associated primarily with Platonic idealism and vagueness, knowledge and pseudo-knowledge, feminine cursiveness or liquidity, and (homo)sexuality and fear of drowning. In both novels, they are also associated, to a greater or lesser extent, with W. B. Yeats, whose ideas Joyce parodies without entirely skewering.

The image of the spiral is similarly pervasive in the work of Marcel Duchamp, who officially "retired" from his career as an artist around the time Joyce began work on what would become *Finnegans Wake*. It is not often recognized that *Nude Descending a Staircase* (1912), on which many myths of the birth of modernist art in the United States are constructed, is actually the second version of the painting, a dull brown *No. 2* (figure 29). Before *No. 2*, there was a yellow-hued *No. 1* (1911), in which the machine-like "nude" (often presumed to be female)[3] comes down a spiral staircase (figure 30). *No. 2*'s staircase is straightened, its descending course lengthened, de-emphasizing depth, de-emphasizing space, and emphasizing the rods, pistons, and partialized body parts layered over one another, unfolded repetitively, kinetically over time—which is to say, the reading time of the canvas. Yet despite its relative rectification of the now-absent spiral, it was this *No. 2*, shown at New York's now-legendary Armory Show, that was famously dubbed a "cyclone in a shingle factory," and the reception of *No. 2*, in turn, that caused the storm that legendarily followed.

According to Duchamp's notebooks, the figure of the spiral was also to have featured prominently in *The Large Glass* (figure 31). Here, there was to have been a spiral on the "Bachelors' Apparatus" on the lower half of the glass, a kind of coiled vas deferens through which male fluids passed on their way, shooting past the "Oculist Witnesses" through the "Region of the Splash" and back up through the horizon, also known in Duchampese as the "Bride's Garment."[4] In both of these cases, to which might be added the "drain" of the famous ready-made

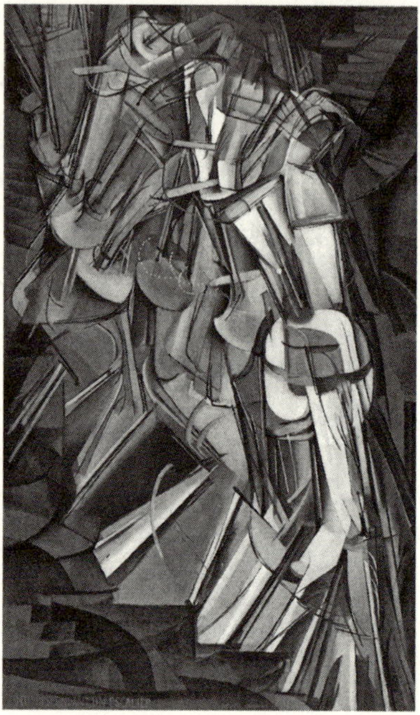

29 Marcel Duchamp (1887–1968), *Nude Descending a Staircase (No. 2)*, 1912. (The Louise and Walter Arensberg Collection, 1950. © Succession Marcel Duchamp / ADAGP, Paris / Artists Rights Society [ARS], New York, 2013. The Philadelphia Museum of Art / Art Resource, New York)

Fountain (1917), the trace of the spiral, more or less unseen by the naked eye, is intimately related not only to sexual difference (which, for Duchamp, is never a vast difference) and gender confusion, but also to desire, mechanical movement, dimensionality (including the "fourth dimension"), and temporal unfolding—constant preoccupations of Duchamp's.

But it is surely in the work grouped under the loose rubric *Precision Optics* (*Rotary Glass*, *Rotary Demispheres*, and *Rotoreliefs*, and especially the film *Anémic*

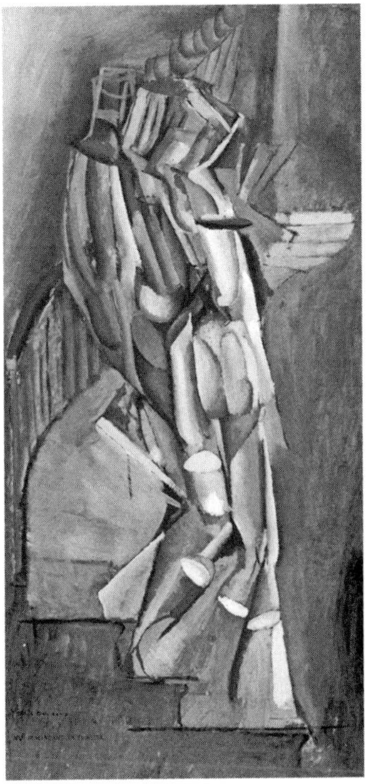

30 Marcel Duchamp, *Nude Descending a Staircase (No. 1)*, 1911. (© Succession Marcel Duchamp / ADAGP, Paris / Artists Rights Society [ARS], New York, 2013. Printed by permission of the Philadelphia Museum of Art and the Louise and Walter Arensberg Collection)

Cinéma) that spirals appear most clearly (if sinuously) and most directly reveal the function of spirality in Duchamp's broader project, blending as it does aspects of Dada and Surrealism but eluding some of the manifested aims of both rubrics. *Anémic Cinéma* (1926), created with the assistance of Marc Allégret and Man Ray, the latter of whom took one of the most famous photographs of Joyce, in 1922 (figure 32), demonstrates the strategies that Duchamp employs to challenge

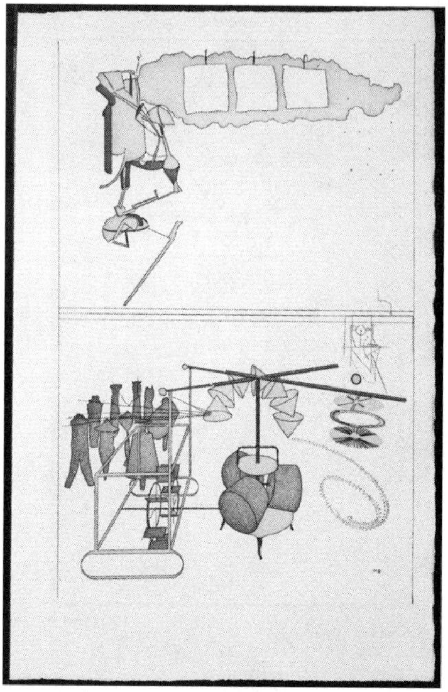

31 Marcel Duchamp, design for *The Large Glass* (lithograph), ca. 1918, in *The Large Glass and Related Works* (1967), vol. 2, ed. Arturo Schwarz. (Private collection / The Stapleton Collection / The Bridgeman Art Library. © Succession Marcel Duchamp / ADAGP, Paris / Artists Rights Society [ARS], New York)

"retinality" (the way images hit the eye) with language—and what both vision and language have to do with desire.

In this chapter, I bring Joyce's work of the late 1910s to the early 1930s into a constellation with Duchamp's work of the same period and focus on the question of the entropy expressed by their spirals. Although the word sounds as though it derives from the ancient Greek, "entropy" is a consummately modern neologism coined in 1865 by German physicist and mathematician Rudolf Clausius, who was pursuing a way to ensure the efficient running of

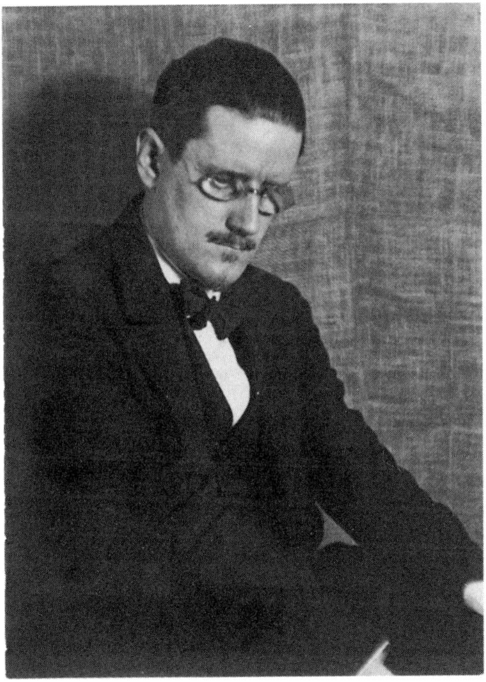

32 Man Ray (1890–1976), *James Joyce*, 1922. (Museum of Modern Art, New York, N.Y., U.S.A. © Man Ray Trust / Artists Rights Society [ARS], New York / ADAGP, Paris, 2013. Digital image © The Museum of Modern Art / Licensed by SCALA / Art Resource, New York / Private collection / Photo © Christie's Images / The Bridgeman Art Library)

engines (later called "thermodynamics"): "I propose to name the quantity S the entropy of the system after the Greek word ἡ τροπή [*trope*], the transformation. I have deliberately chosen the word entropy to be as similar as possible to the word energy: the two quantities to be named by these words are so closely related in physical significance that a certain similarity in their names appears to be appropriate."[5] Clausius stresses the closeness of the pseudo-etymology of "entropy" with the real one of "energy," the prefix "en-" denoting "to put into or on" or "to invest with a certain quality."[6] The word "energy" itself derives from Aristotle, who combined *en-* with *ergon* (work) to describe a product of an activity, an effect; in this sense, *energia* is related, in Aristotle, to *entelechia*, the condition in which a potentiality becomes an actuality. The term "energy" was, for Aristotle, associated not just with things in the world but with language itself: in *Rhetoric*, Aristotle wrote the chapter "Energy and [the] Animation of Language" and was especially interested in the kind of metaphor that calls up a mental picture of something acting or moving.[7] Homer's writing, he claims, is "full of energy," in that his metaphors give life and sense to inanimate objects. Aristotle's first example of an energetic metaphor is "a youth in the vigour of his bloom."[8]

If energy (as entelechy) is thus very much at issue in the figures of early and high modernism whose spirals we have explored thus far (Italian Futurists and British Vorticists, Yeats and Tatlin), the "closely related" entropy, which in Clausius's writing is expressed by the sinuosity of the letter *S*, is the kind of transformation that falls out of or operates against that process of actualization.[9] In titling his spiral-dominated film *Anémic Cinéma*, reflecting the anagrammatic (indeed, near-palindromic) collision of kinesis and an arresting anemia, Duchamp playfully but strategically amplified this tension. As for Joyce, for whom energetic entelechy and "blooming" were obviously crucial ideas, an opposing principle emerges, expressed in spirals, that has drawn less attention among critics: while Brancusi himself saw thrusting or pushing as the *symbole de Joyce*, Joyce's writing may achieve its greatest force in recoiling—a recoiling that has implications for political readings of his work.

In both Duchamp and Joyce, entropic spirals, in addition to calling into question the relation between the seen and the unseen, connect sexual desire to proclivities within language, proclivities that themselves expose aspects of the *polis*. In Duchamp, the whirling, obscene, transatlantic pun is structured like a tendentious Freudian joke that operates against the gender and class dynamics it seems to propound, while in Joyce, the near-Esperantic pun ineluctably flows toward the whirlpools of (homo)eroticism and colonial power relations.

DUCHAMP'S OPTICAL ALLUSIONS

Early advocates of Dada and Surrealism, international movements with which Duchamp was a fellow traveller,[10] drew heavily on spirals to articulate and flesh out a number of their central premises. In the Dada Manifesto of 1918, which emerged in the final year of the Great War, Tristan Tzara exhorted comrades to purify both art and life through destruction:

> Let each man proclaim: there is great negative work of destruction to be accomplished. To sweep, to clean [*Balayer, nettoyer*]. The cleanliness of the individual after the state of madness, aggressive complete madness of a world abandoned to the hands of bandits, who rend one another and destroy the centuries. Without aim or design, without organization: indomitable madness, decomposition. Those who are strong in words or force will survive, for they are quick in defense, the agility of limbs and sentiments flames on their faceted flanks.[11]

In many editions of the manifesto, along with this passage—whose conclusion itself evokes the flaming flanks of Umberto Boccioni's war-lauding sculpture *Unique Forms of Continuity in Space* (1913)—appeared a large hand-drawn image (figure 33). The drawing is reminiscent of playful child-like doodling, yet the *x*'s linking the coils also give it the appearance of patched-together barbed wire.[12] The tension between ludic assertion and sharp-edged recoiling demonstrates the productive ambivalence of the Dada project emphasized in Tzara's passage: destroying in order to oppose the destruction of the "bandits," decomposing in order to counter decomposition wrought by the state of madness, cleaning out in order to challenge the phony proprieties of individuality asserted by the bourgeoisie (to whom too many artists make "nice nice")[13] and usher in a new, genuinely artistic individuality. The drawing gives shape to Tzara's concluding claim that Dada represents the "interlacing of all opposites and contradictions, grotesques, inconsistencies."[14]

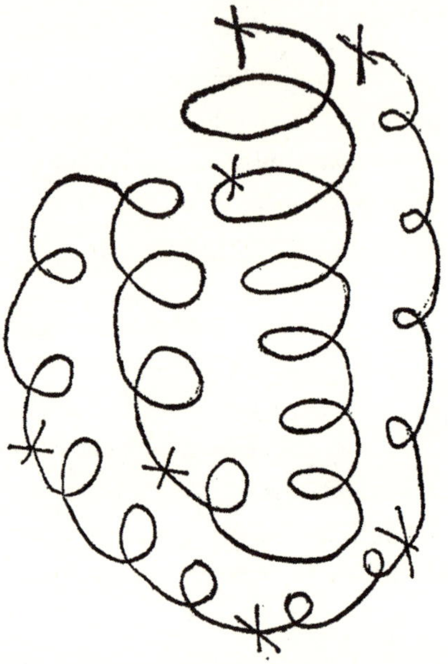

33 Tristan Tzara (1896–1963), doodle in the Dada Manifesto, 1918.

In later Dada works, such as the one that appeared on the cover of *DADA*, number 7, in 1920, Francis Picabia's drawing of an expanding telephone cord depicts an icon of technological modernity and suggests a desire to communicate (figure 34). However, the quasi-poetic text accompanying the drawing evokes reaching out and touching in other ways, in part through excess and abjection:

> Dame! [Lady!]
> La chair qui a trop bu est un boeuf napolitain [Flesh that has drunk too much is a Neapolitan beef]
> Les mains dans la crotte canonique [Hands in the canonical shit]
> Rafistoler son lit [Tinkering (with) her bed]
> Le pont-levis de la dame [Lady's drawbridge] (my translation)

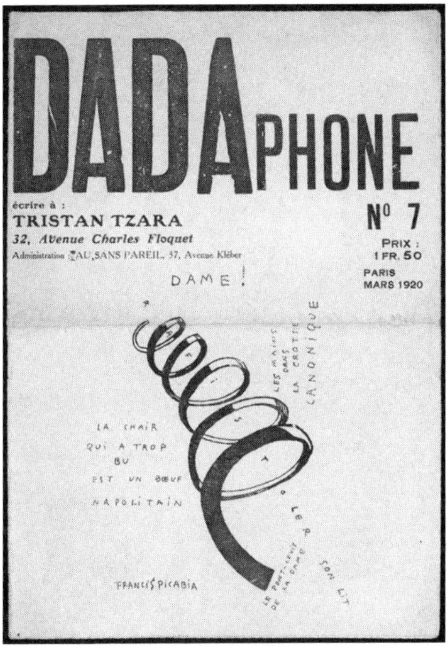

34 Francis Picabia (1879–1953), drawing and poem on front cover of *DADA*, no. 7 (1920). (Private collection. Photo © Christie's Images / The Bridgeman Art Library)

Here, the supposedly non-sense text horizontally and vertically surrounds, and diagonally cuts through, the DADAphone cord, on the one hand providing a kind of map of DAME, and on the other emphasizing through the coils that DAME is unknowable and ultimately impenetrable.

As Tzara-led Dada yielded to André Breton–led Surrealism, there was an ever-more-amplified attention to (typically hetero-)eroticism, often couched in the terms of a liberated unconscious. This attention is evident in Man Ray's rayographs of the early 1920s, in which he put aside the camera entirely and placed coiled objects on photosensitized paper, creating highly stylized, wrapped, black-and-white images, which, through the intervention of light, expose the phenomenology (and commodification) of things themselves while suggesting female body parts and ideas of femaleness (figure 35).

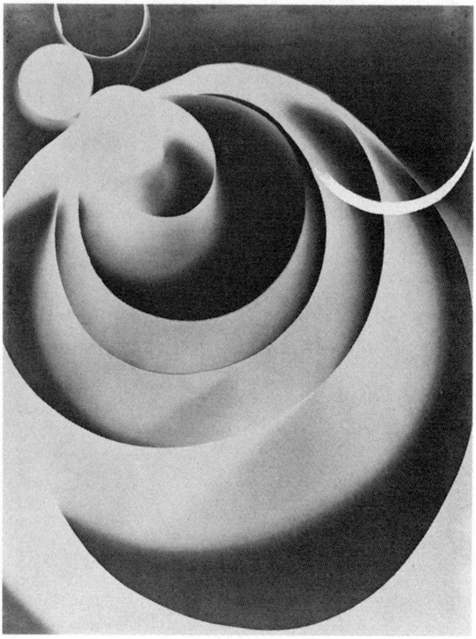

35 Man Ray, untitled rayograph, 1922. (© Man Ray Trust / Artists Rights Society [ARS], New York / ADAGP, Paris, 2013. Printed by permission of the Museum of Modern Art)

Duchamp's fascination with spirals in the *Precision Optics* series took shape in this milieu, combining the eroticism invoked by Ray's rayographs and the technological fascination (and lewdness) of Picabia's DADAphone "poem," while retaining something of the "sweeping" negative work exhorted by Tzara in the text surrounding his barbed coil. This unwieldy combination was sustained by Duchamp, first and foremost, by investigating the connections between perception and deception. Arguably, Duchamp's interest in these connections can be traced back to his work of the early 1910s. In the *Precision Optics* projects, however, they come to the fore.

The *Rotary Demispheres*, which Duchamp initiated in 1924,[15] were modeled after phenakistoscope machines invented by the Belgian scientist Joseph Antoine

Ferdinand Plateau in the 1830s. Plateau's early phenakistoscopes—from φέναξ (cheater, imposter) and σκοπεῖν (to look at, examine)—consisted of two disks, one with evenly spaced slits or windows, and the other divided into sixteen equal segments, on each of which appeared a slightly different image. When the viewer, looking into a tilted mirror, turned the machine's handle, the synchronization of the windows and the images created the illusion of sequence or "animation."[16] In a later, related experiment that also relies on "afterimages" and illusion, Plateau and an assistant created a spiral attached to a circular disc that, when rotating, appeared to be continuously expanding from or contracting toward its center. After being observed for several seconds, it induces a powerful opposite-motion aftereffect, in which an object or a surface that is fixed appears to be contracting or expanding.[17]

Duchamp's *Rotary Demispheres* combine elements of both of Plateau's experiments. When in motion, long spirals appear to spin in a clockwise motion from the center of the demispheres, while shorter spirals appear to fall centripetally back toward the center. I write "appear to," because the disks are made of concentric circles that occur as spirals only in the mind (or, if you prefer the neuroscientific idiom, brain) of the viewer (figure 36). In her canon-revising textbook, *Art Since 1900*, produced collectively with other founding and early members of *October*, Rosalind Krauss summarizes her earlier essays on Duchamp[18] by noting, in her own spiralized sentences, that

> the ironic turn on opticality wrought by these oculist machines was the havoc they were able to wreak with form. For as the turning spirals of the "oculist chart" opened onto a pulsatile movement from concavity to convexity and back again, the throb of this motion dizzied and destabilized the field of vision, eroticizing and carnalizing it instead, by filling it with a suggestive play of "part-objects": now an eye, now a uterus.[19]

To this short list one might add: "now a breast, now a lathe- or caterpillar-like phallus, now a searchlight." The "havoc" Krauss cites as produced by the throb

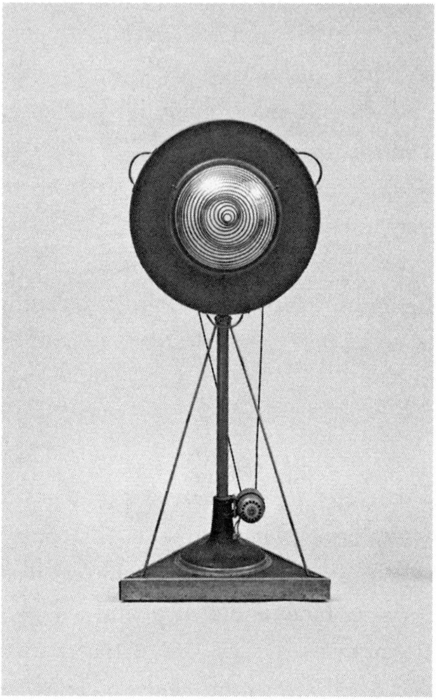

36 Marcel Duchamp, *Rotary Demisphere (Precision Optics)*, 1925. (Museum of Modern Art. Gift of Mrs. William Sisler and Edward James Fund. © Succession Marcel Duchamp / ADAGP, Paris / Artists Rights Society [ARS], New York, 2014)

of spiral motion "cheats" the retina by gesturing toward both the erotic and the process of seeing itself. In this sense, the spiral form is crucial for Krauss precisely because it opens the possibility, or gives the impression, of a liberatory formlessness.[20]

What Krauss describes as Duchamp's ironic and carnal turn on opticality extends beyond what the individual eye perceives and even how the brain translates that vision into sexual desire. Indeed, it implicates a broader scopic regime linking technology to political power. As Jonathan Crary notes, the phenakistoscope's impression of "the persistence of vision . . . substantiates Walter Benjamin's contention that in the nineteenth century 'technology . . . subjected the human sensorium to a complex kind of training'"[21]—the kind of training that required habituating one's very perceptual apparatus to the rational organization of time and movement in production. For Crary, the phenakistoscope was not only a mode of popular entertainment that anticipated modern cinema, but also "isomorphic to [other] apparatuses used to accumulate knowledge about an observer."[22] When Duchamp draws on this (by the 1920s, retrograde) protocinematic form, after its implications have been realized in feature-length Hollywood silent cinema, he is (implicitly, if we follow Crary's logic) calling into question the entire process of technological self-habituation.[23]

This set of interlinked interrogations—of the eye's propensity to be fooled, of the body's propensity to desire, and of governmentality's propensity to want to know and organize political subjects—is extended even further in the seven-minute *Anémic Cinéma*, in which Duchamp (collaborating with Ray and Allégret)[24] alternates a filmic version of ten rotary demispheres set in motion with nine punning phrases shaped into spirals, mounted on revolving phonographic disks. The demispheres each take up between twenty and thirty-two seconds of screen time, while the inscriptions typically run between eleven and nineteen seconds.

Molly Nesbit and Naomi Sawelson Gorse have suggested that Duchamp effectively raises the question "Could language have optics?"[25] Their observation is pertinent when approaching Duchamp's use of language from the perspective of his investigations of the visual, undertaken in the spiralized demispheres. But it seems to me that in juxtaposing the desire-producing machine of the demispheres with a particular *kind* of language in *Anémic Cinéma*, Duchamp goes further, asking how the whirled of language might implicate the whirled of vision, and how both perceivable shapes and language relate (and do not relate) to the world of phenomena, including carnal phenomena. P. Adams Sitney has observed with respect to the film's eroticism, "The sexuality is neither in the literal surface of the words nor in the optical illusion. It is an operation of the viewer's reading of one part of the film into the other."[26] To understand this translation "operation," it is necessary first to address how language itself takes place, spirally, in Duchamp's film.

WRITING AS COUNTER-REPEATING

The puns in *Anémic Cinéma*—Sitney rightly compares them with intertitles of silent films—consist of edited and revised versions of the kind of homophonic, syllabic swapping that characterized Duchamp's aphoristic early-1920s epistolary exchanges with his Dada and Surrealist friends, usually associated with the proper name Rrose Sélavy.[27] Sélavy, whose name itself phonetically suggests both "Eros, c'est la vie" (Eros, that's life) and "arroser la vie" (to make a toast to life), was contrarily a rather masculine-looking, wealthy Jewish patron of the arts and business entrepreneur, photographed in a starlet's pose by Ray in 1920/1921. In this pose, Sélavy, to whom Marjorie Perloff has rightly compared Gertrude Stein,[28] is wearing furs and a colorful hat featuring many odd geometric shapes (including what looks like a squared spiral above her left eye) (figure 37). Sélavy had, in fact, been introduced (in her 1921 business card) as the salesperson of Precision Oculism, offering a "Complete Line of Whiskers and Kicks."[29]

During one of the epistolary exchanges, Robert Desnos correctly suggested that "Rrose Sélavy connaît bien le marchand du sel [Rrose Sélavy knows the seller of salt very well]," thereby syllabically twisting Marcel Duchamp's name to "marchand du sel."[30] In fact, it is Sélavy (Duchamp's creation and alter ego) who is said to be *Anémic Cinéma*'s creator, and it is she who "copyrights" the film (to which copyright she appends her fingerprint) in the film's final frame.[31] From first frame to last, then, gender and individual authorship are two of the many things implicated and "inverted" in this set of language games.

One crucial example of a corrosive pun deployed by the salt seller, in the guise of Sélavy, is the film's very title, *Anémic Cinéma*, which pits cinematic movement against anemic slowness. Note that this title is neither quite English nor quite

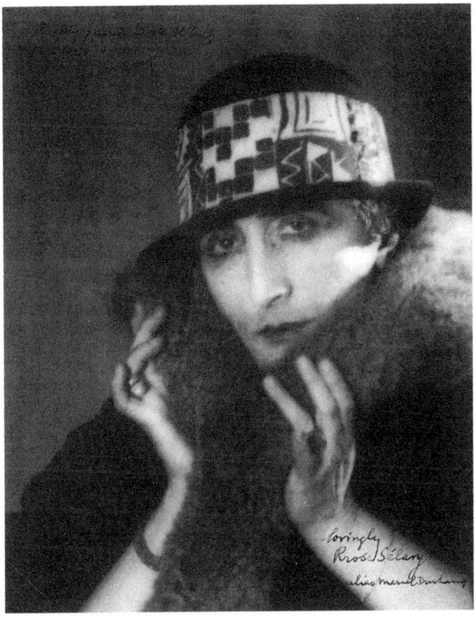

37 Man Ray, *Marcel Duchamp as Rrose Sélavy*, 1920–1921. (The Samuel S. White III and Vera White Collection, 1957. The Philadelphia Museum of Art, Philadelphia, Penn. © Man Ray Trust / Artists Rights Society [ARS], New York / ADAGP, Paris, 2013. © Succession Marcel Duchamp / ADAGP, Paris / Artists Rights Society [ARS], New York, 2013. The Philadelphia Museum of Art / Art Resource, New York)

French: in idiomatic English, there would be no accents, whereas in French the title would be *Cinéma Anémique*. The brief title sequence presents the two words in a kind of inverted *V*, with the letters nearly mirroring one another. This early frame sets the stage for the presentation of phrases and images that constitute the rest of the film.

Placed on the mat of a record player and then shot with a camera mounted over the record player, which moves at different speeds in different scenes, the phrases' white letters invoke the optical illusion of animation insofar as they present words apparently unfolding centrifugally. The words seem to unwind counterclockwise in a spiral pattern but must in effect be closed or wound up centripetally in an act of reading left to right. This epistemological double movement reflects the technological double movement of the record player's own juxtaposition between pure mechanical repetition, the record mat being driven around and around, and the spiral movement caused by the stylus hitting the grooves of the phonograph record.

Yet the viewer cannot easily make such "centripetal" sense of *Anémic Cinéma*, as many of the phrases are examples of *contrepèterie*, a form of spoonerism in which syllables or phonemes are inverted or repeated differently. The French word *contrepèterie*, combining *contre* (against) and *peter* (Old French for "making a sound"),[32] is itself an example of such a spoonerism, as the *re-* from *contre* also turns *petition* into *repetition* (though without the accent). The word thus contains notions of both countering and repeating: repeating, differently, as a kind of countering. What results in *Anémic Cinéma*'s deployment of *contrepèterie* is a set of relayed translations: between spiral image (or "art") and text (or "poetry"), text and spirally "contrepeated" text, and text and what might be called sense or sensibility.[33]

For example, the fourth intertext follows a twenty-three-second scene of a black spiral that seems to be emerging counterclockwise against a white background. In motion, the spiral leads the viewer's eye down into a kind of receding hole, like a drain, but after a few seconds appears to be moving around the contours of a kind of conical, multistepped hill, on the top of which is a small circle. If the viewer focuses on the small central circle, the gyrations around its edges begin to mirror the eye's search for information in the small frame. After a brief fade, spiraling words unfold: "ON DEMANDE DES MOUSTIQUES DOMESTIQUES (DEMI-STOCK) POUR LA CURE D'AZOTE SUR LA CÔTE D'AZUR."

A literal translation of this counterclockwise spiraling passage might read, "SEEKING DOMESTIC MOSQUITOES (HALF-STOCK) FOR THE NITROGEN CURE ON THE AZURE COAST." But this rendering almost completely elides what makes the intertitle both witty and salacious, a salacious wittiness whose circuit of implications even an attentive French reader might not have caught in the nineteen or so seconds during which the phrase spiraled on the screen. Availing ourselves of an interpretive languor that was unavailable to its original audiences confronting the speed of cinema: *On demande* is familiar from the language of newspaper want ads—“One asks [or seeks]” is a more polite way of saying “I want to buy.” From here, excluding the relatively insignificant words *pour la* (for the) and *sur la* (on the), the intertext relies on two puns involving echoic *contrepèterie*: the first is “des moustiques domestiques (demi-stock)” whose first three syllables—“des-mou-stiques”—morph into “do-me-stique” and then “de-mi-stock”; the second pun paronomastically counter-repeats the three syllables “cure-d’a-zote” as “côte-d’a-zur.” As these syllabic contours are shape-shifting, the potential meaning of the apparently non-sense passage is also disclosing itself: *cure d’azote* (nitrogen cure) is not a regularly used expression in French, but one medical use of nitrogen, in liquid form, is to freeze off skin imperfections and especially warts. *La cure d’azote* is thus the kind of cure that “one”—a preferably anonymous person—might seek if one had contracted warts on a delicate part of the body and wanted to have, while on vacation in the south of France, a discreet dermatologist remove them.[34] The novel method suggested in the want ad is to use a half-stock (perhaps the female, blood-sucking half) of domestic mosquitoes for this process.

A second example of the interplay between image and intertext (and counter-repeated text within intertext) presents itself in the fifth scene, in which a thin black spiral orbits among white rings, which themselves gyrate very slowly for twenty seconds. This scene is followed by the seventeen-second “intertextual” pun: “ESQUIVONS LES ECCHYMOSES DES ESQUIMAUX AUX MOTS EXQUIS [LET US AVOID THE BRUISING OF ESKIMOS OF EXQUISITE WORDS]” (figure 38). And once more, the syllabic shape-shifting relies on three alliterative sounds: “es-qui-vons” shifts into “ec-chy-moses” and then “mots-ex-quis.” This sonic shifting again implicates the apparently non-sense phrase: “Eskimos”—the name for indigenous peoples of the Arctic region—were not particularly well known for their “exquisite words” (the first word of this phrase gestures toward the “exquisite corpse” games of the Surrealists). Yet their liberal attitudes about

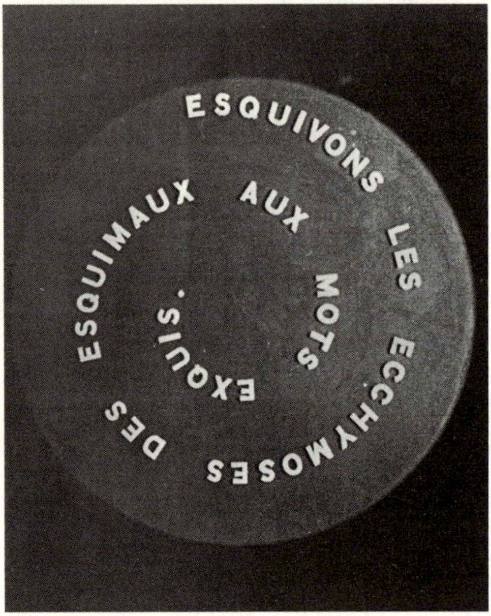

38 Marcel Duchamp, Man Ray, and Marc Allégret (1900–1973), still from *Anémic Cinéma*, 1926. (Courtesy of the Museum of Modern Art, New York. © Succession Marcel Duchamp / ADAGP, Paris / Artists Rights Society [ARS], New York, 2014. © Man Ray Trust / Artists Rights Society [ARS], New York / ADAGP, Paris, 2014)

sex were legendary. One such legend, which Western anthropologists claimed to substantiate, was the practice of asphyxiation to enhance orgasm during sexual intercourse or masturbation.[35] "Bruising" is thus Duchamp's way of insinuating, through *contrepèterie*, the kind of sexual mark or aftereffect already implied in the earlier invocation of *cure d'azote*.

In a final example of the interplay between rotorelief image and spiraling graphic text, the ninth spinning rotorelief,[36] containing the most blank or negative space of any of the rotoreliefs, consists of a series of circles and a couple of half-moons orbiting clockwise around a receded small circle; it looks at times

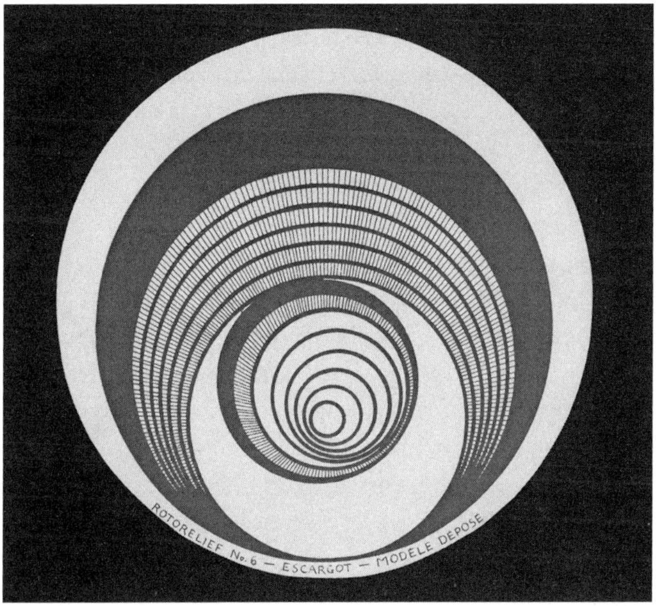

39 Marcel Duchamp, rotorelief, no. 6: *Escargot*, 1935. (© Succession Marcel Duchamp / ADAGP, Paris / Artists Rights Society [ARS], New York)

like a ringed planet, and at others rather like a searchlight coming down a long tunnel (figure 39).

The corresponding intertitle, the film's ultimate one, reads "L'ASPIRANT HABITE JAVEL ET MOI J'AVAIS L'HABITE EN SPIRALE." Here, the syllables of the first phrase (before *et moi*) appear homonymically or near-homonymically in the second: "l'a-spi-rant-ha-bite-ja-vel / j'a-vais-l'ha-bite-en-spi-rale." Such torsions continue when the unfolding syllables' words are provisionally rendered into English: "THE MIDSHIPMAN LIVES [IN] JAVEL," a neighborhood in the then working class and dreary fifteenth arrondissement of Paris, whose argot the passage mimics, "AND ME, I HAD THE HABIT IN A SPIRAL."

Now, in addition to being a midshipman—being a sailor in the French Navy has the same association with louche sexuality (and homosexuality) as it does in the United States Navy—an *aspirant* is, literally, a male who aspires or hopes, both generally for "a better position" and sometimes in the more specific sense of a suitor (compare the aspiring *célibataires* of *The Large Glass*). As *aspirant* draws etymologically on *spirare* (literally, "to breathe"), an *aspirant* is thus also a "breather," which is what Duchamp once famously said he preferred to call himself as opposed to "artist." "Suck" and "suck-up" are also clearly insinuated. *L'habit* (without the feminizing *e*) can mean "habit" in the sense of a priest's or nun's garment, or a uniform or formal clothing in a more general sense: *habits du dimanche* means "Sunday finest"—or even "underwear." Yet in this case, the English language word "habit" (tendency, addiction) also seems to be at or in play: the grammatically correct French expression for "the habit [of being] in a spiral" would be "l'habitude [d'être] en spirale." Meanwhile, "Javel" invokes not only the rundown area of Paris, but also *eau de Javel*, the French term for "bleach," which is olfactorily related to ejaculated semen. If the multilayered, multisensual innuendo is not already evident enough, *l'habite* phonetically invokes *la bitte*, French slang for "penis."

"J'avais l'habite en spirale" thus suggests, among many other possibilities, "I had the spiral habit," "I had the sailor's uniform in a spiral," "I had my knickers in a twist," and phonetically, "I had my cock in a spiral," all while the phrase itself is pictured spinning into (or out of) a spiral form responding intertitularly to a wordlessly throbbing, searching spiral (which, as optical illusion, is not one), shot on a mechanism (the record player) that is associated with spiral movement, and then projected by a filmic apparatus that feeds cellulose spirally from unwinding reel to in-winding reel.

What is at stake in this kind of multiply spiralized counter-repeating, or repeating-with-a-difference, is, thus, not simply making an optical illusion out of language, which, as white type on a black mat, is itself an inversion or negation of "normal" written language. Nor does the appearance of spinning, punning text merely insinuate that language itself is *like* an optical illusion, not to be trusted.

Nor is "carnality" or "sexuality" (including gender inversion and the suggestion of homosexual desire) the sole pertinent issue. Rather, the spiral intertitles, performing rather like X-rays (or rayographs) of some of the functions of language itself, expose language's synonymic and homonymic proclivity toward proliferation as well as the viewer's desire (related to sexual desire) both to follow the proliferation of language and contrarily to give it shape, to master it by closing off the spiral of meaning making.

In his influential work on Duchamp's ready-mades of the later 1910s, Thierry de Duve borrows the Duchampian phrase "pictorial nominalism" to articulate the multilayered effects of Duchamp's abandonment of painting and "common-sense" pictoriality at a given moment in the history of art and in the exhibition of art, an abandonment that he claims produced what he calls "lines of fracture" for the artistic enterprise.[37] Accordingly, what Duchamp demonstrates through the use of puns in *Anémic Cinéma* is a linguistic nominalism, one that followed (perhaps more spirally) the lines of the kind of break from ordinary language sought not only in Dada non-sense but in Ferdinand de Saussure, whose synchronic-based structural linguistics in *Cours de linguistique générale*, first published in Geneva in 1916, was only beginning to gain recognition elsewhere in Europe.

Duchamp's notebook entries—jotted down sometime between 1913 and 1915, and eventually assembled into *Notes on the Large Glass*—make clear that Duchamp was already considering a film, part of whose focus would be "the representation of a group of words. . . . The sentences or words chosen would give a form of meaning to this film. This relation between film and meaning translated into words would be striking [*frappante*] and would serve as a basis for a kind of writing."[38] It is not clear whether this "kind of writing"—writing that would strike (or literally "hit") the viewer in the way that images "hit" the retina—is what actually emerged more than a decade later in *Anémic Cinéma*, Duchamp's only film, but in his notes Duchamp reflects on what he calls "Grammar = i.e. How to connect the elementary signs (like words), then the groups of signs one to the other."[39] Such signs would be "freed from the 'baby talk' of all ordinary languages," but presumably would reveal the adult or adulterated meaning or "form of meaning"

Duchamp suggests. Under this exposed grammar, Duchamp goes on to ask, "What will become of the ideas of action or of being (verbs)[?]"[40]

De Duve stresses, in his provocatively titled *Kant After Duchamp*, how Duchamp's shifting of attention in his ready-mades from object of art to "art as proper name" calls into question not only the enterprise of art making and aesthetic judgment, but also ethics and even, implicitly, Enlightenment reason, not by any means disproving the troika of Kantian critiques but displacing their foundations. Correspondingly, I would suggest that, just as Duchamp's (or R. Mutt's) literal flipping of the habitual use of a urinal in *Fountain* unhitched the grounds of Enlightenment aesthetics, so *Anémic Cinéma*'s (or Rrose Sélavy's) juxtaposition of shape-shifting visual spirals and syllable-inverting linguistic spirals (and their attendant links to desire to make continuous and desire to desire) participates in a similar project. Duchamp himself viewed the puns as sorts of "inscribed ready-mades";[41] if the implications of de Duve's argument are acknowledged, the question necessarily follows: How do the film and its spiralized, counter-repeated puns intervene in the Enlightenment philosophical tradition (including, but not limited to, aesthetic theory)?

It is safe to assume that in deploying spirals in *Anémic Cinéma*, Duchamp was aware that other visual artists relied on the spiral, not only in the early twentieth century but before that, to illustrate the movement of history. As discussed in chapter 1, Hegel, in *Introduction to the Philosophy of History*, asserted, "The life of the ever-present Spirit is a spiral [*Kreislauf*] consisting of steps, in which, looked at from one angle, things seem to exist next to each other, and only when looked at from another point of view appear as past. The elements that Spirit seems to have left behind it, it still possesses in its ever-present profundity."[42] To envision the whole course of history, according to Hegel, requires understanding what appears to be two- dimensional (things "next to each other") as in fact three-dimensional (having a "profundity" rooted in the past). This spiral (or running circle) of history, whose material and spiritual poles were famously flipped by Marx, was thus itself already a kind of optical illusion, revealing to the trained eye an upward-ascending staircase of history. De Duve suggests that it was not with Impressionism or Cubism or Dada, but with Hegel's famous (if incomplete) declaration of the "end of art"—which posits that art after the beginning of the nineteenth century no longer meets civilization's "highest needs"—that the eventual aesthetic theory of modernism (in other words, pictorial nominalism) became possible. In this vein, Duchamp's recycling, screwing, and unscrewing of this familiar form seems to me at least in part a response to a residual Hegelianism implicit in both the aesthetic theory and the (art) historical thinking of his own moment.[43]

Of course, a reader might object that in claiming such an intervention takes place in *Anémic Cinéma*, I am neglecting to acknowledge the whimsical dimension of the film, which after all is less than seven minutes long and intended not to instruct but to delight. Objection sustained. But if one admits that Duchamp's spinning witticisms (and, indeed, much of his art) are indeed funny, one should ask in what way they are funny and what that humor has to do with the "great negative work of destruction to be accomplished" as laid out (itself not unhumorously) by Tzara, to which Duchamp was certainly sympathetic.[44] I submit that *Anémic Cinéma*'s puns, considered alongside the rotary demispheres' optical illusions, can be viewed as jokes or witticisms in the Freudian sense, not as signs of "Duchamp's" (or Rrose Sélavy's) own unconscious but of a broader social, historical, or political unconscious toward which the outer rungs of the film's spirals are reaching.

JOKES AND/AS INVERSION

In his catalogue of types of *Witze*, Freud's first example of the technique of jokes is drawn from Heinrich Heine's *Reisebilder*, in a story called "Die Bäder von Lucca." Here Heine, according to Freud, presents "the delightful figure of the lottery agent and collector of corns Hirsch-Hyacinth," who boasts to Heine of his connections with the fabulously wealthy Baron Rothschild, claiming that Rothschild treated him (Hirsch-Hyacinth) "just like his equal, quite famillionairely.'"[45]

Freud then goes on to chart the word "famillionaire" (as made up of "familiar" and "millionaire") and to explain that what makes the joke "delightful" is how the abbreviation and condensation of the word itself expresses the resentful recognition of the lottery collector/corn-remover of his lower social status. This type of condensation occurs in some of Duchamp's own counter-repeated witticisms, and Freud (of course, without reference to Duchamp) locates it as one of the central processes of the unconscious in both jokes and dreams.

Even more crucial than the condensation technique for Freud, in his description of the relation of wit and the unconscious, is "tendentiousness." The typical tendentious joke (*tendentiöse Witz*) involves a male narrator (whom Freud calls a "first person"), a male listener or group of listeners (a "third person"), and another person, usually an absent or invisible figure (a "second person"), often a female "object of hostile or sexual aggressiveness" or "socially inferior or powerless person" by whom the first person is repulsed or made anxious.[46] Such a scenario in fact aptly describes the general architecture of *The Large Glass*, with its collected bachelors on one side and unreachable "bride" on the other; most of the busywork (like the joke-work) occurs on the bachelors' side. And yet, in Duchamp's writing about *The Large Glass*, it is the "bride" who has ultimate power, especially the power to choose among the suitors.[47]

In *Anémic Cinéma*, the spirally unfolding puns typically involve the suggestion or hint not only of tendentious sexuality but also of a bodily mark or injury. In the examples presented earlier, the *cure d'azote* on the Côte d'Azur is necessary because someone has contracted warts or some other skin ailment (compare Heine's "remover of corns," Hirsch-Hyacinth); Eskimos are claimed to cause ecchymoses (bad, visible bruising); to have one's *bitte en spirale* (penis in a spiral) sounds potentially painful. In other intertitles of *Anémic Cinéma*, one finds euphemistically named "beauty spots" (*grains de beauté*)—more likely moles or warts—to be treated with baths of loose tea (*bains de gros thé*), without too much Ben Gay (*trop de Bengué*); a nursing child is described as a *souffleur de chair chaude* (sucker [literally, "blower"] of hot flesh [*chair* reflecting the "meat" in the poem that surrounds Picabia's telephone cord spiral]); and there is a proposed exchange of a penny (*un sou*) for a pair of scissors/legs (*paire de ciseaux*), itself a linking of the sexual act with castration.[48]

In the most clearly "Freudian" example of an intertext, Duchamp/Sélavy offers "INCESTE OU PASSION DE FAMILLE, À COUPS TROP TIRÉS" (INCEST OR FAMILY PASSION, SHOTS FIRED), though *tirer un coup* is also slang for "having sexual intercourse"; further, the homonym *couteau tiré* also implies "with knife drawn."[49] In these cases, each of which points to scenarios involving the consequences of sexual activity, the body, site of potential pleasure, is also a locus of potential suffering. Of course, much popular humor has long been based on the idea of suffering (in, say, slapstick skits a clown who falls down is considered funny); the difference here is that spirally "twisted" language points, sinuously, to both pleasure and suffering—a potent cocktail that is, in Freud's sense, "delightful."[50]

While the scenes of spinning spirals gesture toward or possibly produce sexual desire in the viewer akin to *dreams*, familiar zone of surrealist exploration and manifestation, I am suggesting that the intertitles, assuming their punning logic can be followed, operate on the level of the *joke*—which Freud calls the "most social of all the mental functions that aim at a yield of pleasure."[51] For Freud, drawing on Herbert Spencer's physiological theories of energy expenditure and balance, the laughter that tendentious jokes entail releases psychical energy and defuses the social antagonisms that they inevitably involve, acting as a sort of funnel for the release of insatiable social or political urges. Duchamp's swirlingly anemic puns, notwithstanding their cleverness, do not exactly *release* energy in this Freudian sense, but recycle it back into the (moving) picture, in the mode of a question mark without a point. It is this aspect of *interrogation*—and it is surely significant that two of the nine intertitles are in the form of questions—that extends the implications of Duchamp's foray into filmmaking beyond optics per se.[52]

The puns' interlinguistic aspect accentuates their connection to the social and political realm. Consider the already mentioned puns *anémic cinéma* and *l'habite en spirale*, neither of which, strictly speaking, makes sense in either French or

English but communicates in the space between languages in the way that contemporary French slang frequently does (much to the dismay of language purists). One such form of working-class argot is, in fact, called *verlan*—a counter-repeated homonymic form of the French word *l'invers* (the reverse). As is the word *contrepèterie*, *verlan* is an instance of the syllable-switching phenomenon it describes; in single-syllable words, phonemes rather than syllables are reversed. A frequently cited example of multisyllabic *verlan* is the word *ripou*, a reversal of *pourri* (rotten or smelly); a slightly more complicated example of the single-syllable variety is *keuf*, a reversal of the already slang word *flic* (cop, pronounced "FLEE kuh," which arrives at *keuf* via *keuf li*). *Verlan* is often compared with pig Latin, but this comparison obscures its social function of "signifying" in a way potentially unintelligible to the politically powerful, especially if spoken quickly; a better equivalent would be Cockney rhyme, although unlike Cockney, contemporary *verlan* is most frequently spoken by the children of working-class French *immigrants*. Even though they were written to be understood and enjoyed primarily by a coterie of French artist friends, *Anémic Cinéma*'s puns enter into a similar signifying circuit—one involving ideas of immigration and expatriation.

T. J. Demos suggests viewing Duchamp's artistic practice and biography under the rubric of *exile*, both because Duchamp spent so much of his adult life on the move and because, according to Demos, Duchamp's art itself points beyond national boundaries and offers a way of thinking and living extranationally—a way that became ever more desirable after the devastation of the war. Claiming that "exile provides an optic that brings Duchamp's subjective attachment to the represented figures from his earlier life into greater focus,"[53] Demos concentrates on Duchamp's work before 1918 and then leaps ahead to the Exposition Internationale du Surréalisme (1938) in Paris and the exhibition of Surrealism in exile (1942) in New York. In doing so, he passes over—largely without comment—the 1920s, when Duchamp was responding directly to Dada and Surrealism and working on the *Precision Optics*, and the 1930s, when Duchamp had ostensibly retired from art practice in order to play chess and sell the rotorelief machines (among other projects). Moreover, Demos neglects to consider the spiral as one such important "represented figure"—even if this figure precisely points *away* from pictorial representation per se. Yet if we follow Demos's lead and consider *Anémic Cinéma*'s spiraling puns as, on the one hand, "jokes" involved in the masculinized circuit of imagined community (in relation to the invisible "second person" suggested by Freud) and, on the other hand, examples of already translated, "interlinguistic" neologisms, partaking in a *verlan*-like inversion, some of the social and political (as well as affective) stakes of Duchamp's "exile" emerge, just as in the rotary demispheres a "relief" emerges out of what appears to be a downwardly spiraling drain.[54] Even Rrose Sélavy's Duchamp-proclaimed cosmopolitan "Jewishness" takes on a new guise—not as merely playful (or sexist) gender inversion but as symptomatic of a silently cunning exilic condition.

ULYSSES AND THE CHARYBDIC DIALECTIC

The word "spiral" appears only four times in *Ulysses*. Its first occurrence is in the fourth episode, "Calypso," when just-introduced Molly Bloom asks her doting and more than slightly masochistic husband, Leopold, the meaning of the word "metempsychosis." Fumbling to offer an explanation that Molly, to whom he has brought breakfast in bed, can understand—"Some [people] say they remember their past lives"[55]—he looks down and observes that "the sluggish cream wound curdling spirals through her tea."[56]

All the other appearances of the word "spiral" occur in the penultimate episode, "Ithaca," in which Leopold Bloom's long-winded and mostly one-sided conversation with his potential houseguest Stephen Dedalus is rendered in catechism-like questions and answers, and key aspects of the long narrative day are recapitulated or newly revealed. Following the question "What two temperaments did [Bloom and Stephen, respectively,] individually represent?" and the unusually direct answer "The scientific. The artistic,"[57] the narrative tracks Bloom's attempt to persuade Stephen that his, Bloom's, "tendency was toward applied, rather than toward pure, science."[58] Among the now-common but once-revolutionary inventions that Bloom claims to admire are the parachute, the telescope, the suction pump, and "the spiral corkscrew."[59]

Later in the same episode, in the garden behind 7 Eccles Street, Stephen is watching and listening to Bloom talk of "meditations of evolution increasingly vaster" and then "obverse meditations of involution increasingly less vast"; Bloom, noting the constellations in the sky, regards and remarks on "the annular cinctures of Saturn: the condensation of spiral nebulae into suns: the interdependent gyrations of double suns."[60] Finally, at the end of "Ithaca," on the verge of discovering the flakes of potted meat that give quasi-scientific proof of Molly's afternoon-long sexual romp with her lover, Hugh "Blazes" Boylan, Bloom is described entering the bed "[w]ith circumspection, as invariably when entering an abode (his own or not his own): with solicitude, the snakespiral springs of the mattress being old, the brass quoits and pendent viper radii loose and tremulous under stress and strain: prudently, as entering a lair or ambush of lust or adders: lightly, the less to disturb: reverently, the bed of conception and of birth, of consummation of marriage and of breach of marriage, of sleep and of death."[61]

While hunting for single words or motifs in *Ulysses* nearly always leads the inquiring reader down a labyrinthine interpretive path, in this case the appearances of the word "spiral" offer a tidy encapsulation of some of the chief large- and small-scale preoccupations of the novel: the relation between the heavens (or gods) and the earth (or human beings), metempsychotic repetition-with-a-difference, the proximity of import and banality, the sinuous attractions of the flesh, and the ethics of betrayal and fidelity. Curiously, the word "spiral" does not appear at all in "Scylla and Charybdis," the ninth of the novel's eighteen episodes. Yet given the Homeric theme of Odysseus's being required to navigate between these two voracious, female monsters—the six-headed rock and the bilious whirlpool—it is in the spiral's Charybdis-like *nearly invisible* presence in *Ulysses*'s "Scylla and Charybdis" that its perils reside.

According to the just-conquered Circe's warning in the *Odyssey*, Odysseus must hew toward Scylla in order to avoid at all costs Charybdis, who vomits black water and "sucks it terribly down,"[62] even though in taking the Scylla route he will lose six men; to veer toward Charybdis, who lies in wait under a large fig tree, would be even more disastrous. The stakes are enormous, not only for Stephen, who in this episode appears as a Telemachus charting a distinctly Odyssean course and whose dreadful fear of water is asserted throughout the novel, but indeed for the understanding of the novel itself, at least if Joyce's own schemas are to be believed. In the Linati schema of 1920, Joyce claimed that the central "science/art" of the episode was "literature," and the episode's "meaning" was "the double-edged sword." In the Gilbert schema, produced a year later, he appended a crucial bodily "organ" ("brain") and a "technic" ("dialectic"). According to the schemas, then, it would seem that Stephen must, using his brain, wield the double-edged sword of dialectic in order to avoid being devoured, and that this process of negotiating between Scylla and Charybdis is intimately related to the enterprise of "literature." In this section, then, we will pursue via the spiral the intertwined questions of doing battle (by means of a particular deployment of dialectic) and succumbing to drowning (by whirlpool), questions that extend the idea of literature into the murkier zones of sexuality and politics.

Although both Plato and his student Aristotle deploy "dialectic," the episode sets up an opposition between Platonic and Aristotelian modes of pursuing truth—an opposition that returns to ideas propounded by a slightly younger Stephen in chapter 5 of *A Portrait of the Artist as a Young Man*. In that chapter, Stephen pompously announces to his university friends his own theory of the ideal stasis or immobility evoked by art, a theory he claims to derive in part from Aristotle. Aristotle also guides Stephen's thinking in the early episodes of *Ulysses*—especially in the "Proteus" episode, where Stephen tests Aristotle's theories of perception by experimenting with his vision and hearing. "Scylla and Charybdis" presents Stephen trying to hew close to the "rock" of Aristotle's comparatively material, bodily, and fact-based deductive reasoning in order to avoid the comparative whirlpool of Platonic idealism favored by his current interlocutors, the literati gathered in the National Library of Ireland, whom he seeks to defeat, or at least impress, by trotting out what appears to be his often-recited theory about Shakespeare, *Hamlet*, and the psychical forces that produce literature.[63]

One of those opponents, AE, based on the well-known poet and Irish Literary Revival figure George Russell, opines that "art has to reveal to us ideas, formless spiritual essences,"[64] a Platonic view with which Stephen profoundly disagrees. Another of the assembly, assistant librarian John Eglinton, based on the essayist William Kirkpatrick Magee, opines, "[I]t makes my blood boil to hear anyone compare Aristotle with Plato,"[65] to which Stephen promptly responds, "Which of the two . . . would have banished me from his commonwealth?"[66] In this sense, the whirlpool of Platonism is associated not only with formless idealism per se but with the kind of republic unsympathetic to would-be poets.

Closely linked to Platonism in the "Scylla and Charybdis" episode is occult knowledge. Indeed, the narrative swirls around and disgorges theosophical ideas associated with the figures of Madame Blavatsky and Yeats.[67] Throughout the episode, Stephen pictures many of the men in the Platonic camp, and especially AE, as theosophists, a belief hinted at when Stephen sees the men "through the cone of lamplight"[68] and when "the auric egg of Russell warn[s] occultly"[69] of the "dangerous" political potential of love songs. Stephen pictures Russell later that evening at a literary soirée to which Stephen has not been invited:

> Yogibogeybox. . . . *Isis Unveiled.* Thei. . . . Crosslegged under an umbrel umbershoot he thrones an Aztec logos, functioning on astral levels, their oversoul, mahamahatma. The faithful hermetists await the light, ripe for chelaship, ringroundabout him. . . . Lotus ladies tend them i'the eyes, their pineal glands aglow. Filled with his god, he thrones, Buddh under plantain. Gulfer of souls, engulfer. He souls, shesouls, shoals of souls. Engulfed with wailing creecries, whirled, whirling, they bewail.[70]

For Stephen, this willy-nilly blending of Hinduism, Tibetan and Chinese Buddhism, and received ideas about Native American religions constitutes the wishy-washy, tongue-twisting theosophical thinking that sucks in Dublin's would-be intellectuals and saps their political opposition to colonialism. Whirled, whirling, and wailing, they cannot, Stephen thinks, "free their sireland."[71]

Part of the irresistibly dangerous sucking of Platonism and theosophy is their association, in Stephen's mind, with homosexuality. When his opponent Eglinton is first introduced, Stephen pictures him as Malacoda, the lead devil from the fifth *bolgia* in Dante's *Inferno*, in which the devils keep shoving the souls of former embezzlers into swirling, scalding water. Where Dante had described this lead devil using his asshole for a trumpet, "Ed elli avea del cul fatto trombetta," Stephen momentarily thinks "Ed egli avea del cul fatto trombetta," substituting *egli* (Eglinton) for *elli* (he).[72] In addition to being immediately linked with a trumpeting anus, Eglinton is repeatedly pictured "frowning" his disapproval of Stephen's ideas—a frown that anticipates the face depicted on the tattoo of the likely homosexual sailor "Murphy" in the "Eumaeus" episode.[73] Most patently, it is the often-frowning Eglinton who is contrarily identified by Stephen as smiling "Cranly's smile."[74] The brilliant and handsome Cranly is Stephen's closest intimate in *A Portrait of the Artist*, the intimate who, as Joseph Valente notes, "embodies the most profound danger to Stephen's heterosexual self-conception."[75]

This "danger" accounts in part for Stephen's attempts to avoid Charybdis-like homosexuality through nearly constant observation and remark. When Richard Best, one of the younger of the assembled men and an ardent admirer of Oscar Wilde, brings up Shakespeare's dedication of the Sonnets to "Mr. W. H." (who could be either the Earl of Pembroke or, according to Wilde, the boy actor Willie Hughes), Stephen thinks, "Love that dare not speak its name."[76] Several times during the episode, Stephen makes a mental note that both Eglinton and Best are unmarried: "He laughed, unmarried, at Eglinton Johannes, of arts a bachelor."[77] Meanwhile, the Quaker librarian (based on Thomas Lyster, a name he is sometimes called), who serves as a sort of moderator among Stephen, AE, Eglinton, and Best, is noted by Stephen as constantly blushing, tiptoeing, and "purring." Finally, in this maelstrom of homosexual associations, toward the end of the episode Stephen's ostensible friend Buck Mulligan warns Stephen about Bloom, who has popped into the National Library to look up an advertisement for "House of Keyes" from the previous year's newspapers. According to Mulligan, who saw Bloom looking at the nether regions of classical sculptures at the National Museum, Bloom "is Greeker than the Greeks."[78] "Kinch," Mulligan warns Stephen again at the end of the episode, "thou art in peril. Get thee a breechpad."[79] Stephen responds by thinking, "Manner of Oxenford,"[80] referring to English public school culture, but then, as elsewhere in the chapter, suggests that the betrayer, Mulligan, is himself homosexual ("Jest on. Know thyself").[81]

While Charybdis is associated in the episode with the swirling snares of Plato, theosophy, "bachelorhood," and, not incidentally, established Irish literary thought—all of which Stephen struggles to avoid by sticking more closely to the Scylla-like rock of Aristotle; a peculiar kind of atheism; and a highly troubled, protest-too-much heterosexuality—Stephen's own avowed sophistry ("'Do you believe your own theory?' —'No,' Stephen said promptly")[82] makes the hidden maelstrom and its figurative annihilation at times seem irresistible. As he begins to propound his theory of paternity as legal fiction, for example, Stephen, suggesting that "a father . . . is a necessary evil," is described as "battling against hopelessness."[83] Momentarily concluding by quoting, without attribution, Cranly's "*amor matris* being the only true thing in life,"[84] he asks, "Who is the father of any son that any son should love him or he any son?"[85] Pondering this question, which has implications for Stephen personally in relation to his father, for his theory of Shakespeare, and more broadly for the Christian doctrine of consubstantiality, Stephen asks himself, "What the hell are you driving at?"[86] and then, "Are you condemned to do this?"[87] His momentary attempt at self-assurance—"I know. Shut up. Blast you. I have reasons"[88]—draws on the rhetoric of the vomiting maelstrom ("blast you") to resist the conceptual maelstrom of his thinking.

In fact, the idea of the whirlpool is crucial to Stephen's own elaborate theory about Shakespeare. Stephen tries to convince the assembled interlocutors, whose number keeps changing as the men pop in and out, that *Hamlet* is a "ghost story" and that Shakespeare did not, as commonly thought, imagine himself in the role of Hamlet the son but in that of the betrayed king and husband of Gertrude. *Hamlet*, Stephen argues, bears witness to Shakespeare's woundedness and resultant fury over Anne Hathaway's sexual infidelities. Drawing on the story of

Odysseus's scar, and speaking with impassioned hyperbolic dialogue drawn from a number of Shakespeare's plays, Stephen suggests,

> The tusk of the boar has wounded him there where love lies ableeding. If the shrew is worsted yet there remains to her woman's invisible weapon. There is, I feel in the words [of *Hamlet*], some goad of the flesh driving him into a new passion, a darker shadow of the first, darkening even his own understanding of himself. A like fate awaits him and the two rages commingle in a whirlpool.[89]

Shakespeare's two rages—rage at Anne Hathaway's infidelities (infidelities, Stephen insinuates, that occurred with Shakespeare's own brothers, among other men) and rage at the fact that his own attempted "dongiovannism" will not quench the initial rage—produce a whirlpool out of which "the words" emerge. In espousing this whirlpool-to-words theory, Stephen recognizes his own rages (at his lack of success attracting women, his homosocial attractions, and his failure to publish) and casts himself as murderer (Claudius, or Milton's Satan), by way of spiraling liquid, of the gathered literati's conventional ideas: "They list. And in the porches of their ears I pour."[90] In this sense, it is ultimately not by avoiding the whirlpool but by *entering* it that Stephen-as-Odysseus-like Telemachus is able to escape. This analysis accords with the Homeric parallel in that, later in his wanderings, stranded alone on a raft, Odysseus is swept back once more through the strait to face Scylla and Charybdis. On that occasion, Odysseus passes toward Charybdis. His raft is sucked into Charybdis's orifice, but he survives by clinging to her fig tree.

The notion of the irresistible whirlpool accounts for Bloom's peculiar role in the "Scylla and Charybdis" episode. Bloom has come to the National Library from the National Museum—two repositories of externally imposed official, colonial culture—not only to look up the "House of Keyes" ad in a newspaper from the previous year, but in part to escape the sight of Boylan, which at the end of "Lestrygonians" nearly gave him a heart attack: "My heart! . . . My heart."[91] In the very middle of "Scylla and Charybdis," after Mulligan mockingly reads a telegram that Stephen sent him earlier in the day, Stephen thinks of the all-too-brief time he spent in Paris, where he received his father's "Nother dying" misspelled telegram calling him home. Echoing Hamlet's response to Polonius's misguided prodding, the phrase "In words of words for words"[92] enters his mind. Bloom is "announced" at this very moment—"There's a gentleman here, sir, the attendant said, coming forward and offering a card"—and is described as "a patient silhouette," waiting and listening.[93] This description of Bloom as silhouette clearly references Plato's parable of the cave, which in Plato's dialogue between Socrates and Glaucon, in book 7 of the *Republic*, is itself used to illustrate the dialectic and is consonant with the impression of vacancy Bloom often leaves when in public, allowing spiteful and malevolent thoughts (and occasionally erotic desires) to be projected onto him. Accordingly, Mulligan mocks Bloom as an "Ikey Moses"–like, assimilationist Jewish petty thief and derisively speculates on his sexual preferences, and the two currents of conversation course throughout the chapter, culminating in Stephen's insinuation that Shakespeare himself was a Jew, a claim he cannot prove. Finally, at the very end of the episode, as Stephen and Mulligan are leaving the library, Stephen "feel[s] [some]one behind" and stands aside. "A man," in other words, Bloom, "passed out between them, bowing, greeting."[94] With considerable narrative pathos, Stephen is described as remembering his dream of the previous night of the man with the creamfruit melon, a momentary identification with Bloom (to materialize later in the "Eumaeus" episode) that Mulligan interrupts: "He looked upon you to lust after you. I fear thee, ancient Mariner."[95]

Notwithstanding its obnoxiousness, Mulligan's snide insinuation is somewhat apt, especially when one considers that in Coleridge's poem the ancient Mariner's ship ultimately sinks "upon the whirl," and the Mariner is saved by suddenly appearing in a boat "sp[inning] round and round." Like Odysseus after encountering Charybdis, the Mariner then escapes: "[A]ll was still, save that the hill / Was telling of the sound." In this multilayered network of associations and allusions, Bloom is thus connected both with the whirlpool (Plato) and with rescue from the whirlpool (ancient Mariner), with dialectic and with escape from the dialectic.

The last spoken words of this deeply verbose episode are Mulligan's "I fear thee, ancient mariner. O, Kinch, thou art in peril. Get thee a breechpad," after which Stephen, seeking a kind of quiet unavailable to him, looks up and, despite the fine June weather, sees two plumes of smoke coming from nearby chimneys: "Frail from the housetops two plumes of smoke ascended, pluming."[96] The two plumes are described as "frail," suggesting both a diminution of the episode's dialectical energy and an amplification of an anemic frailty that, Joyce insinuates, perpetually accompanies the dialectic. In a Joycean gesture similar to the end of "The Dead," the sentence concludes, "pluming, and in a flaw of softness softly were blown."[97] This blowing away of the two frail, flawed plumes of smoke inaugurates the cinematic wandering of "Wandering Rocks."

The charybdic whirlpool of "Scylla and Charybdis" thus repeatedly and differently challenges "the brain" (both Stephen's and, by extension, *Ulysses*'s reader's) to grapple with the limits of dialectic, with profound implications not only for what Joyce, in the schemas, called the science/art of literature, but for history, understood both as an individual's life story in relation to writing (the artist "weav[ing] and unweav[ing] his image,"[98] crucial for all of Joyce's early work) and, more generally, as the whirl of collective, repetitive activity that occasionally, hauntologically, produces not a dialectical resolution but a shout in the street.

"COURSER, RECOURSER, CHANGECHILD": RECIRCULATION AS HISTORY IN THE *WAKE*

In 1929, a young and virtually unknown Samuel Beckett informed bewildered readers about the subtle but important connections between Joyce's *Work in Progress* (the text that would later become *Finnegans Wake*) and the writing of the Neapolitan political philosopher Giambattista Vico.[99] For Beckett, it was not only Vico's approach to history from which Joyce drew—as alluded to in any case in the *Wake*'s scene-setting first sentence, which is itself a continuation of its last sentence ("from swerve of shore to bend of bay, brings us by a commodious vicus of recirculation back to Howth Castle and Environs")—but that cyclical thinking's implications for literature and then-current "civilization." According to Beckett, in book 2 of *Scienza nuova*, Vico "evolved a theory of the origins of poetry and language, the significance of myth, and the nature of barbaric civilization that must have appeared nothing less than an impertinent outrage against tradition. These two aspects of Vico have their reverberations, their reapplications—without however, receiving the faintest explicit illustration—in *Work in Progress*."[100] Notwithstanding their illustrative faintness, these dimensions of Vico's "evolved" thought, in their reverberation and reapplication (the "re" s stressing the importance of repetition in both Vico and Joyce), lend the in-progress Joyce novel a thunderous outrageousness whose novelty consists in part, according to Beckett, in that "it is not to be read—or rather it is not only to be read. It is to be looked at and listened to. His writing is not *about* something; it is *that something itself*."[101]

Beckett alerts potential readers to the visual and sonic dimensions of Joyce's writing while also insisting on the phenomenological dimension of the *Wake* that resists allegorization and asserts its facticity. Vico, according to Beckett, wrote "about" recursivity in history and "about" "barbaric civilization," an ostensible oxymoron also deployed by Walter Benjamin and later by Theodor Adorno, but the *Wake* is not, or not exactly, "about" Vico's positions on history or even the potential for the coexistence of civilization (or enlightenment) and barbarism. Rather, for Beckett, Joyce's novel's "impertinent outrage against tradition" inheres in its recursive, evolved form and its deployment of language—the "something itself" that expresses a gesturing outward by a turning inward. Accordingly, attending to the appearance of spirals in *Finnegans Wake*, a novel that not only is *about* spirals but is *a kind of spiral (or set of spirals) itself*, helps to account for this impertinently outrageous entropic process—a process with implications for imagining both world history in the broadest sense and the more specific geopolitics of the 1920s and 1930s.[102]

An early episode in the *Wake* that makes clear how much Joyce himself was "looking at" spirals occurs in I.5, the chapter concerning the letter written by Anna Livia Plurabelle (ALP), the so-called mamafesta, ostensibly extolling her husband, Humphrey Chimpden Earwicker (HCE).[103] In the course of a long and wayward mock-scholarly description of the letter (whose contents are never directly revealed) appears a section drawing heavily on the Book of Kells—a section that at once describes the intricately illustrated late-eighth-century illuminated manuscript version of the Gospels, considered one of Ireland's cultural treasures, and parodies Edward Sullivan's 1920 study floridly describing the book, which had been buried for several months by monks to keep it safe from invading Danish marauders. On the very first page of his study, Sullivan wrote of the "clean, unwavering sweep of rounded spiral [and] the creeping undulations of serpentine forms that writhe in artistic profusion" in the manuscript; elsewhere he notes the book's "lacertine convolution."[104]

Joyce's parodic treatment of Sullivan's interpretation of the Book of Kells is clearest in the *Wake*'s description of the crucifixion of Christ as told in Matthew 27:38 and as illustrated on the "Tunc" page of the Book of Kells, the old Latin/Vulgate/Greek text of which reads "Tunc crucifixerant XRI cum eo duos latrones" (Then they crucified Chri[st] [and] with him two thieves) (figure 40). Echoing Sullivan, the narrative voice focuses on the spiral at the top of the illuminated manuscript and describes, in an odd tonal admixture, the "strange exotic serpentine, since so properly banished from our scripture, about as freakwing a wetterhand now as to see a rightheaded ladywhite don a corkhorse, which, in its invincible insolence ever longer more and of more morosity, seems to uncoil spirally and swell lacertinelazily before our eyes under pressure of the writer's hand."[105]

Here the narrative voice links spirals first and arrestingly with a serpentine, sinful sexual attraction and then, explicitly, with the act of writing: the spiral in its "invincible insolence" seems to uncoil and, "under pressure of the writer's hand," to swell. In this passage, Joyce clearly casts doubt on the unmediated pious communication of the Christian "word": with mock offense, the narrator suggests that the monk-illustrator has inscribed a residual pre-Patrick Irish snake worship, one that survives domination—all the while ventriloquizing the awful narrative of Christ's killing, along with the "latrones," by the biblical-era Roman forces, which appear related to the forces that invaded and conquered Ireland.[106]

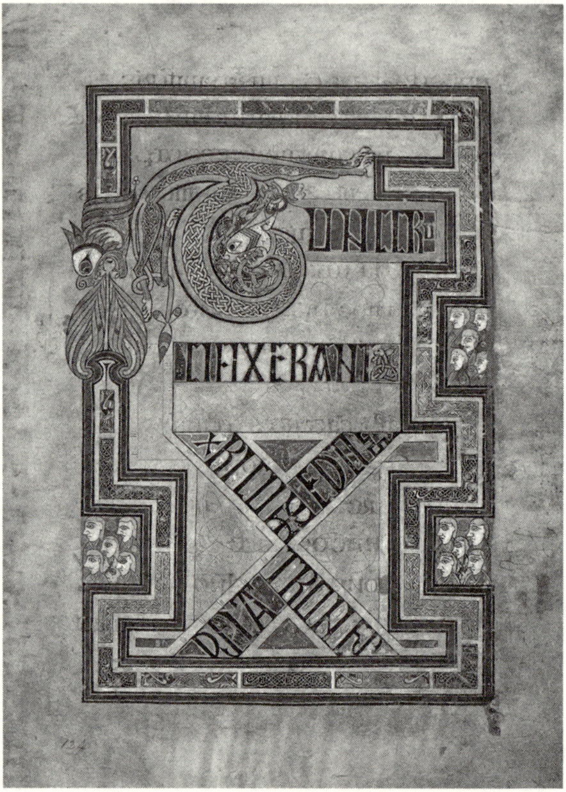

40 The Book of Kells (ms. 58), folio 124r, page concerning the crucifixion of Christ, with text from the Gospel of Saint Matthew, showing roaring lions in profile (vellum, ca. 800). (© The Board of Trinity College, Dublin, Ireland / The Bridgeman Art Library)

Some *Wake* commentators have suggested that the "Tunc" page is a kind of "skeleton key" to the "entire puzzle of the *Wake*."[107] In part because in Joyce keys are often easily lost and puzzles go unsolved, it suffices for our purposes to note how this headlined spiral, associated, if loosely, with the "mamafesta" and thereby with a male-scribed *écriture feminine*, links the very act of writing letters to a productive insolence that challenges civilization's barbarities. This connection among spirals, gender, writing, insolence, and a critique of historical-political barbarism is further made evident in I.8, the famous chapter linking ALP to the names of hundreds of the world's rivers—from the "Reeve Gootch" (Rive Gauche in Paris), to the "Nore" of Ireland and the "Bloem" of British-controlled South Africa (together making a "Nora Bloom," connecting Joyce's wife, Nora Barnacle, to Molly Bloom), to the "Kishtna" (Kistna or Krishna of southern India, in the 1920s also still controlled by the British Empire);[108] all told, the river names alone could fill dozens of pages of graphs in a data-mined "distant reading" approach to the text, but, unless read closely and, in a sense, translated, this approach would never reveal their cultural geography and links to (and challenge of) notions of civilizational history.

The "story" of ALP is told by two washerwomen washing clothes in the Liffey, who begin by gossiping about the fall of HCE, who was accused, like Charles Parnell, of sexual indiscretions,[109] and then lay out several possible origins for ALP's arrival in Ireland and, in doing so, of the *Ursprung* of the very river in which they are working. In describing the rumored elopement of HCE and ALP, one woman tells the other how HCE was so smitten that he did not mind ALP's terrible voice—"She'd bate the hen that crowed on the turrace of Babbel"[110]—and then, in a Babel-like profusion of languages, focuses on how ALP flicked her fan to excite him: "Is that a faith? That's the fact. Then riding the ricka and roya romanche, Annona, geboren aroostokrat Nivia, dochter of Sense and Art, with Sparks' pirryphlickathims funkling her fan, anner frostivying tresses dasht with virevlies—[.]"[111]

The born-"aroostokrat" Anna Livia/Anona (the Roman goddess associated with supplying food to the people and hence with fertility and political stability), her long hair dashed with fireflies, practically freezes HCE with her artful beauty, enhanced by her wiles. Embedded in this ventriloquistic passage on ALP's riding/writing are references to the rivers Roya (France and Italy), Romanche (France), Ebro (Spain), Aroostook (Maine, United States, and New Brunswick, Canada), Nive (France near the Basque Country), Sense (Switzerland),

Pyriphlegethon (Greek underworld river of fire), Dasht (Baluchistan, now Pakistan), and Vire (France)—many of them rivers that divide two nation-states (or colonies) or flow through more than one. The passage concludes with the word "virevlies," suggesting not only fireflies but *hvirvel*, the Danish word for "whirlpool"; the Danes are one of the ethnic groups that sacked Hibernia. In this short passage, not even a complete sentence, it is as though the plethora of rivers that flow through the text, along with the profusion of languages that they carry, are brought together in a whirlpool that suggests both a pre-Babel origin (*Ursprung*) and national and civilizational confusion.

Nowhere is the spiral made more evident in its hiddenness in the *Wake* than in II.2, in the "Night Lessons" episode in which HCE and ALP's three children—the twin boys, Shem and Shaun, and the girl, Issy—are studying upstairs in a pub, after having been called inside at the end of the previous chapter, itself marked by HCE's arrival accompanied by Viconian thunder ("the Clearer of the Air from on high has spoken in tumbuldum tambaldam to his tembledim tombaldoom worrild").[112] Their lessons ostensibly concern geometry, and all three children are involved in "writing" the first half of the chapter, the twin boys (in the chapter also called Dolph and Kev) penning the utterly tangential marginal notes and an unnamed Issy in charge of the equally oblique and at times infantile footnotes.

But much of the lessons' main text parodies Yeats's *A Vision*, as is clear in the following colloquial mathematical explanation: "So, bagdad, after those initials falls and that primary taincture, as I know and you know yourself, begath, and the arab in the ghetto knows better, by nettus, nor anymeade or persan . . . construct ann aquilittoral dryankle Probe loom."[113] Here "primary tincture," the term with which Yeats described the "objectivity of mind," becomes "primary taincture," something akin to an original sin, with the hint of the deflowering of a male with the mention of [G]anyme[a]de, considered the most beautiful young male god, associated with pederasty. Meanwhile, Joyce pokes fun at Yeats's/Michael Robartes's "desert geometry," especially the story of Giraldus/Kusta ben Luka, expanding Yeats's geographical reach by using "bagdad" instead of "bedad"; mentioning "arab," "Me[a]de," and "persan" (Persian); and ventriloquizing "Nothus"

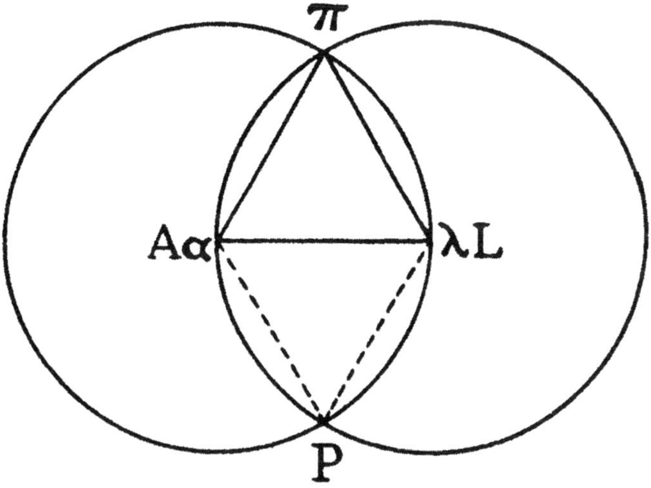

41 James Joyce, diagram in *Finnegans Wake*. (Copyright 1939 by James Joyce; copyright renewed © 1967 by Giorgio Joyce and Lucia Joyce. Used by permission of Viking Penguin, a division of Viking Penguin Group [USA] LLC)

(a Persian king) in "nettus" (which also sounds like "net us" or "ensnare us"). The description of an "aquilittoral dryankle," or equilateral triangle, which also recalls the frontispiece to Vico's *Scienza nuova*, generates a spiral interruption ("husk, hisk, a spirit spires"),[114] and for several pages there are no marginal notes or footnotes, only a sustained description of the creation of a diagram, the presentation in the text of the diagram itself, and a mock-scholarly defense of that diagram, one as outrageous in its own way as Stephen's *Hamlet* pedagogy described earlier.

The diagram that appears in the text is introduced by text that draws amply from Yeats (figure 41):

> Your parn! You, you make what name? (and in truth, as a poor soul is between shift and shift ere the death he has lived through becomes the life he is to die into, he or he had albut—he was rickets as to reasons but the balance of his

> minds was stables—lost himself or himself somnione sciuiones . . . in the lazily eye of his lapis, Vieus Von DVbLIn, 'twas one of the dozedemams a darkies ding in dewood) the Turnpike under the Great Ulm (with Mearingstone in Fore ground). Given now ann linch you take enn all.[115]

"Your parn!" signifies both "beg your pardon?" and Yeats's "pern"—Sligo-ese for "spool."[116] The parenthetical remark about "the death he has lived through" becoming "the life he is to die into" certainly refers to Yeats's often-repeated paraphrase of Heraclitus—living each other's death, dying each other's life—through which he describes the interpenetrating spirals of *A Vision*. Lapis lazuli (referenced in the phrase "lazily eye of his lapis") was a figure associated by Yeats in his poetry with creation and destruction and thus with the running of the gyres.[117] Finally, the diagram itself, with its invocation of ALP's genitals, is similar to Yeats's quasi-mathematical diagrams in *A Vision*.

While the references to Yeats pile up in the pages-long description of the diagram—"circumscript a cyclone"; "dunloop into eath the ocher"; "nether nadir is vertically where . . . its naval's napex will have to beandbe"; "whereapool"; and, ultimately, in a combination of Yeats and Vico, "Gyre O, gyre O, gyrotundo! Hop lala"[118]—what it is especially important to recognize is how Joyce undermines Yeats's civilizational worldview. One clear example of this parodic undermining is in the collision between these Yeats references and idioms of blackness. The expression "Given now ann linch you take an all," embedded in the passage that immediately follows the diagram, is at once a parody of a German-accented geometry professor, a description of the width of ALP's vagina (measuring from Aα to λL), and an invocation of the apocryphal saying "Give a nigger an inch and he'll take an ell," found both in *The Autobiography of Frederick Douglass*, to describe a slave owner's resistance to his wife's teaching Douglass to read the Bible, and in Huck's complaint about a suddenly free-talking Jim in Mark Twain's *The Adventures of Huckleberry Finn*, which is later in the schoolroom episode referred to as "Hurdlebury Fenn." Here, the racist phrase is complicated significantly by the alteration that reads "Given now ann linch," invoking the dismal history of lynching to punish African American suspects in vigilante justice.[119] That Charles Lynch, who gave the name to these extrajudicial hangings, was descended from an Irish indentured servant would surely have been of interest to Joyce. Meanwhile, "darkies ding in dewood" seems to reference either "savage" Africans or American slaves singing in the woods, while also mimicking the supposed sound of American black speech as well as asserting the German word for "thing" (*ding*), important for a phenomenologically inclined mathematics.

As the detailed description, ostensibly offered by her own children, of ALP's nether regions and their different parts' functions continues, this theme of blackness returns in several guises:

> ... fastness firm of Hurdlebury Fenn, distinct and isoplural in its (your sow to the duble) sixuous parts, flument, fluvey and fluteous, midden wedge of the stream's your muddy old triagonal delta, fiho miho, plain for you now, appia lippie pluvaville, (hop the hula, girls!) the no niggard spot of her safety vulve, first of all usquiluteral threeingles, (and why wouldn't she sit cressloggedlike the lass that lured a tailor?) the constant of fluxion, Mahamewetma, pride of the province and when that tidled boare rutches up from the Afrantic, allaph quaran's his bett und bier![120]

The portrayal of ALP's "old triagonal delta," itself, as in Yeats's *Vision* triangles, containing a spiral, dredges up a reference to the muddy Mississippi Delta, while "no niggard spot of her safety vulve," with its own insinuated fear of interracial sex, morphs into a quasi-theosophical "Mahamewetma," evoking both the disciple-seeking "mahamahatma" mentioned in *Ulysses*'s "Scylla and Charybdis" episode and a "wet" mother. Meanwhile, the "Afrantic" references both the Atlantic and Africa as well as the adjective "frantic"—thereby drawing attention to the triangular Atlantic slave trade (as well as Yeats's spiritual "daimon," Leo Africanus)—and "allaph quaran" returns to the rhetoric of Islam of earlier passages, poking fun at Yeats's *Vision*-fiction. As for the hula dancing, it returns to the "hop lala" of Yeats and Vico's "Gyre O, gyre O, gyrotundo! Hop lala."

Why does Joyce here infuse passages about Yeatsian gyres (related to ALP's genitals) with idioms of blackness—including African American, Indian, Arab, and Hawaiian versions of blackness? On the one hand, Joyce appears simply to be gently reminding us of Yeats's dermatological complexion, which, as noted in chapter 3, was so dark that he was frequently mistaken for an Indian. Yet surely also in or at play in these sentences are Yeats's (and by extension Spengler's and other) civilizational theories, which promote a grandiose vision of "aroostokratic" European culture that portrays a West perpetually at odds with an encroaching or retreating East. Although Joyce's novels certainly recirculate stories from many texts often considered Western (the *Odyssey*, the Hebrew Bible and the Roman Catholic Bible, *Tristan and Isolde*, *Hamlet*), Joyce always expands his narrative's cultural geography to challenge decisively any strict West–East divide: hence the focus on Gibraltar and Hungary (as well as Dublin) in *Ulysses* and, in *Finnegans Wake*, the Middle East and the black "Afrantic." Joyce was also well aware that in England and in the United States in the nineteenth and early twentieth centuries, the Irish themselves were often considered "black," only eventually "becoming white" in relation to the perpetually marginalized African American population.[121] The repeated reference to the image of the swirling spiral in the "Night Lessons" episode thus helps to illustrate a sort of counterprinciple to the hierarchical spiral models of history in Yeats and Hegel.[122]

POINT CARRIED!

Of course, Yeats is only one of many quasi-mathematical thinkers whose ideas are circulated and parodied in the gyrational "Night Lessons." Another, significantly, is the French mathematician and physician Jules Henri Poincaré, whose name is invoked toward the end of the section in a phrase in which Shem/Dolph apparently acknowledges the validity of Shaun/Kev's argument: "Thanks eversore much, Pointcarried!"[123] Poincaré is often considered the last universalist in the field of mathematics. In the 1880s, he researched curves defined by a particular type of differential equation, investigating whether solutions "spiral into or away from" a point.[124] Extending his curved thinking to the dimensionality of the physical globe, Poincaré later worked on ways to accurately determine time zones. Like Plateau (and later Duchamp), Poincaré also undertook studies in the field of optics; that Joyce was aware of this is clear when, shortly after exclaiming "Pointcarried," Shem/Dolph exclaims, "I'm seeing rayinbogeys rings round me."[125] (*Regenbogen* is German for "rainbow"; in optics, a prism reveals the spectrum of visible light reflected in rainbows.) Finally, it is crucial to note that Poincaré was a major European proponent of the work of James Clerk Maxwell, the Scottish theoretical physicist who made significant advances in the field of thermodynamics; indeed he, like Poincaré, is associated with the development of the concept of entropy.

Accordingly, the spiral-heavy "Night Lessons" scene entropically winds down with a long Joycean list of academic or pseudo-academic subjects ("Art, literature, politics, economy, chemistry, humanity, & c"), before moving into cliché essay topics or magazine headlines ("The Voice of Nature in the Forest, Your Favorite Hero or Heroine, On the Benefits of Recreation," and the Nietzsche-inspired "The Uses and Abuses of Insects"), and then to such apparently vapid questions as "Should Ladies learn Music or Mathematics?" and "When is a Pun not a Pun?"[126] It ends with a marginal note/simple drawing (one of two in the text, both in this episode) of what appears to be a nose being thumbed over a crossed fork and spoon (figure 42).[127]

Rather like the discussion of *Hamlet* in *Ulysses*'s "Scylla and Charybdis" (or, for that matter, the lesson on Pyrrhus in "Nestor"), *Wake*'s "Night Lessons" episode, viewed from its endpoint, thus appears to function as a parody of education, with the thumbed nose representing the ultimate "winding up" of the reader for having bothered to wade through the previous several dozen pages. And yet, just as the disavowed *Hamlet* argument advances an aesthetic theory that provides an important lens through which to understand *Ulysses*'s idea of the whirlpool of life that produces words (as well as the whirlpool of perceived obstacles to becoming an artist), so "Night Lessons" makes clear that accessing even the

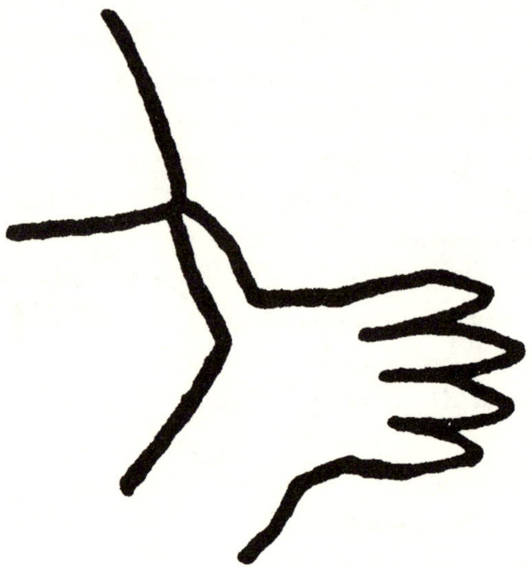

42 James Joyce, detail of drawing in *Finnegans Wake*. (Copyright 1939 by James Joyce; copyright renewed © 1967 by Giorgio Joyce and Lucia Joyce. Used by permission of Viking Penguin, a division of Viking Penguin Group [USA] LLC)

least nuanced understanding of *Finnegans Wake* requires a great deal of erudition, attention to language as not "about" something but *that something itself*, and, especially, a willingness to read puns as not (just) puns. In fact, it requires reading punningly, entropically against the energetic grain, a mode of analysis also promoted by Duchamp's punning, anemic spirals in *Anémic Cinéma*, one that generates new ways to think about language, sexual desire, and opticality as well as about history and geopolitics. Just as Duchamp's obscenely spiraling joke-work, in limning the infra-thin difference between direct phrase and insinuated meanings, critiques the persistence of national boundaries in the wake of the First World War, so Joyce's nose-thumbing deployment of language, rather like a better, more difficult Esperanto,[128] gestures, in the swirling geopolitical whirlpool

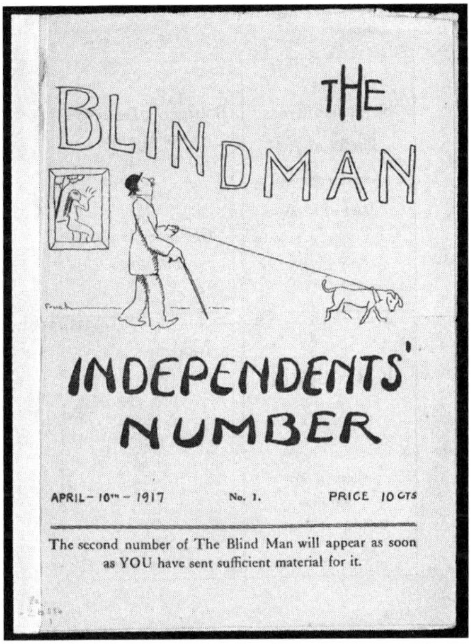

43 Marcel Duchamp, drawing on front cover of *The Blindman*, no. 1 (1917). (Courtesy of Yale University Beinecke Library. © Succession Marcel Duchamp / ADAGP, Paris / Artists Rights Society [ARS], New York)

leading up to the Second World War, toward a zone of feeling, of understanding, beyond a nation-state but short of a "universal" political entity.[129]

Lest this closing analogy seem a bit forced, readers might consider where Joyce, who hand-drew the nose and thumb, might have gathered inspiration for his drawing. In 1917, in New York, Duchamp drew the cover for the first number of the Dada journal *Blindman*. It features a possibly blind gentleman with small black bowler hat, small mustache, and ashplant-like walking stick (figure 43). (This was the same year as R. Mutt's *Fountain*.) The man looks up in the air as he is pulled along by a dog, to which he is connected by a long leash. In the

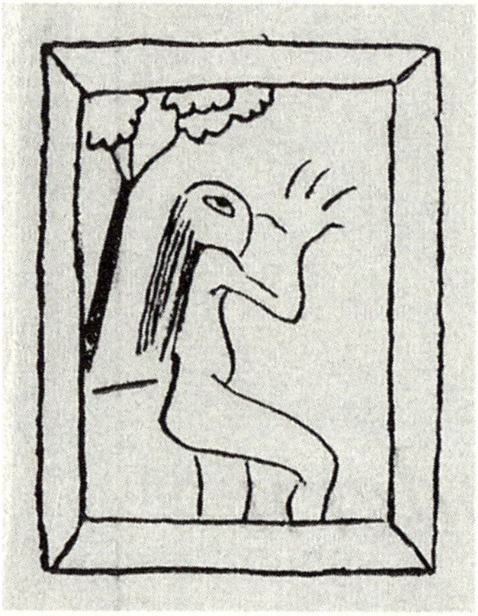

44 Marcel Duchamp, detail of drawing on front cover of *The Blindman*, no. 1 (1917). (Courtesy of Yale University Beinecke Library. © Succession Marcel Duchamp / ADAGP, Paris / Artists Rights Society [ARS], New York)

upper-left-hand corner of the drawing, just under the *B* of *Blindman*, and in the background of the dog-walking scene, appears a sort of inset-framed image of a woman, in front of a few hastily sketched trees, thumbing her nose (figure 44). The hand and nose are in almost exactly the same position as they are in Joyce's drawing, which is one of only two drawings in *Finnegans Wake* (the other one, as we have seen, clearly referencing Yeats's gyres).

This affiliation, while not in itself indicative of a thoroughgoing similarity in technic or science in Joyce's and Duchamp's broader projects, nevertheless attests the kind of parodic spiral entropy effectuated in *Precision Optics* and in *Ulysses* and *Finnegans Wake*, one that negotiates between vision and thing, body and world, and art and life, and by turning "work" inward, opens it up to the globe.

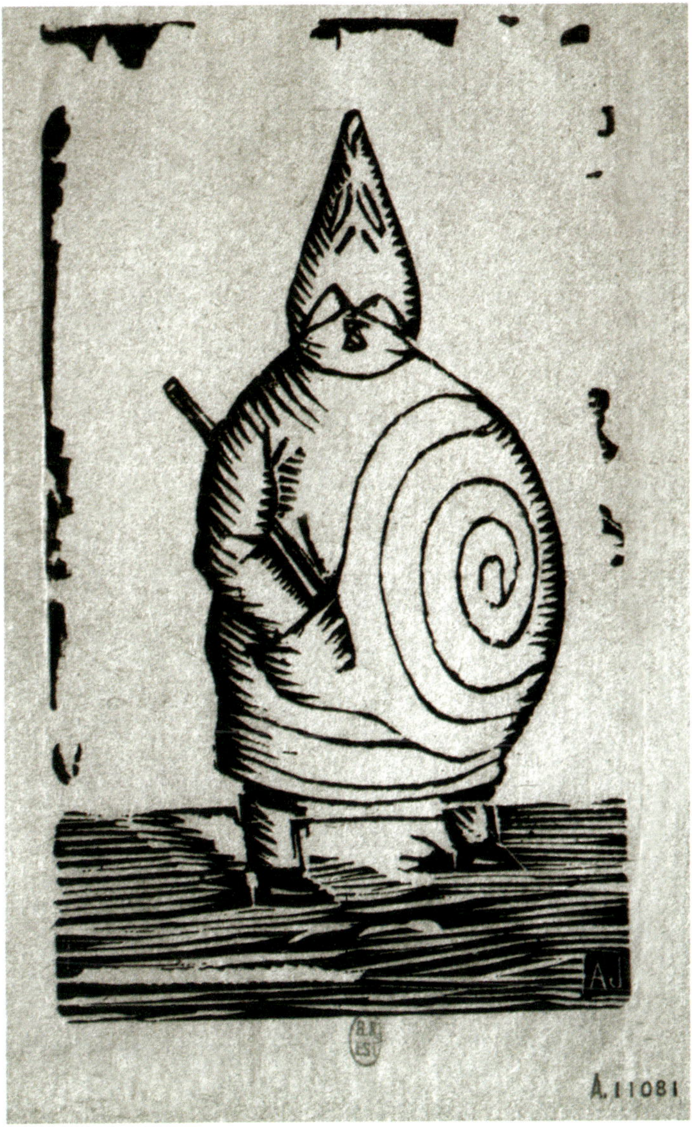

PLATE 1

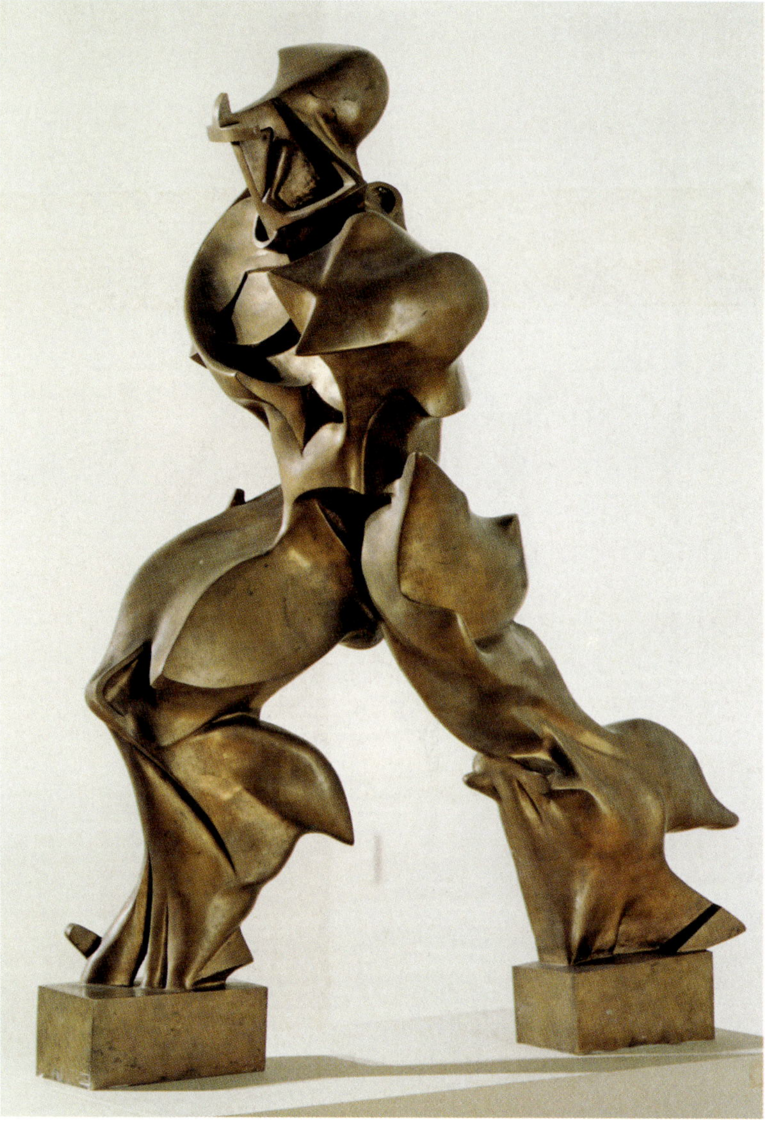

PLATE 2

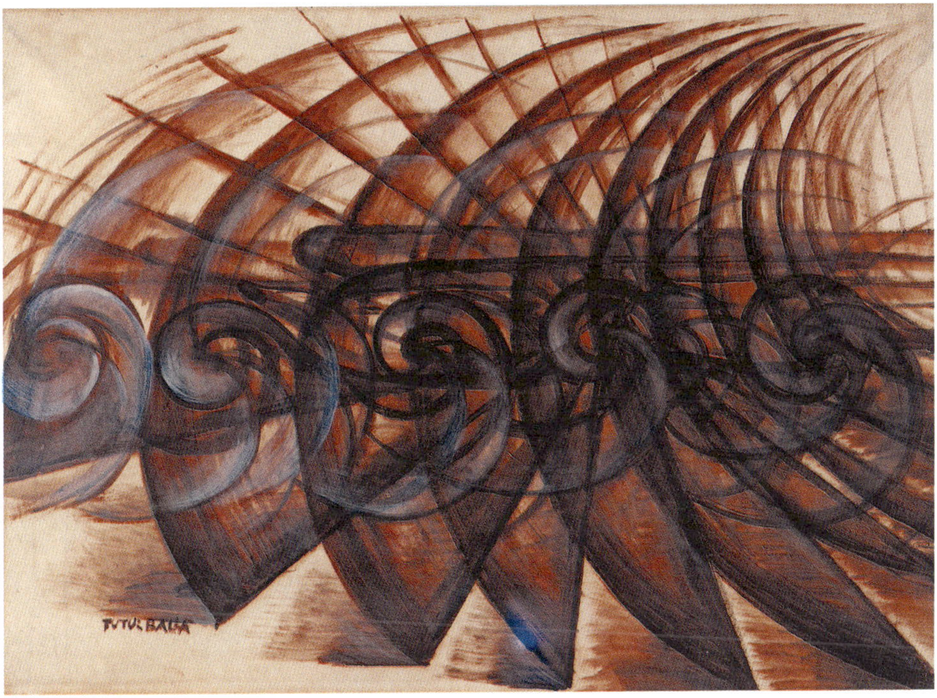

PLATE 3

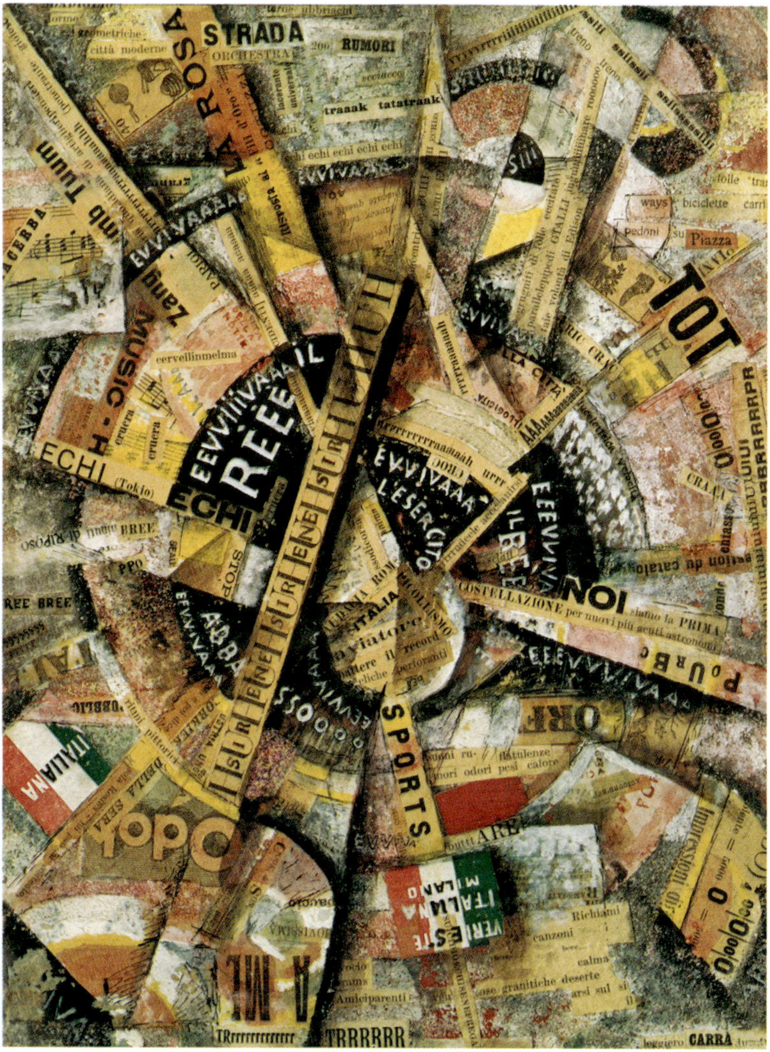
STRADA
RUMORI
ORCHESTRA
LA ROSA
città moderne
geometriche
traaak tatatraak
echi echi echi echi
EVVIVAAA
ways biciclette
pedoni
Piazza
TOT
MUSIC - H
cervellinmelma
ECHI
(Tokio)
EEVVIIIVAAAA IL
REEE
EVVIVAAA L'ESERCITO
NOI
COSTELLAZIONE per muovi più acuti astronomi
SPORTS
ITALIANA
ITALIA
MILANO
Richiami
canzeni
calma
TRrrrrrrrrrrr
TRRRRRR
CARRA

PLATE 4

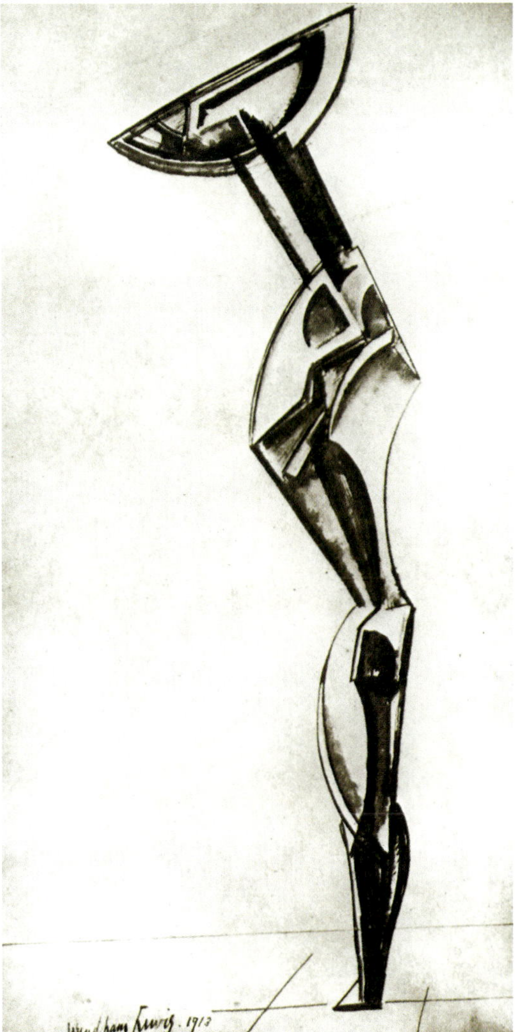

PLATE 5

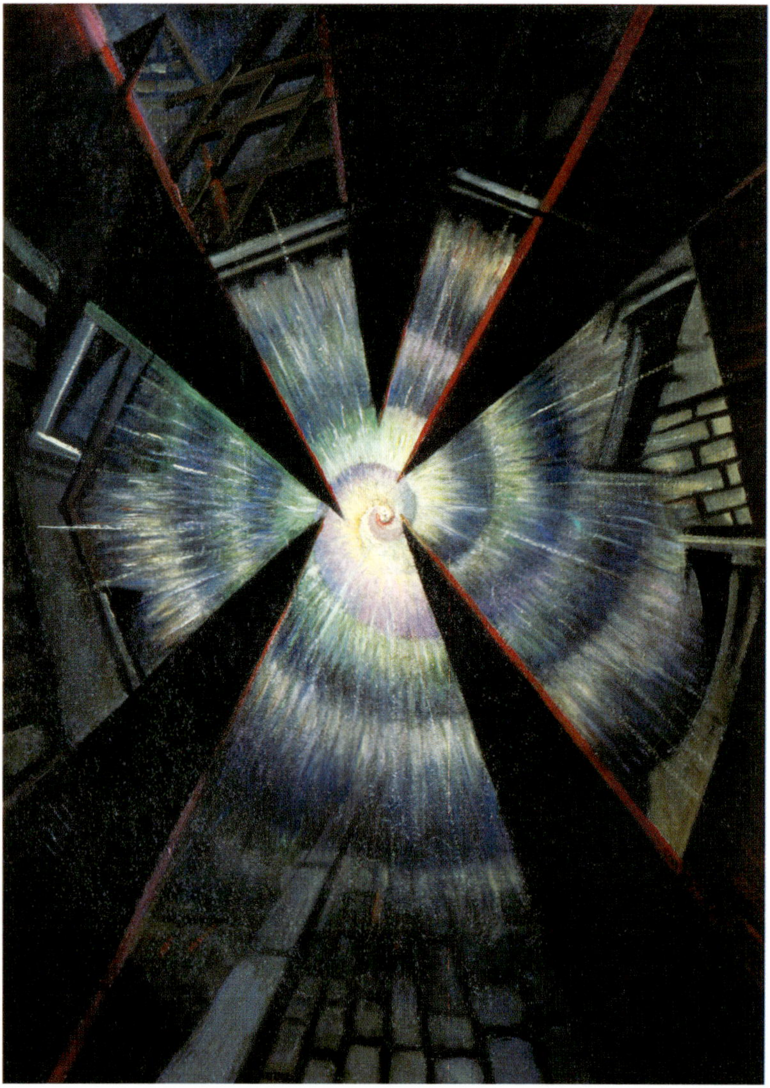

PLATE 6

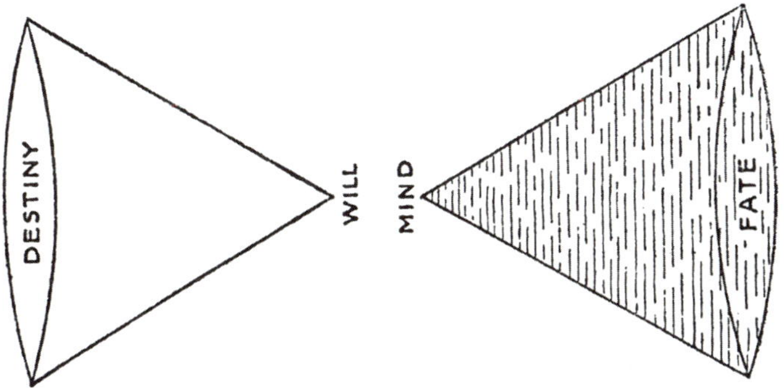

PLATE 7

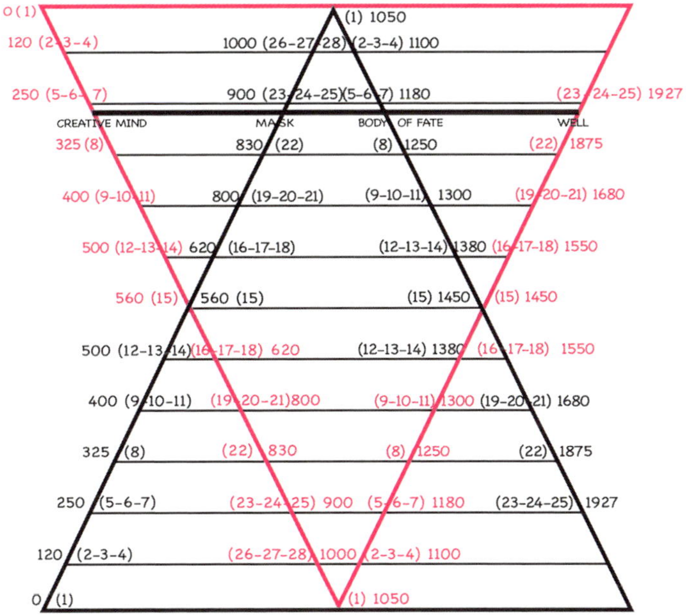

PLATE 8

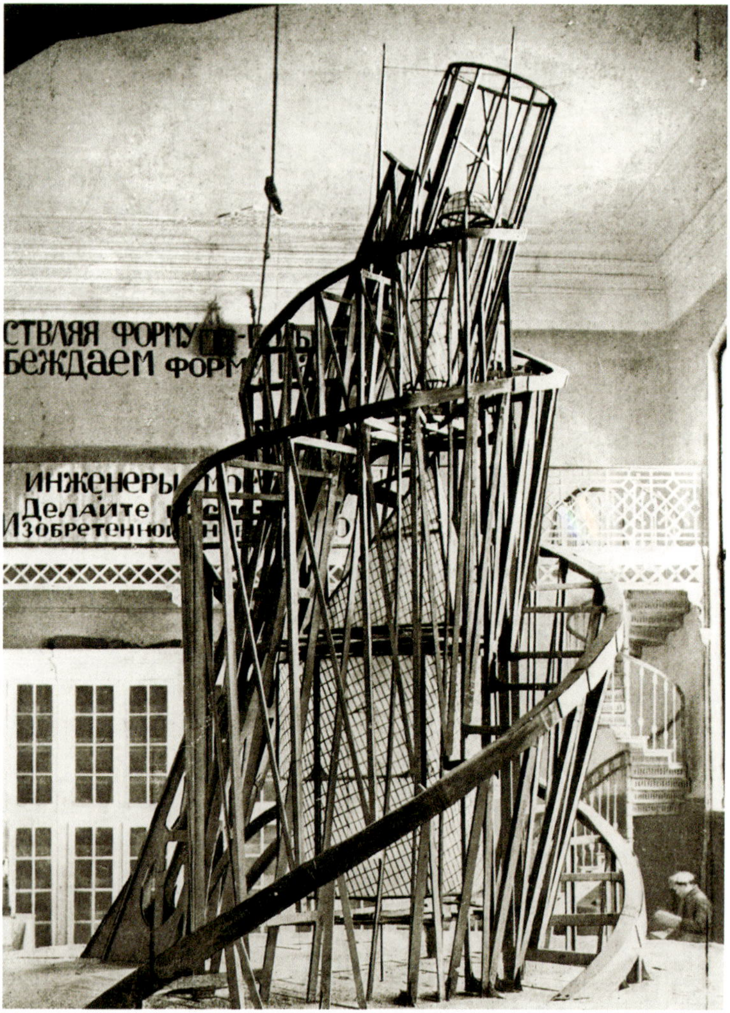

PLATE 9

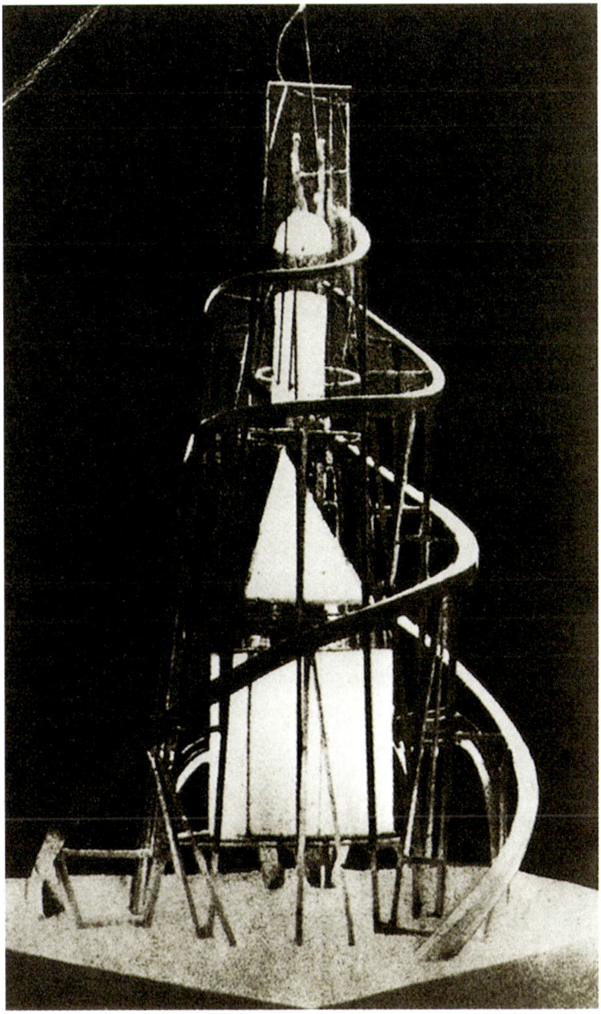

PLATE 10

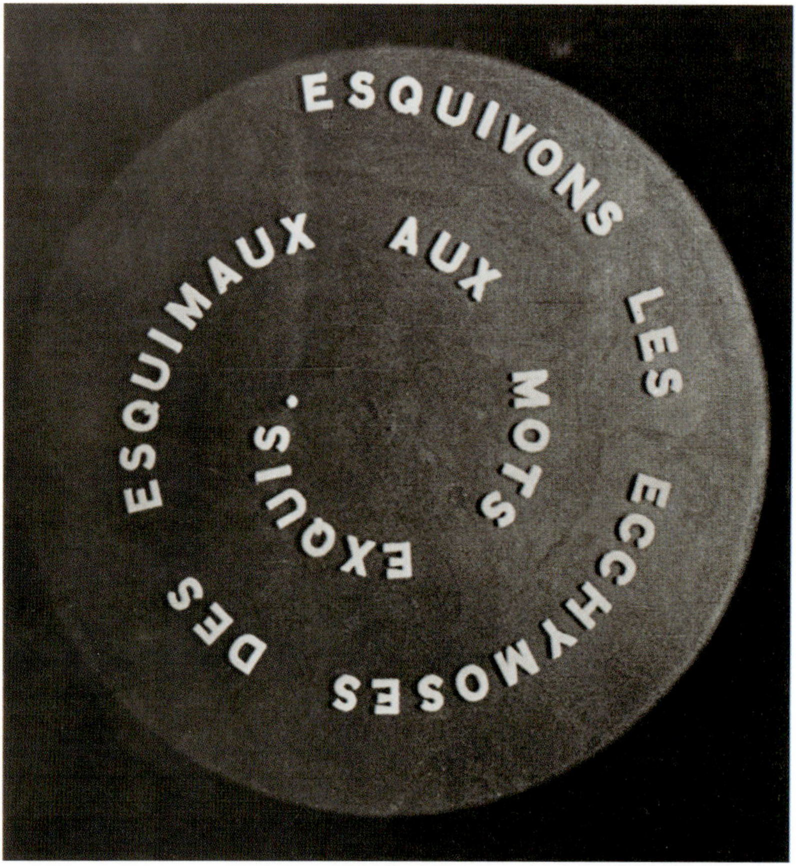

PLATE 11

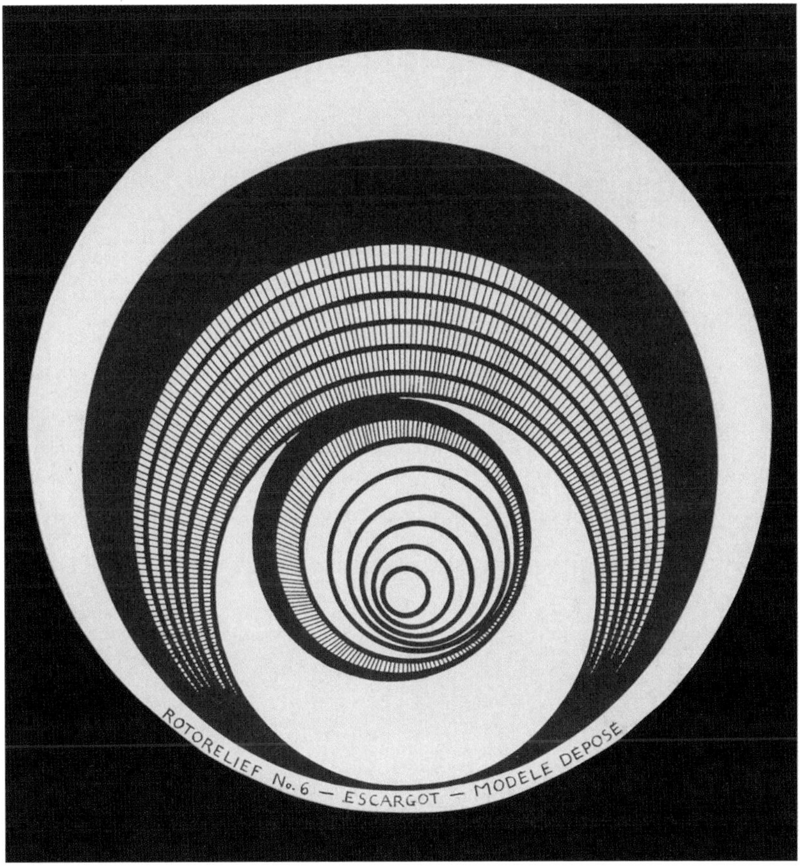

PLATE 12

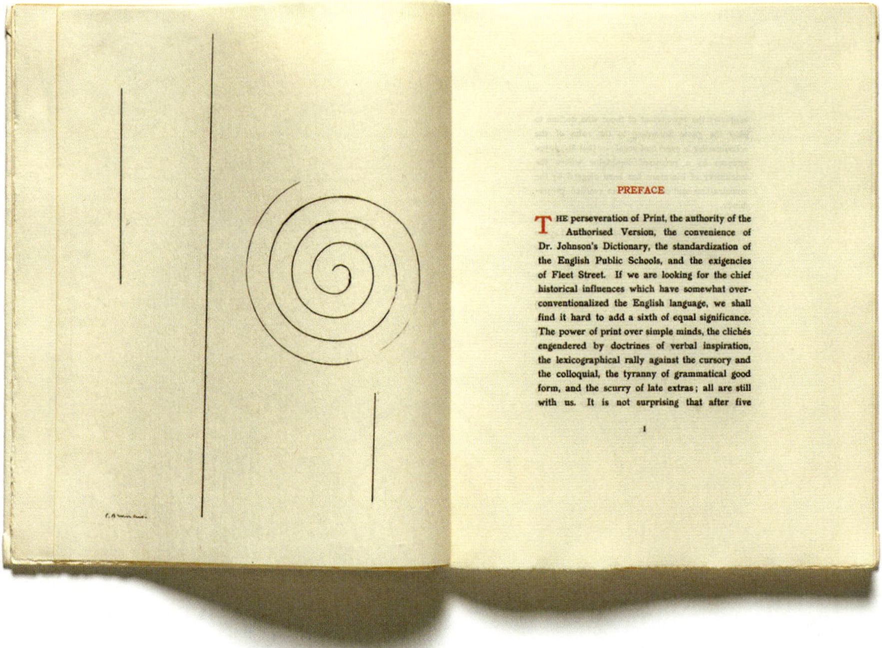
PREFACE
THE perseveration of Print, the authority of the Authorised Version, the convenience of Dr. Johnson's Dictionary, the standardization of the English Public Schools, and the exigencies of Fleet Street. If we are looking for the chief historical influences which have somewhat over-conventionalized the English language, we shall find it hard to add a sixth of equal significance. The power of print over simple minds, the clichés engendered by doctrines of verbal inspiration, the lexicographical rally against the cursory and the colloquial, the tyranny of grammatical good form, and the scurry of late extras; all are still with us. It is not surprising that after five
1

PLATE 13

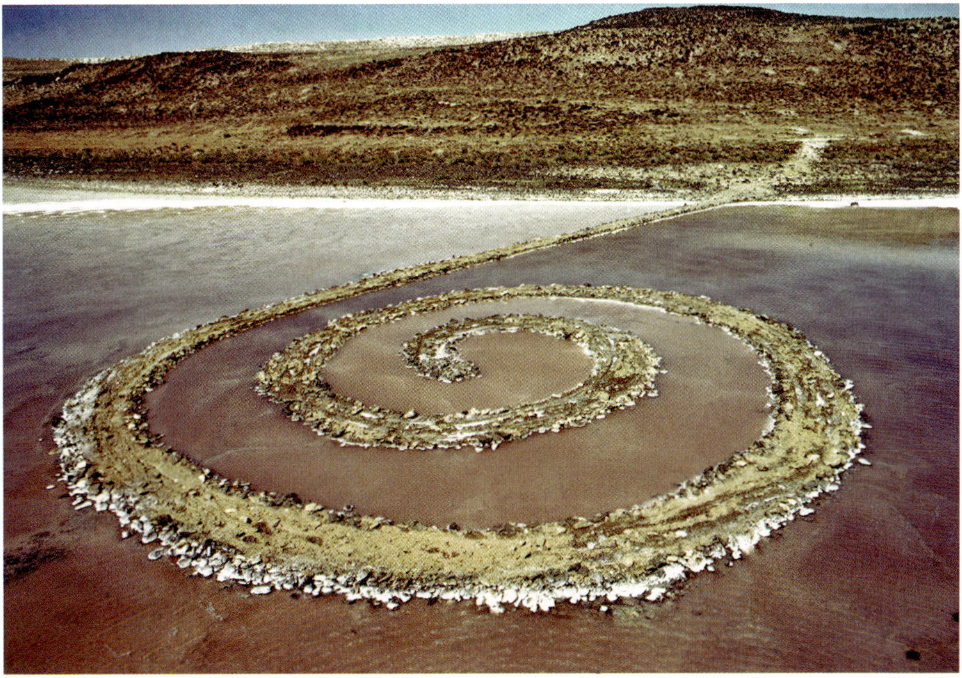

PLATE 14

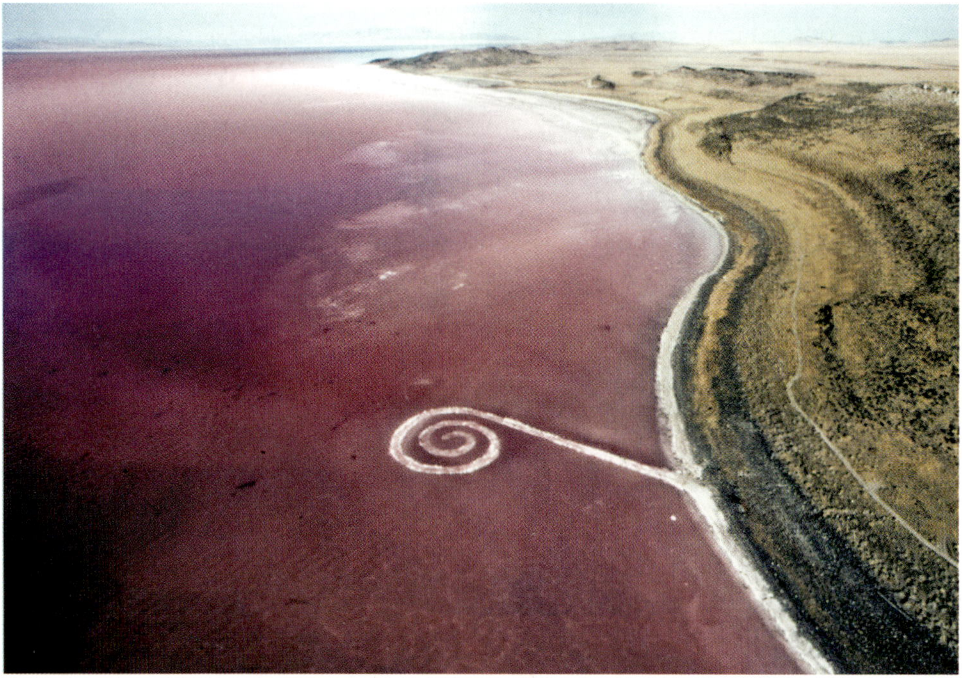

PLATE 15

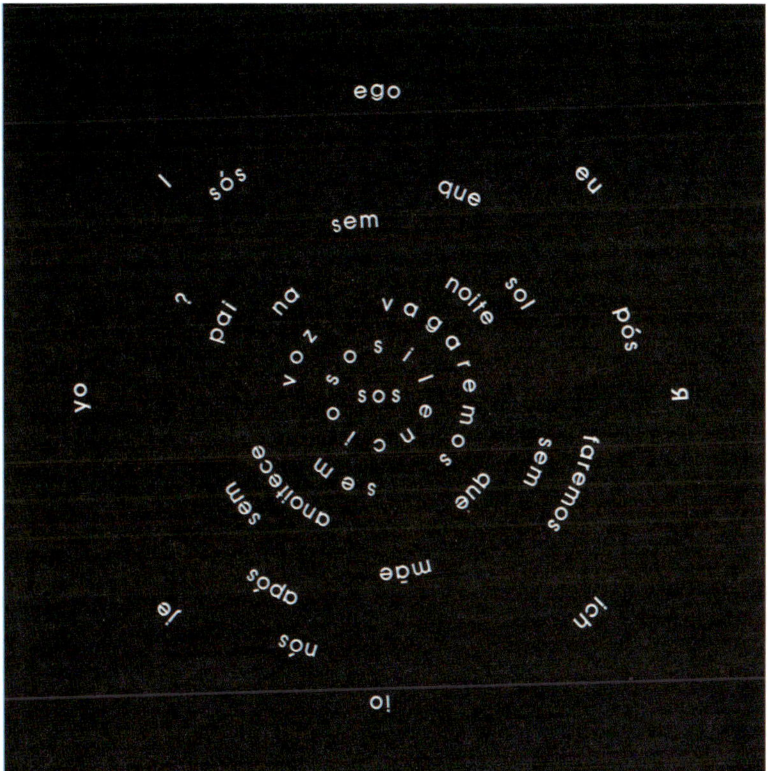
ego
I
sós
sem
que
eu
?
pai
na
noite
sol
pós
yo
vagaremos
voz
sos
я
faremos
sem
que
anoitece
sem
mãe
após
ich
je
nós
io

PLATE 16

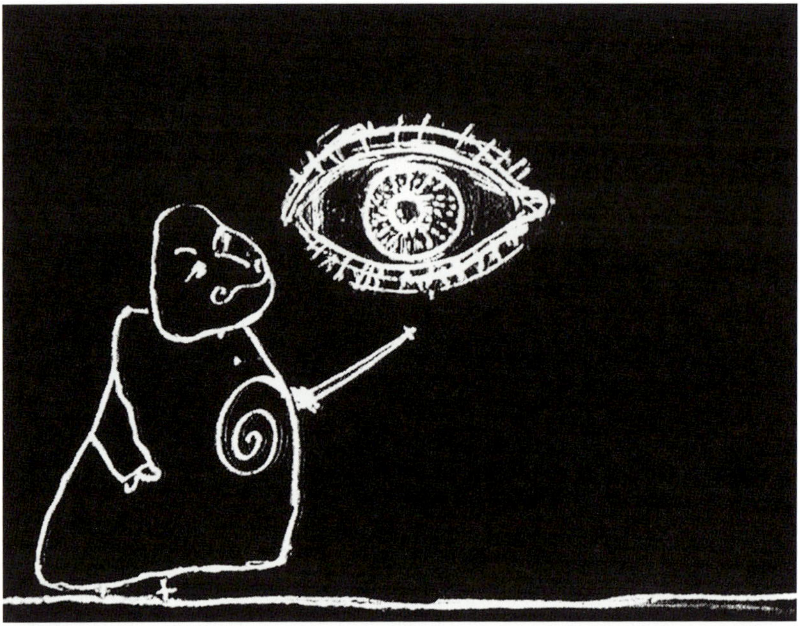

PLATE 17

FIVE

AT THE END OF THE JETTY

BECKETT . . . SMITHSON. RECOIL . . RETURN

I must have got embroiled in a kind of inverted spiral, I mean one of the coils of which, instead of widening more and more, grew narrower and narrower and finally, given the kind of space in which I was supposed to evolve, would come to an end for lack of room.

• SAMUEL BECKETT, *THE UNNAMABLE*

There is a political centrifugal force that throws the blood of atrocities onto those working for peace. . . . Conscience-stricken, the artist wants to stop the massive hurricane of carnage, to separate the liberating revolution from the repressive war machine. Of course, he sides with the revolution, [but] then he discovers that real revolution means violence too.

• ROBERT SMITHSON, "THE ARTIST AND POLITICS"

EXAGMINATING ROUND

In the fall of 1930, fresh from contributing his essay "Dante . . . Bruno. Vico . . Joyce" to *Our Exagmination Round His Factification for Incamination of Work in Progress* about Joyce's *Finnegans Wake*, and winning a substantial cash prize for his own hastily written, footnote-laden poem, *Whoroscope*, Samuel Beckett returned to Dublin from Paris, where he had been residing for three years, and took a post at his alma mater, Trinity College, teaching foreign languages. Invited soon after his return by the Modern Language Society of Dublin to present a November lecture, Beckett announced he would discuss the Concentrisme movement, and in particular the esteemed works of the movement's Toulouse-born leader, Jean du Chas, author of the Concentrist Manifesto and of the titlularly Descartes-inflected *Discours de la sortie* (*Discourse on the Exit*), whose title seemed to have been borne out by du Chas's recent suicide. By some accounts, Beckett's presentation, though rather recondite, was well received by his audience.[1] In fact, however, the entire lecture, from conception to completion, was a spoof designed by Beckett to mock what he would later call the "loutishness of learning"—particularly in its Irish variety.[2] Jean du Chas, it turned out, was a concocted persona, and, as such, there was no Concentrist movement at all.[3]

The "du Chas" lecture has become legendary among Beckett scholars as evidence of the young Beckett's wicked sense of humor, as well as his tendency to sabotage his own career. Not only would Beckett leave academia for good the following year, but he would soon afterward seek treatment in London for severe depression, with the Freudian psychoanalyst Wilfred Bion. For those with a psychoanalytic inclination, it is certainly of interest that the fictional du Chas's biography shared many significant details with the little-known Beckett's own, including a birthday (April 13, 1906), a childhood summer vacation destination (Kragenhof on the Fulda, near Kassel, Germany), and more than a passing familiarity with the works of Descartes, Racine, and Proust. Moreover, although it is obviously parodic of the influence of the rapidly disseminated Parisian "–isms," the idea of "concentrisme" is not at all an inaccurate description of much of Beckett's own eventual literary and dramatic output. Consider the many examples of "revolving it all" (or of *exagminating round*)—the cylindrical trap chambers; cycling bicycle wheels; obsessively rotating stones; and orbiting, almost-colliding atomic figures—that appear in Beckett novels and dramatic productions; or Hamm's insistence, in *Endgame*, of being "right in the center," "bang in the center," after his abortive Clov-assisted wheelchair journey "right round the world"; or, more generally, Beckett's extremely concentrated and distilled sentences and phrases.

A special form of finding, and not finding, the center is at issue in the many spirals that play a significant role in Beckett's writing. Nowhere is this more powerfully the case than in Beckett's most sustained and yet arguably most "concentrated" novel, *L'innommable*, written in 1948/1949 and published in its French original in 1953, translated into English by Beckett as *The Unnamable*, and published by Grove Press in 1958. The final novel of the trilogy of the mid- to late 1940s that, as Hugh Kenner notes, "carries the Cartesian process backwards, beginning with a je suis and ending with a bare cogito," *The Unnamable* "concerns itself to no end with a baffling intimacy between discourse and nonexistence."[4] It does so, at least in part, through the repeated presentation of spiral journeys and spiralized thinking.

In this chapter, I read *The Unnamable*'s spiral figurations in collision and conjunction with American artist Robert Smithson's *Spiral Jetty*: the earthwork, film, and essay that Smithson produced between 1969 and 1972—in the latter two components of which Smithson directly cites *The Unnamable*.[5] Of all the visual artists whose work is explored in this book, Smithson may have been the most genuinely obsessed with spirals. As I mentioned in the introduction, in Smithson's handwritten notes for the *Spiral Jetty* film, which he curiously titles "A Metamophoses [*sic*] of Spirals," Smithson directly quotes, without comment, short passages of some twenty-one texts. Where one might have expected to see excerpts from or about such visual artists as Umberto Boccioni, Marcel Duchamp, and Bruce Nauman, each of whom had created and/or written about spirals in a way that clearly influenced Smithson's thinking, he instead excerpts passages from, or concerning, Yeats, Joyce, Beckett, and many other literary writers. Without directly declaring that he is doing so, Smithson, in his notes, which present these figures largely in chronological order, traces a metamorphosis (or some metamorphoses) of the spiral from the late nineteenth through the mid-twentieth century and on into his own jetty project. *Spiral Jetty*, like much of Smithson's artistic output, presents *writing* and *placing* as intertwined acts.

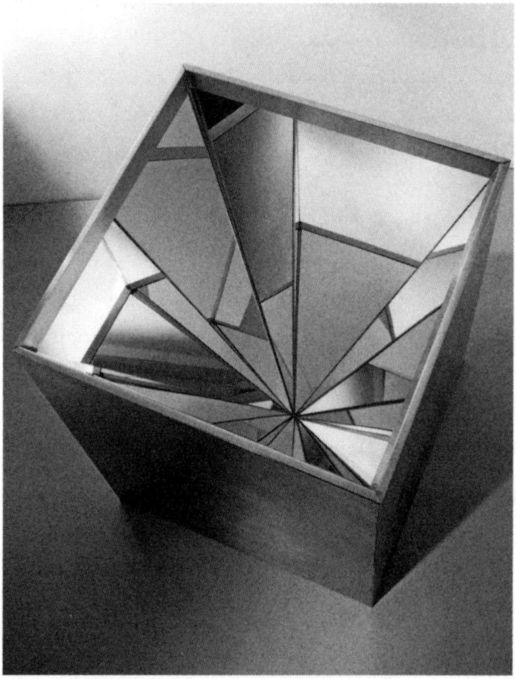

45 Robert Smithson (1938–1973), *Four-Sided Vortex*, 1965. (© Estate of Robert Smithson / Licensed by VAGA, New York. Courtesy James Cohan Gallery, New York / Shanghai)

As early as 1965, Smithson, then a twenty-seven-year-old former painter, created a number of experimental, mathematically conceived sculptures using mirrors, including *Four-Sided Vortex* (figure 45), a work that gives early evidence of what Marjorie Perloff calls Smithson's "cool futurism"[6]—or better, in this case, cool vorticism. The sculpture consists of a three-foot-high Donald Judd–like square, stainless-steel box with an open top, into which Smithson glued four mirrors cut into twelve downward-pointing triangles that meet at the center at the bottom of the inside of the box. The mirrors are angled in such a way that the viewer, upon peering into the box, sees his or her own reflection, as well as that of the surrounding room, refracted and reshuffled. The tension between weighty objectivity (the apparently heavy box) and dispersal and extension of agency and architecture (through the mirrors) certainly draws on the work of such precursors as Boccioni and Wyndham Lewis, though *Four-Sided Vortex* is stripped of those precursors' enthusiastic, expansionist rationales. This "cool," minimalist reflection of concerns of earlier geometric modernism is equally evident as Smithson moved his sculptures outdoors and created them in larger and larger scales, and as he began publishing essays in *Artforum* and elsewhere.

And yet, despite the multiplicity of references that Smithson consistently made to other literary and visual-art texts throughout his brief but astoundingly productive career, the notion of simple "influence" seems especially problematic and insufficient in the case of *Spiral Jetty*, an earthwork that from aerial photographs resembles a giant stuck drain (figure 46).[7] To be sure, this obstacle has not stopped art and architectural historians from producing a steady stream of critical texts tracing other thinkers' potential impact on Smithson's ways of seeing and thinking—from George Kubler and György Kepes, to Alfred Hitchcock and Chris Marker, to William Carlos Williams and J. G. Ballard, to the archaeologist John Lloyd Stevens—and, indeed, from asserting the impact of Smithson's work on contemporary artists such as Mark Dion, Alexis Rockman, Diana Thater, and Wade Guyton, among others.[8]

Thus far largely unacknowledged, both in earlier Smithson criticism and in the resurgent attention to the *Spiral Jetty* since the earthwork emerged in 2002, after having spent almost thirty years underwater,[9] is the artist's significant debt to Beckett, and specifically to *The Unnamable*.[10] Smithson recites a long excerpt from the novel at a crucial moment in the *Spiral Jetty* film, as a voice-over during a scene shot in the Hall of Late Dinosaurs in the American Museum of Natural History in New York; he refers both to this scene and to *The Unnamable* itself at the end of "The Spiral Jetty"; and he cites a different part of the same Beckett text in the handwritten quotations concerning spirals and spirality assembled during the period in which he was working on the

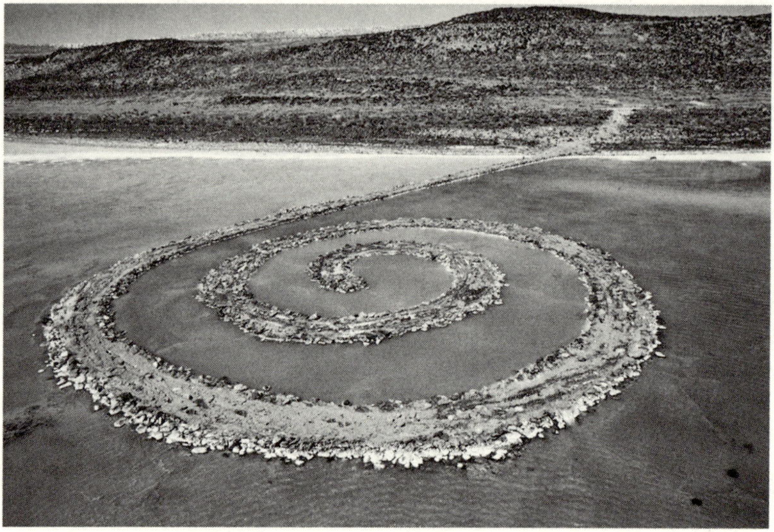

46 Robert Smithson, *Spiral Jetty*, 1970. (Photo by Gianfranco Gorgoni. © Estate of Robert Smithson / Licensed by VAGA, New York. Courtesy James Cohan Gallery, New York / Shanghai)

film. Yet Smithson's encounter with Beckett is far from limited to these references. As revealed in the (still incomplete) list of the contents of Smithson's library, the artist possessed copies not only of *Three Novels*, but also of many other Beckett texts, including *Murphy*, *Stories and Texts for Nothing*, *How It Is*, *Poems in English*, *Endgame*, the book version of *Film*, the essay "Proust," and *Bram Van Velde* (coauthored with Georges Duthuit and Jacques Putman), on the Dutch-born artist. In fact, with nine volumes, Beckett ties with Nabokov for the most-represented author in Smithson's library, surpassing Flaubert (seven) and Borges (six), whose impact on Smithson's thinking and artistic production are likewise estimable and equally unexplored. The Beckettian reverberations extend from eye to ear: nestled in Smithson's record collection—among LPs of Arnold Schoenberg, Richard Wagner, Pink Floyd, Neil Diamond, Nico, and

Big Hot Rod Hits—were sound recordings of parts of Beckett's novel trilogy read by the South African–born Irish Shakespearean actor Cyril Cusack, as well as of *Endgame*, *Krapp's Last Tape*, and *Waiting for Godot* (the last featuring former *Wizard of Oz* Tin Man Bert Lahr in the role of Estragon).[11]

Rather than merely demonstrating Beckett's "influence" on Smithson, then, my aim in reconsidering the kinds of inscriptions offered by both Beckett's and Smithson's spirals is to demonstrate how both Beckett's and Smithson's texts specifically refer to and revise the spiral form's connection to entropy, drawing Duchamp's and Joyce's nascent forays in *Precision Optics*, *Ulysses*, and *Finnegans Wake* into the era of the Cold War, which both Beckett and Smithson respond to with a certain affective coldness of their own. In *The Unnamable* and *Spiral Jetty*, Beckett and Smithson not only expose the presumptions and limits of the project of philosophical modernity, but also reveal the multiple temporalities of the geopolitical, problematizing (by spiralizing) the relation of the "local" to the "global." Reading (and looking at, and hearing) Smithson and Beckett together both clarifies crucial aspects of Smithson's project and spins back on Beckett's as well, elucidating some of the ethical dimensions of Beckett's work—a recoiling that is apposite, considering that over the course of his career, as Smithson's work became more cinematic, Beckett's output (even his work in television) arguably became more sculptural.

MAHOOD AND THE DINOSAUR MUMMY

The *Spiral Jetty* earthwork unfolds like a giant question mark without a *punctum* from the shore of the Great Salt Lake in Rozel Point, Utah, reframing the landscape around the desolate northern part of the lake, which in turn reframes the jetty (figure 47). Thousands of basketball-size rocks climb an abandoned-looking hillside. Several tons of these "local" rocks were ripped from the hillside and dumped on the water, into which Smithson had staked a spiral shape and had workers prepare an embankment, or bedding, thereby extending the already

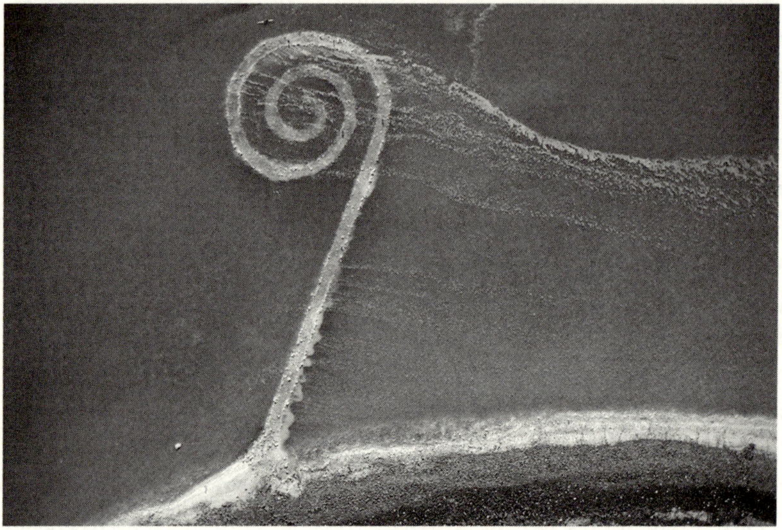

47 Robert Smithson, *Spiral Jetty*, 1970. (Courtesy of Dia Art Foundation. Photo by George Steinmetz. © Estate of Robert Smithson / Licensed by VAGA, New York. Courtesy James Cohan Gallery, New York / Shanghai)

existing dirt road, sinuously, out into the water. The earthwork took about a week to construct.[12]

Like the unpedestaled, horizontally inclined geometric shapes of the 1960s minimalist sculpture that Smithson knew well (works by Judd, Carl Andre, and Robert Morris, among others), *Spiral Jetty* can be viewed from a distance—from the shore or up the hill—or directly walked upon, its meanings unfolding in and through time. But Smithson's notion of the temporal departs from that of minimalist sculptors, most of whom embraced the logic of phenomenology. Against its liquid background, the jetty (looked at from the shore) literally turns counterclockwise, both in the sense of physically closing inward toward a center and in its rejection of clock time in favor of a notion of time in which extreme past, present, and future interpenetrate. Smithson had already written, in 1966, of the confluence of extreme past and science-fiction future in the American Museum of Natural History in New York, where, as he puts it, "the 'cave-man' and the 'space-man' may be seen under one roof."[13] In the *Spiral Jetty* film, which in part documents the making of the earthwork and in part sends up the documentary mode, Smithson draws on Beckett to elaborate on, and literalize, this temporal confusion.

The Unnamable is quoted at length quite early on in the film, during a long, four-minute scene shot in the Hall of Late Dinosaurs (HoLD) in the selfsame American Museum of Natural History. In the narrative context of the film, the HoLD scene serves as a bridge between early images of roads and maps and later scenes showing the construction of the jetty, whose roaring machines are, on two occasions, directly juxtaposed with models of dinosaurs. Immediately preceding the scene is a long-held shot of an unidentified dirt road filmed from behind a fast-moving vehicle, dust kicking up from the vehicle's tires; immediately following it is the same road shot from the front of the same vehicle, toward the end of which a lake begins to come into view. Two scenes away, the camera surveys maps of radically different scales.[14] Still to come are images of the dump truck and tractor and the apparently placid, pink water; and it will be ten filmic minutes until the completed jetty is shown, shot from a helicopter (a word that Smithson, in his essay, asserts is itself derived "from the Greek word *helix*, or spiral"). In this sense, while the HoLD scene is certainly not as central as the film's longest and best-known scene, in which the helicopter traces the contours of the jetty while redundant words—inspired by a "found" geological survey in William Carlos Williams's epic poem *Paterson* ("North – Mud, salt crystals, rocks, water, / North by East – Mud, salt crystals, rocks, water")—are recited in a voice-over,[15] it is nevertheless of critical importance, introducing *topoi* (and *tropoi*) that will be continually returned to later in the film and in the essay, and that are arguably already embedded in the earthwork itself.[16]

When Smithson, at the very end of "The Spiral Jetty," refers to *The Unnamable*, he is in a sense offering Beckett *Spiral Jetty*'s final words. Smithson describes the HoLD scene thus:

> The camera focuses on a[n] Ornithomi[m]us Altus embedded in plaster behind a glass case. A pan across the room picked up a crimson chiaroscuro tone. There are times when the great outdoors shrinks phenomenologically to the scale of a prison, and times when the indoors expands to the scale of the universe. So it is with the sequence from the Hall of Late Dinosaurs. . . . The bones, the glass cases, the armatures brought forth a blood-drenched atmosphere. . . . The ghostly cameraman slides over the glassed in compounds. These fragments of a timeless geology laugh without mirth at the time-filled hopes of ecology. From the soundtrack the echoing metronome vanishes into the wilderness of bones and glass. Tracking around a glass containing a "dinosaur mummy," the words of *The Unnamable* are heard.[17]

Here Smithson condenses several of his far-flung preoccupations, many of which are by now familiar to workers in what Pamela Lee has aptly called "the Smithson industry"[18]—scientific classification, the mausoleal quality of museums, display, extinction—all the while never completely tamping the final enthusiastic traces of a boyhood fondness for dinosaurs or, for that matter, of painterliness, here possibly ironized ("crimson chiaroscuro tone"). A Pascalian reflection on the relation between room and universe slips into a dig at the then-burgeoning ecology movement, whose practitioners, for Smithson, succumb to the Romantic logic of "the great outdoors," and whose "time-filled hopes" are made mirthlessly risible by earth's comparative timelessness. Even the passage itself conveys, through its shifting verb tenses—the camera "focuses," the pan "picked up," the bones "brought forth," the cameraman "slides"—a persistent temporal confusion.

Accordingly, and somewhat contrary to Smithson's retrospective recollections of the film, the metronomic soundtrack from the earlier part of the scene never quite "vanishes"; it persists at diminished volume, and it is over its still-echoic ticking that "[t]he words of *The Unnamable* are heard," in Smithson's own idiosyncratic, low-affect northern New Jersey–accented reading of them, which bears as little resemblance to Cyril Cusack's sometimes tormented-sounding South African–Irish brogue (on *The Unnamable* phonograph record Smithson owned) as fossils do to a living being, and which slightly stumbles and pauses, as though *The Unnamable* were not a novel but a heavily enjambed poem:[19]

> Nothing has ever changed since I have been here. But I dare not infer from this that nothing ever will change. Let us try to see where these considerations lead. I have been here, ever since I began to be, my appearances elsewhere having been put in by other parties. All has proceeded, all this time, in the utmost calm, the most perfect order, apart from one or two manifestations the meaning of which escapes me. No, it is not that their meaning escapes me, my own escapes me just as much. Here all things, no, I shall not say it, being unable to. I owe . . . existence to no one, these faint fires are not of those that illuminate or burn. Going nowhere, coming from nowhere.[20]

Recently, when Smithson's critics have written about the artist's use of *The Unnamable* in this passage, the last five words of the excerpt have been privileged and magnified to suggest a negation or dislocation of the spatial realm in favor of the temporal or, analogously, of the sculptural realm in favor of the cinematic; what Smithson calls "the words of *The Unnamable*" are boiled down and reduced to "going nowhere, coming from nowhere" or, occasionally, even by such astute critics as Lynne Cooke and George Baker, the latter of whom draws on the cinematic theories of Gilles Deleuze, "going nowhere" or "coming from nowhere."[21] This is a tempting deduction, as the final words dovetail easily with Smithson's rhetoric of (useless or obsolete) maps and roads in the early scenes of the film, and anticipate the drifting, hallucinogenic tone of the latter part of the film and much of "The Spiral Jetty." But if Smithson wanted to use only the five (or three) words, he was perfectly capable of excising the rest of the passage to suit his needs. After all, the film's soundtrack is peppered with short snippets like "The Lost World" (a reference to Arthur Conan Doyle's 1912 novel about a region in South America where dinosaurs are found alive) or "Ripping the Spiral Jetty" (the brief spasm of voice-over that accompanies the film's images of Rozel Point's crusty soil being loosened by a blade attached to the tractor). Moreover, Smithson did not hesitate to lop off the last two words of the final sentence of Beckett's passage, which read "Malone passes"—a clause that would make little sense in the context of the film—or, notably, to eliminate the word "my" in the phrase "I owe my existence to no one." A closer, more nuanced analysis of this passage in the context of Beckett's novel, and of its function in Smithson's film and essay, reveals further twists and turns in Smithson's Beckettian presentation of place, spatiotemporality, and history (as well as laughter-without-mirth)[22] encountered, first and foremost, and persistently, through the problem of the name.

This passage, Smithson's take on "the words of *The Unnamable*," points immediately to a question of attribution, of authorship, that haunts Beckett's novel from its beginning ("Where now? Who now? When now? Unquestioning. I, say I")[23] to its oft-cited, tenacious end ("I can't go on, I'll go on")[24]—and, by extension, the *Spiral Jetty* film, which draws on, through quotation, materialization, and elaboration, Beckett's *The Unnamable*.[25] (This is a crucial question: it is no accident that it is Beckett whom Michel Foucault quotes at the beginning of his groundbreaking late-structuralist essay "What Is an Author?" and precisely Beckett whom Giorgio Agamben rereads in "The Author as Gesture," his ethically minded revision of Foucault's thesis.)[26] In the novel, the name of the narrator—or, as Richard Begam has aptly called him, "locutor"[27]—who churns out text on his "wordy-gurdy," is withheld, and a variety of character names from the other parts of the trilogy as well as elsewhere in Beckett's fiction circulate. At times, this locutor seems on the verge of disclosing himself—"All these Murphys, Molloys and Malones do not fool me. They have made me waste my time, suffer for nothing, speak of them when, in order to stop speaking, I should have spoken of me and me alone"[28]—but this "I" is equally elusive, save for the fact of *Inferno*-like suffering: "I, of whom I know nothing, I know my eyes are open, because of the tears that pour from them unceasingly."[29]

Early in the text—and the passage Smithson excerpts begins on the novel's third page—the "I" seems a figure distinct from these temporarily used and discarded names, but of course "he" isn't ever actually named, much less named "the Unnamable." For an extended period in the novel, the locutor takes the name Mahood, as if compelled to do so, and later imagines himself as earless, creeping Worm[30]—but the "I" who at the end of the novel appears to be waiting to be extinguished or to be born remains unnamed, and it is this "I" who tries (and fails) to deduce itself via a confrontation with its location and temporality, its own historicity.

Consequently, given that this is the one passage in the *Spiral Jetty* film's voice-over in which the first-person singular is used, the analogous question emerges: Who or what says "I"? Of course, it is tempting to assume that the first-person singular is the "Robert Smithson" one sees repeatedly in the film, standing alongside a dump truck or in a frog suit staking out the spiral; or, as if a quasi-fugitive, walking or running the length of the jetty (figure 48); or, white-dress-shirted and leather-pants-wearing, windblown by the helicopter's blades, his back turned to the camera, caught in or near the spiral's center. Indeed, despite his consistent disavowal of the Romantic myth of the artist as all-controlling "maker," and the collective nature of building and filming and editing *Spiral Jetty*, which points away from restrictive notions of artistic agency, Smithson's repeated self-presentation in the *Spiral Jetty* film exceeds the necessity of providing photographic scale—that the jetty or the trucks needed a body to reveal their comparative size. One might go even further and suggest that the expeditionary and landscape-transforming dimensions of the project are inherently linked to the rhetoric of giving a name and making a name for oneself.

And yet, in the context of the Hall of Late Dinosaurs scene, the "I" seems to be giving voice not to "Smithson" but to the fossilized dinosaurs pictured in "chiaroscuro crimson" (which itself mirrors what Smithson called, with a nod toward Warhol, the "tomato-soup" color of the northern Great Salt Lake). The voice might be said to belong to the frozen-in-mid-stride *Ornithomimus altus* or the prone "mummy," a carcass of a Mesozoic-era duck-billed dinosaur, its impressions of skin, flesh, and tendons preserved in the sandstone (and the American Museum of Natural History's prized possession) (figure 49).[31]

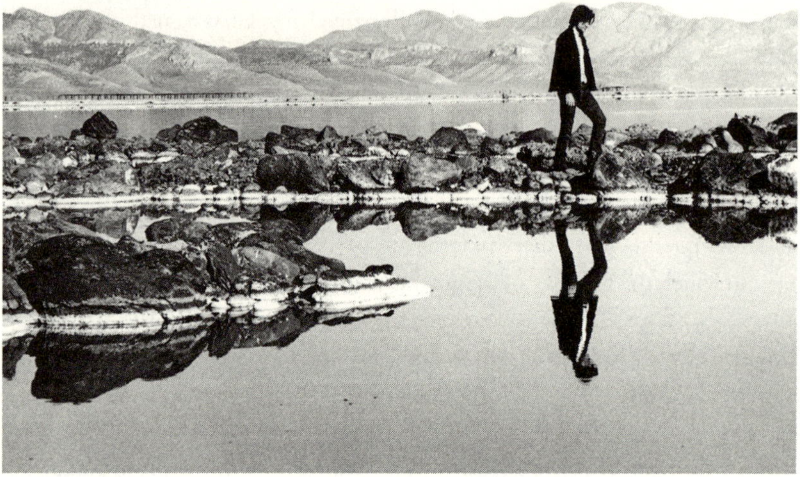

48 Robert Smithson on *Spiral Jetty*, 1970. (Photo by Gianfranco Gorgoni. © Estate of Robert Smithson / licensed by VAGA, New York. Courtesy James Cohan Gallery, New York / Shanghai)

Like *The Unnamable*'s locutor, who speaks (or utters, or mutters) from the position of being stuck in a large jar, virtually paralyzed, armless, legless, and limbless (save for his "onetime virile member"), the dinosauric "specimen squeezed flat by the weight of sediments"[32] peers out of its glass confinements only to find, as its outermost frame of vision, still more glass: the windows of the room itself (a classically Beckettian motif). This fossilized and/or mummified "I," as ventriloquized by Smithson, would, it follows, seem to deny the possibility of any "change" since being "here"—a location that could be understood as either specifically in the museum or, more broadly, "here" on earth since "prehistoric" times.

In the Beckett excerpt (and, indeed, throughout *The Unnamable*), the question of being is inherently connected to the problem of location; there is a persistent sense of having-been-thrown, *jetté*, into the world—a thrownness that is made all the more sinister and bewildering by the presence of unnamed

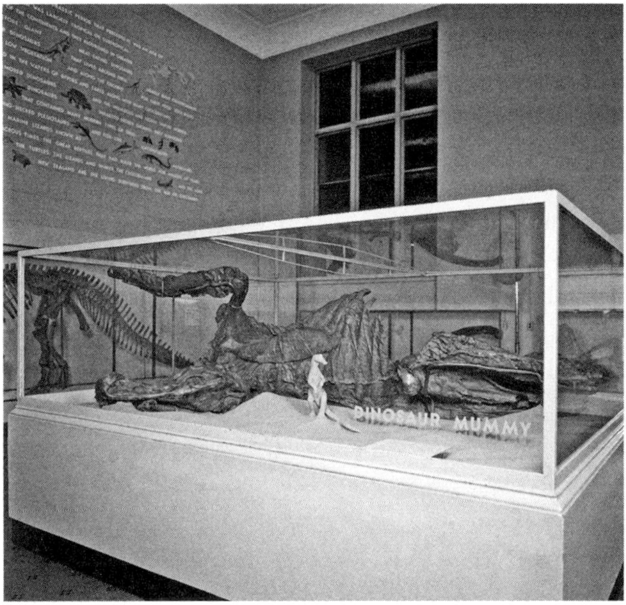

49 Mummy of a duck-billed dinosaur, discovered in 1908. (Image 3759 American Museum of Natural History, New York)

"other parties." As Leo Bersani has noted, the locutor of *The Unnamable* portrays himself as "the victim of a conspiracy to force him just to live."[33] The quasi-historical deductions that follow—"nothing has changed, but that doesn't mean nothing will change. Let us see where these considerations lead"—emerge from that position of dim awareness of conspiracy, of having been duped, trapped, incarcerated, and potentially tortured, an awareness that, in the *Spiral Jetty* film, could fairly be claimed to be both Smithson's and the dinosaur's, Smithson-as-dinosaur's: from the perspective of the archived specimen, held in place by "other parties," history—even one's own history—seems an impossibility.

For *The Unnamable*'s narrator, "All has proceeded, all this time"—the second troika bears with it much of the ambivalence of Eliot's Prufrock's "There will be time"—"in the utmost calm, the most perfect order, apart from one or two manifestations the meaning of which escapes me."[34] About these disordering manifestations, the locutor provides no further clue. As often happens in Beckett's fiction and theater (*Happy Days* and *Footfalls* spring to mind), the reader senses that there has been some kind of unmentionable traumatic event, one that in the case of *The Unnamable*'s locutor ruptured the veneer of "utmost calm" and the seamless continuum of (his own) history—the negative horizon of Bergsonian involuntary memory—but these suspicions are quickly routed back into a self-loathing self-questioning and (at least in the way Smithson has excised the passage) a pervasive sense of aimlessness, of obscure origin and impossible destination. If, in the context of the *Spiral Jetty* film, the voice is to be understood as that of the *Ornithomimus altus* or that of the "dinosaur mummy," then it follows that what Smithson elsewhere calls "the hells of geology" and the "nightmare" of "natural history" remain unknown to their victims—victims whose fossils, presented in glass cases and named, bear witness to their own extinction.[35] If, at the same time one still recognizes an autobiographical trace of "Robert Smithson" in *The Unnamable*'s mirthlessly funny vocalizations, one can also perceive a proleptic resistance to archivalization, to being unearthed and reassembled—the task of the art historian as modern-day paleontologist.

INVERTED SPIRALS

Lest this analysis of the Hall of Late Dinosaurs scene, its voice-over, and its relation to Beckett's text has thus far produced only "faint fires" of illumination concerning the Beckettian strains in the *Spiral Jetty* project, I propose turning now, or returning, to another passage from *The Unnamable* cited, though never recited, by Smithson. This is to be found in the Robert Smithson and Nancy Holt Papers in the Archives of American Art, lodged, appropriately, in the Smithsonian Institution. Here, sandwiched between a humorous anecdote from Eugène Jolas about James Joyce's father's response to Constantin Brancusi's portrait of his son (quoted in chapter 4)[36] and a lovely, if technical, description concerning spirals in Nabokov's *Speak: Memory*, one finds the following excerpt from *The Unnamable*: "I must have got embroiled in a kind of inverted spiral, I mean one of the coils of which, instead of widening more and more, grew narrower and narrower and finally, given the kind of space in which I was supposed to evolve, would come to an end for lack of room."[37] This preposition-filled excerpt gives voice to the notion of centripetal motion familiar to readers of Beckett, whose narrative and dramatic characters often find themselves in culs-de-sac—holes, ruts, obscure rooms. Here, the locutor, who at this point in the novel "took [him]self for Mahood," finds himself embroiled (*empêtr[é]*) in an "inverted" spiral—"inverted" would have a barbed meaning in Beckett, linked to the faint but persistent (and literally insatiable) erotic urges that flicker in the locutor's jar—and, winding himself up into an ever-tighter space (one in which he was "supposed to evolve"), would eventually run out of room ("vu l'espace d'espèce ou j'etais censé me trouver"[38] offers an echo of "species" in "space"). It is not hard to imagine that this quotation might have served Smithson well as a voice-over for the scene in the *Spiral Jetty* film in which he finds himself coursing the length of his earthwork toward its center, pursued, *North by Northwest*–style, by the helicopter; the scene ends with Smithson at a standstill, gazing into the pitiless sun. Beckett's passage would seem in this case to accord with the kind of "constriction or concentration" that Smithson, in his writing, associates with the inner coils of the jetty and, indeed, with his rhetoric of the "non-site" that he outlines in a long footnote in "The Spiral Jetty" (closed limits, determinate uncertainty, center, no place, and the like).[39]

But, as one might expect of Beckett, this journey is by no means unidirectional. Immediately following the passage from *The Unnamable* hand-copied by Smithson emerges the possibility, even necessity, of a spiral reversal:

> would come to an end for a lack of room. Faced then with the material impossibility of going any further I should no doubt have had to stop, unless of course I elected to set off again at once in the opposite direction, to unscrew myself as it were, after having screwed myself to a standstill, which would have

> been an experience rich in interest and fertile in surprises if I am to believe what I once was told, in spite of my protests, namely that there is no road so dull, on the way out, but it has quite a different aspect, quite a different dullness, on the way back, and vice versa.[40]

While the deliberate tedium of the locutor's circuitous reasoning could prove a distraction, viewers of the *Spiral Jetty* film might recall that Smithson, after the long scene of walking in toward the elusive center of the spiral, "screwing himself," as it were, before coming to a stop, "elects" to set off in the opposite direction, toward the shore and out toward the dull road that brought him in, which he had extended into the Great Salt Lake. The shot of Smithson "unscrewing himself" is much shorter than that on the way in and has quite a different aspect—Smithson walks casually and no longer seems pursued by the helicopter—but this movement must nevertheless be acknowledged and reckoned with, as it concerns, as the art historian Jennifer Roberts has recognized, "the possibility and necessity of history," history wound into the shape of a spiral.[41]

About the possibility of history, as we have already seen, Beckett has a great deal to say, none of it straightforward. In the context of *The Unnamable*, which Beckett wrote in the aftermath of the Second World War, these quoted passages appear toward the beginning of a pages-long meditation on spiral journeys (*girations*) in which the locutor describes how he came to find himself in the jar from which his story issues forth. In a similarly worded and structured elaboration of the passage quoted and handwritten by Smithson ("I must have got embroiled"), Beckett's locutor-as-Mahood describes, with considerable murkiness and frequent scale shifting, how and when his inward journey began:

> I must have been coming to the end of a world tour, perhaps not more than two or three centuries to go. My state of decay lends colour to this view, perhaps I had left my leg behind in the Pacific, yes, no perhaps about it, I had, somewhere off the coast of Java and its jungles red with rafflesia stinking of carrion, no that's the Indian Ocean, what a gazetteer I am, no matter, somewhere round there. In a word I was returning to the fold, admittedly reduced.[42]

Mahood's return "to the fold" begins, then, at the tail end of a "world tour," an outward-bound spiral journey lasting for "two or three centuries," a time frame whose duration is impossible for any individual human being to have experienced, but that happens to coincide roughly with the lifespan of philosophical modernity—as emphasized in Beckett's French original, in which "what a gazetteer I am" appears as *quelle encyclopédie*, a word that not only invokes the eighteenth-century *encyclopédistes* but also amplifies the sense of cyclical motion.[43] Moreover, given his recurrent return to the limits of Cartesian thought and intimate knowledge of Descartes's biography and his own interest in mathematics, Beckett would surely have been aware of the fact that Seigneur du Perron, the geometer of Geneva, in addition to inaugurating Enlightenment critical rationality, discovered the formula of the equiangular or logarithmic spiral (later called the "miracle spiral") and hypothesized the "vortex theory of creation," in which space was filled with matter in various states, whirling about the sun. Beckett also would undoubtedly have been cognizant of the fact that, some two centuries later, Hegel idealistically described a world-historical "spirit" winding in the shape of a spiral toward the fulfillment of historical destiny, a spiritual quest that, in *The Unnamable*, is flattened and distended. Finally, if another of Beckett's nearly silently offered spiral allusions is worthy of unearthing, *The Unnamable*'s gyrational "world tour" is also almost certainly parodic of Yeats's esoteric, astrological-cum-millenarian Vision, the all-encompassing occult system in which Yeats describes in great detail how both an individual life and human history move ineluctably in and through time in the shape of widening and narrowing gyres, the coils of which can take centuries to "come round."[44]

Whatever its allusive propensities and provenances, Mahood's centuries-long spiral world tour has taken him to faraway places like "the Pacific" and "off the coast of Java"; he (or the locutor) seems not quite sure where. Aside from having somehow lost his leg, the first of many such lost limbs, the only detail recollected from his amazing intercontinental journey is the appearance of red *Rafflesia*, a genus of large flowering plants named after the British colonial administrator Sir Stamford Raffles—which sounds pretty enough until one immediately learns that they are parasitic and carnivorous and "stinking of carrion." In fact, a little research reveals that the plants lure the flies that pollinate them by mimicking the smell of rotting flesh.[45] In this way, Beckett subtly but caustically links Mahood's spiral "world tour" (with its associations with the history of modern philosophy and the outsized ambitions of high modernist literature) to bloodshed and woundedness, including the locutor's own, thereby invoking a highly concentrated version of what Theodor Adorno, later one of Beckett's most perspicacious readers,[46] and Max Horkheimer—themselves following Walter Benjamin—called the dialectic of enlightenment and barbarism.[47]

Indeed, the recognition that "the fully enlightened earth . . . radiates disaster triumphant" is driven home, literally though also humorously, in *The Unnamable*. After his long and treacherous world tour, Mahood's inward spiral journey eventually takes him back to his unnamed home village, where he is watched by his parents and his wife and children ("born"—and presumably even conceived—"in my absence"),[48] who cheer him on as, with the aid of a pain-killer, he pulls himself on crutches around and around his native abode, growing ever closer to arriving. But over time, the children take ill from botulism (or "sausage poisoning," from bad corned beef), die, and begin to rot; and without particular malice, he grinds their organs spirally into the soil. Eventually abandoning his crutches, he finds himself virtually immobile in his jar, serving as an "undeniable asset" to the *restaurateuse* who has affixed a menu to it in order to attract customers to her "chop shop" right next to the slaughterhouses, and even festooned it with colorful Chinese lanterns. From world traveler he thus, jarringly, becomes a hideous trinket.

Seemingly concluding these spiraling reflections, the locutor-as-Mahood wants to know, if he could unscrew himself and "launch" himself in the opposite direction, "Should I not normally unfold ad infinitum, with no possibility of ever stopping, the space in which I was marooned being globular, or is it the earth[?], no matter, I know what I mean."[49] In this halting, paratactic fashion, his rhetoric by turns centripetal and centrifugal, abyssal and vertiginous, Beckett's narrator calls into question the relation between the utterly local and the global; indeed, it is no accident that the jar in which he finds himself marooned (*foutu* also implies "screwed") is described as "globular." In doing so, he not only reveals a fundamental perspectival and experiential problem in the modern understanding of space—knowing the difference between "earth" and "globe" is, after all, hardly inconsequential in the age of the world picture—but also gives the idea of the geopolitical a different spatiotemporal spin.

SCALES OF EDGES

Much as Beckett does with Descartes's, Hegel's, and Yeats's (and, arguably, Joyce's) spirals, Smithson flattens and evacuates art-historical precursor grand spiral "visions," turning them inward while never entirely relinquishing their rhetorical power or energy. And yet, as is the case with Beckett, whose aversion to "allegorical" readings is well known,[50] Smithson's projection of the (geo-)political is subtle and nuanced, even involuted.

In 1970, in an oft-cited response to a question about contemporary artists' political responsibilities, Smithson, during an *Artforum* symposium, opined that

> there is a political centrifugal force that throws the blood of atrocities onto those working for peace. . . . Conscience-stricken, the artist wants to stop the massive hurricane of carnage, to separate the liberating revolution from the repressive war machine. Of course, he sides with the revolution, [but] then he discovers that real revolution means violence too. Gandhi is invoked, but Gandhi was assassinated.[51]

Such statements led many early critics to assume that Smithson's artistic practice was simply apolitical or even reactionary. But it is clear from this passage that, rather than advocating a "dropping out" or retreat into "geological" history, Smithson is instead cannily warning against the assumption that art can ever stand outside of that which it would diagnose, arrest, and ameliorate. Readers of this passage might hear an echo of Benjamin's thesis 9 on the concept of history in Smithson's "wants to stop the massive hurricane of carnage," as well as recognizing another series of "revolutionary" spirals, this time meteorological. Just as Benjamin's angel of history cannot stop the storm of progress, the "committed" artist cannot escape the bloody whirlwind of atrocity and, indeed, in standing resolutely against atrocity, might actually increase it. The problem for Smithson, as for Benjamin and, I suggest, Beckett, is the very conception of progress and amelioration that frequently undergirds political analysis.

The way Smithson draws on Beckett's *The Unnamable* helps to clarify that geopolitical questions are, quite literally, involved in all aspects of Smithson's *Spiral Jetty* project, connecting what he calls their "scale of edges" to their "scale of centers." It is worth noting that Smithson, who was fascinated with the rhetoric of travel and exploration, claims at the very beginning of "The Spiral Jetty" initially to have wanted to make the jetty in Bolivia, at a site where, he had read in a book called *Vanishing Trails of Atacama*, flamingos had evolved to mimic the reds and pinks of volcanic lava and exposed salt.[52] This may sound like mere Darwinian whimsy, but in the late 1960s, Bolivia, the country where Ernesto "Che" Guevara had been captured and killed (in 1967), was embroiled in political unrest over the proposed nationalization of the country's foreign-owned mines (a history repeating itself with only a modicum of difference in the early twenty-first century). Lest South America seem a bit out of Smithson's geopolitical ambit, it is also worth recalling that, in 1969, he joined a group of other American artists (North and South), pulling his contribution out of the São Paulo Biennial in order to protest the actions of Brazil's United States–supported right-wing military government.

It is striking that the words "Cold War" and "Vietnam" are so noticeably absent from most recent critical discussion of Smithson's work, even those studies directly raising the question of "history," as if even to invoke these rubrics would be to succumb to a naïve form of "mere" contextualization obscuring what is truly radical about Smithson's project.[53] Yet in "The Spiral Jetty," Smithson himself alludes, albeit in a rather recondite fashion, to Vietnam in another passage concerning mapping, one that connects the Hall of Late Dinosaurs scene (intimately linked, as we have already seen, with Beckett's *The Unnamable*) with the shot of the map that follows it. For Smithson, maps not only expose what is under the cartographer's purview, but also, perhaps inadvertently, reveal what is not: "One is able to see things in maps that are not there. One must be careful of the hypothetical monsters that lurk between the map's latitudes. . . . In the pan shot one doesn't see the flesh-eaters walking through what today is called Indochina."[54]

Here, in what initially may appear to be a non sequitur, Smithson first refers to "monsters" that may not appear on a map but are nevertheless "hypothetically" present "between . . . latitudes," lurking and poised to attack.[55] Then he addresses another, similar kind of invisibility: in the pan shot of the map, one does not, or cannot, see "today" 's "flesh-eaters" roaring through the horror movie of "what is called" Indochina, whose imprecise binational name itself is a product of colonial domination, mapping. The clear implication is that, despite their invisibility, the presence of the flesh-eaters, which in the film's previous scene had been shown in their fossilized form in yet another pan shot, can still be discerned. Smithson's reference to the Vietnam War and the United States's use of napalm, a flesh-eating weapon produced by an American-owned multinational corporation,[56] is as unmistakable as Beckett's persistent, if muted, reference to colonialism and to the carnage of the Second World War via, for example, the flesh-eating *Rafflesia* brought centripetally into *The Unnamable*'s locutor's jar: it is simultaneously elsewhere and now here, shadowing the present.[57]

If one accepts, even only hypothetically, the Vietnam War as such an invisibly visible presence in the *Spiral Jetty* project, or at least as one layer of possible meaning among several other sedimented, partially buried layers, then perhaps the many invocations of blood in the film and essay, which have recently been read by art historians as a continuation of Smithson's fascination in his early paintings with scenes of crucifixion and redemption, may be cast in a different, more explicitly geopolitical light. Moreover, such an interlatitudinal reading might help account for the thus-far almost entirely untheorized role of the helicopter, which supplies the film with its breathtaking aerial images of the jetty but is itself pictured only in shadow.

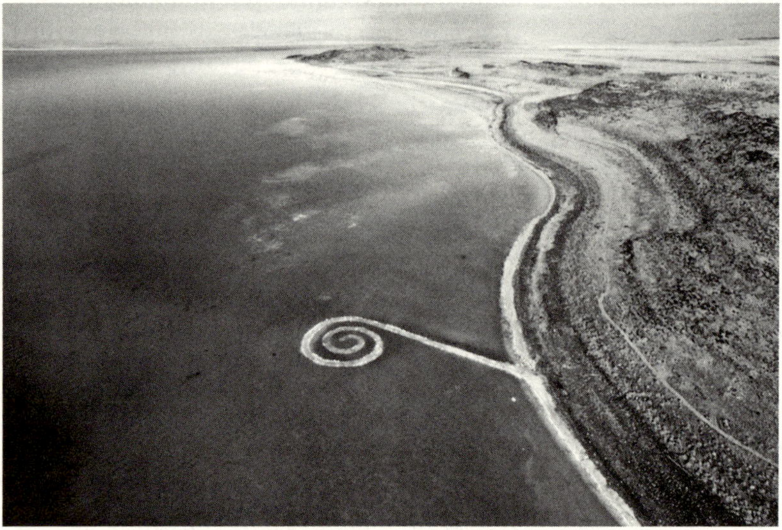

50 Robert Smithson, *Spiral Jetty*, 1970. (Courtesy Dia Art Foundation. Photo by Nancy Holt. © Estate of Robert Smithson / licensed by VAGA, New York. Courtesy James Cohan Gallery, New York / Shanghai)

As Miriam Hansen has perceptively written concerning the Vietnam War movies that began to emerge within a few short years of the completion of the *Spiral Jetty* film, "helicopters, which usually hover and rise and descend vertically, became [in the Vietnam War] a symbol of the impossibility of forward movement."[58] Undoubtedly, Smithson would have been invested in precisely such a notion of spatiotemporal arrest, especially one associated with the *helix* (figure 50). Finally, concerning the earthwork jetty, evidence of Vietnam and the Cold War was not only a geographically distant phenomenon, requiring a kind of afterimage cognitive mapping. Within six miles of the Golden Spike National Historic Site, and unavoidable on approach to the jetty by road from Brigham City (named for Mormon leader Brigham Young)—the very road that appears at the beginning of the film version of *Spiral Jetty*—is the Thiokol Propulsion plant, formerly owned by Morton, the salt company, where during the 1960s and 1970s, LGM-30 Minuteman intercontinental nuclear missiles were built and where, in the 1980s, the defective "O-rings" for the space shuttle *Challenger* were made.[59] While Smithson does not mention the existence of the weapons plant per se, he includes in an early scene the menacing sound of a Geiger counter, aurally registering, as if in a spiral ear, the earth's resonant radioactivity. *Spiral Jetty*'s symptomatic twists and turns thus signal not merely a retreat from institutional space or an advocacy of the long duration of geologic time, but—and simultaneously—a blade-sharp critique of a particular "flesh-eating" war, one conceived in and through a spiral, projecting from real to reel and back.[60]

Spirals, in both Beckett's and Smithson's work, are thus both form and forum for challenging the vexed relationship between "I" and "not I," "site" and "non-site," past and present, and, irresistibly, local and global, both ends of which "jetties" the artists call into question, reroute, approach without quite ever reaching. Just as Beckett (through *The Unnamable*'s locutor) responds to the history of philosophy (and the philosophy of history) as well as the overblown aspirations of an energetic high modernism with morbidly hilarious tales of globetrotting and homecoming, in which "globalization" comes to signify both the anxiety of spinning out of control and the anxiety of perpetual imprisonment, so Smithson responds to historical and geopolitical "elsewheres" with fractalized tropes of discovery and enmirement, entropy and vertigo. It is habitual, following the periodistic contours of much contemporary literary and art history, to deduce that the postmodernist Smithson simply *succeeded* the "late" (or last) modernist Beckett, and that through pastiche, appropriation, and horizontality, Smithson (and his generation) "broke" from the earlier kind of practice emblematized by the existentially weighty—though still recognizably parodic—Beckett. A closer analysis of the Beckett–Smithson relation demonstrates that such a conception does not hold much water. After all, Beckett survived Smithson by fifteen years, writing fragmentary narratives and plays through the 1970s and 1980s that seem to echo the *Spiral Jetty*'s portrayal of stasis and movement (sometimes even approaching Beckettian "earth art") and, of course, not dying until 1989, the frequently proclaimed year of the "birth" of the post–Cold War era of globalization—a term the psychical and geopolitical stakes of which, in *The Unnamable*, he seems proleptically to comprehend.

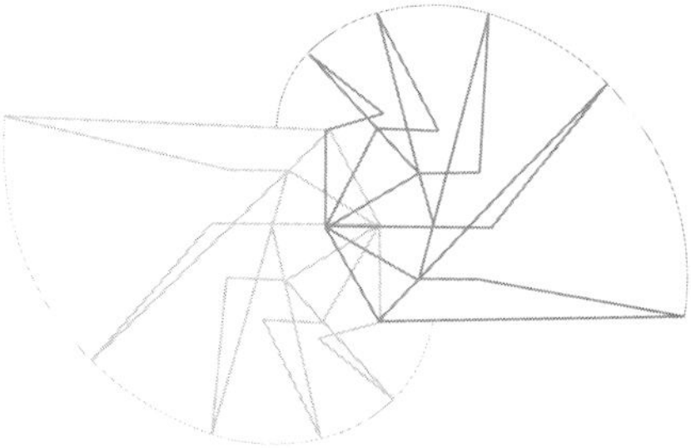

IN CONCLUSION

THE SPIRAL AND THE GRID

Day after day I have sat in my chair turning a symbol over in my mind, exploring all its details, defining and again defining its elements, testing my convictions and those of others . . . attempting to substitute particulars for an abstraction like that of algebra.

• W. B. YEATS, "THE END OF THE CYCLE," IN *A VISION*

. . . It is life englobed.
One would like to stick one's hand
Out of the globe, but its dimension,
What carries it, will not allow it.

• JOHN ASHBERY, "SELF-PORTRAIT IN A CONVEX MIRROR"

WINDING UP

In the preceding chapters, I have traced a metamorphosis of the spiral image from the early twentieth century, in which the spiral was often passionately embraced as associated with modernity, energy, and spatiotemporal expansion, through the pivotal work of James Joyce and Marcel Duchamp, in which the spiral began to serve as a sign for an anemia that challenged those early-century associations, to the later-century work of Samuel Beckett and Robert Smithson, in which spirals expressed a recoiling entropy that calls into question the very foundation of the project of modernity and the colonial-imperial project and human-centered histories it subtended. I have also simultaneously tried to demonstrate how spirals resist this depiction of a metamorphic "story" by embodying a different mode of understanding history, as arrested *image* into which history, as Walter Benjamin describes it, "decays." The collision between these two modes of apprehending historicity has also revealed the intimate connection between twentieth-century spirals and geopolitical situations at specific moments in the century, from the conquering of territory urged by the Italian Futurists to the links, exposed by Smithson, between the rhetoric of American exploration and the napalm assaults on Vietnam. I will now, in conclusion (and, appropriately for a study of spirals, "inconclusion"), turn to a few significant examples of spirals in visual art and literature of the very end of the twentieth century and chart how they respond to the century as century, as that century itself has faded into "what has been."

Curiously, spirals appear rather infrequently in what might be called the high or classic postmodernism of the 1980s—which is to say, in literature, art, and architecture that Fredric Jameson famously described as low-affect, pastiche-ridden, high/low–blending examples of the new cultural dominant exemplary of a globally driven consumer society. But in the 1990s, as that mode of ironic postmodernism began to wane, a number of artists deployed spirals as central to their projects in ways that, rather than participating in or smirking at that cultural dominant, sought, to the extent possible, to address (and resist) it both formally and conceptually. In this final chapter of *Spirals*, I explore the appearance of the spiral image in works produced in the years 1989 to 2002, particularly those artworks of South African artist William Kentridge and Mexican artists Melanie Smith and Rafael Ortega, as well as a concrete poem and an Internet poem/film by Brazilian writer Augusto de Campos and (at greater length) a novel by German-born Briton W. G. Sebald. All these works refer directly to earlier "spiral-imaged" twentieth-century literature, art, or theory that I have discussed in previous chapters in the book—Alfred Jarry's *Ubu Roi*, Duchamp's

Anémic Cinéma, Smithson's *Spiral Jetty*, and Benjamin's "storm of progress"—but the effects of this revision are anything but flat or "blank" parody, as we shall see. Rather, these works' spiral repetitions-with-a-difference reveal the intimate linkages among spirals, modernity, and extranational politics that we have been exploring over the course of these pages.

I read these works in relation to the writing produced in this early post–Cold War period by Italian philosopher Giorgio Agamben, as it is Agamben who has most forcefully and provocatively extended the implications of Benjamin's writings on ethics and politics in the age of what Agamben has called the "new planetary order," an age replete with "bloody mystifications."[1] Indeed, Agamben, who edited Italian translations of Benjamin for over twenty years and is credited with discovering the original manuscript of Benjamin's "On the Concept of History," repeatedly draws on Benjaminian insights to complicate the challenge to political agency—and the concept of history—posed by Martin Heidegger's early work, a challenge that extends through Heidegger's entire project to the work of his intellectual post-structuralist successors. Although my references to Agamben's work amid the chapter's engagement with spirals in literature and visual art will be recursively occasional rather than sustained, my focus remains on the questions of violence, sovereignty, and community raised by Agamben, and the end of the chapter bears witness to Agamben's complication of the Benjaminian image that has given shape to my entire project.

Throughout the chapter, I juxtapose the two crucial figures reflected in the chapter title, reiterating one of the interventions I hope to make in the field of twentieth-century art history—that of the spiral as responding to, and to a certain extent counteracting, the grid. It will be recalled that in the introduction, I addressed Rosalind Krauss's well-known argument about the prevalence of the grid in visual art beginning in the early part of the twentieth century. "Surfacing in pre-War cubist painting and subsequently becoming ever more stringent and manifest, the grid announces, among other things," Krauss argues, "modern art's will to silence, its hostility to literature, to narrative, to discourse."[2] It has been one of the central aims of this book to suggest that the spiral's coordinates, though clearly related to the grid's, are decidedly other. In the late twentieth and early twenty-first centuries, the grid in all its globalizing geopolitical manifestations, including that of surveillance (think "Google Earth" and drone weaponry), has proved ever harder to escape; I offer the spiral as a way artists and writers attempt to swerve around the spatiotemporal and geopolitical axes of the grid, and a way, too, of avoiding the kind of historicity and foreclosed agency that might be seen as following from it.[3]

UBU REWOUND: TRUTH, RECONCILIATION, COMPLICITY

William Kentridge's multimedia project *Ubu and the Procession* (1999), drawing on the legacy of spiral-chested Ubu as radically evil force, addresses the legacy of apartheid in South Africa and the predicament of refugees worldwide. *Ubu and the Procession* consists of two seven- to eight-minute animated films, *Ubu Tells the Truth* (1997) and *Shadow Procession* (1999), as well as several drawings.[4] In *Ubu Tells the Truth*, as in his work of the earlier 1990s, Kentridge pursues a distinctive animation technique, in which he makes successive charcoal and pastel drawings on the same sheet of paper and films each drawing on a stop-action camera, a technique opposed to traditional cartoon animation, in which each movement is drawn on a separate sheet. The technique relies fundamentally on erasure—there is a key frame that is subject to partial effacement and then redrawing—and the filmic result is anything but the seamless cinematic movement that tricks the eye: in this sense, both Duchamp and Sergei Eisenstein are clear influences. In fact, Kentridge's films make their seamed palimpsestic sequentiality readily visible, thereby invoking not only the question of the filmic apparatus but the phenomenology of time and memory more generally.[5]

In *Ubu Tells the Truth*, the puppet-like anti-hero appears more loosely drawn than in Kentridge's earlier films and, instead of being shown against a white background, is negatively scratched out on a black charcoal background, the scratching accentuating the film's thematics of extreme violence. The title of *Ubu Tells the Truth* invokes the mission of the Republic of South Africa's Truth and Reconciliation Commission (TRC), established in 1995, in which the new republic, led by the African National Congress, sought to provide "restorative justice" by allowing both victims of apartheid state–sponsored violence and amnesty-seeking perpetrators of that violence a forum for testimony. As described by Mary Burton, a white South African former anti-apartheid activist on the commission, "Guilt for wrongdoing needs to be translated into positive commitment to building a better society."[6] The film, which explores the extraordinary difficulty of discerning, confronting, and expressing such pervasive "guilt for wrongdoing," as well as of "telling the truth," blends together several of Kentridge's filmic preoccupations: the ethics of witnessing, the relation between the domestic sphere and the reach of the state, and the possibility for redemption or newness or "positive commitment"—all under the repeated sign of the Ubu-esque spiral.

The plot of *Ubu Tells the Truth*, if it can be called a plot, requires detailed description to convey its complexity. The first two, very brief, scenes concern, first, spiral-chested and handlebar-mustached Ubu on a stroll and, second, an illustrated eye facing the viewer. Ubu approaches the eye, pokes it out with his stick (figure 51), and steals its pupil, quickly himself transforming into an arachnoid walking surveillance device with the eye as a head, a camera for a midsection, and a tripod for legs—the tripod mirroring the actual tripod on which the screen displaying *Ubu Tells the Truth* is balanced. The surveillance device begins a grotesque dance, which is intercut with brief shots of a real human eye rolling around in its socket as if in astonishment (figure 52), but the eye soon morphs into a long, thin shower with rotating taps for legs and a large sprinkler as head. As the shower turns on, parts of the body of the now-recognizable Ubu drop into the drain, along with the scissors that continue to slice the body parts. The camera follows the sprinkling water up from the drain to the showerhead, and the stream of water morphs into a spiral-chested and -nippled, naked, large female figure, gyrating coquettishly but grotesquely to muffled South African folk music.

The next part of the film begins when this Mère Ubu–like form soon sprouts the death's head, and her body becomes a sort of ghoulish composite of skeletons;

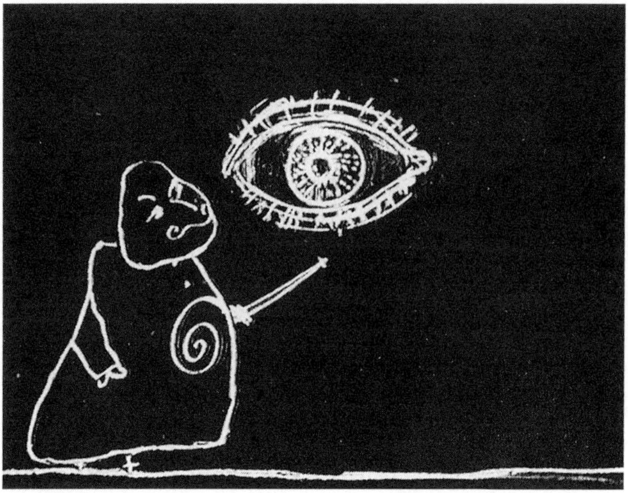

51 William Kentridge (b. 1955), still from *Ubu Tells the Truth*, 1996–1997. (Image courtesy Marian Goodman Gallery. © William Kentridge)

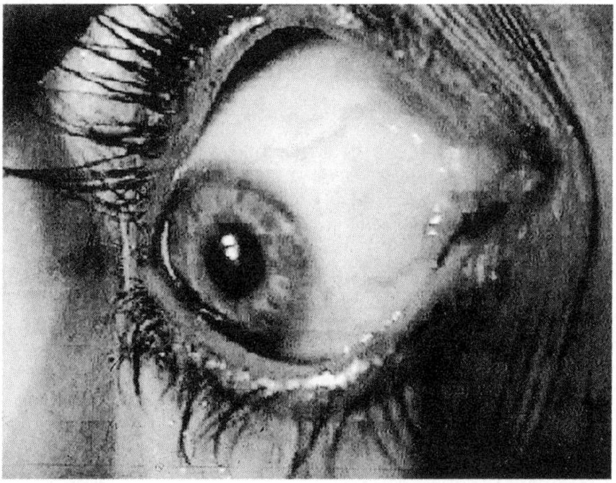

52 William Kentridge, still from *Ubu Tells the Truth*, 1996–1997. (Image courtesy Marian Goodman Gallery. © William Kentridge)

she waves the scissors threateningly and almost immediately is hanged from a tree. The film switches back to the first image of the eye, which soon becomes a pig-snouted dog, on whose ears suddenly appear a headset for electroshock therapy or execution. The dog is immediately electrocuted, producing a brief flash of a mushroom cloud, though the dog's head again returns. A new scene begins with momentarily cheerier, active music accompanying Père Ubu in a spiral-fronted woman's dress on his way to a kind of stadium. He becomes the arachnoid apparatus again; then a helicopter; then, after a brief helicopter flight, a radio with a spiral screen on the same tripod; then, accompanied by Hawaiian hula music, a cat on a tripod languidly cleaning itself; and then a radio broadcasting a wailing sound. An Ubu-headed figure with a debonair spiral handlebar mustache and tripod legs then arrives and intimately tangos with the cat.

The radio on a tripod disgorges through spiralized sound a showerhead, which then sprouts water and becomes a white film screen against which is projected a domestic scene: now black-faced, mustachioed, Latin lover–type Ubu and now fully white-faced cat, accompanied by sinister music, put something, possibly a bomb, inside a square package, wrap the package, and toss it across a map of South Africa as, in the audio track, an Afrikaner politician speechifies.

The final part of the film intercuts the humanoid and animal figures with actual historical footage—ranging from police confronting a running crowd with whips in Cato Manor in 1960 and storming a group of students at Wits University during a state of emergency in 1985, to scenes from the Soweto Uprising of 1976. These images are interspersed with animated episodes suggesting torture and other forms of violence behind closed doors. As the film winds down, these episodes congeal into an enormous, animated city apartment block with windows opening out to the viewer (figure 53), behind each of which an interrogation or a violent confrontation appears to be taking place. The film cuts away to a giant spiral constellation in the sky.

As will surely have been noticed, *Ubu Tells the Truth* engages many precursor texts besides Jarry's *Ubu Roi*. The camera with its tripod recalls Dziga Vertov's *Man with a Movie Camera*; the real human eye rolling around in its socket, Luis

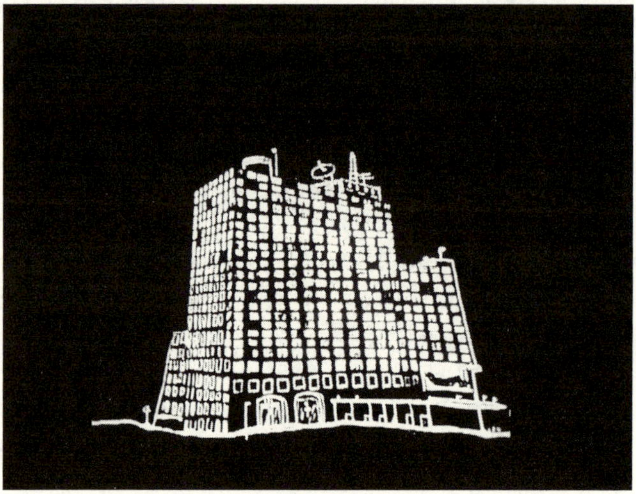

53 William Kentridge, still from *Ubu Tells the Truth*, 1996–1997. (Image courtesy Marian Goodman Gallery. © William Kentridge)

Buñuel and Salvador Dalí's *Un chien andalou*; and the radio's discordant sounds and politician's speeches, Rainer Werner Fassbinder's *The Marriage of Maria Braun*. At least three Alfred Hitchcock films are referenced: *Psycho* in the shower scene, *Rear Window* with the depiction of apartment block windows, and *Vertigo* with the giant spiral constellation. The precursor filmic scenes themselves portray different aspects of violence and witnessing, and *Ubu Tells the Truth*'s reiteration of them in negatively animated form accentuates the ethical responsibilities and quandaries of historical testimony.

As Agamben notes, "[T]he value of testimony lies essentially in what it lacks."[7] Because, for Agamben, there can be no "complete" witness to extreme forms of victimization, the very possibility of not being able actively to bear witness creates an authority beyond the testimony of the individual subject—one that stands in for the absent subject. This ethical predicament is confronted in

Ubu Tells the Truth not only by the repeated presentation of the "eye," but by the spiral-fauceted shower and its drain, which seem to represent both an attempt to forget or wash away and, through association to holocaust iconography, mass killing by the state.[8] Meanwhile, the depiction and suggestion of violence on individual human bodies abounds and is linked to spectacularity (the stadium lights, the burlesque dance) and a sharp questioning of spectacle. The final juxtaposition of the gridded apartment block and the giant spiral constellation conveys both how state violence extends its tendrils into the domestic sphere and how radical, Ubu-esque evil persists even after the "truth" is told—if, indeed, it can ever be told.

Ubu Tells the Truth has often been accompanied by, and played on a separate screen simultaneously with, its eight-minute partner film *Shadow Procession*, for the filming of which Kentridge fabricated a series of cardboard humanoid figures shot behind a screen to give the impression of passing shadows. In the longest section of the film, these shadows move from left to right across the screen; for the first several minutes, an accordion-accompanied South African version of "What a Friend We Have in Jesus" (by Alfred Makgalemele and Philip Milla) plays in the background, sounding far more desperate for than confident of this friendship. A shadow version of Eugène Delacroix's *Liberty Leading the People* is followed by a number of wounded figures on crutches, weary soldiers porting rifles, a father with a child on his back, and miners carting a wounded woman in a wheelbarrow, as well as an occasional European-looking refugee. Blurry shadows cross the foreground again, creating a sense of receding depth to the now-backgrounded, clearer shadow images.[9] Some of the figures seem to repeat: a woman carries her dead or wounded husband, and a man holds his lifeless-looking child. An old woman limps with a walking stick; a figure with a rudimentary prosthetic leg walks proudly, arms holding crutches aloft. Miners carry shovels, and another carries a hanged man. A shadow-man pulls along another man, who is showering and leaning his head backward. (The shower image is one of many that connect *Ubu Tells the Truth* with *Shadow Procession*; in the latter film, the European-looking figure once appears as though smashed over the head violently by his attendant.) A shadow-woman in nineteenth century–style dress lugs a huge megaphone on a mine cart and then seems to proclaim something through it. Some bent-backed men carry a city's high-rises on their backs—the apartments again mirroring those of *Ubu Tells the Truth*. In fact, the procession is immediately followed by a ninety-second vignette of a kabuki-like, moving Ubu (played by a live actor)[10] pictured entirely in shadow, slicing his arms and enormous puppet hands through the air as though they were attached to giant whips, and dancing in satisfaction to the rhythm of the militant "toyi-toyi" chants, drums, and combative slogans.

While *Ubu Tells the Truth* bears witness to the impossibility of "completely" bearing witness to the effects of state-sponsored violence and a state-centered liberation struggle, *Shadow Procession*, whose title invokes ritualized, funerary movement, focuses on the production by the state of refugees, a production that exceeds the boundaries of the state and troubles linear, narrative versions of national history—including, especially, the very idea of procession toward a historical destiny. Indeed, although the appearance of wounded figures and the pathos-filled soundtrack gesture toward some notion of eventual redemption, the images loop continuously, suggesting an eternal recurrence of harm, of wandering.

Much of *Shadow Procession* bears a remarkable visual similarity to Kara Walker's silhouette-based art, which, like Kentridge's work, began to be exhibited internationally in the mid-1990s and confronts the politics of race and extreme violence through black-and-white shadows, sometimes cast stationary on the wall and sometimes sequentially in film. Walker's exaggerated cutout depictions of grotesque stereotypes of "house negroes," fieldhands, and plantation slave owners, in predatory and sexualized positions, display the unconscious underbelly of slave society and its persistent impact on subsequent generations of Americans, both black and white. As in Walker's work, Kentridge's figures abound in woundedness—amputations, peg legs, hideously bent backs—but, unlike Walker's work and unlike its paired film *Ubu Tells the Truth*, *Shadow Procession*, with the couple of exceptions mentioned, does not generally depict violence per se. Rather, in showing the procession of shadow refugees, both physiognomically European and African, Kentridge's focus seems to be on the *aftermath* of that violence.

The figure of the refugee further complicates the truth-telling and restitution demanded by the TRC's mission, grounded as it is in the rhetoric of human rights. As Hannah Arendt suggests in an analysis crucial to Agamben's own, "The concept of the Rights of Man, based on the supposed existence of a human being as such, collapsed in ruins as soon as those who professed it found themselves for the first time before men who had truly lost every other specific quality and connection except for the mere fact of being humans."[11] The paradox Arendt reveals is that the figure that incarnates the idea of human rights, the refugee, instead and increasingly over the course of the twentieth century, reveals the radical insufficiency of the concept of human rights—while by no means dispensing with the need for genuine human rights.[12] Arendt's analysis thereby exposes another aspect of Kentridge's films' connection to Jarry's *Ubu Roi*—a play whose subtitle *ou, les Polonais* effectively conveys the biopolitical plight of the country's effectively stateless South African black majority before the end of the apartheid system.

SOS: EXTENDING THE LYRIC

While Kentridge's *Ubu and the Procession* thus adumbrates (and re-umbrates) the sketchy non-place of biopolitical ethics, Augusto de Campos's spiralized digital poem/film project *SOS* presents a meditation on the durability of the phenomenality of language-as-such in the nascent age of the World Wide Web. De Campos, a Brazilian writer who has published poetry and translations of poetry since the early 1950s and poetics essays since the early 1960s, penned the essay "Theory of Concrete Poetry" (1956), in which he emphatically defined the movement as "TENSÃO DE PALAVRAS-COISAS NO ESPAÇO-TEMPO" (TENSION OF WORDS-THINGS IN SPACE-TIME).[13] De Campos posited that "the concrete poet sees the word in itself—a magnetic field of possibilities—like a dynamic object, a living cell, a complete organism, with psycho-physico-chemical properties [com propriedades psicofisicoquímicas]."[14] Given the magnetism of words-in-themselves, the concrete poet "does not turn away from words, does not glance at them obliquely: he goes directly to their center, in order to . . . vivify their facticity."[15]

In advocating the attentive pursuit of words' "center," de Campos was clearly responding to the traditions of Euro-American high modernism. This is evident not only in the manifesto-like form and bold typography of "Theory of Concrete Poetry," but in its series of Vorticist (and Surrealist) blessings of precursors: "mallarmé (*un coup de dés*), joyce (*finnegans wake*), pound (*cantos*, ideograma), cummings . . . apollinaire (*calligrammes*) e as tentativas experimentais futuristasdadaistas [and the tentative futuristdadaist experimental efforts]."[16] These are "na raíz do novo procedimento poético [at the root of the (then-)new poetic procedure]."[17] And yet the rigorous procedure advocated by de Campos and his colleagues in publishing the anthologies they called *Noigandres* also clearly drew impetus from an earlier generation of Brazilian modernists, including Oswald de Andrade and the "anthropophagic" instantpoem, and a tendency, shared with Brazilian modernist visual art, toward organicism. For example, de Campos, throughout "Theory of Concrete Poetry," stresses the life-filled and vivifying dimension of concrete poetry.[18]

SOS was written in 1983, and published in book form (part of the collection *Expoemas*) in 1991. In the same year that the book was published, de Campos and his son Cid began work on a short, computer-animated version of the poem with the computer science department at the University of São Paulo; this was completed the following year and then reworked into a more fully fledged digital work in 2000. In these latter projects, concrete poetry's "direct" phenomenological investigation is extended and complicated by the animating potentialities of the digital sphere. In its published book form, the title appears at the center of seven concentric circles of mostly monosyllabic words, letters set (as Kentridge's *Ubu Tells the Truth* is drawn, and as Duchamp's *Anémic Cinéma*'s puns are printed) in white against a black background. In the inner circles, blank black

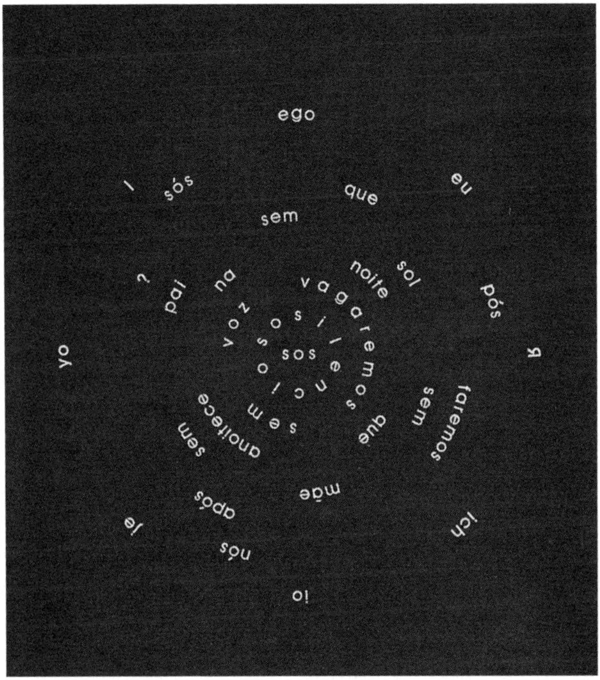

54 Augusto de Campos, *SOS*, 1984. (© Augusto de Campos. Image courtesy of Augusto de Campos)

space between many of the words creates a vacancy that encourages the reader to leap in at various possible points, the potential continuity of the reading act thereby creating a spiral out of the circles' rungs (figure 54).

The pictogram can be read clockwise and counterclockwise, from the outer to the inner rungs and vice versa. Reading from out to in, the reader first encounters the outermost circle of eight short words in eight different European languages: "ego eu я ich io je yo I." These versions of the first-person pronoun "I" serve as at once gatekeeper for the rest of the poem and invitation to proceed inward. They both invoke the expressive lyrical tradition (long shunned by the objectivist concrete poets) and, by having the pronouns appear in multiple languages, problematize unmediated lyricality. Some of these languages likely will be unfamiliar to the reader (even the reader of Portuguese); the foreignness of language—even that of the native tongue—motivates the poem. Depending on where the reader begins reading the second-outermost circle, the poem's rungs or levels might appear as "nós sós pós," "sós pós nós," or "pós nós sos": different iterations of "we alone dust"; "pós" also implies "post"—not in its verb form (as it might be in English), but as an adverb or a prefix indicating a belatedness or "coming after."[19] The rest of *SOS*, following the same combinatory logic, might read, in translation, "What will we do afterward? / Without sun without mother without father / In the night that night falls / We wander voiceless silent."

Not only is the order of particular rungs subject to randomness, but the monosyllabic blurting quality of the work invites conjunction with other syllables to create longer words—for example, "sem mãe" (motherless) invokes the Greek *seme* (seed, semantics) and "sem pai," the Latin *semper* (always). As Marjorie Perloff has shown, de Campos's interest in syllabic connectivity owes a debt to the language-based speculations of the Russian polymath Velimir Khlebnikov, which, as discussed in chapter 3, also significantly influenced the conception of Tatlin's Tower.[20]

This notion of connectivity in the poem extends to crossing one rung of the spiral onto another level to create or continue a word: "silencio," the penultimate rung, is a command for silence, but "silenciosos" is an adjective suggesting "we are silent." What serves as a shifter for these two different but possibly enjambed words is the titular and terminal (or, reading inside-out, inaugural) "sos," a word that in Portuguese signifies (with an acute accent over the *o*) the plural form of the adjective "alone," but also, in the international language of Morse code, . . . – – – . . . , a sign of extreme distress (sometimes erroneously thought to signify "Save Our Souls"). Returning for a moment to the facticity of poetry advocated in de Campos's "Theory of Concrete Poetry," "sos," pronounced as distinct letters in English, also suggests, in Spanish, the declarative "it [or that] is."[21] As concrete (post-) poem, the logic of the poetic lines therefore suggests a movement from nominalized subjectivity or individual consciousness to the (difficult) possibility of a kind of community, itself indicated by the connectivity implied in the spiral reading experience. The central oppositions that drive the poem, "voice" / "silence" and "night" / "sun," are visually rendered or, better, "translated" in the spiral image itself, which at once gestures toward the cosmological mystery of origin (in the Cartesian vortical sense) and deep, empty space as a sort of destination.

When the poem was first digitalized in 1991/1992, set into motion in a way similar to that through which Duchamp, in *Anémic Cinéma*, cinematized anemic-seeming language on a record player, the effects on the reading experience were multiple.[22] The rungs of letters, which now appear in blue squares against a white background, wheel around alternately clockwise and counterclockwise, such that one line cannot easily be connected to the next line. The soundtrack contains disorienting music redolent of science-fiction films, making the words seem as though they were being slowly churned out by a machine. Over this music, a voice-over echoically and distantly intones the words of the poem.

Because the poem is now read on the voice-over, what was, in its earlier, printed form, a potentially multidirectional reading experience, on film (or as digits) becomes unidirectional, wending its way to "silencio/SOS." The "sos" at the center of the spiralized concentric circles itself rotates around the *o* at its center, which then explodes like a biological cell structure, evoking the founding ethos of concrete poetry—that the word is "a living cell, a complete organism, with psycho-physico-chemical properties"—but then spinning that cell, as though placing it in a centrifuge.

As was the case in Duchamp's *Rotoreliefs* and *Anémic Cinéma*, the idea of rotation in the original digital version of *SOS* tests the limits of the eye as a perceiving apparatus, as well as the connection between the eye and the "I" in which it is housed. And, as was the case with Duchamp's salty investigations in *contrepèterie*, *SOS* invites (but also resists) multilingual translation on the level of the syllabic—though de Campos's poem tends more toward the metaphysical than the bodily.

In the revised digital version of *SOS*, the poem begins with a smattering of little circular *o*'s, which appear like stars in dark night sky, forming, as they multiply, constellations. The music in this version is less "techie"-sounding and more discordant and foreboding. The *o*'s begin to form words: *vóz*, *sós*, *pós*, *vagaremos*, *noite*, *sol*, and so on, and the now fully formed words begin to spin slowly. The reading on the voice-over is identical to that on the original digital version, but here the recording is manipulated so that voices combine to create a series of echoic "rounds," until the speakers reach "SOS" and the bomb-like "O" in the middle fizzles into dust and disappears into the distance.

This later, remediated digital version accentuates the spiral movement from *o* to *I* to *O* to .—insinuating that the declaration of I-ness is at once a blunt fact ("eso es") and a call for help ("SOS"). In doing so, it exposes what Agamben, in *The Coming Community*, calls "the false dilemma that obliges knowledge to choose between the ineffability of the individual and the intelligibility of the universal," a universality literally invoked in *SOS* by the evocation of the stars in the night sky.[23] In this collection of essays, Agamben explores the possibility of a politics not premised on substantive identities that fix subjects in the way that the proper noun "I" fixes a self. When identities are fixed, they must, for Agamben, rely on sovereign power to grant rights and to police the borders of both identity and class privilege. In Agamben's approach to the question of community, the desacralization of the self allows for an opening into the kind of singularity that he calls *quodlibeticità* (whatever being), which itself signals the possibility of a human community free of any *essential* condition of belonging.

In a remarkably bold claim that demonstrates that the fact of language is more primary to his political philosophy than is the economic sphere or the society of the spectacle, Agamben asserts, "Even more than economic necessity and technological development, what drives the nations of the earth toward a single common destiny is the alienation from linguistic being, the uprooting of all peoples from their vital dwelling in language [dalla sua dimora vitale nella lingua]."[24] In what Agamben calls "the new planetary humanity"—that is, the community under the regimes of globalization—there is no way back to this "dwelling" and certainly no universal language to replace that displaced dwelling, but to be "common," the coming community must at once acknowledge this alienation and confront the political task of resisting both clannishness and false universalism.

The digitalized versions of the spiral *SOS*, in their remarkably early incursions into the World Wide Web, encounter the possibility that the Web is one more tool for control—dictatorship by other means.[25] Indeed, in confronting the possibility of extinction, of evaporation, *SOS* issues a cry for help. But, in line with the utopianism of the Web's early advocates, they also explore the potential saving power of connectability, a community-to-come, a planetary democratization in which the "whateverness" that is revealed in any interlinguistic iteration resists the dictatorship of the sovereign.[26] The spiral in this sense becomes a sign of both this destruction and this saving power.[27]

BEYOND UTAH: SURVEILLING THE MEGALOPOLIS

Melanie Smith, born in the United Kingdom and a resident of the Distrito Federal since the late 1980s, and Mexico City–born Rafael Ortega created their collaborative multimedia project *Ciudad Espiral/Spiral City* (2002) in response to Smithson's *Spiral Jetty*: earthwork, film, and essay. As discussed at length in chapter 5, Smithson's 1972 color film documents the creation of the isolated earthwork at the northern end of Utah's Great Salt Lake, juxtaposes this collaborative act of creation (ripping, dumping, shaping, laying of earth) with scenes of maps and images of dinosaur fossils, and features the earthwork's completed spiral contours in vertigo-inducing scenes shot from a helicopter hovering and spinning directly above the installation (also picturing the artist walking on the jetty, the jetty reflecting the sunlight, and the like). In decided contrast, Smith and Ortega set their black-and-white six-minute video (part of a project that also contains Smith's paintings, photographs, and drawings) in the megalopolis of the turn-of-the-millennium Distrito Federal. As was the case with the final few minutes of Smithson's longer film, *Ciudad Espiral/Spiral City* is shot from above by a camera mounted to an open door of a helicopter. But, unlike Smithson's jetty, the city itself is not spiral shaped, and it is not set against "tomato soup"–colored salt water. Instead, the helicopter itself travels in a slowly ascending and widening clockwise spiral, and the city, shot at an oblique angle, appears as one enormous gray and dull white grid, with little to distinguish one building from another.[28]

Fading in from a generic blurred, snowy background, the video begins by featuring what seems to be a mixed-use (industrial and residential) part of a city on a hazy morning, with large, squat one- and two-story buildings with corrugated tin roofs, and a sprinkling of old cars parked in driveways and inner courtyards. Aside from the occasional bus or taxi moving as though in slow motion along obscure roads—an effect created by slowing the video down 40 percent in post-production—visible human activity is minimal (figure 55). Within one minute of the video's beginning, as the helicopter continues its slow ascent, almost all details from the buildings have disappeared; they appear jammed against one another, and one street seems interchangeable with another, save for the occasional large thoroughfare with a motley street island and scrubby trees. Only the occasional appearance of moving cars breaks the extreme monotony of gray-and-white buildings, and they, too, are soon indistinct (figure 56). The grid keeps expanding, with no horizon to give it shape. It grows and grows until a snowy fade-out ends the video.

Whereas *Spiral Jetty*'s soundtrack features loud trucks, plashing water, metronomes, Geiger counters, and voice-overs of Smithson reading from snippets of many texts—including, as we have seen, Beckett's *The Unnamable*—Smith and Ortega's video presents a monotonous, vacuum-like sound that might be compared with that of a large seashell placed over one's ear.[29] While the ear (and its spiral receptors) thus plays a central role in establishing the odd temporal affect of the video, *Ciudad Espiral/Spiral City* focuses primarily on the eye and highlights the act of surveillance itself, in the mode of drones that will become more widely deployed in the second U.S.–Iraq War and in images of missile strikes from later in the first decade of the twenty-first century. Yet much of the chief visual

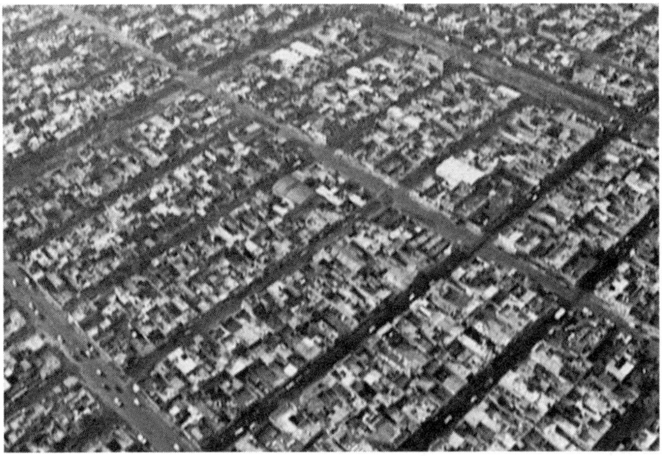

55 Melanie Smith (b. 1965) and Rafael Ortega, still from *Ciudad Espiral/Spiral City*, 2002. (© Melanie Smith. Printed by permission of Melanie Smith)

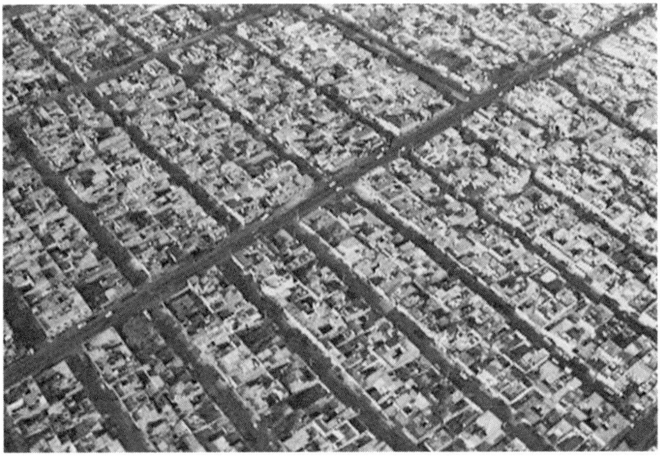

56 Melanie Smith and Rafael Ortega, still from *Ciudad Espiral/Spiral City*, 2002. (© Melanie Smith. Printed by permission of Melanie Smith)

information presented in *Ciudad Espiral/Spiral City* is obscure, if not useless, and becomes, as the film drones on, ever more so. In this sense, what Smithson theorized as a spiralized entropy that countered early American entrepreneurial energy is, in Smith and Ortega's work, drawn into an urban, "underdeveloped" setting and thereby complicated, raising questions about development more broadly.

The video was shot in Iztapalapa, a part of the Distrito Federal to the southeast of the international airport and one of the most highly populated and poorest areas of the district. Yet because of the lack of monuments or rivers or mountains or any other means of orientation, the area is virtually impossible to recognize from above. This unrecognizability extends to the city as a whole, which could theoretically be any expanding "third world apocalyptic city"—Delhi, Karachi, Manila, Guangzhou.[30] In part, the obscure quasi-industrial, quasi-domestic architecture of this part of the Distrito Federal quietly bears witness to the neoliberal policies of successive pro-U.S. governments, including especially that of the massively corrupt Carlos Salinas de Gortari, which encouraged internal migration from the countryside into the city, creating a large pool of cheap labor for both local industries and, through a series of "free trade agreements," the expansion of maquiladoras, typically assembly plants owned by foreign corporations.[31]

The population of the city and its environs increased from around 5 million in 1960, to 13 million in 1980, to over 21 million in 2010,[32] making it the third-largest such megalopolis in the world. Under the sign of global modernity, the physical size of the city has kept growing, swallowing up former agricultural zones and causing enormous traffic congestion. Yet even though the city is, in *Ciudad Espiral/Spiral City*, being surveilled from above, what is actually being *produced* by human labor is unclear—visually so, in fact, thanks to the air pollution that dominates the horizon throughout *Ciudad Espiral/Spiral City* and makes Mexico City seem endless. The most distinctive feature of the video is not the city's architecture but its dismal smog.

Shortly before making *Spiral Jetty*'s earthwork, Smithson undertook a project called *Yucatan Mirror Displacements (1–9)*, in 1969, in which the artist placed small rectangular mirrors in the earth in various locations in Mexico's easternmost state, photographed those mirror placements, and wrote an essay, "Incidents of Mirror-Travel in the Yucatan," about his journey, to accompany the photographs, which was published in *Artforum* later that year. As was the case with "The Spiral Jetty," Smithson's essay on Yucatán both partakes in the customary exoticization that informs travel writing—"one becomes aware of the indifferent horizon . . . [;] one is always crossing the horizon, yet it always remains distant. In this line where sky meets earth, objects cease to exist"—and undercuts that exoticization by focusing on the tedious details of tourist information:

> Looking down on the map (it was all there), a tangled network of horizon lines on paper called "roads," some red, some black. Yucatan, Quintana Roo, Campeche, Tabasco, Chiapas and Guatemala congealed into a mass of gaps, in a neat row: archeological monuments (black), colonial monuments (black), historical site (black), bathing resort (blue), spa (red), hunting (green), fishing (blue), arts and crafts (green), aquatic sports (blue), national park (green), service station (yellow). On the map of Mexico they were scattered like the droppings of some small animal.[33]

This late-1960s list of potential educational and physical diversions, most likely written with the American traveler in mind, represents the nascence of what will become, by the turn of the millennium, a fully fledged international tourist mecca, part of which is widely trumpeted as the "Mayan Riviera," in which much of the choice land is owned by foreigners and the Mayans themselves are employed primarily in service industry roles.

By directly and indirectly invoking Smithson's "earth art" projects, Smith and Ortega call into question the residually organic presumptions of Smithson's spiral, and the exoticism (even if at times an ironized exoticism) and fetishization (especially of Native Americans) that drove much of his work. The airport-abutting area of Iztapalapa is surely not the Mexico promoted by the tourist board—the tourism sector is Mexico's third-largest employer nationally—yet descendants of Mayans, Nahuatls, Zapotecs, and Otomí (not to mention Toltecs and Olmecs) live down there, "on the ground," though they are not visible in the helicopter's view. The video's highly neutral tone makes Smithson's film *Spiral Jetty*, designed itself to appear anti-Romantic and anti-"Art," seem comparatively grandiose and masculinist.

While *Spiral Jetty* poetically encounters the history of modernization and the rhetoric of exploration and expansion, *Ciudad Espiral/Spiral City* more prosaically encounters modernization and its attendant massification. It bears witness to Benjamin's crucial assertions in "The Work of Art in the Age of Its Technical Reproducibility," that "[t]he mass is a matrix from which all traditional behavior toward works of art issues today in a new form" and that "architecture has always represented the prototype of a work of art the reception of which is consummated by a collectivity in a state of distraction."[34] In *Ciudad Espiral/Spiral City*, *Die Masse* is certainly *eine matrix*, though this mass is not watching the film; rather, it is being watched by the film, through the intermediary of quickly erected urban architecture. Unlike popular films of the 1920s, which brought masses together to "consummate" collectivities, this slapdash architecture does not unify; it distracts and imprisons.

In its final shot of a film projector against a photograph of the completed earthwork, Smithson's *Spiral Jetty*, in the spirit of 1960s structuralist film, calls direct attention to the materiality of celluloid shuttling from reel to reel. Without advertising that it is doing so, Smith and Ortega's *Ciudad Espiral/Spiral City* interrogates the technical shift from film to video technology. The scene of the city was shot using not film, or the then-latest-available digital technology, but Betacam SP, a professional video cassette recorder widely used in the 1980s and early 1990s, giving *Ciudad Espiral/Spiral City* its grainy and slightly anachronistic, already archival feel, rather like the long-recording video cassettes used in security cameras.

Smith and Ortega's exploration of the apparatus of video does not stop with the idea of medium specificity. Rather, it extends to "apparatus" in Michel Foucault's much wider application of the term. In his interview "The Confession of the Flesh" (1977), Foucault describes "apparatus" (*dispositif*) as a "thoroughly heterogeneous ensemble consisting of discourses, institutions, architectural forms, regulatory decisions, laws, administrative measures, scientific statements, philosophical, moral and philanthropic propositions—in short, the said as much as the unsaid. Such are the elements of the apparatus. The apparatus itself is the system of relations that can be established between these elements."[35]

In his millennial revisiting of Foucault's late work, Agamben expands the idea of apparatus still further to include

> anything that has in some way the capacity to capture, orient, determine, intercept, model, control, or secure the gestures, behaviors, opinions, or discourses of living beings. Not only, therefore, prisons, madhouses, the panopticon, schools, confession, factories, disciplines, judicial measures, and so forth (whose connection with power is in a certain sense evident), but also the pen, writing, literature, philosophy, agriculture, cigarettes, navigation, computers, cellular telephones and—why not—language itself, which is perhaps the most ancient of apparatuses—one in which thousands and thousands of years ago a primate inadvertently let himself be captured, probably without realizing the consequences that he was about to face.[36]

Agamben's addition of newer ("computers, cellular telephones") and older ("pen, writing, literature, philosophy, agriculture, cigarettes, navigation") apparatuses to the now-familiar catalogue of Foucauldian institutional sites of power relations ("prisons, madhouses, the panopticon, schools, confession") extends the notion of regimes of control to almost any technique that organizes the "gestures, behaviors, opinions, or discourses of living beings."[37] Again, we see the crucial role of language-as-such in Agamben's work on the biopolitical. Agamben's little fable of the primate indicates that writing, approached from the perspective of apparatus, is not a zone of freedom or resistance but a mode of imprisonment, of captivation in both senses.

To be sure, Smith and Ortega's nearly silent video surveillance of a working-class part of the Distrito Federal is not able directly to depict, in six minutes of black-and-white video projection, "prisons, madhouses, the panopticon, schools, confession, factories, disciplines, judicial measures" and "the pen, writing, literature, philosophy, agriculture, cigarettes, navigation, computers, [and] cellular telephones," much less "language" as such, but despite its hazy projection and droning sound, it loudly and with startling acuity exposes how the late twentieth-century megalopolis is itself a site of power relations that extend to the very frame of the globe. It does so primarily by juxtaposing (as does Kentridge's *Ubu and the Procession*, to which *Ciudad Espiral/Spiral City* otherwise bears little resemblance) spirals and grids, the former conveying both the impression of organic expansion and Ubu-like inorganic absorption, and the latter, modes of control, of rendering legible and hence, at least in part, captive.

THE GRID, THE SILKWORM, AND THE ANGEL OF MELANCHOLY

Captivation in this dual sense is also repeatedly invoked in W. B. Sebald's *The Rings of Saturn*, a novel whose very title gestures toward a tension between holding in place and cycling satellitically. *The Rings of Saturn* consists of a narrative of a walking tour undertaken by the author through the economically depressed seaside towns along the southeastern coast of England, a travelogic tale that is interspersed with black-and-white photographs taken by Sebald himself or with other images supposedly discovered along the way. The narrative follows Sebald's ambulations through varied physical and intellectual terrains: there are extended meditations on the works and lives of other famously saturnine writers—Thomas Browne, Edward FitzGerald, Joseph Conrad, Roger Casement, Jorge Luis Borges—as well as encyclopedic expositions on the area's moribund fishing industry, munitions factories, and maritime involvement in the British colonial and imperial projects stretching to China and India. The photographs, placed directly into the typographic text, sometimes directly follow from, respond to, or illustrate the nearby narrative—as when, for example, in a discussion of southeast England's once-active fishing industry appears a re-photographed early-twentieth-century postcard titled "A Morning Catch of Herring," featuring dozens of fishermen and fish packers standing amid tens of thousands of dead herring spread at the men's feet. At other times, the uncaptioned photographs bear at best a tangential relation to the text that surrounds them: a few pages after the appearance of the herring catch postcard, during a brief mention of a British army major from the local area who had served in the Second World War regiment that liberated Bergen-Belsen in 1945, appears a two-full-page documentary image of a pile of hundreds of dead bodies amid a number of tall trees, presumably at Bergen-Belsen. Sebald's careful curation of photographs allows the two eerily similar images of massive destruction (herring amid standing humans, dead human bodies amid standing trees) to constellate, without direct acknowledgment of or comment on their relation.

The constellation of word and image (and image and image), the extended quotations and paraphrases, and the descriptions of the long filiations of destruction are but a few of the numerous structural and thematic aspects of *The Rings of Saturn* that convey Sebald's familiarity with, and deep imbrication in, the thought of Walter Benjamin. As Eric L. Santner notes (using a rather odd formulation) in his study *On Creaturely Life*, "Benjamin functions as a kind of patron saint . . . of Sebald's fictional universe."[38] For Santner, "Sebald shows himself to be a modern master of Benjaminian poetics, a mode of writing in which the materiality of human artifacts and habitations pulsates with the rhythms of natural history."[39] Indeed, *The Rings of Saturn* likely draws its very name from one of the first pieces that Benjamin wrote for what became *The Arcades Project*: "Ring of Saturn" (1929), a brief treatment of how iron construction epitomized a rift between artistry and engineering. If, for the later Benjamin, one of the most crucial tasks of the historical materialist is to honor the memory of the *Namenlosen*—those anonymous victims, human and animal, who have borne the brunt of the *longue durée* of modernization[40]—Sebald pursues this most difficult of tasks with intense melancholic concentration.

While *The Rings of Saturn* catalogues the harms that history inflicts on the nameless, it also registers through the voice of its narrator (Max Sebald) the affective impact of knowledge of that infliction.[41] The narrative begins with a first-person explanation of the inception of the book: "In August 1992, when the dog days were drawing to an end, I set off to walk the county of Suffolk, in the hope of dispelling the emptiness that takes hold of me whenever I have completed a long stint of work."[42] The hope for recuperation is rather quickly dashed, because the walker is everywhere "confronted with the traces of destruction, reaching far back into the past, that were evident even in that remote place," and a year to the day after he began the tour, he ends up being "taken into hospital in Norwich in a state of almost total immobility."[43] The novel thus commences by juxtaposing slow movement over a wide area with bedridden stasis bordering on *Unnamable*-like paralysis, and by demonstrating the infinite traces linking one geographic region with the rest of the globe, usually through political and economic exploitation.

The first photograph displayed in the text immediately follows the narrator's description of the room in which he first decided to write the pages that would comprise *The Rings of Saturn*:

> I can remember precisely how, upon being admitted to that room on the eighth floor, I became overwhelmed by the feeling that the Suffolk expanses I had walked the previous summer had now shrunk once and for all to a single, blind, insensate spot. Indeed, all that could be seen of the world from my bed was the colourless patch of sky framed in the window.[44]

This window, shot on an angle and placed in the text against a black framing backdrop (figure 57), is the kind of gridded window found in a hospital, ostensibly to ensure the safety of those institutionalized within. Its grid effectively reduces the Suffolk expanses to a sign of imprisonment, recalling the modern latitudinal and longitudinal mapping of the globe that eventually abetted the earth's conquering. Here the gesture of mapping and conquering extends, from the perspective of the bedridden narrator, to the sky.

This "blind, insensate spot" evoked by the window's grid is soon repeated in another image in the first chapter, in an extended discussion of seventeenth-century English thinker Thomas Browne, who had written on burial urns that

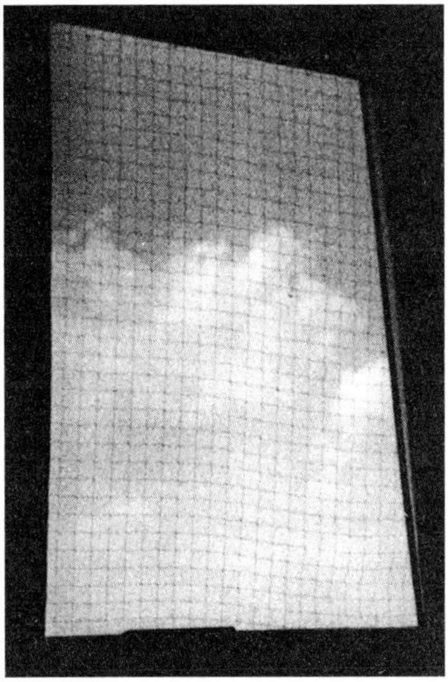

57 Gridded window, in W. G. Sebald, *The Rings of Saturn* (1995). (Source of original image unknown. Photographic excerpt from *The Rings of Saturn* by W. G. Sebald used with permission of the Wylie Agency LLC. All rights reserved. Used by permission of the Wylie Agency LLC)

had recently been excavated in the Norfolk area as well as on the quincunx, the arrangement of five units, through which Browne (rather like Theodore Andrea Cook, author of *The Curves of Life*, discussed at the beginning of chapter 2) claimed to demonstrate that intelligent design exists throughout nature. This quincunx, according to *The Rings of Saturn*'s narrator, paraphrasing Browne, appears in "animate and inanimate matter: . . . in starfish and sea urchins, in the vertebrae of mammals and the backbones of birds and fish, in the skins of various species of snake . . . in butterflies . . . [and] within young oak shoots."[45] It also can be found in "the creations of mankind, in the pyramids of Egypt[,] the mausoleum of Augustus[, and] the garden of King Solomon."[46] Whereas for Browne the quincunx attests to the plenitude of nature and its connection to the heavens, in *The Rings of Saturn*, it resonates instead with the grid stared at by the bedridden narrator and appears as a kind of chain-link fence, barring insight and knowledge.[47]

The spatiotemporal figure of the grid—as mapped and interlinked world, sign of destruction, and instigator of and response to melancholy—is reinforced in the text's numerous portrayals of views from above. One such portrayal comes fairly early in the novel, when the narrator is in a museum in The Hague (home of the International Court of Justice), where he has gone to see Rembrandt's painting *The Anatomy Lesson of Dr. Nicolaes Tulp*, by which he is greatly affected (and into which *The Rings of Saturn* delves at length). Seeking to recover from Rembrandt's image of an executed thief being dissected while "men of science" look coolly away, the narrator claims to have spent a full hour in front of Jacob van Ruisdael's painting *View of Haarlem with Bleaching Fields.* Although this painting, unlike Rembrandt's, is not shown as a photograph in *The Rings of Saturn*, the narrator describes it at length:

> The flatland stretching out towards Haarlem is seen from above, from a vantage point generally identified as the dunes, though the sense of a bird's-eye view is so strong that the dunes would have to be veritable hills or even modest mountains. The truth is of course that Ruisdael did not take up a position on the dunes in order to paint; his vantage point was an imaginary position some distance above the earth. Only in this way could he see it all together: the vast cloudscape . . . the dark bosks and bushes; the farm in the foreground; and the bright field where the sheets of white linen have been laid out to bleach and where, by my count, seven or eight people no taller than a quarter of an inch, are going about their work.[48]

While this elegant description of techniques of perspective and landscape painting's typical diminution of human labor may seem merely incidental, it, like many of the narrative details in *The Rings of Saturn* linked together apparently haphazardly, resonates with data presented and repeated elsewhere in the text:

"the vast cloudscape" harks back to the constrained, gridded view from the hospital window and to the broader theme of temporal fugitivity; the linen, to textile production (especially in relation to silk, as we will explore); and, especially, the "bird's-eye view," to the inherent falsity of total vision, especially a totalizing view of history.

This thread is picked up again as the narrator recounts having taken a trip to Waterloo, where he recalls suddenly deciding to buy a ticket for the Waterloo Panorama. Housed in "an immense domed rotunda," the panorama featured "a raised platform" from which "one can view the battle . . . in every direction. It is like being at the center of events."[49] On a landscaped proscenium, the scene is portrayed in extraordinary detail: life-like but lifeless horses, "cut down infantrymen . . . eyes rolling in pain or already extinguished."[50] Gazing at the "circus-like structure," the narrator reflects that this "is the representation of history":

> It requires a falsification of perspective. We[,] the survivors, see everything from above, see everything at once, and still we do not know how it was. The desolate field extends all around where once fifty thousand soldiers and ten thousand horses met their end within a few hours. The night after the battle, the air must have been filled with death rattles and groans. Now there is nothing but the silent brown soil. Whatever became of the corpses and mortal remains? . . . Are we standing on a mountain of death? Is that our ultimate vantage point?[51]

In asking these concluding questions about "survival," which clearly resonate with Benjamin's portrayal of the angel of history, the storm, and the angel's vision of "one single catastrophe" hurling rubble before his feet, Sebald not only grapples with the disastrous residues of nineteenth-century historiography, but implicates our own potential consumption of that narrative, whose aestheticization and enjoyment would from the angel's perspective represent still another disaster.

In *The Rings of Saturn*, Sebald extends this question of vantage point for discerning the slow and competing temporalities of human and natural history to that of the possibility of surveying the unfolding present. In yet another scene depicting an aerial view, the narrator reflects on the disorienting experience of flying in an airplane:

> No matter whether one is flying over Newfoundland or the sea of lights that stretches from Boston to Philadelphia after nightfall, over the Arabian deserts which gleam like mother-of-pearl, over the Ruhr or the city of Frankfurt, it is as though there were no people, only the things they have made and in which they are hiding. One sees the places where they live and the roads that link them, one sees the smoke rising from their houses and factories, one sees the vehicles in which they sit, but one sees not the people themselves. And yet they are present everywhere upon the face of the earth, extending their dominion by the hour, moving around the honeycombs of towering buildings and tied into networks of a complexity that goes far beyond the power of any one individual to imagine, from the thousands of hoists and winches that once worked the South African diamond mines to the floors of today's stock and commodity exchanges, through which the global tides of information flow without cease. If we view ourselves from a great height, it is frightening to realize how little we know about our species, our purpose and our end.[52]

This description of the aerial view of cities and landscapes, which with remarkable acuity describes aspects of the filmic work of Kentridge and of Smith and Ortega, discussed earlier in this chapter, begins with the narrator noting the invisibility of people among "the things they have made"—houses, factories, cars, in which they are not living and moving but "hiding." Then, human beings, as a "species," are portrayed as a colonizing force, "extending their dominion" (rather like Wallace Stevens's jar) through "networks of . . . complexity," networks that stretch from the bluntest type of extraction of resources to a global information flow that is compared to a naturally occurring tide.

In the photograph accompanying this text, where one might have expected to see, say, a view from an airplane window, we find a blurry image featuring

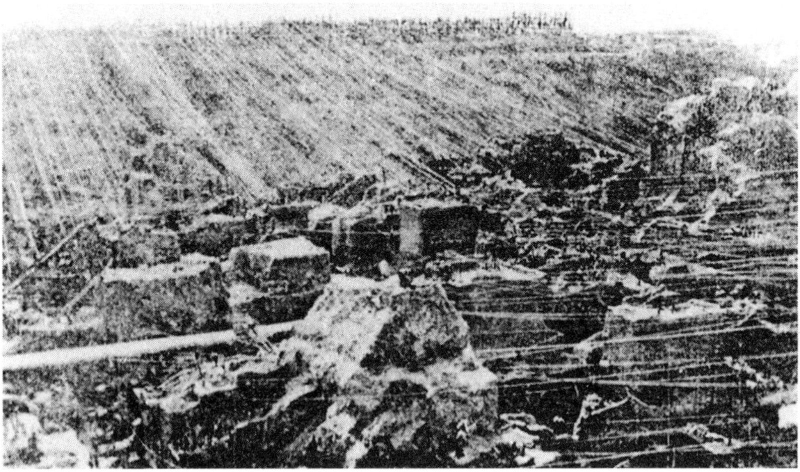

58 Landscape, in W. G. Sebald, *The Rings of Saturn*. (Source of original image unknown. Photographic excerpt from *The Rings of Saturn* by W. G. Sebald used with permission of the Wylie Agency LLC. All rights reserved. Used by permission of the Wylie Agency LLC)

a barren, hilly landscape of what looks to be a mining area, perhaps the South African diamond mine mentioned in passing in the text that surrounds it. In this image is faintly pictured an immense grid of "hoists and winches" covering the landscape (figure 58). The image conveys the "network of . . . complexity" that almost entirely obscures the brute extraction of a natural resource and gross exploitation of human labor in the service of a worldwide commodity fetishism in which exchange value absolutely trumps use value: diamonds, often virtually useless in themselves though ceaselessly promoted in advertising, through a remarkable catachresis, as emblem of faithful love, in this sense truly are "forever" in Sebald's textual landscape.

While the grid and its bedridden and aerial views are the primary figures through which Sebald, in *The Rings of Saturn*, conveys "global positioning" in the broadest sense,[53] he juxtaposes this figure with that of the spiral image, associated in the text with writing, with the silkworm, and with redemption. Early in the novel, the narrator notes Browne's erudition, his deployment of "a vast repertoire of quotations," and his construction of "labyrinthine sentences that resemble processions or a funeral cortège in their sheer ceremonial lavishness."[54] Because of the "immense weight of the impediments" Browne is consequently "carrying," the narrator continues, "Browne's writing can be held back by the force of gravitation, but when he does succeed in rising higher and higher through the circles of his spiraling prose, borne aloft like a glider on warm currents of air, even today the reader is overcome by a sense of levitation."[55] In this sense, Brown's "spiraling prose," on which Sebald's own is clearly modeled, evades the gravitational pull of inevitable impediments; indeed, it both relies on and generates levitation. And yet, this figure of spiral uplift is reversed a few pages later, as the narrator notes Browne's overall melancholic disposition and his conviction that in nature's continuous process of living things consuming other living things and being consumed, "nothing endures." Paraphrasing Browne's view, the narrator asserts,

> On every new thing there lies already the shadow of annihilation. For the history of every individual, of every social order, indeed of the whole world, does not describe an ever-widening, more and more wonderful arc, but rather follows a course which . . . leads without fail down into the dark. Knowledge of that descent into the dark, for Browne, is inseparable from his belief in the day of resurrection, when, as in a theatre, the last revolutions are ended and the actors appear once more on stage, to complete and make up the catastrophe of this great piece.[56]

This assertion of a downward spiraling, annihilating melancholy, prefiguring and engendering a resurrection, draws on an extraordinary metaphor of theatricality to convey that redemption. It is when "the last revolutions are ended"—a clear reference, at least in the English translation, to Prospero's melancholy reflection toward the end of Shakespeare's *The Tempest*, with a nod to the connection between revels and revolution—that the "catastrophe" (in both the dramatic and the historical sense) is completed.

The connection among spirals, catastrophe, and resurrection is made especially clear in the text's depiction of silkworms. Early in the novel, Sebald notes that Browne, whose father happened to be a wealthy silk merchant, "scrutinize[d] that which escaped annihilation for any sign of the mysterious capacity for transmigration he [. . .] so often observed in [silk] caterpillars."[57] Silk—made by silkworm caterpillars, which, though captive, produce the material that can be spun into something both useful and beautiful for human beings—becomes the central textual figure through which Sebald, in *The Rings of Saturn*, evades the annihilation of the grid.[58]

In the middle of his description of his walking tour, the narrator takes a lengthy detour through the legend of Cixi (T'zu-hsi)—the notoriously cruel Dowager Empress of China in the late nineteenth and early twentieth centuries who "had a daily blood sacrifice offered in her temple to the gods of silk" and who regarded silkworm moths, "which would give their lives for the fine thread they were spinning," as her only "true loyal followers."[59] This connection between silkworms and sacrifice returns in the text's final chapter, in which the narrative chiefly concerns sericulture. Ventriloquizing an encyclopedia entry supposedly from 1844, Sebald begins this section by describing the short life of silkworms, their cocooning process (during which silk is spun as a form of self-protection), and their metamorphosis into moths. He describes silk cultivation in China as beginning around 2700 B.C.E.; the "unraveling of the cocoons and the weaving and embroidering of the materials . . . [became] the principal occupation of all . . . empresses" and eventually "passed from their hands into those of the entire female sex."[60] Although it began to be valued abroad and widely traded, silk for some three millennia was produced exclusively in China, owing to an imperial demand for secrecy that was militarily enforced, until—thanks supposedly to two friars who smuggled some Chinese silkworms in their hollowed-out walking sticks—it appeared in (Yeats's beloved) Byzantium and from there spread throughout Europe.

Remarking on the collision of sericulture with European labor techniques at the dawn of the industrial age, Sebald's narrator reflects on the plight of weavers in Norwich, who "spent their lives with their wretched bodies strapped to looms made of wooden frames and rails, hung with weights, and reminiscent of instruments of torture or cages,"[61] noting the inevitable association of the work of weaving with melancholy but also, through a hand-drawn diagram of a weaver at his loom, subtly connecting the weaving of silk with the act of writing, including his own writing. (The silkworm moth family Saturnidae is, Sebald claims in passing, among the most beautiful of moths.) From here, he traces modern silk production in various parts of Europe through to its waning in the early twentieth century, concluding by noting its attempted revival by German fascists "with that peculiar thoroughness they brought to everything they touched."[62] Following "the Führer's pronouncement" at the 1936 party rally in Nuremberg that "Germany must become self-sufficient within four years in all the materials it lay in the nation's power to produce itself,"[63] silk production began in earnest. According to an educational pamphlet that Sebald claims to have discovered, authored by a certain Professor Lange, "the significance of silk cultivation in Germany lay not only in obviating the need to buy from abroad . . . but also in the importance silk would have in the dawning era of aerial warfare."[64] Sebald describes a related Nazi-era German film on sericulture he claims haphazardly to have come across, in which

> a silk worker receiv[es] eggs dispatched by the Central Reich Institute of Sericulture in Celle, and deposit[s] them in sterile trays. We see the hatching, the feeding of the ravenous caterpillars, the cleaning out of the frames, the spinning of the silken thread, and finally the killing . . . by suspending them over a boiling cauldron. The cocoons, spread out on shallow baskets, have to be kept in the rising steam for upwards of three hours, and when a batch is done, it is the next one's turn, and so on until the entire killing business is completed.[65]

Sebald here not only notes the connection between the worms' silk spinning and silk's potential use in the Reich's buildup for war, but demonstrates how the putatively modern, humane treatment of this form of creaturely life anticipates the ordered, routinized "killing business" of the Holocaust, and its own slow and grotesque extractions of value.

Yet while silk weaving (like writing) can never entirely be extricated from the all-too-human cruelties of resource extraction and inequitable distribution, the very fact of spiral silk spinning, its cultivation by humans, and its appearance in fabrics of use and beauty bears witness in the text to a different mode of apprehension than that of the grid, even if most weaving must follow the weft and the warp of the loom. The novel's conclusion and its final accompanying image demonstrate how Sebald proposes an affective temporality of repetition, and emanation, through the figure of the spiral:

> Today, as I bring these notes to a conclusion, is the 13th of April 1995. It is Maundy Thursday, the feast day on which Christ's washing of the disciples' feet is remembered. . . . On this very day three hundred and ninety-seven years ago, Henry IV promulgated the edict of Nantes; Handel's *Messiah* was first performed two hundred and fifty-three years ago, in Dublin; Warren Hastings was appointed Governor-General of Bengal two hundred and twenty-three years ago; the Anti-Semitic League was founded in Prussia one hundred and thirteen years ago; and, seventy-four years ago, the Amritsar massacre occurred, when General Dyer ordered his troops to fire on a rebellious crowd of fifteen thousand that had gathered in Jallianwala Bagh square, to set an example. Quite possibly some of the victims were employed in silk cultivation, which was developing at that time, on the simplest of foundations, in the Amritsar region and indeed throughout India. Fifty years ago to the day, British newspapers reported that the city of Celle had been taken and that German forces were in headlong retreat from the Red Army, which was advancing up the Danube valley. And finally, Maundy Thursday, the 13th of April 1995,

> was also the day on which Clara's father, shortly after being taken to hospital in Coburg, departed this life. Now, as I write, and think once more of our history, which is but a long account of calamities, it occurs to me that at one time the only acceptable express of profound grief, for ladies of the upper classes, was to wear heavy robes of black silk taffeta or black crêpe de chine.[66]

This passage, which epitomizes Sebald's interweaving of world history with the ephemera of everyday life, traces the occurrence of "calamitous" events on this particular apparently random day, which happens to be the anniversary of the day before Christ's crucifixion: these include atrocities perpetrated by both the British Empire and the soon-to-be-German Reich, but also the first performance of the rousing, redemption-promising *Messiah*—in (British-dominated) Dublin. A decade before the advent of "Google searches," which would make such date-driven connections easy to produce, it is precisely Sebald's laborious assemblage of apparently unrelated data, and the strikingly sudden, almost confessional connection to an aspect of his own marriage (the loss of a father-in-law), that makes the tour of historical calamities resonate, levitate.

The accompanying image—the final one in the text—is of three Indian men holding in front of them, as though they were shields, three spiral-shaped frames for the cultivation of silkworms (figure 59). Like little rings of Saturn themselves, orbiting spirally around empty emanation zones, the silkworm frames illustrate the accompanying text's description of history as repetitive catastrophe driven ceaselessly by exploitation of nature and human labor; yet, through the rungs or levels of the image, they also assert the possibility of historical change, be it through a royal edict diminishing the power of the Church or a mass gathering provoking the unleashing of the martial power of the empire but setting in motion the possibility for national independence, or, just as "evental" though more abstract, the Resurrection, ending with the resounding final victory over sin and death, promised (though not delivered) by Handel's *Messiah*.

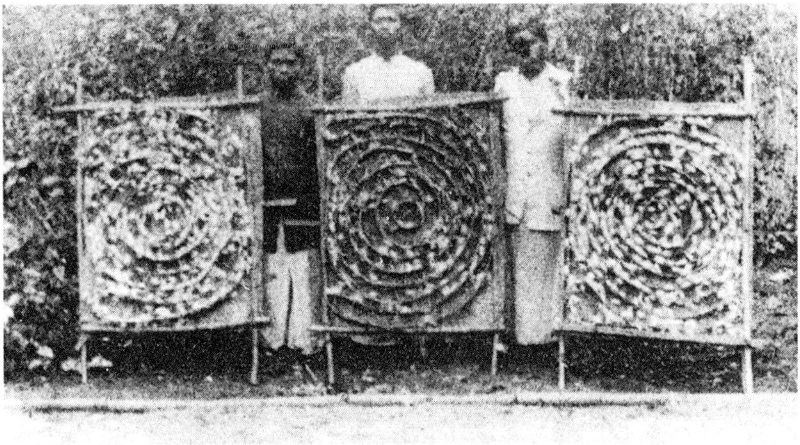

59 Silkworm frames, in W. G. Sebald, *The Rings of Saturn*. (Source of original image unknown. Photographic excerpt from *The Rings of Saturn* by W. G. Sebald used with permission of the Wylie Agency LLC. All rights reserved. Used by permission of the Wylie Agency LLC)

These three final silkworm spirals, like all the spiral images discussed in this chapter and many in the latter half of the book, in which the spiral increasingly serves as both a sign of and an alternative to the gridded world, engender a melancholy (signaled by the black silk garments to which the narrator refers) that, while painful for the sufferer in itself, is nevertheless productive—a melancholy of the type described by Benjamin in *Ursprung des deutschen Trauerspiels*.

Given Benjamin's exalted status in Sebald's writing, it is unsurprising that Sebald frequently refers to Benjamin's *Trauerspiel* reading of Dürer's etching *Melencolia I* (figure 60). In fact, the novel's first paragraph contains two references to dogs—the aforementioned "dog days" and, soon afterward, the helically rising "dog star," Sirius. In the section of *Trauerspiel* that directly follows his discussion "The Doctrine of Saturn," Benjamin calls the starving, immobile dog one

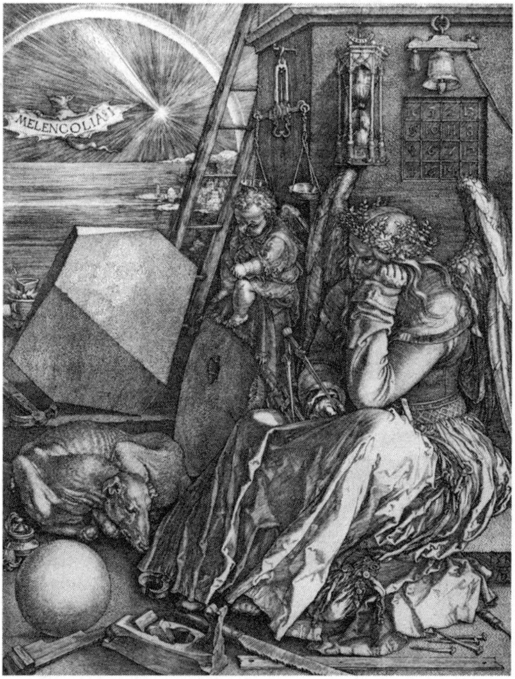

60 Albrecht Dürer (1471–1528), *Melencolia I* (engraving), 1514. (The Art Archive at Art Resource, New York)

of the etching's three most important "allegorical emblems" or "meaning-images" (*Sinnbilder*); the others are the heavy stone and, as discussed in chapter 1, the sphere or globe (*Kugel*). For Benjamin, the dog's gaze indicates that melancholy is "the most creaturely of the contemplative impulses [den kontemplativen Intentionen die eigentlich kreatürliche],"[67] and in a sense the canine's saturnine expression repeats the angel's. That Sebald had Dürer's image in mind at the outset is made clear when later in the chapter he refers directly to the etching with its angel "steadfast among the instruments of destruction."[68]

Sebald invokes Dürer's image in relation to silk spinning as well, not simply to gesture toward human beings' treatment of animals (and insects), or humans' and animals' mutual creaturely fate under the heavy weight of the global, or merely to demonstrate the powerlessness of art or science to arrest the relentless destructions engendered by modernity, but to gesture, through a particular recasting of history, toward a possible redemptivity that art can expose through its own inevitable failure. In his essay "The Melancholy Angel," Agamben sketches the contours of an angel of art that constantly shadows Benjamin's angel of history. "If Klee's *Angelus Novus* is the angel of history," Agamben writes,

> nothing could represent the angel of art better than the winged creature in Dürer's engraving. While the angel of history looks toward the past, yet cannot stop his incessant flight backward toward the future, so the melancholy angel in Dürer's engraving gazes unmovingly ahead. . . . The utensils of active life and other objects scattered around him have lost their significance. . . . The storm of progress that has gotten caught in that angel's wings has subsided here, and the angel of art appears immersed in an atemporal dimension, as though something, interrupting the continuum of history, had frozen the surrounding reality in a kind of messianic arrest.[69]

For Agamben, the apparently frozen, atemporal dimension invoked by *Melencolia* references an "arrest" that he (like Sebald, and, according to Sebald, like Browne) mines for its messianic, redemptive, or resurrective potential. Drawing again on Benjamin, Agamben asserts that art's function is to "perform the same task that tradition performed before [tradition's] interruption" at the dawn of modernity: "knotting up . . . the broken thread [of] past"—rather like a weaver of silk—in this way "opening a space between past and future in which [human beings] can found [their] action and [their] knowledge."[70] In modernity, this space, Agamben continues, "is the aesthetic space, but what is transmitted in it is precisely the impossibility of transmission, and its truth is the negation of the truth of its contents."[71]

In art's failure in modernity genuinely to transmit tradition in itself, a failure that is exacerbated in an ever-more-globalized world, Agamben paradoxically asserts its "truth": since "knowledge of the new is possible only in the nontruth of the old,"[72] the old's nontruths, including the grand nontruth of art's separateness itself, must be art's central domain. The spiral rings of *The Rings of Saturn*, which is also to say, the spiral rings of *Spirals*, from roaring race-car's serpent-hood to lowly silkworm's modest spinning, expose this arrest, this untruth, and this melancholically redemptive knowledge.

NOTES

INTRODUCTION

Walter Benjamin, *The Arcades Project*, trans. Howard Eiland and Kevin McLaughlin (Cambridge, Mass.: Harvard University Press, 1999), Convolute N11,4 (476). The original, "Geschichte zerfällt in Bilder, nicht in Geschichten," plays on the even closer filiation in German between history (*Geschichte*) and stories (*Geschichten*). See also Benjamin, *Das Passagen-Werk*, vol. 5.1 of *Gesammelte Schriften*, ed. Rolf Tiedemann (Frankfurt: Suhrkamp, 1983), 596.

1. Jacques Rancière defines "le partage du sensible" (which in French also implies not only "distribution" but "partition" of the "sensible" or of "sensitivity") as "the system of . . . forms determining what lends itself to sense experience[:] a delimitation of spaces and times, of the visible and the invisible" (*The Politics of Aesthetics: The Distribution of the Sensible*, trans. Gabriel Rockhill [New York: Continuum, 2006], 19). Put plainly, Rancière asks why something becomes perceivable in a particular way at a particular time, and how that sensibility marks off ideas of expertise and social class. He declares that there is "aesthetics at the core of politics," and that the distribution of the sensible "simultaneously determines the places and the stakes of politics as a form of experience." See also Rancière, *Le partage du sensible: Esthetique et politique* (Paris: Fabrique, 2000). I propose the spiral as one way of thinking about this distribution.
2. Benjamin, *Arcades*, Convolute N2a,3 (462); *Passagen*, 577.
3. Benjamin, *Arcades*, Convolute N1a,2 (459); *Passagen*, 573.
4. Benjamin, *Arcades*, Convolute N11,2 (476). In the original, "Geschichte schrieben heißt, Jahreszahlen ihre Physiognomie geben," *Jahrezahlen* implies "yearly accounts" as well as "dates" (*Passagen*, 595). Concerning this "exposure": for more on Benjamin and

photography, see Eduardo Cadava, *Words of Light: Theses on the Photography of History* (Princeton, N.J.: Princeton University Press, 1998).

5. "[T]he historical index of . . . images not only says that they belong to a particular time; it says, above all, that they attain to legibility only at a particular time. And, indeed, this acceding 'to legibility' constitutes a specific critical point in the movement at their interior [Bewegung in ihrem Innern]" (Benjamin, *Arcades*, Convolute N3, 1 [462]; *Passagen*, 578).
6. Alain Badiou, *The Century*, trans. Alberto Toscano (Malden, Mass.: Polity, 2007), 148. See also Badiou, *Le siècle* (Paris: Seuil, 2005). The part of the "century" whose "art" Badiou endorses actually consists of about seventy-five years, from around 1905 to 1980; it excludes what Badiou views as the reactionary retrenchments of the last two decades of the century's art and politics. My study rethinks literature and art of the entire one hundred years, and does not presume that post-1980s art is inherently reactionary.
7. Badiou, *Century*, 3. It has been Badiou's project to describe the contours of such "events," a term through which he seeks to revise and politicize the Heideggerian conception of *Ereignis*. In *Century*, Badiou goes on to raise the question of "how the century thought its own thought, how it identified the thinking singularity of the relation it entertained with the historicity of its own thought" (3). He later silently invokes Carl Schmitt by defining "avant-garde" as those who "decide on a present." The literary and artistic figures whom Badiou engages—Breton, Mandelstam, Brecht, Malevich, Celan, Pessoa, and Beckett, among others—are those Badiou views as vanguard in this sense. My study proceeds from the premise that it is crucial to understand "how the century thought its own thought," but I propose that that thinking often takes place in and through spirals.
8. Benjamin, *Arcades*, Convolute N2a,3 (462); *Passagen*, 577.
9. Susan Buck-Morss, *The Origin of Negative Dialectics: Theodor W. Adorno, Walter Benjamin, and the Frankfurt Institute* (New York: Free Press, 1977); Anselm Haverkamp, "Notes on the 'Dialectical Image': How Deconstructive Is It?" *Diacritics* 22, nos. 2–3 (1992): 69–80.
10. To do justice to this question of the "place" of language, one must address Benjamin's earlier essay "On Language as Such [*or* in General] and on the Language of Man [Über Sprache überhaupt und über die Sprache des Menschen]," in which Benjamin suggests that "[f]or an understanding of artistic forms, it is of value to attempt to grasp them all as languages and seek their connection with natural languages [*Natursprachen*]." But for Benjamin (and for Giorgio Agamben, who draws heavily on these Benjaminian ideas), such natural language is "not only communication of the communicable, but also, at the same time, a symbol of the non-communicable [nicht allein Mitteilung des Mitteilbaren, sondern zugleich Symbol des Nicht-Mitteilbaren]" (*Selected Writings*, vol. 1, *1913–1926*, ed. Marcus Bullock

and Michael W. Jennings [Cambridge, Mass.: Harvard University Press, 2004], 73–74; *Aufsätze, Essays, Vorträge*, vol. 2.1 of *Gesammelte Schriften*, ed. Rolf Tiedemann and Hermann Schweppenhäuser [Frankfurt: Suhrkamp, 1980], 156–157).

11. In Convolute N, the word *Erwachen* (awakening) is repeatedly rendered in bold type. Early in the convolute, Benjamin writes of "the awakening of a not-yet conscious knowledge of what has been" (*Arcades*, Convolute N1,9 [458]).

12. Among the best-known literature scholars who have written about the connections between literary and visual-artistic modes of expression in the twentieth century are Daniel Albright, Marjorie Perloff, and Jean-Michel Rabaté.

13. In the "Paralipomena" to his very late, aphoristic "On the Concept of History," Benjamin succinctly defines the dialectical image as "the involuntary memory of redeemed humanity" (*Selected Writings*, vol. 4, ed. Howard Eiland and Michael W. Jennings [Cambridge, Mass.: Harvard University Press, 2003], 403). This formulation demonstrates the consummately Benjaminian blending of Bergsonian memory (almost certainly via Proust's deployment of it) with a term from Jewish theology, and likewise clarifies the ethical import of "image." As Peter Szondi succinctly observes, Proust "listens attentively for the echo of the past; Benjamin listens for the first notes of a future" ("On Walter Benjamin," in *On Textual Understanding and Other Essays*, trans. H. Mendelson [Manchester: Manchester University Press, 1986], 153). Concerning the recent debates in literary studies over the "hermeneutics of suspicion," my position in this book is that when it comes to globalization and the capitalist economic forces that motor it, one has a right to be suspicious—but that this suspicion need not produce the kind of "bunny out of the hat" interpretations of literary texts that are sometimes caricatured in such critiques of suspicious reading.

14. The earthwork went underwater within two years of its construction and stayed submerged for most of the 1970s, 1980s, and 1990s. The water level of the northern end of the Great Salt Lake depends on a variety of environmental factors, including the amount of precipitation the area receives.

15. Robert Smithson, "The Spiral Jetty," in *Robert Smithson, Collected Writings*, ed. Jack Flam (Berkeley: University of California Press, 1966), 146.

16. We would soon learn that this "oil jetty" had been built in the early 1980s, after *Spiral Jetty* was submerged. The oil explorer Kenneth Pixley said he did not know that his pier was less than a quarter-mile from what would later be considered one of the twentieth-century's most influential artworks. The debate about oil extraction in this part of the lake was renewed in the first decade of the twenty-first century, when, because of rising oil prices, new oil leases were granted. A campaign to halt the drilling was led by Smithson's wife, the artist Nancy Holt, and no new excavation has taken place.

17. With impeccable timing, the earthwork emerged in the summer of 2002, just as my essay on the road trip to *Spiral Jetty* was published as "Non-site Unseen," *Artforum* 41, no. 1 (2002): 172–177. It stayed above water until around 2009, and has not been reported to have been seen since.
18. Benjamin describes the "method of [his] project" as "literary montage" and goes on to write "I needn't say anything. Merely show" (*Arcades*, Convolute N1a,8 [460]).
19. The increasingly deployed term "anthropocene," which emphasizes the effect of human beings on ecological (and natural) history, is associated with the work of ecologist Eugene Stoermer and atmospheric chemist Paul Crutzen, but it has quickly spread into ecocritical scholarship in the humanities.
20. In his well-known essay "Form and Intent in the American New Criticism," Paul de Man describes how hermeneutically inclined critics conflate the idea of form with "the organic circularity of natural processes" (*Blindness and Insight: Essays in the Rhetoric of Contemporary Criticism* [Minneapolis: University of Minnesota Press, 1983], 29). Although, as we shall see, the spiral is often likewise associated with the organic, it has the benefit of being an open as opposed to a closed form.
21. Rebecca L. Walkowitz, *Cosmopolitan Style: Modernism Beyond the Nation* (New York: Columbia University Press, 2007). Walkowitz borrows this concept of "thinking and feeling" from Bruce Robbins, who, in turn, borrows the idea of "structure of feeling" from Raymond Williams. See Pheng Cheah and Bruce Robbins, eds., *Cosmopolitics: Thinking and Feeling Beyond the Nation* (Minneapolis: University of Minnesota Press, 1998).
22. Jessica Berman, *Modernist Fiction, Cosmopolitanism, and the Politics of Community* (Cambridge: Cambridge University Press, 2001); Jed Esty, *A Shrinking Island: Modernism and National Culture in England* (Princeton, N.J.: Princeton University Press, 2003); Laura Doyle, ed., *Geomodernisms: Race, Modernism, Modernity* (Bloomington: Indiana University Press, 2006). See also Berman's more recent *Modernist Commitments: Ethics, Politics, and Transnational Modernism* (New York: Columbia University Press, 2012).
23. The terms "downward spiral" and "death spiral," although recent, seem likely linked to the idea of airplane battle in the two world wars.
24. Douglas Mao and Rebecca L. Walkowitz describe (and call for) "expansion" of the period of modernism, interdisciplinary studies of forms and genres, and transnational historicization, in their much-discussed essay "The New Modernist Studies," *PMLA* 123, no. 3 (2008): 737–748. This book can be considered part of such an expansion—but also, as befits a study of spirals, a contraction that returns to question the very terms of the discipline, including the "newness" of the "new modernist studies," which seems to adopt the logic of innovation

endorsed by Pound, Greenberg, and other high modernists whose grip on the period the reading orientation wants to loosen.

25. Samuel Weber, *Mass Mediauras: Form, Technics, Media* (Stanford, Calif.: Stanford University Press, 1996).
26. Samuel Weber, *Targets of Opportunity: On the Militarization of Thinking* (New York: Fordham University Press, 2005).
27. See, for example, David Damrosch, *What Is World Literature?* (Princeton, N.J.: Princeton University Press, 2003); and Emily Apter, *Against World Literature: On the Politics of Untranslatability* (New York: Verso, 2013).
28. Rosalind E. Krauss goes on to note perceptively of the grid that "the barrier it has lowered between the arts of vision and those of language has been almost totally successful in walling the visual arts into a realm of exclusive visuality and defending them against the intrusion of speech. The arts, of course, have paid dearly for this success, because the fortress they constructed on the foundation of the grid has increasingly become a ghetto" ("Grids," in *The Originality of the Avant-Garde and Other Modernist Myths* [Cambridge, Mass.: MIT Press, 1986], 9).
29. Krauss has herself written often and persuasively about spirals, most notably those in Duchamp's work. At times, she seems to associate spirals with her (and Yves Alain Bois's) concept of "formlessness," itself theorized in Georges Bataille's writing from the 1930s. For Krauss, formlessness is an operational tool, a third term that negotiates between theme (or content) and form. While such formlessness has indeed been repressed in art history's narrative of itself, and perhaps no less so in literary history, my own analysis will pursue the related route of viewing spirals as Benjaminian "image." See Yves Alain Bois and Rosalind E. Krauss, *Formless: A User's Guide* (New York: Zone Books, 1997). Krauss herself has perceptively drawn on Benjamin in *The Optical Unconscious* (Cambridge, Mass.: MIT Press, 1994).
30. Alfred Jarry refers to 1898 as the year when "the 20th century was (−2) years old" (*The Exploits and Opinions of Doctor Faustroll, Pataphysician*, trans. Simon Watson Taylor [Boston: Exact Change, 1996], 7).
31. Umberto Boccioni, *Pittura e scultura Futuriste: Dinamismo plastico*, ed. Zeno Birolli, Saggi e documenti del Novecento 72 (1914; Milan: SE, 1997), 196 (my translation).
32. Ezra Pound, "Vortex," *Blast: Review of the Great English Vortex*, no. 1 (1914): 153.
33. "The greater the decrease in the social significance of an art form, the sharper the distinction between criticism and enjoyment by the public" (Walter Benjamin, "The Work of Art in the Age of Its Technical Reproducibility," in *Illuminations: Essays and Reflections*, ed. Hannah Arendt, trans. Harry Zohn [New York: Schocken, 1969], 234).

1. DEFINITIONS

Franz Kafka, "In the Penal Colony," in *The Complete Stories*, ed. Nahum N. Glatzer, trans. Willa Muir and Edwin Muir (New York: Schocken, 1971), 149.

1. Early in *Toward a New Architecture*, Le Corbusier writes of "the great primary forms" that are "distinct and tangible within us without ambiguity." Calling these forms "the most beautiful forms," he posits, "Everybody is agreed to that [their beauty], the child, the savage, and the metaphysician" (*Toward a New Architecture*, trans. Frederick Etchells [1923; New York: Praeger, 1960], 31). Carl Jung, in *Modern Man in Search of a Soul* (1933) and later in *Mandala Symbolism* (1972), draws on spiral figures to express ideas of selfhood and growth.
2. Roland Barthes, "Réquichot and His Body," in *The Responsibility of Forms: Critical Essays on Music, Art, and Representation*, trans. Richard Howard (New York: Hill and Wang, 1985), 219. See also Barthes, "Réquichot et son corps," in *Essais critiques* (Paris: Seuil, 1982), 211.
3. Barthes coins the term "bathmology" for a kind of conceptual spiral that accounts for what he calls "degrees of language." See both *Roland Barthes by Roland Barthes*, trans. Richard Howard (New York: Hill and Wang, 2010); and Pierre Force's analysis of bathmology in "Beyond Metalanguage," in *Writing the Image After Roland Barthes*, ed. Jean-Michel Rabaté (Philadelphia: University of Pennsylvania Press, 2011), 187–195.
4. Paul de Man, "Semiology and Rhetoric," in *Allegories of Reading: Figural Language in Rousseau, Nietzsche, Rilke, and Proust* (New Haven, Conn.: Yale University Press, 1982), 9.
5. Edward Grant, *Planets, Stars, and Orbs: The Medieval Cosmos, 1200–1687* (Cambridge: Cambridge University Press, 1994).
6. Plato, *Timaeus, Critias, Cleitophon, Menexenus, Epistles*, trans. R. G. Bury, Loeb Classical Library 234 (Cambridge, Mass.: Harvard University Press, 1929).
7. T. L. Heath, introduction to *The Works of Archimedes. Edited in Modern Notation*, ed. T. L. Heath (Cambridge: Cambridge University Press, 1897).
8. This condensation applies as well to the "Archimedean spiral" pictured in figure 1, which the *OED* defines as "a curve traced by a point moving uniformly along a line which at the same time revolves uniformly round a fixed point in itself." In his letter to Dositheus, Archimedes shows little interest in this kind of spiral that moves (like the players in William Carlos Williams's poem "At the Ball Game") "uniformly"; his diagrams instead demonstrate that the primary object of his study was what would later be called the *equiangular* or logarithmic spiral, in which (as defined by the *OED*) "the angle between the radius vector and the tangent is constant"—giving the impression of widening (or shrinking)

proportionally with each gyration of the coils, as is the case in, say, the nautilus shell. For more on the equiangular spiral, see my brief discussion of Descartes later in this chapter. Although there are in fact many kinds of spirals, helixes, and vortices, I am less concerned with their specific geometry than with the rhetoric associated with them and the affect this rhetoric seeks to generate. For this reason, I will in these pages often use the adjective "spiral-like."

9. The Latin word *clinamen* signifies "inclination" or "bias." As part of his description of the Epicurean system, Lucretius surmised a *clinamen principorum* (first swerve), in which free-floating atoms, at undetermined moments and in undetermined points of space, deviate ever so slightly, just sufficient to modify equilibrium; thus are solid bodies formed. For a popular account of how the idea of the *clinamen* was picked up in early modern Europe, see Stephen Greenblatt, *The Swerve: How the World Became Modern* (New York: Norton, 2012).
10. John Freccero, "Dante's Pilgrim in a Gyre," *PMLA* 76, no. 3 (1961): 168–181.
11. As Peter Sloterdijk succinctly puts it in an interview about *Sphären*: "First the universe was globalized with the help of geometry, then the earth was globalized with the help of capital" ("Against Gravity," *Bookforum*, February–March 2005, 27). "World systems analysis," as undertaken by such theorists as Immanuel Wallerstein, Giovanni Arrighi, and Janet Abu-Lughod, among others, similarly traces histories of globalization over centuries, usually only as far as the late Middle Ages. Significantly, Arrighi claims that the current, U.S.-dominated world system "seems to be moving 'forward' [toward a new system of rule] and 'backward' [toward early modern forms of state-making] at the same time. This double movement has always been a major feature of the modern world system" (*The Long Twentieth Century: Money, Power, and the Origins of Our Times* [New York: Verso, 1994], 79).
12. Recent research has demonstrated that Renaissance conceptions of the golden or "miracle" spiral were mathematically imprecise. See John Sharp, "Spirals and the Golden Section," *Nexus Network Journal* 4, no. 1 (2002): 59–82; and Rory Fonseca, "Shape and Order in Organic Nature: The *Nautilus pompilius*," *Leonardo* 26 (1993): 201–204.
13. René Descartes, *The World*, trans. Michael Sean Mahoney (New York: Abaris Books, 1979). *Le monde* was written in the early 1630s but not published until 1664, in part due to the furor over Galileo's revelations.
14. Johan Wolfgang von Goethe, *Über die Spiraltendenz der Vegetation* (1831; Weimar: Böhlaus, 1892), 131.
15. Jocelyn Holland, *German Romanticism and Science: The Procreative Poetics of Goethe, Novalis, and Ritter* (New York: Routledge, 2009).

16. G. W. F. Hegel, *Vorlesungen über die Philosophie der Geschichte*, vol. 12 of *Gessamelte Werke* (Hamburg: Meiner, 1981), 85 (my translation).
17. In *Philosophy of Right*, Hegel speaks of international relations as follows: "It is as particular entities that states enter into relations with one another. Hence their relations are on the largest scale a maelstrom of external contingency and the inner particularity of passions, private interests and selfish ends, abilities and virtues, vices, force, and wrong. All these whirl together, and in their vortex the ethical whole itself, the autonomy of the state, is exposed to contingency" (*Philosophy of Right*, trans. T. M. Knox [Oxford: Oxford University Press, 1940], 340).
18. Hiroshi Uchida traces Marx's *Kreislauf* back to Hegel's, in *Marx's Grundrisse and Hegel's Logic* (New York: Routledge, 1988).
19. V. I. Lenin, "Karl Marx: A Brief Biographical Sketch with an Exposition of Marxism," in *Collected Works*, trans. Julius Katzer (Moscow: Progress, 1964), 21:54.
20. Ralph Ellison, *Invisible Man* (New York: Random House, 1952), 6.
21. Friedrich Nietzsche, *The Gay Science*, ed. Bernard Williams, trans. Josefine Nauckhoff (Cambridge: Cambridge University Press, 2001), 194.
22. Pierre Klossowski, *Nietzsche and the Vicious Circle*, trans. Daniel W. Smith (Chicago: University of Chicago, 1997), 66 (emphasis in original).
23. As we will explore briefly in chapter 3 (on Yeats and Tatlin), Nietzsche shares with William Blake a fascination with spirals. In both his writings and his paintings, Blake presents abyssal and vertiginous vortexes. Concerning the drawings, see "Eve Tempted by the Serpent" (no. 44), and "Every man also gave Him a piece of money" (no. 79), in William Blake, *Pencil Drawings*, ed. Geoffrey Keynes (New York: Dover, 1970).
24. There are, of course, other possible approaches. In her recent book, *Haiti Unbound: A Spiralist Challenge to the Postcolonial Canon* (Liverpool: Liverpool University Press, 2011), Kaiama L. Glover explores the "spiralist" movement that emerged in Haiti in 1965 and proposes that spiralism expresses a kind of organic response to Haiti's cyclical history of disaster, as well as resistance to domination.
25. See, for example, Vincent Pecora, *Households of the Soul* (Baltimore: Johns Hopkins University Press, 1997); and Paul Peppis, *Literature, Politics, and the English Avant-Garde: Nation and Empire, 1901–1918* (Cambridge: Cambridge University Press, 2009).
26. In the *Passagen-Werk*, Walter Benjamin describes Nietzsche's intervention simply but dramatically: "In the idea of eternal recurrence, the historicism of the nineteenth century capsizes" (*The Arcades Project*, trans. Howard Eiland and Kevin McLaughlin [Cambridge, Mass.: Harvard University Press, 1999], Convolute D8a,2 [116]). Several pages of the *Passagen-Werk*'s Convolute B concern the eternal return. At times, Benjamin refers to the

eternal return as a "boring" idea (see the note "Boredom, Eternal Return"), as he associates Nietzsche with what he calls "mythical thinking," the kind of thinking that he tries to reject but cannot completely avoid.

27. Walter Benjamin, *The Origin of German Tragic Drama*, trans. John Osborne (New York: Verso, 1998), 57. See also Benjamin, *Ursprung des deutschen Trauerspiels*, vol. 1.1 of *Gesammelte Schriften*, ed. Rolf Tiedemann (Frankfurt: Suhrkamp, 1991), 238.
28. Benjamin, *Trauerspiels*, 226 (my translation, with gratitude to Samuel Weber).
29. Benjamin was well aware of the challenge to history posed by Nietzsche's eternal return. In the *Passagen-Werk*, Benjamin defends his version of the dialectic for its political potentiality: "It is the inherent tendency of dialectical experience to dissipate the semblance of eternal sameness, and even of repetition, in history. Authentic political experience is absolutely free of this semblance" (*Arcades*, Convolute N9,5 [473]).
30. Stéphane Mallarmé, "Igitur," in *Selected Poetry and Prose*, ed. and trans. Mary Ann Caws (New York: New Directions, 1982), 94.
31. Benjamin, *Arcades*, Convolute N10a,3 (475).
32. Benjamin, *Origin of German Tragic Drama*, 155.
33. Benjamin, *Origin of German Tragic Drama*, 157.
34. "Zu den Sinnbildern Hund, Kugel und Stein und zu Dürer" (Benjamin, *Trauerspiels*, 329ff.). As I demonstrate in the conclusion, Giorgio Agamben elegantly rereads the "Melancholy Angel" through a Benjaminian lens in *The Man Without Content*, trans. Georgia Albert (Stanford, Calif.: Stanford University Press, 1999), 104–115.
35. Benjamin, *Origin of German Tragic Drama*, 157.
36. While "storms" are not necessarily spiral shaped, as significant ones appear to be in satellite technology that emerged later in the twentieth century, it is certain that Benjamin in the years shortly before his death was closely reading the work of nineteenth-century philosopher and polymath Hermann Lotze, who posited in *Mikrokosmos* (1856–1864) that thought and history proceeded in spiral patterns of "progress" and "regress," the latter particularly interesting Benjamin. In a very late (post-1937) note in Convolute N, Benjamin repeatedly calls Lotze a "critic of the concept of progress," and cites Lotze as writing that "the course of history takes the form of spirals [die Geschichte winde sich in Spirallinien fort (winds itself into spirals)]." Benjamin crucially goes on: "If the idea of progress extended over the totality of recorded history is something peculiar to the satiated bourgeoisie, then Lotze represents the reserves called up by those on the defensive" (*Arcades*, Convolute N13,2 and N13,3 [478–479]; *Das Passagen-Werk*, vol. 5.1 of *Gesammelte Schriften*, ed. Rolf Tiedemann [Frankfurt: Suhrkamp, 1983], 599).

37. Walter Benjamin, *Illuminations: Essays and Reflections*, ed. Hannah Arendt, trans. Harry Zohn (New York: Schocken, 1969), passim. My use of the term "Extreme" also alludes to Eric Hobsbawm's rubric for the years 1914 to 1989 in his influential book *The Age of Extremes* (1994). Note that Jacques Derrida links Benjamin with spirality in "Des tours de Babel," in *Psyché: Inventions de l'autre* (Paris: Galilée, 1998), 1:203–236. We return to this essay on translation in chapter 3.
38. Shoshana Felman, "Turning the Screw of Interpretation," *Yale French Studies* 55–56 (1977): 94–207.

2. ENTERING THE WHIRLPOOL

Umberto Boccioni, "Plastic Dynamism," in *Futurist Manifestos*, ed. and trans. Umbro Apollonio (New York: Viking, 1973), 92.

Ezra Pound, "Vortex," *Blast: Review of the Great English Vortex*, no. 1 (1914): 153.

1. Theodore Andrea Cook had already published *Spirals in Nature and Art* (1903). *The Curves of Life*, which was widely reviewed in 1914 and 1915 and is still in print, was intended as a comprehensive account of his research since that earlier time. The magazine he edited, *The Field*, is mentioned in Ford Madox Ford's novel *The Good Soldier: A Tale of Passion* (1915); narrator John Dowell describes the apparently gentlemanly Teddy Ashburnham as follows: "[H]e never more than once or twice in all the nine years of my knowing him told a story that couldn't have gone into the columns of the *Field*" (*The Good Soldier* [Harmondsworth: Penguin, 1984], 18). This dazzling overture to *The Good Soldier* was published in the first issue of the Vorticist organ *Blast* (with the quoted sentence included verbatim, though its clauses are reversed).
2. Theodore Andrea Cook, *The Curves of Life: Being an Account of Spiral Formations and Their Application to Growth in Nature, to Science, and to Art; With Special Reference to the Manuscripts of Leonardo da Vinci* (1914; New York: Dover, 1979), 166.
3. Cook, *Curves of Life*, 266.
4. Alfred Jarry, *The Exploits and Opinions of Doctor Faustroll, Pataphysician*, trans. Simon Watson Taylor (Boston: Exact Change, 1996), 21. See also Jarry, *Gestes et opinions du docteur Faustroll, pataphysicien*, ed. N. Arnaud (Paris: Gallimard, 1980), 31.
5. The "pun" apostrophically displaced is not so "simple": *pataphysique* might invoke *pas ta physique* (either "not your physics" or "not your physique").
6. Jarry, *Faustroll*, 20.
7. Jarry, *Faustroll*, 21; *Gestes*, 31.

8. Lest this link from Jarry to Benjamin seem tenuous, note that Gilles Deleuze, in a late essay, links Jarry to Heidegger. See Gilles Deleuze, "Unrecognized Precursor to Heidegger: Alfred Jarry," in *Essays Critical and Clinical*, trans. Daniel W. Smith (Minneapolis: University of Minnesota Press, 1997), 91–98.
9. Jarry writes that "Doctor Faustroll was sixty-three years old when he was born in Circassia in 1898 (the 20th century was [−2] years old)" (*Faustroll*, 7).
10. Jarry, *Faustroll*, 87.
11. Jarry, *Faustroll*, 87.
12. Jarry, *Faustroll*, 88.
13. Jarry, *Faustroll*, 89.
14. Note the echo of this geopolitical theme in Faustroll's "Circassian" birthplace: like the Poles (see Ubu), the Circassians, or Adyghe (an ethnic group from the Eurasian region around the northern Caucasus), were dominated by czarist Russia in the mid-nineteenth century. Also like the Poles, many fled their homeland and dispersed throughout Europe and the Near East.
15. The manifesto was first published in Italian as "Il 'Futurismo,'" *Gazzetta dell'Emilia* (Bologna), February 5, 1909, and then in French as "Manifeste du futurisme," *Le Figaro*, February 20, 1909; my translations into English take into account both versions. See F. T. Marinetti, "La fondation du futurisme et son manifeste," in *Le Premier Manifeste du Futurisme de F. T. Marinetti*, ed. Jean-Pierre de Villers (Ottawa: University of Ottawa Press, 1986), 47. For more on the influence of Jarry on Futurism, and especially Marinetti, see Christine Poggi, *Inventing Futurism: The Arts and Politics of Artificial Optimism* (Princeton, N.J.: Princeton University Press, 2008), 37.
16. For an excellent historicization and reading of the Futurist Manifesto, including an account of its rapid dissemination, see Martin Puchner, *Poetry of the Revolution: Marx, Manifestos, and the Avant-Gardes* (Princeton, N.J.: Princeton University Press, 2006).
17. Marinetti, "Fondation du futurisme et son manifeste," 47 (my translation).
18. Marinetti, "Fondation du futurisme et son manifeste," 47 (my translation).
19. Curiously, an account of the accident in the newspaper *Il Corriere della Serra* mentions only *one* bicyclist. See Lawrence Rainey, "Introduction: F. T. Marinetti and the Development of Futurism," in *Futurism: An Anthology*, ed. Lawrence Rainey, Christine Poggi, and Laura Wittman (New Haven, Conn.: Yale University Press, 1989), 5–6.
20. Marinetti, "Fondation du futurisme et son manifeste," 47 (my translation).
21. Marinetti, "Fondation du futurisme et son manifeste," 54 (my translation).
22. Marinetti, "Fondation du futurisme et son manifeste," 53 (my translation).

23. See also Balla's *Speeding Automobile (Auto en Course, Etude de Vitesse,* 1913), in Poggi, *Inventing Futurism*, 29.
24. Balla was so entranced with spirals and helixes that he gave his second daughter, born in 1914, the unusual name Elica (Italian for "helix, propeller").
25. Boccioni, "Plastic Dynamism," 92 (translation altered). The original Italian reads "Il dinamismo è l'azione simultanea del moto caratteristico particolare dell'oggetto (moto assoluto) con le trasformazioni che l'oggetto subisce nei suoi spostamenti in relazione all'ambiente mobile o immobile (moto relativo)" (Umberto Boccioni, *Pittura e scultura Futuriste: Dinamismo plastico*, ed. Zeno Birolli, Saggi e documenti del Novecento 72 [1914; Milan: SE, 1997], 195).
26. Boccioni, "Plastic Dynamism," 92. The original Italian reads "creazione de una nuova forma che dia la relatività tra peso ed espansione. Tra moto di rotazione e moto di rivuluzione" (Boccioni, *Pittura e scultura Futuriste*, 196).
27. Boccioni, "Plastic Dynamism," 92. The original Italian reads "vita stessa afferrata nella forma che la vita crea nel suo *infinito succedersi*" (Boccioni, *Pittura e scultura Futuriste*, 196 [emphasis in original]).
28. Boccioni, "Plastic Dynamism," 92; *Pittura e scultura Futuriste*, 196. In "Plastic Dynamism," Boccioni does mention that "immobility is one of the main features of Cubist sculpture" (92).
29. Boccioni, "Plastic Dynamism," 92; *Pittura e scultura Futuriste*, 196.
30. According to Poggi, Boccioni "strives to represent the Nietzschean ideal of the heroic superman by realizing the dreamed-of fusion of human flesh and metal" (*Inventing Futurism*, 170). Poggi intriguingly notes that the work was initially executed in plaster and that after Boccioni's death Marinetti ordered it cast in bronze, "although perhaps steel, rather than bronze (a material Boccioni had rejected as traditional and 'passatista') . . . would have been preferable" (170). Wyndham Lewis writes, "Futurism . . . is largely Impressionism up-to-date. To this is added [their] Automobilism and Nietzsche stunt" ("The Melodrama of Modernity," *Blast: Review of the Great English Vortex*, no. 1 [1914]: 143).
31. Henri Bergson, *L'évolution créatrice* (Paris: Alcan, 1911), 157.
32. Mark Antliff, "The Fourth Dimension and Futurism: A Politicized Space," *Art Bulletin* 82, no. 4 (2000): 730.
33. Antliff, "Fourth Dimension and Futurism," 730.
34. James Joyce, whose work will be explored in chapter 5, was living in Trieste at this time.
35. Marinetti's *Zang Tumb Tumb* depicted the siege of Adrianopoli in October 1912; during this period, encompassing the breakup of the Ottoman Empire, Italy occupied the Dodecanese islands.

36. Marinetti's bombastic lecture at London's Lyceum Club, "Futurist Speech to the English," was attended by many future members of the Vorticist contingent. That the Vorticists borrowed the bold, emphatic, advertising-like typographical style of the Futurists is often remarked upon.
37. Wyndham Lewis, "Manifesto—I," *Blast: Review of the Great English Vortex*, no. 1 (1914): 11.
38. Lewis, "Manifesto—I," 30.
39. Nevinson gave the name *Blast* to the Vorticist journal, from which his work was excluded.
40. Hal Foster, *Prosthetic Gods* (Cambridge, Mass.: MIT Press, 2004), 137.
41. Lewis uses "it's" as a possessive so frequently that it's hard to view this as a mere printer's or editor's error.
42. Wyndham Lewis, "Vortices and Notes: Our Vortex," *Blast: Review of the Great English Vortex*, no. 1 (1914): 147.
43. Lewis, "Our Vortex," 147.
44. Wyndham Lewis, "Vortices and Notes: 'Life is the Important Thing!,'" *Blast: Review of the Great English Vortex*, no. 1 (1914): 129.
45. Lewis, "Our Vortex," 147.
46. Ezra Pound, "Before Sleep," *Blast: Review of the Great English Vortex*, no. 1 (1914): 47.
47. Pound, "Before Sleep," 47.
48. Pound, "Before Sleep," 47.
49. The *OED* defines the noun "rocket" as "a cylindrical projectile that can be propelled to a considerable height or distance by the combustion of its contents and the backward ejection of waste gases, usually giving a burst of light and used for signaling, in maritime rescue, for entertainment, and as a weapon; spec. a firework of this form, typically giving a brilliant visual display at the apex of its ascent." Pound draws on the valences of weaponry and "burst of light," but a more thorough reading of the Vorticist rhetoric of explosivity must also account for the consummately Poundian "backward ejection of waste gases."
50. Pound, "Vortex," 153.
51. Pound, "Vortex," 153.
52. "If you compare several representative passages of the greatest poetry you see how great is the variety of types of combination, and also how completely any semi-ethical criterion of 'sublimity' misses the mark. For it is not the 'greatness,' the intensity, of the emotions, the components, but the intensity of the artistic process, the pressure, so to speak, under which the fusion takes place, that counts" ("Tradition and the Individual Talent," in *Selected Prose of T. S. Eliot*, ed. Frank Kermode [New York: Harcourt Brace Jovanovich, 1975], 47).

53. Walter Benjamin, "Theses on the Philosophy [Concept] of History," in *Illuminations: Essays and Reflections*, ed. Hannah Arendt, trans. Harry Zohn (New York: Schocken, 1969), 256. This maxim clearly inspired Max Horkheimer and Theodor Adorno's conception of the dialectic of enlightenment and barbarism.
54. Benjamin, "Theses on the Philosophy [Concept] of History," 262.
55. Pound, "Vortex," 153.
56. Henri Gaudier-Brzeska, "Vortex," *Blast: Review of the Great English Vortex*, no. 1 (1914): 155.
57. Gaudier-Brzeska, "Vortex," 155.
58. Gaudier-Brzeska, "Vortex," 156.
59. Gaudier-Brzeska, "Vortex," 156.
60. Gaudier-Brzeska, "Vortex," 156.
61. Gaudier-Brzeska, "Vortex," 156.
62. Gaudier-Brzeska, "Vortex," 157.
63. Gaudier-Brzeska, "Vortex," 157.
64. Gaudier-Brzeska, "Vortex," 157.
65. Gaudier-Brzeska, "Vortex," 158.
66. In the Futurist Manifesto, Marinetti announced, "We will glorify war—the world's only hygiene—militarism, patriotism, the destructive gesture of freedom-bringers, beautiful ideas worth dying for and" in something of a non sequitur, "scorn for woman."
67. Henri Gaudier-Brzeska, "Vortex Gaudier-Brzeska (Written from the Trenches)," *Blast: Review of the Great English Vortex*, no. 2 (1915): 33–34.
68. Despite the obvious dissimilarities between the aesthetic visions of Gaudier-Brzeska and Cook, note that the latter does claim that his "life-affirming" spiral is common to ancient Egyptians, Hindus, Mayans, and Renaissance Europeans. Complicating the literary and art historian's tendency to separate figures into entirely opposed schools, note further that Cook's book was reviewed enthusiastically by Huntly Carter in 1915 in an issue of the influential little magazine *The Egoist* (the journal edited by Pound, which would publish Joyce, Eliot, and Lawrence). Carter himself, former editor of the *New Spirit*, was an enthusiastic promoter of certain strands of vanguardism, and was a friend of the so-called Rhythmistes, who gathered around the short-lived magazine *Rhythm*, edited by John Middleton Murry. Included among the Rhythmistes were a number of artists who later joined the Vorticists; hence the emphasis in *Blast* on "rhythm"—not usually known as a British strong suit. This magazine, which operated from 1911 to 1913, printed art by Picasso and Gaudier-Brzeska, among others.

3. TWINNED TOWERS

W. B. Yeats, *A Vision*, vol. 13 of *The Collected Works of W. B. Yeats*, ed. Catherine E. Paul and Margaret Mills Harper (New York: Simon and Shuster, 2008), 174 (cited hereafter as *A Vision A*).

Vladimir Yevgrafovich Tatlin, "My Answer to 'Letter to the [Russian] Futurists,'" in *Tatlin*, ed. Larissa Alekseevna Zhadova (Budapest: Corvina, 1984; New York: Rizzoli, 1984), 185. Written under the pseudonym Baian Plamen, the essay originally appeared in the art journal *Anarkhia* in March 1918. Regarding the pseudonym: the noun *baian* means "accordion," and the noun *plamen*, "flame"; in Russian, the juxtaposition of two nouns does not yield a compound, so the name cannot be translated as "The Accordion Flame." As the *baian* was an instrument that Old Russian poet-singers would use to accompany their narratives, Tatlin could be suggesting that his own voice—in this case a voice promoting an orientation toward the future—was like a "flame."

1. Quoted in Harold Bloom, *Yeats* (Oxford: Oxford University Press, 1972), 318.
2. Yeats wrote to his friend and fellow theosophist George Russell ("AE") just after the revolution: "I consider the Marxian criterion of values as in this age the spearhead of materialism and leading to inevitable murder" (quoted in Richard Ellmann, *Yeats: The Man and the Masks* [New York: Norton, 1978], 232). Yeats recognized the connection between Hegel and Marxism: "I remember a Communist described by Captain White in his memoirs ploughing on the Cotswold Hills, nothing on his great hairy body but sandals and a pair of drawers, nothing in his head but Hegel's *Logic*" ("The End of the Cycle," in *A Vision* [1937; New York: Collier, 1966], 301 [cited hereafter as *A Vision B*]).
3. While Yeats is generally disparaging of most early-twentieth-century -isms, he eventually compares the "system" of *A Vision* to "cubes in the drawing of Wyndham Lewis and . . . ovoids in the sculpture of Brancusi" (*A Vision B*, 25).
4. It is almost certain that Tatlin eventually became familiar with Yeats's name, as the latter won the Nobel Prize in Literature in 1923.
5. Of course, it is also the late, disastrous period of the Great War and the Black and Tan incursions in Ireland, to be explored later in this chapter.
6. According to art historian John Milner, "to employ two concentric conical spirals," as Tatlin does in his monument, "is as rare in structures of an architectural scale as the single cylindrical spiral is common" (*Vladimir Tatlin and the Russian Avant-garde* [New Haven, Conn.: Yale University Press, 1985], 156). Yeats was also drawn to this type of doubled spiral.

7. W. B. Yeats, *The Poems*, vol. 1 of *The Collected Works of W. B. Yeats*, ed. Richard J. Finneran (New York: Scribner, 1997), 137, 232, 145, 136.
8. Yeats, *The Only Jealousy of Emer*, in *Poems*, 566.
9. Claire Nally, *Envisioning Ireland: W. B. Yeats's Occult Nationalism* (Oxford: Lang, 2010), 133. See also Catherine E. Paul and Margaret Mills Harper, editors' introduction to *A Vision A*. As Harper notes elsewhere, Yeats's wife, Bertha Georgiana Hyde-Lees, known as Georgie, dropped the *i* from her nickname for numerological purposes soon after her marriage to Yeats, but it is not incidental that for many years she also largely effaced her personal involvement in the project that would become *A Vision*. (Yeats claimed in *A Vision B* that his "wife was unwilling that her share [in *A Vision A*] should be known"; intriguingly, upon being initiated into Golden Dawn, she chose the Ulyssean name Nemo, which is Latin for "Nobody.") See Margaret Mills Harper, *The Wisdom of Two: The Spiritual and Literary Collaboration of George and W. B. Yeats* (Oxford: Oxford University Press, 2006). For more on the George–W. B. collaboration, see also Bette London, *Writing Double: Women's Literary Partnerships* (Ithaca, N.Y.: Cornell University Press, 1999), 179–209.
10. The laboriousness of this endeavor was not widely known until the publication of 36 notebooks of automatic writing produced in 450 sittings between November 1917 and March 1920, including some 8,600 questions posed by Yeats and 3,600 pages of answers from the "Educators" in George's hand; 270 pages on the visionary dreams recorded from March 1920 to March 1924; an index of 780 cards in which Yeats tried to organize the information from the automatic writing; and 2 notebooks containing the early drafts of the book itself. The scholar most associated with this project is George Mills Harper, *Yeats's "Vision" Papers*, 3 vols. (Iowa City: University of Iowa Press, 1994), and *Yeats and the Occult* (London: Macmillan, 1976). Regarding the male poet's questionings and the female hearer's envisionings, Paul and Harper ask a pertinent question that we cannot presume to address here: "What levels of automaticity and volition are represented by the writing that began to flow from GY's hand in response to her husband's questions?" (editors' introduction to *A Vision A*, xxvi). For more on the collaboration between the Yeatses, see Harper, *Wisdom of Two*; and Anne Saddlemyer, *Becoming George: The Life of Mrs. W. B. Yeats* (Oxford: Oxford University Press, 2002).
11. Yeats, introduction to *A Vision A*, lix. In early printings of *A Vision A*, Yeats uses the name "Giraldus" in the title and "Gyraldus" throughout much of the rest of the "explanation"; perhaps he had Giraldus's "gyre" in mind. He also used the incorrect Latin title "Hominorum" instead of "Hominum."
12. Yeats, introduction to *A Vision A*, lx.
13. Yeats, introduction to *A Vision A*, lx.

14. Yeats, introduction to *A Vision A*, lx–lxi. In 1924, Yeats published a poem called "The Gift of Harun Al-Rashid," which elaborates on the Kusta–Harun linkage. This Harun (766–809) became the fifth caliph of the Abbasid dynasty in 786: "Under him . . . the caliphate reached the height of its power, its empire extending from the Mediterranean to India. His court at Baghdad, famous for its splendor, was a noted center of arts and learning." Harun (also rendered Haroun) is also a central character in the *Arabian Nights*. Meanwhile, the "real" Qusta ibn Luqa (820–912) was a doctor and translator of Greek and Syrian texts into Arabic; but for Yeats, he is essentially a fictional figure "who epitomizes a noble commitment to literary and cultural learning" (Lawrence S. Rainey, headnote to "The Gift of Harun Al-Rashid," in *Modernism: An Anthology*, ed. Lawrence S. Rainey [London: Blackwell, 2005], 335).
15. Yeats, introduction to *A Vision A*, lxi.
16. Ellmann, *Yeats*, 25.
17. Yeats, *A Vision A*, 5.
18. Among the generations of Yeats scholars to delve in detail into *A Vision* are George Mills Harper, Hazard Adams, and Catherine Paul and Margaret Mills Harper.
19. Yeats, *A Vision A*, 103.
20. Yeats, *A Vision A*, 103. The hero of "La Spirale" was to have experienced an inverse emotional economy: "Plus il sera malheureux dans le fait, plus il sera heureux dans le rêve." Yeats seems primarily drawn to Flaubert's notion of inversion, largely leaving the description of affect aside. But note Emma's strongly affective response in *Madame Bovary*; while in a coach en route to visiting Léon, her lover, she sees the "wretched beggar" who "wandered with his stick in the midst of the traffic," displaying "two gaping, bloody sockets in place of eyelids." The beggar's "plaintive cry of distress" . . . "gave Emma a shudder of horror. The sound spiraled down into the very depths of her soul, like a whirlwind in an abyss, and swept her off into the reaches of a boundless melancholy" (Gustave Flaubert, *Madame Bovary*, trans. Francis Steegmuller [New York: Random House, 1982], 304). For an analysis of Yeats's response to the Flaubert fragment, see John R. O'Connor, "Flaubert: *Trois contes* and the Figure of the Double Cone," *PMLA* 95, no. 5 (1980): 812–826.
21. Yeats, *A Vision A*, 103.
22. Yeats, *A Vision A*, 107.
23. Quoted in Ellmann, *Yeats*, 316n.137.
24. Yeats, *A Vision A*, 156.
25. Yeats, *A Vision A*, 157. Yeats mentions "the drilled pupil of the eye" again a couple of pages later, noting that "when the drill is in the hand of some Byzantine worker in ivory, [it] undergoes a somnambulistic change for its deep shadow among the faint lines of the tablet" (159).
26. Yeats, *A Vision A*, 166.

27. Yeats concludes his late poem "The Gyres" with the lines "The workman, noble and saint, and all things run / On that unfashionable gyre again." A similar indeterminacy infuses the title of Nietzsche's *Unzeitgemässe Betrachtungen*, in which the adjective *unzeitgemässe* implies both "unfashionable" and, literally, "untimely, not in time." This is the volume that contains the essay "On the Use and Abuse of History for Life." In a letter responding to his then twenty-something son William's reference to Nietzsche to support his claim of being no longer in need of family affection, Jack Yeats wrote, "The men whom Nietzsche's theory fits are only great men of a sort, a sort of Yahoo great men. The struggle is how to get rid of them, they belong to the clumsy and brutal side of things" (quoted in Ellmann, *Yeats*, 181).
28. Quoted in Ellmann, *Yeats*, 316n.137.
29. William Blake, "Vala: Night the Sixth," in *Poetical Works*, ed. E. J. Ellis (London: Chatto and Windus, 1906), 2:94.
30. Yeats, *A Vision A*, 142.
31. I discuss these alternative models of history in chapter 2. As Paul de Man notes in his famous essay on Yeats, "[t]here may be true incoherence at the core of a system . . . which claims to be both cyclical . . . and dialectical" ("Image and Emblem in Yeats," in *Rhetoric of Romanticism* [New York: Columbia University Press, 1984], 146). It is precisely this possibly "true incoherence" in which we are interested.
32. Yeats, *A Vision A*, 152.
33. Yeats, *A Vision A*, 152.
34. In preparing for *A Vision B*, Yeats read a good deal of philosophy, history, and philosophical history, as if to close evident gaps in *A Vision A*'s system. One of the figures he clearly read is Oswald Spengler. Hazard Adams writes that "Yeats surely read Spengler with his eye on a set of oppositions that is evident everywhere in *The Decline of the West*. The principle one is what Spengler calls world-as-history and world-as-nature" (*The Book of Yeats's Vision: Romantic Modernism and Antithetical Tradition* [Ann Arbor: University of Michigan Press, 1995], 128). Adams points out that in Spengler these two forms of history are also called the "physiognomic" and the "systematic." Concerning Yeats's shifting definitions of what constitutes "civilization," see Lucy McDiarmid, *Saving Civilization: Yeats, Eliot, and Auden Between the Wars* (London: Cambridge University Press, 1984).
35. Yeats, *A Vision A*, 150.
36. On the tendency to use the capital letter to distinguish "history" from "History," see Samuel Weber, "Capitalizing History: Notes on *The Political Unconscious*," *Diacritics* 13, no. 2 (1983): 14–28.
37. Yeats, *A Vision A*, 184. Mithraism was a Roman cult dedicated to the worship of the Persian god Mithra.

38. Yeats, *A Vision A*, 197.
39. Yeats, *A Vision A*, 171.
40. Yeats, *A Vision A*, 172.
41. Yeats, *A Vision A*, 173.
42. Yeats, *A Vision A*, 165.
43. Yeats, *A Vision A*, 174. In the manuscript version, Yeats states more baldly, "We have in our great war repeated the wars of Alexander" (*A Vision A*, 317n.143). Presumably, Yeats is suggesting that European colonization efforts during the years 1870 to 1920 will follow Alexander's example and "fall apart."
44. Yeats, "On Being Asked for a War Poem," in *Poems*, 155.
45. Yeats, *A Vision A*, 174.
46. Yeats, *A Vision A*, 174. As mentioned earlier, Yeats would later compare the completed *A Vision* to Wyndham Lewis's and Constantin Brancusi's work.
47. Yeats, *A Vision A*, 175.
48. Yeats, *A Vision A*, 175.
49. These numbers are simply reproduced in *A Vision B*, even though they are no longer "timely," as what was the near future has, by the publication of the second volume, receded into the as-yet-unrealized past.
50. Even Immanuel Kant suggested that philosophical thought tended toward prophecy, especially the three options for prophecy: "the human race is either continually regressing and deteriorating [Kant calls this "moral terrorism"], continually progressing and improving [Eudaemonism], or at a permanent standstill [Abderitism]" ("The Contest of the Faculties," in *Political Writings*, ed. H. S. Reiss, trans. H. B. Nisbett [Cambridge: Cambridge University Press, 1991], 178–180). Yeats's spirals, like Hegel's though in a different way, combine the two former "forms" of prophecy.
51. Quoted in Ellmann, *Yeats*, 248.
52. Yeats, *A Vision A*, 176–177.
53. Yeats, *A Vision A*, 320n.154.
54. Yeats, *A Vision A*, 214–215. Almost enthusiastic, anticipatory, quasi-sci-fi language like this, all eventually scrapped in *A Vision B*, cast in retrospect a peculiarly jaundiced light on the red and black Historical Cones, such that they might be said to resemble the badges worn by Jewish political prisoners in Nazi concentration camps. Regarding Yeats's fascist sympathies, about which much has been written, Paul and Harper note that *A Vision A* happens to "share a publication date with the first English edition of Margherita Sarfatti's biography of Mussolini" (editors' introduction to *A Vision A*, xliv).
55. Quoted in Ellmann, *Yeats*, 25.

56. Victor Shklovsky, "The Monument to the Third International (The Most Recent Work by Tatlin)," in *Tatlin*, 343 (translation slightly altered).
57. Initially, the cube was supposed to house the Soviet of the People's Commissars of the World (Sovnarkom) and make one revolution a year; the pyramid, intended for the executive and administrative committees of the Third International, would rotate once a month; and the cylinder, home to the information and propaganda section, would complete one revolution every day. The proposed shapes changed over the course of the project and its various exhibitions. A fifteen-foot-high model built of wood, tin, paper, nails, and glue was exhibited in Petrograd in the fall of 1920; it featured a hemisphere on top of the cylinder, but the speed of the hemisphere's movement was not described. Tatlin and his collaborators I. A. Meerzon, M. P. Vinogradov, and T. M. Shapiro revised the model for exhibition in a more simplified form in Paris (at the Grand Palais) in 1925, where it was exhibited next to a samovar, and, again simplified and shrunk, in the (newly named) city of Leningrad in 1926, when it was placed on a truck and paraded through the streets during a May Day parade. The hemisphere is discussed in more detail later in the chapter.
58. Shklovsky, "Monument to the Third International," 343.
59. Punin had first written about Tatlin's project as early as March 1919, when it was first being formulated. Some of these ideas were reworked in the eight-page brochure essay of early 1920. In 1953, Punin died in a Stalin-era gulag.
60. Nikolai Punin, "The Monument to the Third International," in *Tatlin*, 345.
61. Whether Meerzon, Vinogradov, and Shapiro were actual collaborators or simply assistants has long been debated. See Anatoly Strigalev, "From Painting to the Construction of Matter," in *Tatlin*, 13–43.
62. Punin, "Monument to the Third International," 345. For Punin, this critique of the individual hero extended to the idea of the individual artist: "It is finally time to get rid of the sharply romantic idea of the artist as a high priest carrying out a solemn rite in front of the altar of art" (345). Mayakovsky also mocked these supposedly outmoded heroic memorials and praised Tatlin's Tower as being the first "monument without a beard."
63. Punin, "Monument to the Third International," 346.
64. Punin, "Monument to the Third International," 345.
65. V. I. Lenin, "Karl Marx: A Brief Biographical Sketch with an Exposition of Marxism," in *Collected Works*, trans. Julius Katzer (Moscow: Progress, 1964), 21:54.
66. Punin, "Monument to the Third International," 345. The Russian word колебаться implies the "oscillating" rising of a charmed cobra. In an extension of the snake metaphor, Punin would claim that the "spiral is the ideal expression of liberation; with its heel pressed into

the soil it escapes the ground and becomes a sign, as it were, of the liberation of [everything] animal, earthbound and reptile" (346).

67. Velimir Khlebnikov, Tatlin's friend and collaborator, led the protest against Filippo Marinetti when he visited Russia in early 1914, distributing leaflets decrying the reactionary implications of the Italians' thinking. Mayakovsky (who would also write a poem about Tatlin) had already challenged them as early as November 1913. Likewise, Tatlin opposed Marinetti's manifesto; he claimed that his own aim, *pace* the Italian Futurists (and their disciples in Russia), was not to celebrate the machine but to "overcome the tyranny of the machine" ("My Answer to 'Letter to the [Russian] Futurists,'" 185).
68. Punin, "Monument to the Third International," 345.
69. Punin, "Monument to the Third International," 346. The city of Saint Petersburg was itself long viewed as Russia's "gateway to Europe." As noted, a version of the model appeared in the international exhibition in Paris in 1925.
70. During his first trip to Berlin, Tatlin was asked to appear in Russian peasant garb and dance. During another trip to Paris, he supposedly met Picasso and played the bandura, a traditional, zither-like Russian instrument.
71. In 1920, Naum Gabo attacked Tatlin's proposal, calling it a "medieval idea . . . like the Tower of Babel," new only in its incorporation of moving parts (quoted in Norbert Lynton, *Tatlin's Tower: Monument to Revolution* [New Haven, Conn.: Yale University Press, 2009), 170).
72. Lynton, *Tatlin's Tower*, 93–94, passim.
73. In the 1920s and 1930s, Kolli collaborated with Le Corbusier and Corbusier's cousin Pierre Jeanneret, most famously on the international modernist Centrosoyuz building in Moscow.
74. Marxists tended to view the second international as ending in failure, as many European national social democratic movements supported World War I.
75. Leon Trotsky, "The Manifesto of the Communist International," in *The First Five Years of the Communist International* (New York: Pathfinder, 1979), 1:19.
76. For an exploration of the rhetoric of incorporation in United Nations (successor to the League of Nations) charter documents as well as a critique of the notion of "development" that both capitalist and Communist rhetoric depends on, see Joseph Slaughter, *Human Rights, Inc.: The World Novel, Narrative Form, and International Law* (New York: Fordham University Press, 2007) .
77. Trotsky, "Manifesto," 20.
78. As noted, some of these functions were initially intended for the cylinder, to which the hemisphere was in a sense connected through its time of rotation.
79. Lynton, *Tatlin's Tower*, 65.
80. Shklovsky, "Monument to the Third International," 343.

81. According to Tatlin's early critic, Sergei Isakov, the idea of the counter-relief shared strategies of "counter-attack" that emerged during the Great War. See Strigalev, "From Painting to the Construction of Matter," 19.
82. Leon Trotsky, *Lenin*, translator unknown (New York: Blue Ribbon Books, 1925), n.p.
83. Trotsky, *Lenin*, n.p.
84. Trotsky saw a model of Tatlin's Tower in 1919; he was generally quite positive, opining that Tatlin was "unreservedly right" to exclude "national styles, allegorical sculpture, stucco-work, ornamentation, decoration and all sorts of nonsense." But he also asked, apropos of the shapes of the inner structures, "Is not the whole thing untimely?" (quoted in Lynton, *Tatlin's Tower*, 103). Trotsky was referring to the idea of building a state-of-the-art tower in a city without adequate sewage, but his is a curious question to pose about a building for which "timeliness," and the Unzeitgemässe, are so crucial.
85. Whether Lenin had a personal reaction to the monument's design is unclear, but the fact that Tatlin was concerned with rumors that may have been reaching Lenin about the planned monument is certainly clear from a 1918 letter he wrote to his Narkompros colleague Anatoly Lunacharsky: "We have learned that comrade Vinogradov . . . is bringing his totally unfounded opinion to the attention of c[omrade] V. I. Lenin and in this way is attempting to cast a shadow on the activity of the Fine Arts Department" (*Tatlin*, 187).
86. The narrative of Genesis 11 suggests a direct relation between the place the Babylonians called "Babel" (for "gate of God") and the Hebrew word for "confusion": "That is why it was called Babel—because there the Lord confused the language of the whole world" (Genesis 11:9 [NIV]).
87. "Tour" as in a limited duration—for example, "tour of duty"—is also implied in Derrida's title, as is, phonetically, "detours."
88. Jacques Derrida, "Des Tours de Babel," in *A Derrida Reader: Between the Blinds*, ed. Peggy Kamuf (New York: Columbia University Press, 1991), 244.
89. Derrida, "Des Tours de Babel," 243. In deploying the word "dominate," which I am italicizing for emphasis, Derrida insinuates both the Latin name of God, *domine*, and the idea of uncomprehending "nations" in the Babel story.
90. Strigalev claims that Soviet engineering was up to the task of constructing the ambitious tower, in "From Painting to the Construction of Matter," 34. In any case, compared with the unlikelihood of pulling off the total political revolution that had just occurred, building a large edifice must have seemed a snap.
91. As noted earlier in this chapter, Khlebnikov had led a protest against Marinetti when he came to Russia in early 1914.
92. Vladimir Yevgrafovich Tatlin, in *Tatlin*, 248. Tatlin goes on to quote Khlebnikov's "principle" that "'[t]he word is the building unit, the material is the unit of organized space'

and that 'the supernarrative is "architecture from stories" and a story is "architecture from words"'" (248).

93. Milner, *Vladimir Tatlin*, 117.
94. Nikolai Punin, in *Tatlin*, 396. Theater reviewer A. V. Tufanov notes, concerning Tatlin's production of two types of transrational "unintelligible" languages in song—that of the birds (primarily consonants) and that of the gods (primarily vowels)—that the song of the gods "is less perfect since there exist only five vowel phonemes. Even in ancient languages [such as] Arabic [and] Hebrew, vowel alternation had . . . a purely formal significance, and not a material one" (*Tatlin*, 401). These reflections relate directly to my analysis of the Tower of Babel episode.
95. Samuel Weber, *Theatricality as Medium* (New York: Oxford University Press, 2009), 3.
96. Weber, *Theatricality as Medium*, 3.
97. *Tatlin* contains Tatlin's written responses (1928) to the question, "Have you been abroad, and where?": "France[. . . ,] Germany, Egypt, Syria, Turkey, and Italian colonies in Africa" ("Autobiography," in *Tatlin*, 263), the last clarified as "Tripoli" (now Libya) in an autobiography/narrative résumé in 1929. In another such piece, "Curriculum Vitae of Honored Art Worker Tatlin," he claims to have also been to Bulgaria. Elsewhere he added Greece, Lebanon, Egypt, and what is now called Israel, parts of which would earlier have been considered "Turkey" (as might Iraq); no direct mention is made of Iraq or Babylonia.
98. Lynton, *Tatlin's Tower*, 82.
99. Another kind of misconstrual seems to be taking place in the more recent attempt to associate Tatlin's project too narrowly with "modern functionalism." Gilles Deleuze and Félix Guattari briefly mention Tatlin's Tower, in relation to Franz Kafka's castles and their "infinite paranoiac spirals," and claim, "It seems that the most modern functionalism more or less voluntarily reactivated the most archaic or mythical forms" (*Kafka: Toward a Minor Literature*, trans. Dana Polan [Minneapolis: University of Minnesota Press, 1986], 76). To be sure, these forms were "reactivated," but not, I think, in a way that is as intrinsically linked to fascism or to paranoia as Deleuze and Guattari imply that they were.
100. Milner claims that Tatlin "approaches astrology" in his interest in the movements of heavenly bodies, and in the regular rhythm of the "various halls' revolutions about the axis" (*Vladimir Tatlin*, 164–165).
101. Svetlana Boym, *Architecture of the Off Modern* (Princeton, N.J.: Princeton University Press, 2008), 13. As was the case with many artists of this period, Tatlin was somewhat rehabilitated in the later 1940s and early 1950s. It is worth remembering that the adjective "formalist," deployed as a pejorative, emerged in the Stalin era in the Soviet Union.

4. L'HABITE EN SPIRALE

Calvin Tomkins, *The Bride and the Bachelors: Five Masters of the Avant-garde* (New York: Penguin, 1968), 33.

James Joyce, *Ulysses: The Corrected Text*, ed. Hans Walter Gabler (New York: Vantage, 1986), episode 4: line 438 (page 55). Here, in the "Calypso" episode, Leopold Bloom is thinking of his daughter Milly; Bloom later thinks "Your head it simply swurls" twice: once in relation to maggots around dead bodies in the soil, in the "Hades" episode (*Ulysses* 6:784 [89]), and once in response to Hugh "Blazes" Boylan's scheduled assignation with Leopold's wife, Molly Bloom (*Ulysses* 11:688 [225]); Bloom thinks "Your head it simply swirls" again in relation to Gerty MacDowell and their *onanisme à deux*, in the "Nausikaa" episode (*Ulysses* 13:942 [305]). In each case, Bloom is misremembering the chorus to the popular song "Seaside Girls" (1898) by Harry B. Norris. The song was identified by Zack Bowen in *Musical Allusions in the Works of James Joyce* (Albany: State University of New York Press, 1974), 89–90.

1. The book was eventually called *Tales Told of Shem and Shaun: Fragments from Work in Progress* (Paris: Black Sun, 1929).
2. Quoted in Richard Ellmann, *James Joyce* (Oxford: Oxford University Press, 1982), 614.
3. The French title, *Nu descendant un escalier*, is gender neutral.
4. The diagram appears in Marcel Duchamp, *Notes and Projects for the Large Glass*, selected, ordered, and with an introduction by Arturo Schwarz, trans. George H. Hamilton, Cleve Gray, and Arturo Schwarz (New York: Abrams, 1969), 19. Most of the notes from which Schwarz created Duchamp's glossary/lexicon were written by Duchamp between 1913 and 1915. In one note, Duchamp describes a section of the glass as being akin to "a form of a toboggan but more of a corkscrew, and the splash . . . [as] an uncorking" (174). Note that as the liquid shot up toward the bride there was also supposed to be a "Handler of Gravity," which Duchamp proposed as a kind of "spring," whose "center [would be] suppress[ed]" (178).
5. Salvatore Califano, *Pathways to Modern Chemical Physics* (New York: Springer, 2012), 7. The German original appeared as Rudolf Clausius, *Ueber verschiedene für die Anwendung bequeme Formen der Hauptgleichungen der mechanischen Wärmetheorie* (Zurich: Fäsi and Beer, 1865).
6. *Oxford English Dictionary*, 2nd ed., 20 vols. (Oxford: Oxford University Press, 1989), s.v. "energy."
7. See, especially, Aristotle, *Rhetoric*, trans. John Gillies (London: Cadell, 1823), bk. 3, chap. 11, 405–413.

8. Aristotle, *Rhetoric*, 406.
9. Beginning in the later 1940s, entropy began to be associated with information theory, especially the "lost information" in telephone communication. Claude Elwood Shannon's *Mathematical Theory of Communication* (1962) is perhaps the best-known early text in this field. As Thomas Pynchon's character John Nefastis notes in the novel *The Crying of Lot 49*, the two definitions of entropy, "heat or energy loss" and "information dispersal," have little to do with each other, but tend to be confused.
10. Duchamp's ready-mades of the late 1910s, including *Fountain* and *LHOOQ*, are often associated with New York Dada. In the Manifesto of Surrealism of 1924, André Breton mentions Duchamp by name: in the "castle" of Surrealism, in the "hall of mirrors, we received a certain Marcel Duchamp whom we had not hitherto known" (*Manifestoes of Surrealism*, trans. Richard Seaver and Helen R. Lane [Ann Arbor: University of Michigan Press, 1969], 17).
11. Tristan Tzara, "Dada Manifesto, 1918," in *Modernism: An Anthology*, ed. Lawrence S. Rainey (London: Blackwell, 2005), 483. See also Tristan Tzara, *Oeuvres completes* (Paris: Flammarion, 1975), 357–358.
12. Tzara actually uses this drawing four times in manifestos; it is depicted in each of four directions, as if inclined from north, south, east, and west. The drawing was probably made by Francis Picabia. See Tristan Tzara, *Seven Dada Manifestos and Lampisteries*, trans. Barbara Wright (London: Calder, 1981).
13. Tzara pointedly asks, "Is the aim of art to make money and cajole the nice nice bourgeois?" ("Dada Manifesto, 1918," 480).
14. Tzara, "Dada Manifesto, 1918," 484.
15. See Duchamp's brief letters to Jacques Doucet, concerning Duchamp's struggles to get the machine (or "instrument") working. On October 25, 1924, Duchamp wrote, "I've finally seen something turn. Tomorrow I'll see the motor in place; I'd like to see you at Man Ray's and take you to meet the mechanic. You'll see the instrument there in its unfinished state" ("On the Second Optical Machine," in *The Writings of Marcel Duchamp*, ed. Michel Sanouillet and Elmer Peterson [1973; New York: Da Capo, 1989], 184).
16. Plateau's phenakistoscope is credited as being the precursor to the zoetrope, the essence of modern cinema until the advent of digital technology.
17. By the time of this experiment, Plateau was already almost completely blind, having stared into the sun too long during previous research.
18. Rosalind Krauss's most sustained treatment of Duchamp's optical machines and interest in opticality is in *The Optical Unconscious* (Cambridge, Mass.: MIT Press, 1994). In this text, her polemic against Clement Greenberg, and the twentieth-century art and artists who

gained notice by Greenberg's promotion of "opticality," is made clearest. Her revaluation of Duchamp, whose art Greenberg did not admire, is crucial to this polemic. According to Krauss, "what Greenberg detests in Duchamp's art is its pressure toward desublimation[:] the attempt to erase distinctions between art and not-art, between the absolute gratuitousness of form and the commodity" (139).

19. Rosalind Krauss, in *Art Since 1900: Modernism, Antimodernism, Postmodernism*, vol. 1, *1900–1944*, ed. Hal Foster, Rosalind Krauss, Yve-Alain Bois, and Benjamin H. D. Buchloh (London: Thames and Hudson, 2004), 631.
20. Krauss, citing what Jean-Francois Lyotard called "the cuntishness" of Duchamp's model of vision, refers to Duchamp's own reference to the mind's grasping of ideas as being "the way the penis is grasped by the vagina" (*Optical Unconscious*, 119).
21. Jonathan Crary, "Techniques of the Observer," *October* 45 (1988): 20.
22. Crary, "Techniques of the Observer," 20. In this essay, and in the later book of which it is a part, Crary writes of a progressive "eradication of the point of view" (30) beginning in the mid-nineteenth century.
23. Concerning the demispheres' links to the cinematic apparatus and to eroticism, note that Duchamp wrote to Doucette, in April 1924, "I would like to glue a velvet backing on the metal plate which supports the spiral. An English velvet, a silky velvet? A velvet that will bring to mind the absolutely mat[te] backdrop that you see in movie-houses" ("On the Second Optical Machine," 183).
24. Marc Allégret, who was twenty-five and André Gide's lover at the time of *Anémic Cinéma*, went on to direct over fifty films, including *Fanny*, *Les Beaux Jours*, and *L'Amant de Lady Chatterley*, which was banned for three years before ultimately being allowed into U.S. cinemas. Allégret is credited with "discovering" the actress Brigitte Bardot in the early 1950s.
25. Molly Nesbit and Naomi Sawelson Gorse, "Concept of Nothing: New Notes by Marcel Duchamp and Walter Arensberg," in *The Duchamp Effect*, ed. Martha Buskirk and Mignon Nixon (Cambridge, Mass.: MIT Press, 1996), 173.
26. P. Adams Sitney, "Image and Title in Avant-Garde Cinema," *October* 9 (1979): 104.
27. Duchamp's puns are collected, and casually translated, in "Rrose Selavy & Co," in *Writings*, esp. 104–119.
28. Marjorie Perloff, "A Cessation of Resemblances: Stein, Picasso, Duchamp," *Battersea Review* 1, no. 1 (2012).
29. The business card is reproduced in "Rrose Selavy & Co," 105. Sanouillet and Peterson suggest that the "whiskers and kicks" "probably have reference to what was added to the Mona Lisa" in *LHOOQ*.

30. Further links between Duchamp and Sélavy are suggested, raunchily, in the rare (for Duchamp) strictly English-language pun "oh! Do shit again! . . . / Oh! Douche it again" ("Rrose Selavy & Co," 115), which picks up on the American pronunciation of Duchamp as "douche."
31. In adding Sélavy's fingerprint to his/her signature, Duchamp is almost certainly parodying French couturière Madeleine Vionnet's gesture of having her signature and fingerprint appear on labels for her clothing. Vionnet is credited with popularizing bias-cut dresses in the early 1920s.
32. The French word *péter*, which is also insinuated, means "fart."
33. In the following set of translations, I have been aided by Katrina Martin's attempt to explain the film's elaborate puns in her short essay "Marcel Duchamp's *Anémic- Cinéma*," *Studio International* 189 (1975): 53–60. (While my references to the sexual nature of Duchamp's puns may at times seem strained, they are in fact rather *re*strained in comparison with the erotic force Martin grants them.)
34. The use of liquid nitrogen in cryotherapy and cryosurgery—the freezing off of warts, moles, and skin tags—was first performed in the early twentieth century, and had become the favored treatment for these ailments by the 1920s.
35. Lawrence Hennigh traces the history of this practice in *Functions and Limitations of Alaskan Eskimo Wife Trading* (Montreal: Arctic Institute of North America, 1970). Wife trading was mentioned in passing as early as 1900 in American Edward William Nelson's *The Eskimo About Bering Strait*. Closer to the year of *Anémic Cinéma*'s production, Inuit families had been featured in Robert J. Flaherty's documentary film *Nanook of the North* (1922).
36. This ninth spinning spiral image in *Anémic Cinéma* is similar to, but not exactly identical with, the rotorelief appearing in figure 39, which Duchamp/Sélavy called *Escargot* (*Snail*).
37. Thierry de Duve, *Kant After Duchamp* (Cambridge, Mass.: MIT Press, 1998), 6. De Duve goes on to note modernism's turn from art as an object to art as a "proper name" (77).
38. Duchamp, "A l'Infinitif," in *Writings*, 78.
39. Duchamp, "A l'Infinitif," 77.
40. Duchamp, "A l'Infinitif," 77.
41. Martin, "Marcel Duchamp's *Anémic-Cinéma*," 54.
42. G. W. F. Hegel, *Vorlesungen über die Philosophie der Geschichte*, vol. 12 of *Gessamelte Werke* (Hamburg: Meiner, 1981), 85 (my translation).
43. De Duve astutely asks of Duchamp, "Is he really free of Hegel, of the Hegel that lies dormant in every theoretician?" (*Kant After Duchamp*, 367).
44. According to Duchamp, "Dada was an extreme protest against the physical side of painting. It was a metaphysical attitude. It was intimately and consciously involved with 'literature.' It

was a sort of nihilism to which I am still very sympathetic" ("The Great Trouble with Art in This Country" [interview with James Johnson Sweeney], in *Writings*, 125).

45. Sigmund Freud, *Jokes and Their Relation to the Unconscious*, trans. James Strachey (1905; New York: Norton, 1989), 136.
46. Freud, *Jokes*, 117–118.
47. One of the best-known accounts of Duchamp and gender critique remains Amelia Jones, *Postmodernism and the En-Gendering of Marcel Duchamp* (Cambridge: Cambridge University Press, 1995).
48. Michel Sanouillet and Elmer Peterson suggest that "the French custom is to give a sou [penny] to preserve friendship when offered a sharp or pointed object. Duchamp reverses what might be expected, saying in effect, 'If I am good to you will you cut me out of your life?'" ("Rrose Selavy & Co.," 113).
49. Martin, "Marcel Duchamp's *Anémic-Cinéma*," 58. Note also that the intertitle "AVEZ-VOUS DÉJÀ MIS LA MOËLLE DE L'ÉPÉE DANS LE POÊLE DE L'AIMÉE?" borrows from the sport of fencing to ask, "HAVE YOU ALREADY PUT THE MARROW OF THE SWORD INTO THE LOVED ONE'S STOVE?"
50. This idea of suffering has been insufficiently explored in studies of Duchamp's life and work. See his positively Beckettian, pseudo-mathematical notebook entry: "Étant donné que . . . ; si je suppose que je sois souffrant beaucoup [Given that . . . ; if I suppose that I am suffering very much]" (Duchamp, "The 1914 Box," in *Writings*, 23). *Étant donné* is, of course, the singular version of the beginning of the title of Duchamp's late, supposed "masterpiece" installation *Étant donnés: 1° la chute d'eau/2° le gaz d'éclairage* (1966).
51. Freud, *Jokes*, 179.
52. As I note in chapter 5, Robert Smithson dismissed Duchamp's practice as "joke art"; in a technical sense, then, Smithson's diagnosis is correct, although I believe his devaluation of Duchamp is off base.
53. T. J. Demos, *The Exiles of Marcel Duchamp* (Cambridge, Mass.: MIT Press, 2011), 44.
54. Lest the puns' emphasis on suggestive sexual scenarios seem at times distant from these more explicitly sociopolitical questions, it ought to be noted that two of the aphoristic counter-repeated puns that Sélavy/Duchamp created in the early 1920s, but did not use in *Anémic Cinéma*, were "Eglise, exile" (church, exile) and "Étrangler l'étranger" (strangle the foreigner).
55. Joyce, *Ulysses*, 4:365 (53).
56. Joyce, *Ulysses*, 4:366 (53).
57. Joyce, *Ulysses*, 17:559–560 (558).
58. Joyce, *Ulysses*, 17:561–562 (559).
59. Joyce, *Ulysses*, 17:567–568 (559).

60. Joyce, *Ulysses*, 17:1042, 1057 (572–573), 1107–1108 (575).
61. Joyce, *Ulysses*, 17:2114–2121 (601).
62. *The Odyssey of Homer*, trans. Richmond Lattimore (New York: Harper, 2007), book 13, lines 105–106 (page 188).
63. In the inaugural "Telemachus" episode, Buck Mulligan claims that Stephen tries to "prove . . . by algebra that Hamlet's grandson is Shakespeare's grandfather and that he himself is the ghost of his own father" (Joyce, *Ulysses*, 1:555–557 [15]).
64. Joyce, *Ulysses*, 9:48–49 (152). The real George Russell published early versions of three of the stories that later appeared in *Dubliners* in the journal Russell edited, *The Irish Homestead*, but Russell rejected "Clay," and Joyce was angry at the slight. See Ellmann, *James Joyce*, 190.
65. Joyce, *Ulysses*, 9:80–81 (153).
66. Joyce, *Ulysses*, 9:82–83 (153).
67. Yeats is referred to several times in "Scylla and Charybdis." Early in the episode, John Eglington teasingly tells Stephen that he has six medical students who will write *Hamlet* at Stephen's dictation but needs a seventh: "Seven is dear to the mystic mind. The shining seven W. B. calls them" (Joyce, *Ulysses*, 9:27–28 [151]).
68. Joyce, *Ulysses*, 9:292 (158).
69. Joyce, *Ulysses*, 9:103–104 (153).
70. Joyce, *Ulysses*, 9:279–286 (157).
71. Joyce, *Ulysses*, 9:36 (152).
72. Joyce, *Ulysses*, 9:34 (151). For the Dante passage, see canto 21 in *The Inferno of Dante: Bilingual Edition*, trans. Robert Pinsky and John Freccero (New York: Farrar, Straus and Giroux, 1996), 172.
73. "Seeing they were all looking at his chest he accommodatingly dragged his shirt more open so that on top of the timehonoured symbol of the mariner's hope and rest they had a full view of the figure 16 and a young man's sideface looking frowningly rather" (Joyce, *Ulysses*, 16:673–675 [516]).The figure 16 is repeated throughout the sixteenth episode, and here, accompanying the tattoo, it juxtaposes a straight line and a spiral, borrowing part of the iconography of "69" to insinuate one man anally penetrating another.
74. Joyce, *Ulysses*, 9:21 (151).
75. Joseph Valente, "'Thrilled by His Touch': The Aestheticizing of Homosexual Panic in *A Portrait of the Artist as a Young Man*," in *Quare Joyce*, ed. Joseph Valente (Ann Arbor: University of Michigan Press, 2000), 66.
76. Joyce, *Ulysses*, 9:659 (166).
77. Joyce, *Ulysses*, 9:1061 (175).
78. Joyce, *Ulysses*, 9:615–616 (165).

79. Joyce, *Ulysses*, 9:1210–1211 (179).
80. Joyce, *Ulysses*, 9:1212 (179).
81. Joyce, *Ulysses*, 9:1153 (177).
82. Joyce, *Ulysses*, 9:1065–1067 (175).
83. Joyce, *Ulysses*, 9:828 (170).
84. Joyce, *Ulysses*, 9:843–844 (170).
85. Joyce, *Ulysses*, 9:844–845 (170).
86. Joyce, *Ulysses*, 9:847 (170).
87. Joyce, *Ulysses*, 9:849 (170).
88. Joyce, *Ulysses*, 9:848 (170).
89. Joyce, *Ulysses*, 9:459–464 (161).
90. Joyce, *Ulysses*, 9:465 (161).
91. Joyce, *Ulysses*, 8:1179, 1190 (150).
92. Joyce, *Ulysses*, 9:577 (164).
93. Joyce, *Ulysses*, 9:589, 597 (164, 165).
94. Joyce, *Ulysses*, 9:1197, 1203 (178, 179).
95. Joyce, *Ulysses*, 9:1210–1211 (179).
96. Joyce, *Ulysses*, 9:1218–1220 (179).
97. In "The Dead," snow is described as "falling softly upon the Bog of Allen" and then, chiasmatically, "softly falling into the dark mutinous Shannon waves" (James Joyce, *Dubliners*, Norton Critical Edition, ed. Margot Norris and Hans Walter Gabler [New York: Norton, 2006], 223).
98. Joyce, *Ulysses*, 9:377–379 (159).
99. That Joyce connected Vico's thinking to spirals (and not simply cycles) is clear. See Joyce's notebook *VI.B.1.*029c (r): "zigzag vs. spiral corsi ricorsi Vico"—the note that provided the Joyce quotation (James Joyce, *Finnegans Wake* [New York: Penguin, 1976], 481) appears in the heading to this section.
100. Samuel Beckett, "Dante . . . Bruno. Vico . . Joyce," in *Our Exagmination Round His Factification for Incamination of Work in Progress: A Symposium* (1929; New York: New Directions, 1972), 5.
101. Beckett, "Dante . . . Bruno," 14 (emphases in original).
102. The approach I propose is meant to negotiate between the two poles of *Wake* criticism long ago identified by Margot Norris, *The Decentered Universe of Finnegans Wake: A Structuralist Analysis* (Baltimore: Johns Hopkins University Press, 1976): on the one hand, the "quantum" approach, which asserts the text's seeming randomness, chaos, and complexity (extended recently by Thomas Jackson Rice, Dirk Vanderbeke, and Donald Theall, among

others); and, on the other, the "mythological" approach, which asserts the repetitiveness of the book's motifs and narrative strands (Edmund Epstein, Clive Hart, and Joseph Campbell). To these two I wish to add a sociopolitical valence, which was, until fairly recently, generally ignored by the *Wake* industry.

103. Textual and genetic criticism scholars claim that this section is one of the first things Joyce wrote after finishing *Ulysses*. See Laurent Milesi, "Metaphors of the Quest in *Finnegans Wake*," in *Finnegans Wake: Fifty Years*, ed. Geert Lernout (Amsterdam: Rodopi, 1990), 95.
104. Sir Edward Sullivan, *The Book of Kells* (London: The Studio, 1920), 1, 21.
105. Joyce, *Wake*, 121.
106. For a reading of this passage in relation to Jacques Derrida's *Glas*, see Peter Mahon, *Imagining Joyce and Derrida: Between Finnegans Wake and Glas* (Toronto: University of Toronto Press, 2007), 347.
107. Joseph Campbell and Henry Morton Robinson suggest that "the reader of *Finnegans Wake* will not fail to recognize in this page something like a mute indication that here is the key to the entire puzzle; and he will be all the more concerned to search its meaning when he reads Joyce's boast on p. 298[:] 'I've read your tunc's dismissage'" (*A Skeleton Key to Finnegans Wake: Unlocking James Joyce's Masterwork* [1939; New York: New World Library, 2005], 101). Note that several recent paperback editions of *A Skeleton Key* feature a reproduction of the "Tunc" page on their covers.
108. Joyce, *Wake*, 197, 203, 215.
109. Both the theme of washing and the accusations of sexual indiscretions represent a recirculation of central topoi of *Ulysses*'s "Nausikaa" episode.
110. Joyce, *Wake*, 199.
111. Joyce, *Wake*, 199.
112. Joyce, *Wake*, 258.
113. Joyce, *Wake*, 286.
114. Joyce, *Wake*, 287.
115. Joyce, *Wake*, 293.
116. As noted in chapter 3, Yeats, in *Wild Swans at Coole*'s "Shepherd and Goatherd," writes,

> He unpacks the loaded pern
> Of all 'twas pain or joy to learn,
> Of all that he had made. . . .
> Knowledge he shall unwind
> Through victories of the mind[.]

117. See not only the famous poem "Lapis Lazuli" but the lesser-known "Oil and Blood":

> In tombs of gold and lapis lazuli
> Bodies of holy men and women exude
> Miraculous oil, odour of violet.
>
> But under heavy loads of trampled clay
> Lie bodies of the vampires full of blood;
> Their shrouds are bloody and their lips are wet[.] (W. B. Yeats, *The Poems*, vol. 1 of *The Collected Works of W. B. Yeats*, ed. Richard J. Finneran [New York: Scribner, 1997], 243)

Concerning the political implications of Yeats's poem (which in part seems to invoke "soil and blood"), see Michael Golson, *Rhythm and Race in Modernist Poetry and Science* (New York: Columbia University Press, 2007), 239–240.

118. Joyce, *Wake*, 294, 295, 297, 300, 295.
119. Lynching also plays an important role in *Ulysses*'s "Cyclops" episode, where the men gathered in the bar joke about the erect penis of a hanged man, and the narrator mentions a newspaper headline reading "Black Beast Burned in Omaha, Ga.," describing the accompanying photograph: "A lot of Deadwood Dicks in slouch hats and they firing at a Sambo strung up in a tree with his tongue out and a bonfire under him." The narrator adds, sarcastically, "Gob, they ought to drown him in the sea after and electrocute him and crucify him to make sure of their job" (Joyce, *Ulysses*, 12:1324–1328 [269]). There is an implicit comparison between lynching and hanging by the state in the figure of the Croppy Boy in "Circe" and elsewhere.
120. Joyce, *Wake*, 297.
121. See, for example, Noel Ignatiev, *How the Irish Became White* (New York: Routledge, 2008).
122. In addition, just as "Dolph" tries to get "Kev" to view his mother's genitals as a means of convincing him to "kill" his parents in the way the Olympians killed the Titans (with a near-certain allusion to the Freudian Oedipal complex), so is Joyce effectively "killing off" his great Irish literary predecessor and one-time benefactor, Yeats. The Duchampian pun "Inceste ou passion de famille, à coups trop tirés" applies.
123. Joyce, *Wake*, 304.
124. Poincaré also refers to "forward and backward asymptotes" (Jeremy Gray, *Henri Poincaré: A Scientific Biography* [Princeton, N.J.: Princeton University Press, 2012], 259).

125. Joyce, *Wake*, 304.
126. Joyce, *Wake*, 306–307.
127. The fork and spoon are not pictured in the detail.
128. I intend to develop elsewhere this connection between Joyce's language and the international constructed language Esperanto. For now, it should simply be noted that the question of "universal language" is broached at the beginning of the "Circe" episode in Stephen's conversation with his university friend Lynch, and is parodied later in the same episode both during Bloom's "New Bloomusalem speech" (". . . bonuses for all, esperanto the universal language with universal brotherhood . . .") and when Bloom mistakes a doorman's request for a password, in Irish, for Esperanto ("Haha. Merci. Esperanto. *Slan leath*") (Joyce, *Ulysses*, 15:1691–1692 [399], 15:220 [356]). Joyce also includes several Esperanto and mock-Esperanto phrases in *Finnegans Wake*, among them a sequence in III.4 in which the central protagonists, Mr. and Mrs. Porter, stand-ins for or reiterations of HCE and ALP, speak of their son Kevin's troubled sleep, which has caused him to speak a child-like babble:

    —Li ne dormis? [Didn't he sleep?]
    —S! Malbone dormas. [Shh!, he slept badly]
    —Kia li krias nikte? [What does he cry he at night?] [In correct Esperanto, "in notko" would be used to signify "at night." Perhaps Joyce had in mind the modern Greek τη νύχτα (in nichta)]
    —Parolas infanetes. S! [Infant words, Shh!] (565)

    One page later, Porter/HCE is admonished by his wife, with whom he wants to have sex, to cover his loins, since his children can see his nakedness: "Vidu, porkego! Ili vi rigardas. Returnu, porkego. Maldelikato! [Watch out, you big lug, they see you. Turn it over, you oaf, you're being rude!]" (556). Whereas "infant words" in the previous passage invoked Babel and the profusion of unintelligible languages, Mrs. Porter's admonishment points to the primal scene of Ham's curse (by Noah), spilling out (as Porter's genitals do) into a scenario with geopolitical dimensions in that Ham in the biblical narrative is inheritor of land that medieval theologians assumed was Africa, and hence justified the slave trade.
129. Jacques Derrida offers a magisterial reading of the *Wake* phrase "He war" in his self-declared "modest" essay, "Deux mots pour Joyce," translated as "Two Words for Joyce," in *Post-Structuralist Joyce: Essays from the French*, ed. Derrick Attridge and Daniel Ferrer (Cambridge: Cambridge University Press, 1984), 145–160.

5. AT THE END OF THE JETTY

Samuel Beckett, *The Unnamable*, in *Three Novels: Molloy, Malone Dies, The Unnamable* (New York: Grove Press, 2005), 293–294.

Robert Smithson, "The Artist and Politics: A Symposium" (1970), in *Robert Smithson: The Collected Writings*, ed. Jack Flam (Berkeley: University of California Press, 1996), 134.

1. James Knowlson recounts the episode in *Damned to Fame: The Life of Samuel Beckett* (New York: Grove Press, 2004), 124–125.
2. Knowlson, *Damned to Fame*, 124. "Loutishness of learning" is from Beckett's poem "Gnome," *Dublin Magazine* 9 (1934): 8.
3. For the alert listener, the rather comical name (du Chas) and place (Toulouse, which contains the English word "louse," a frequently invoked Beckettian insect) would have been tip-offs.
4. Hugh Kenner, *Samuel Beckett: A Critical Study* (Berkeley: University of California Press, 1968), 128, 129.
5. *Earthworks* (1965) is the title of a dystopian novel by the British science-fiction writer Brian Aldiss. Smithson, curating an exhibition at the Dwan Gallery in New York in 1968, gave the show this sci-fi name, which stuck. Other artists associated with "earth art" include Walter de Maria, Michael Heizer, Richard Long, and, a bit later, James Turrell.
6. Marjorie Perloff, *The Futurist Moment: Avant-Garde, Avant Guerre, and the Language of Rupture* (Chicago: University of Chicago Press, 1987).
7. As Thomas Crow—an art historian who has written, albeit in passing, about *The Unnamable*'s connection to *Spiral Jetty*—has argued, concerning the plethora of texts of various genres from which Smithson draws, "[I]n no sense could the products of [Smithson's] reading"—to which we might add "viewing" or "listening"—"be relegated to a supporting role in the presence of 'the work of art.' It would be far truer to regard the massive . . . edifice of rock and earth as just one more addition to this nested array of inscriptions" ("'Cosmic Exile': Prophetic Turns in the Life and Art of Robert Smithson," in *Robert Smithson*, ed. Eugenie Tsai [Berkeley: University of California Press, 2004], 34).
8. Recent book-length studies include Ann Reynolds, *Robert Smithson: Learning from New Jersey and Elsewhere* (Cambridge, Mass.: MIT Press, 2004); and Jennifer L. Roberts, *Mirror Travels: Robert Smithson and History* (New Haven, Conn.: Yale University Press, 2004), both of which make extensive use of Smithson's archives. For informative postmillennium essays, see Pamela Lee, "'Ultramoderne': or, How George Kubler Stole the Time in Sixties Art," *Grey Room* 2 (2001): 46–77; Reinhold Martin, "Organicism's Other," *Grey Room* 4 (2002): 34–51; and Andrew Uroskie, "La Jettée en Spirale: Robert Smithson's Stratigraphic

Cinema," *Grey Room* 19 (2005): 54–79. These texts, along with others gathered in two substantial essay collections coinciding with large retrospective exhibitions at the Los Angeles County Museum of Art and the Whitney Museum of American Art in New York, have significantly clarified aspects of Smithson's practice that had been unrecognized or inadequately theorized, especially concerning the explicitly temporal and historical dimensions of Smithson's project, which an earlier generation of critics tended to downplay. See Tsai, ed., *Robert Smithson*; and Lynne Cooke and Karen Kelly, eds., *Robert Smithson, Spiral Jetty: True Fictions, False Realities* (New York: Dia Art Foundation, 2005). Other critics who have recognized Beckett's impact on Smithson include Caroline Jones, who offers a Lacanian psychoanalytic reading of the *Spiral Jetty* film's "mode of signification" in which *The Unnamable* makes a brief appearance: "The unnamable is . . . both the narrator's own mangled identity (Smithson's, in the case of the film we watch and hear), and the incomplete (unnamable) memory that must be retrieved if that fragmented identity is ever to be made whole" (*Machine in the Studio: Constructing the Postwar American Artist* [Chicago: University of Chicago Press, 1995], 337). Jones views *The Unnamable*, and by extension Smithson, as presenting "a symbolically castrated figure who queries 'Why should I have a sex, who have no longer a nose?'" (337). Yet this otherwise illuminating reading of the artwork's presentation of the novel's presentation of "castration" is perhaps complicated by the fact that the narrator of *The Unnamable has* a "sex" (referred to as a "onetime virile member") but, being armless and legless, no means to satisfy his persistent sexual urges. He is not symbolically castrated but symbolically unarmed.

9. The earthwork was constructed when the water levels in the northern Great Salt Lake were unusually low; it went completely underwater within a couple years of its documentation. It reemerged in the new millennium, thanks in part to the effects of global warming. As of the date of the printing of this book, the earthwork has gone underwater again.
10. Likewise, Beckett criticism has not taken notice of Beckett's text's appearance in Smithson's artwork. The only prominent Beckett critic to mention Smithson is Herbert Blau, who speculates about the impact of Beckett's oeuvre (particularly the theater) on the work of a number postminimalist and performance artists, in "'The Commodius Vicus' of Beckett: Vicissitudes of the Arts in the Science of Affliction," in *Beckett After Beckett*, ed. S. E. Gontarski and Anthony Uhlmann (Gainesville: University Press of Florida, 2006), 22–38. Blau notes correctly that in Smithson's article "Quasi-Infinities and the Waning of Space" (1965), the budding-artist-as-writer cites Beckett's essay "Proust" (1930); Blau also mentions *Spiral Jetty*, but only in passing, noting its "commodius Viconian" shape (27).
11. The contents of Smithson's library were first published in 1973 and republished, in identical fashion, as "The Library List," with an introductory essay, Alexander Alberro, "The Catalog

of Robert Smithson's Library," in *Robert Smithson*. Of course, as is the case with any bibliophile's library, there would have been books in Smithson's collection that he hadn't yet read at the time of his death. Still, that Smithson read widely in Beckett's oeuvre is certain.

12. For an account of the construction process, see Bob Phillips, "Building the Jetty," in *Robert Smithson, Spiral Jetty*, 185–198.
13. Robert Smithson, "Entropy and the New Monuments" (1966), in *Robert Smithson: Collected Writings*, 15.
14. The map of the Early Jurassic period features the continents Australis, Europa-Angara, Tethys, Gondwanaland, and Atlantis (parts of which cover today's North America); the box-filled Location Diagram for NK 12-7 then shows the part of the western edge of the "Atlantis" continent, the northern part of Utah (in the center of the map) in relation to other parts of the American West (Pocatello, Idaho; Elko, Nevada); moving in still closer, a modern road map shows the way from Brigham City through Promontory through the Golden Spike National Historic Site (and its abandoned railway line) and then along a smaller road (in point of fact, the dirt road that had just been shown), to an unnamed Rozel Point, to the *Spiral Jetty* site, and, finally, on into the Great Salt Lake.
15. Clark Lunberry, "So Much Depends: Printed Matter, Dying Words, and the Entropic Poem," *Critical Inquiry* 30, no. 3 (2004): 627–653. Lunberry points out that Williams was the Passaic-born Smithson's pediatrician. The long aerial scene is viewable at http://www.robertsmithson.com/films/films.htm (accessed June 30, 2014).
16. The linguistic dimensions of Smithson's project are asserted in Craig Owens's two influential essays on Smithson (written in the late 1970s): "Earthwords" and "The Allegorical Impulse: Toward a Theory of Postmodernism," in *Beyond Recognition: Representation, Power, and Culture* (Berkeley: University of California Press, 1994), 40–51, 52–69. But to think of Smithson's earthworks as (or in relation to) a heap of language (or languages) also invites thinking of language as (or in relation to) a heap of earth. This thought process would be in line with Smithson's own declarations about the *materiality* of language: "I'm . . . in favor of a view of language as, not even a fact, but a terrain, a patch of ground within the page that you could extract various meanings from" (Kenneth Baker, "Talking with Robert Smithson," in *Robert Smithson, Spiral Jetty*, 154). For more on Smithson, place, and language, see Lytle Shaw, *Fieldworks: From Place to Site in Postwar Poetry* (Tuscaloosa: University of Alabama Press, 2013).
17. The essay's concluding sentence appears as follows: "The camera shifts to a specimen squeezed flat by the weight of sediments, then the film cuts to the road in Utah" (Robert Smithson, "The Spiral Jetty," in *Robert Smithson, Spiral Jetty*, 13). The essay initially appeared in György Kepes, ed., *Arts of the Environment* (Oxford: Aidan Ellis, 1972), with

photographs reproduced in the spirally unfolding manner that Smithson intended. Referring to his own *Yucatan Mirror Displacements*, in an essay originally published in *Artforum* in 1969, Smithson wrote, "The unnamable tonalities of blue that were once square tide pools of sky have vanished into the camera and now rest in the cemetery of the printed page" ("Incidents of Mirror-Travel in the Yucatan," in *Robert Smithson, Collected Writings*, 97), suggesting that the Beckett novel may have signified for Smithson—even before *Spiral Jetty* was turned into a film—both the metamorphic and the extinct.

18. Pamela Lee, "The Cowboy in the Library," *Bookforum*, December–January 2004–2005, 8.
19. To my knowledge, there has been little or no commentary on Smithson's voice (or mode of reading) in the *Spiral Jetty* film, which seems deliberately deadpan and anti-theatrical. In this sense, it is not insignificant that Smithson should have been drawn to Beckett's fiction rather than his better-known plays.
20. Beckett, *Unnamable*, 293–294.
21. Lynne Cooke, "a position of elsewhere," in *Robert Smithson, Spiral Jetty*, 53; George Baker, "The Cinema Model," in *Robert Smithson, Spiral Jetty*, 84. Deleuze himself has suggested that Beckett's writing is "nowhere" in this sense; drawing on his own debt to Bergson, he emphasizes Beckett's temporal investigations over the spatial. While I am sympathetic to Deleuze's aims in his reading of Beckett, I stress toward the end of this chapter that Smithson helps to reveal a spatial dimension in Beckett's writing (one that by no means privileges it over the temporal).
22. It seems not incidental that Smithson writes "laughs without mirth" so near to mentioning Beckett's *The Unnamable*, a text that may at times provoke a similar response from its readers. Indeed, Theodor Adorno locates this kind of laughter as a crucial aspect of Beckett's theater, and a major reason why the rubric "tragicomedy" does not apply. Adorno further suggests that in "plays like *Godot* and *Endgame* . . . scene[s] in which the protagonists decide to laugh are more the tragic presentation of comedy's fate than they are comic; in the actors' forced laughter, the spectator's mirth vanishes" (*Aesthetic Theory*, trans. Robert Hullot-Kentor [1972; New York: Continuum, 2005], 340).
23. Beckett, *Unnamable*, 291. Beckett's auto-translation is by no means neutral. Any text that renders its opening six words "Où maintenant? Quand maintenant? Qui maintenant?" as "Where now? Who now? When now?"—thereby shifting the question of the subject from a tertiary position to the very middle of a spatiotemporal quandary—raises the question of its own translatability. See Samuel Beckett, *L'innomable* (Paris: Minuit, 1953), 7. In the rest of this chapter, I will refer to the French original when (as here) contextually appropriate.
24. Beckett, *Unnamable*, 414.

25. Smithson drew on other Beckett texts as well. Aside from the quote from "Proust," consider that Murphy (in the novel *Murphy*) speaks of his mind as "a matrix of surds." Smithson liberally uses the word "surd" in "Spiral Jetty" ("The equation of my language remains unstable, a shifting set of coordinates, an arrangement of variables spilling into surds" [8]) and elsewhere. For more on Beckett and set theory, see Reuben J. Ellis, "'Matrix of Surds': Heisenberg's Algebra in Beckett's *Murphy*," *Papers on Language and Literature* 25 (1989): 120–123.
26. Michel Foucault, "What Is an Author?," in *The Essential Foucault: Selections from the Essential Works of Foucault, 1954–1984*, ed. Paul Rabinow and Nikolas Rose (New York: New Press, 2003), 377–391; Giorgio Agamben, "The Author as Gesture," in *Profanations*, trans. Jeff Fort (New York: Zone Books, 2007), 61–72. Part of Agamben's ethical project involves rescuing the "gestural" author/witness from mechanistic conceptions of textuality.
27. Richard Begam, *Samuel Beckett and the End of Modernity* (Stanford, Calif.: Stanford University Press, 1996), 159.
28. Beckett, *Unnamable*, 303.
29. Beckett, *Unnamable*, 304.
30. Among other critics to note Beckett's frequent use of dentally mirroring *M*'s and *W*'s, John Paul Riquelme has suggested that, "in *Company*, Beckett could have presented M and W, like the figures in 'Imagination Dead Imagine,' as man and woman, but male pronouns are applied to both. 'W' could be writer, whose creature 'M,' perhaps W's me, is his double, though orthographically inverted in a curious mirroring" ("The Way of the Chameleon in Iser, Beckett, and Yeats: Figuring Death and the Imaginary in *The Fictive and the Imaginary*," *New Literary History* 31, no. 1 [2000]: 61).
31. According to the AMNH's Web site, "[i]t is one of the most complete pieces of Mesozoic dinosaur remains ever found, and is one of the greatest discoveries in the history of paleontology." In the years since Smithson filmed the scene from *Spiral Jetty* there, the classical vitrines have been replaced by sleeker contemporary glass displays. The room is now called the Hall of Ornithischian Dinosaurs, one of two halls of the museum's David H. Koch Dinosaur Wing. (In addition to their philanthropy toward museums, David H. Koch and his brother Charles G. Koch have financially supported ultraconservative political advocacy groups.)
32. Smithson, "Spiral Jetty," 13.
33. Leo Bersani, *Balzac to Beckett: Center and Circumference in French Fiction* (New York: Oxford University Press, 1970), 24.
34. Beckett, *Unnamable*, 293–294.

35. Smithson explicitly compares this geological history to more recent, extreme forms of what he elsewhere dismissively calls "human history": "Deeper than the ruins of concentration camps are worlds more frightening, worlds more meaningless" ("Art Through the Camera's Eye" [1971], in *Robert Smithson: Collected Writings*, 375).
36. Notably, Smithson changes the elder Joyce's quip to make it even funnier. Where Richard Ellmann has John Joyce saying "The boy seems to have changed a good deal" (quoted in *James Joyce* [Oxford: Oxford University Press, 1982], 614), Smithson has "Well, Jim hasn't changed much." Smithson describes the portrait of Joyce as one of a "spiral ear."
37. Beckett, *Unnamable*, 316.
38. Beckett, *L'innomable*, 50.
39. "If you're walking on the Jetty, you're in a sense thrown out onto an outer edge, and then you move into a kind of interior situation, and in the film I did allude to this, to the prison aspect of the Jetty. Once again, the constriction or concentration exists within the inner coils of the Jetty, whereas on the outer edge you're kind of thrown out, you're aware of the horizons and how they echo through the Jetty" (quoted in Baker, "Cinema Model," 156–158).
40. Beckett, *Unnamable*, 316–317.
41. Roberts, *Mirror Travels*, 139. Roberts recognizes full well the "perpetual slippage of history that Smithson's work suggests," and acknowledges that Smithson, through his work (and as articulated in his many interviews), sought to "pull . . . the bottom out from under history"—a deconstructive bottom-pulling accentuated and celebrated by an earlier generation of Smithson scholarship—but she nevertheless seeks to recuperate a notion of the materially historical (even Hegelian) after its bottoming out. For Roberts, an Americanist, such history is primarily national (or, considering her chapter on the *Yucatan Mirror Displacements*, continental) in scope: she reads the *Spiral Jetty* earthwork as in a kind of dialogue with the Golden Spike National Historic Site, and with the Golden Spike's rhetoric of national expansion ("repeated" on the hundredth anniversary celebration, which took place in the year Smithson secured his Rozel Point lease). While Roberts's attempt to (re-)ground Smithson historically is admirable, and a project to whose aims I am sympathetic (Nico Israel, "Non-Site Unseen: How I Spent My Summer Vacation," *Artforum*, September 2002, 172–177, which also reads *Spiral Jetty* in relation to Golden Spike), I suggest here that the proper understanding of the dimensions of Smithson's historicity hinges at least in part on an understanding of Beckett's notion of historicity, which itself points beyond the merely national, and responds to the perilous ambivalences of the "global."
42. Beckett, *Unnamable*, 317. Curiously, in the original French, Beckett had written of the Indonesian island of Sumatra, not Java. See *L'innommable*, 51.

43. That Smithson recognized the link between Cartesian thought and Beckett is clear. In a 1973 interview, Smithson claimed that Beckett "sees the burnt-out aspects of the Cartesian world" (Moira Roth, "Interview with Robert Smithson," in *Robert Smithson*, 90). For Smithson, as perhaps for Beckett, such "burn out" is not necessarily to be construed negatively.
44. W. B. Yeats, *A Vision*, vol. 13 of *The Collected Works of W. B. Yeats*, ed. Catherine E. Paul and Margaret Mills Harper (New York: Simon and Shuster, 2008). James Joyce himself parodies the gyres in various episodes in *Finnegans Wake*, a text for which Beckett famously served as an amanuensis. In quoting Beckett directly after citations pertaining to Yeats and Joyce, Smithson, in his notes, perceptively reveals an important trajectory not only of Irish modernist literature, but of the "Metamorphosis of Spirals" in modernist literature more generally. For a recent take on the intricate way Beckett acknowledges and undermines Yeats, see Minako Okamuro, "Words and Music; . . . but the clouds . . . and Yeats's 'The Tower,'" in *Beckett at 100: Revolving It All*, ed. Linda Ben Zvi and Angela Moorjani (Oxford: Oxford University Press, 2008), 217–229.
45. It is thus a rather unpleasant, olfactory version of Deleuzian deterritorialization. See the "Introduction: Rhizome," in Gilles Deleuze and Félix Guattari, *A Thousand Plateaus: Capitalism and Schizophrenia*, trans. Brian Massumi (Minneapolis: University of Minnesota Press, 1991).
46. Theodor Adorno, "Trying to Understand Endgame," in *Notes to Literature*, ed. Rolf Tiedemann, trans. Shierry Weber Nicholsen (New York: Columbia University Press, 1991), 1:37–54.
47. Smithson himself used the term "dialectics" as loosely (and frequently) as he did "entropy," distinguishing, for example, his own practice from what he viewed as Marcel Duchamp's more "mechanical" one (which he dismisses as "joke art," a claim I addressed in my notes to chapter 4). See, especially, Roth, "Interview with Robert Smithson," 81–94, passim. In "Spiral Jetty," he claims that when he first saw the northern end of the Great Salt Lake, "[his] dialectics of site and nonsite whirled into an indeterminate state."
48. Beckett, *Unnamable*, 317.
49. Beckett, *Unnamable*, 317.
50. Note again Beckett's early claim that Joyce's writing in what would become *Finnegans Wake* "is not about something; it is that something itself" ("Dante . . . Bruno. Vico . . Joyce," in *Our Exagmination Round His Factification for Incamination of Work in Progress: A Symposium* [1929; New York: New Directions, 1972], 14), a maxim that certainly applies to Beckett's own work.
51. Smithson, "Artist and Politics," 134.

52. Smithson does not name the site, but it is almost certainly the Salar de Uyuni in the southwest of the Andean country.
53. Roberts correctly notes, concerning Smithson's *Yucatan Mirror Displacements*, that the artist "could not have been unaware of the alarming rise in guerilla and terrorist violence in Guatemala. . . . Even the primordial junglescapes of the mirror displacements must have seemed synonymous with guerilla warfare to a Vietnam-era artist" (*Mirror Travels*, 111), but to my knowledge this is her sole direct reference to Vietnam. Similarly, in *Robert Smithson: Learning from New Jersey*, Reynolds links the *Partially Buried Woodshed* (1970) to the (subsequent, 1970) Kent State demonstrations/massacre, but, similarly, the words "Vietnam" and "Indochina" are largely absent from her study of Smithson.
54. Smithson, "Spiral Jetty," 12.
55. Concerning Smithson's tendentious, though etymologically correct, deployment of the term "hypothetically," see again the beginning of *The Unnamable*: "Where now? Who now? When now? Unquestioning. I, say I. Unbelieving. Questions, hypotheses, call them that."
56. Martin Harries, in response to the essay version of this chapter, suggests that Smithson's invocation of "flesh-eaters walking through what is today is called Indochina" conveys something even starker than napalm: that U.S. soldiers might themselves be the walking dead flesh-eaters, reincarnated versions of the fossilized raptors that so fascinated Smithson.
57. Several of Beckett's recent critics have attempted to read the Irish author's work in relation to colonial—particularly Irish colonial—history. Yet Beckett seems almost to want to distance or inoculate himself from association with postcolonial criticism, avant la lettre: "I am a kind of tenth-rate Toussaint l'Ouverture, that's what they're counting on" (*Unnamable*, 349). There is a difference, as I hope to establish elsewhere, between a "postcolonial" Beckett and the more (but not quite) "global" Beckett I am trying to begin to develop here. I explore Beckett's references to Toussaint l'Ouverture—whose very name cannot not have been interesting to Beckett, who himself had translated several essays for Nancy Cunard's *Negro: An Anthology* (1934)—in another context.
58. Miriam Hansen, "Traces of Transgression in *Apocalypse Now*," *Social Text* 3 (1980): 125.
59. "Thiokol" is, unlike Morton, not a proper name; it derives from the Greek words for sulfur (*theio*) and glue (*kola*). While it is not clear that Smithson himself was aware of the existence of the plant, it is easy to imagine that he would have embraced the (well-nigh futurist) relation between art and destruction that it exposes. On the other side of the lake, and still in what Smithson called "Mormon Country," is the Deseret chemical depot, which housed (and still reportedly houses) the United State's largest stockpile of biochemical weapons. It is not insignificant that on any visit to *Spiral Jetty* (as earthwork), the Thiokol plant

precedes the Golden Spike National Historic Site, where the Central Pacific and Union Pacific Railroads were united in 1869. See Israel, "Non-Site Unseen"; and Roberts, *Mirror Travels*. As Roberts points out, the 1969 Golden Spike ceremony sought to replicate the highly publicized 1869 ceremony, and both events took place in periods of national disunity. The Golden Spike National Historic Site was established in 1965.

60. The earlier film, *Swamp* (1969), which Smithson made with his wife, Nancy Holt, in the same year as the *Spiral Jetty* earthwork, similarly renders Vietnam a kind of spectral site. In the film, shot in southern New Jersey, reeds crash against the camera lens, creating a sense of dislocation and confusion. The effect was produced by having Holt walk through the swamp with her camera strapped on but not seeing where she was going, while Smithson gave her verbal instructions that he recorded. "Indochina" is never mentioned, but just as the helicopter (in the *Spiral Jetty* film) presents one iconic view of war, the swamp (in *Swamp*) presents an uncannily familiar topos.

IN CONCLUSION

1. Giorgio Agamben, *Homo Sacer: Sovereign Power and Bare Life*, trans. Daniel Heller-Roazen (Stanford, Calif.: Stanford University Press, 1998), 12 [16].
2. Rosalind Krauss, "Grids," in *The Originality of the Avant-Garde and Other Modernist Myths* [Cambridge, Mass.: MIT Press, 1986], 9.
3. A brief word on my method here: whereas chapters 3, 4, and 5 each pair one literary and one visual-art text, in this conclusion I am exploring, in less sustained fashion, four texts: two literary (de Campos's poem and Sebald's novel) and two art (Kentridge's and Smith and Ortega's films). This is in part because none of these texts has yet achieved the "monumental" status of those earlier-century works, and consequently may not constellate through the kinds of juxtapositions pursued earlier, and in part because the very status of "literature" and "art" have changed, partly because of economic and cultural globalization in the post–Cold War period.
4. According to the Marian Goodman Gallery, which represents Kentridge, the *Ubu* project began with a portfolio of eight etchings, followed by *Ubu and the Truth Commission* (1997), a theatrical production that was directed and animated by Kentridge. It also includes the figurative-drawing works on paper *Cartographer*, *The Sleeper*, *Flagellant*, *Project Drawing Figure 1 (Man with the Microphone)*, *Project Drawing Figure 2 (Listener)*, three drawings of *Cyclist: Ubu on a Bicycle*, and a series of four large etchings entitled *Sleeper* (1997). In Kentridge's play, Ubu briefly becomes a member of the South African special forces. The film version of *Ubu Tells the Truth* was shot on 35mm film and transferred to video. *Ubu*

Tells the Truth and *Shadow Procession,* although two separate films made two years apart, have been shown together in numerous exhibitions, including the large-scale retrospective at the Museum of Modern Art in New York.

5. For a thorough consideration of the implications of Kentridge's technique, see Rosalind Krauss, "'The Rock': William Kentridge's Drawings for Projection," *October* 92 (2000): 3–35.
6. Jeremy Sarkin-Hughes, *Carrots and Sticks: The TRC and the South African Amnesty Process* (Oxford: Hart, 2004), 219.
7. Giorgio Agamben, *Remnants of Auschwitz: The Witness and the Archive,* trans. Daniel Heller-Roazen (New York: Zone, 1999), 34.
8. It is not incidental that Agamben's tracing of the history of the camp as "nomos of the modern" begins with the so-called Boer War, in which Afrikaners were rounded into what were called concentration camps.
9. According to the Goodman Gallery, these shadows were created by the intrusion during the filming process of Kentridge's son and his family's house cat.
10. According to the Goodman Gallery, this Ubu was played by Adrian Kohler from the Handspring Puppet Company, which made all the puppets. Kohler appears in a large Ubu suit, which was used both in the film and during the aforementioned stage production. Ubu also appears in Kentridge's more recent work of the 2010s.
11. Quoted in Giorgio Agamben, "Beyond Human Rights," in *Means Without End: Notes on Politics,* trans. Vincenzo Binetti and Cesare Casarino (Minneapolis: University of Minnesota Press, 2000), 13.
12. Joseph R. Slaughter, *Human Rights, Inc.: The World Novel, Narrative Form, and International Law* (New York: Fordham University Press, 2007).
13. Augusto de Campos, "Poesia concreta: Um manifesto," *AD-Arquitetura e Decoração* 20 (1956). The essay was republished in *Teoria da poesia concreta,* ed. Augusto de Campos, Décio Pignatari, and Haroldo de Campos (São Paulo: Invenção, 1965).
14. De Campos, "Poesia concreta."
15. De Campos, "Poesia concreta."
16. De Campos, "Poesia concreta." De Campos has published translations into Portuguese of texts by Mallarmé, Mayakovsky, Cummings, Stein, Joyce, and, especially, Pound.
17. De Campos, "Poesia concreta." According to de Campos, in an interview from the early 1990s, "Concrete poets can be distinguished from their antecedents by the radicalization and condensation of the means of structuring a poem, on the horizon of the means of communication of the second half of the century." Other comparisons include "greater constructive rigor in relation to the graphic experiences of Futurists and Dadaists; greater

concentration of vocabulary; emphasis on the nondiscursive character of poetry, suppression or relativization of syntactic links; making explicit the materiality of language in its visual and sonorous dimensions; free passage between verbal and nonverbal levels" (Roland Greene, "From Dante to the Post-Concrete: An Interview with Augusto de Campos," *Harvard Library Bulletin* 3, no. 2 [1992]: 34–35).

18. Marjorie Perloff explains that the name *Noigandres*

> was taken from Ezra Pound's Canto XX, in which the poet seeks out the venerable Provençal specialist Emil Lévy, a professor at Freiburg, and asks him what the word *noigandres* (used by the great troubadour poet Arnaut Daniel) means, only to be told by Lévy that for six months he has been trying without success to find the answer: "Noigandres, NOIgandres! / You know for seex mons of my life / Effery night when I go to bett, I say to myself: / Noigandres, eh *noigandres*, Now what the DEFFIL can that mean!" But despite this colorful disclaimer with its phonetic spellings, "Old Lévy" had, in fact, gone on to crack the difficult nut in question: the word, he suggested, could be divided in two—*enoi* (*ennui*) and *gandres* from *gandir* (to ward off, to remove)—and in its original troubadour context, the word referred to an odor (probably of a flower) that could drive ennui away. (*Unoriginal Genius: Poetry by Other Means in the New Century* [Chicago: University of Chicago Press, 2010], 66)

19. As a prefix, *pós* invokes the words *pós-modernismo*, *pós-utopico*, or what de Campos calls, in the neologistic title of a poem, also from 1984, "Pós-tudo"—"after everything." For a cogent treatment of the debates in Brazilian poetry circles around de Campos's claims about "Pós-tudo," see Charles A. Perrone, *Seven Faces: Brazilian Poetry Since Modernism* (Durham, N.C.: Duke University Press, 1996), 149–182.
20. In a 1913 essay on cognates of the word солнце (*solntse*; Russian for "sun"), Khlebnikov speculates that "the syllable *so* [with] is [[in]] a field that encompasses *son* [sleep], *solntse* [sun], *sila* [strength], *solod* [malt], *slovo* [word], *sladkii* [sweet], *soi* ["calm," in the Macedonian dialect], *sad* [garden], *selo* [settlement], *sol'* [salt], *slyt'* [to be reputed], [[and]] *syn* [son]." In her analysis of this speculation, Perloff shows that "to make the relationships more vivid, Khlebnikov sketches them as the rays of a sun bearing the key word 'SO.'" "Logically," she notes, "the relationship between these verbal units is largely arbitrary—what does salt have to do with sun?—but poetically, Khlebnikov shows, they can be made to inhabit the same universe" (*Unoriginal Genius*, 58). It is worth noting that de Campos's *SOS* also derives much of its energy from the phoneme "SO."
21. In Argentinian Spanish, the word *sos* signifies "you are." Aside from the aforementioned Khlebnikov, another acknowledged precursor for *SOS* is the Bolivian-born poet Eugen

Gomringer's concrete poem "Silencio" (1953), which features repeated iterations of the word *silencio*, with a rectangular blank space in the center of the poem.

22. Although Duchamp is not listed by name in the precursor-blessing section of "Theory of Concrete Poetry," he is surely one of the "futurist-dadaist" experimenters referred to by de Campos. In 1976, de Campos published an art-critical poem-essay/book called *Reduchamp*, with ideograms by Julio Plaza. Not incidentally, the Portuguese "de campos" is very nearly a direct translation of the French "du champ."
23. Giorgio Agamben, *The Coming Community*, trans. Michael Hardt (Minneapolis: University of Minnesota Press, 1993), 1; *La comunità che viene* (1990; Torino: Bollati Boringhieri, 2001), 9.
24. Agamben, *Coming Community*, 83; *La comunità che viene*, 66.
25. As Perrone demonstrates in *Seven Faces*, much of concrete poetic production must be understood in the context of the Brazilian dictatorship, which lasted from 1964 until 1985.
26. In numerous interviews, Augusto de Campos and his brother Haroldo de Campos have rejected the implication that literary works from Brazil must follow the contours of national allegory prescribed by Fredric Jameson in "Third-World Literature in the Era of Multinational Capitalism" (1986). Haroldo de Campos has suggested different international routes for literature to travel.
27. The spiral is also featured in de Campos's poems "Caracol" (Snail, 1960), and "Poema-bomba" (1983), both of which were made into short animated digital films in the mid-1990s.
28. According to Melanie Smith, the video was originally shot in color, and then changed to black-and-white in postproduction to give it what she has called an "archival" feeling (correspondence with author, February 2, 2013).
29. Smith has claimed that the soundtrack is meant to convey the "leftovers of what once was" (correspondence with author, February 2, 2013).
30. Smith, correspondence with author, February 2, 2013.
31. Over three thousand maquiladoras countrywide employ approximately 1.5 million people. The majority are found in areas of northern Mexico that share a border with the United States, but there are around fifty in Mexico City, many near the international airport. Since 2000, lower costs of offshore assembly in China and some Central American countries have caused employment in maquiladoras to decline. See Marjorie Hodges Shaw, *Economic Determinants of Demand for Maquiladora Export from Mexico to the United States and Canada* (Charleston, S.C.: BiblioLabsII, 2011). For an immensely important fictional treatment of maquiladoras, see Roberto Bolaño's novel *2666* (2004).
32. Mexico, National Institute of Statistics and Geography (INEGI).

33. Robert Smithson, "Incidents of Mirror-Travel in the Yucatan," in *Robert Smithson: The Collected Writings*, ed. Jack Flam (Berkeley: University of California Press, 1996), 119.
34. Walter Benjamin, "The Work of Art in the Age of Its Technical Reproducibility," in *Illuminations: Essays and Reflections*, ed. Hannah Arendt, trans. Harry Zohn (New York: Schocken, 1969), 239.
35. Michel Foucault, "The Confession of the Flesh," trans. Alain Grosrichard, in *Power/Knowledge: Selected Interviews and Other Writings*, ed. Colin Gordon (New York: Harvester Press, 1980), 194–195.
36. Giorgio Agamben, *"What Is an Apparatus?" and Other Essays*, trans. David Kishik and Stefan Pedatella (Stanford, Calif.: Stanford University Press, 2009), 14.
37. For more on "gesture," a crucial concept in Agamben's writing, see, especially, *Means Without End*. Note that Agamben's catalogue of "gestures and opinions" (probably unintentionally) invokes the title of Alfred Jarry's *Gestes et opinions du docteur Faustroll, pataphysicien* (1898), discussed in chapter 2.
38. Eric L. Santner, *On Creaturely Life: Rilke, Benjamin, Sebald* (Chicago: University of Chicago Press, 2009), xix.
39. Santner, *On Creaturely Life*, xx.
40. "Schwerer ist es, das Gedächtnis der Namenlosen zu ehren als das der Berühmten. Dem Gedächtnis der Namenlosen ist die historische Konstruktion geweiht [It is far harder to honor the memory of the nameless than that of the famous. . . . History is consecrated to the memory of the nameless]" (Walter Benjamin, in *Abhandlungen*, vol. 1.3 of *Gesammelte Schriften*, ed. Hermann Schweppenhäuser and Rolf Tiedemann [Frankfurt: Suhrkamp, 1974], 1241 [my translation]).
41. Because attempting to account for these various narrative and affective strands would require greater detail and nuance than can be supplied in a book's conclusion, I will focus on a few brief narrative excursuses and their accompanying images, mostly from the beginning and end of *The Rings of Saturn*, which in a sense surround Sebald's walking tour, precipitating it and concluding the narrative in the manner of planetary rings, in Saturn's case actually dense spiral waves moving tiny particles of debris.
42. Winfried Georg Sebald, *The Rings of Saturn: An English Pilgrimage*, trans. Michael Hulse (New York: New Directions, 1998), 3; *Die Ringe des Saturn: Ein englische Wallfahrt* (Frankfurt: Eichborn, 1995). The German-born Sebald, who taught in England for over three decades, wrote in German and closely supervised the translations, which are regarded as excellent.
43. Sebald, *Rings of Saturn*, 3.

44. Sebald, *Rings of Saturn*, 4.
45. Sebald, *Rings of Saturn*, 21.
46. Sebald, *Rings of Saturn*, 21.
47. The theme of grid-like containment appears a third time in the opening chapter as the narrator describes seeing "a solitary Chinese quail, evidently in a state of dementia, running to and fro along the edge of the cage and shaking its head every time it was about to turn" (Sebald, *Rings of Saturn*, 36). The accompanying photograph shows a bird looking out of a gridded cage.
48. Sebald, *Rings of Saturn*, 83.
49. Sebald, *Rings of Saturn*, 124.
50. Sebald, *Rings of Saturn*, 124.
51. Sebald, *Rings of Saturn*, 125.
52. Sebald, *Rings of Saturn*, 92.
53. For more on Sebald's aerial views and high vantage points, see Andreas Huyssen, "Rewritings and New Beginnings: W. G. Sebald and the Literature of the Air War," in *Present Pasts: Urban Palimpsests and the Politics of Memory* (Stanford, Calif.: Stanford University Press, 2003), 138–157; Simon Ward, "Ruins and Poetics in the Works of W. G. Sebald," in *W. G. Sebald: A Critical Companion*, ed. J. J. Long and Anne Whitehead (Seattle: University of Washington Press, 2004), 58–71; and Rebecca L. Walkowitz, *Cosmopolitan Style: Modernism Beyond the Nation* (New York: Columbia University Press, 2006), 153–170.
54. Sebald, *Rings of Saturn*, 19.
55. Sebald, *Rings of Saturn*, 19.
56. Sebald, *Rings of Saturn*, 23–24.
57. Sebald, *Rings of Saturn*, 26.
58. David Darby, "Landscape and Memory: Sebald's Redemption of History," in *W. G. Sebald: History–Memory–Trauma*, ed. Scott Denham and Mark McCulloh (Berlin: de Gruyter, 2006), 271.
59. Sebald, *Rings of Saturn*, 151.
60. Sebald, *Rings of Saturn*, 276.
61. Sebald, *Rings of Saturn*, 282.
62. Sebald, *Rings of Saturn*, 290.
63. Sebald, *Rings of Saturn*, 290.
64. Sebald, *Rings of Saturn*, 290.
65. Sebald, *Rings of Saturn*, 294.
66. Sebald, *Rings of Saturn*, 295.

67. Walter Benjamin, *Ursprung des deutschen Trauerspiels*, vol. 1.1 of *Gesammelte Schriften*, ed. Rolf Tiedemann (Frankfurt: Suhrkamp, 1991), 324; *The Origin of German Tragic Drama*, trans. John Osborne (New York: Verso, 1998), 146.
68. Sebald, *Rings of Saturn*, 9.
69. Giorgio Agamben, *The Man Without Content*, trans. Georgia Albert (Stanford, Calif.: Stanford University Press, 1999), 109–110.
70. Agamben, *Man Without Content*, 110.
71. Agamben, *Man Without Content*, 110.
72. Agamben, *Man Without Content*, 110.

ACKNOWLEDGMENTS

I, too, dislike academic writing. But if, with an imperfect contempt for it, having approached the end, at last, of a long and sometimes thankless-seeming project, I imagine myself, however fleetingly, to have found something approaching a "place for the genuine" in it, I acknowledge that this discovery could not have occurred without the support and assistance of the many people and institutions that helped make the project possible. Among them are

- My former teachers, including Peter Brooks, Shoshana Felman, John Guillory, Geoffrey Hartman, Michael Holquist, David Marshall, Craig Owens, Sara Suleri Goodyear, and Samuel Weber, none of whom read a word of this book, but whose insights flashed up in my mind a quarter-century after I attended their classes.
- My students at Hunter College and the City University of New York Graduate Center, Paris VIII: Vincennes-Saint-Denis, Otis College of Art and Design, Bard College Center for Curatorial Studies, and Duke University, who helped give shape to my ideas.
- The Andrew W. Mellon Foundation; the president, provost, and deans of Hunter College, CUNY; and the PSC-CUNY/CUNY Research Foundation, which each granted me generous funding for the research and writing of the book and for subventing the images herein.

▸ The organizers of and fellow participants on numerous panels and roundtables at Modern Language Association, Modernist Studies Association, and American Comparative Literature Association annual conferences, at which I first tried out many of the ideas that made their way into this book.

▸ My colleagues at the CUNY Graduate Center who participated on the Committee on Globalization and Social Change's "Globalization and Temporality" yearlong seminar, who challenged me to clarify the geopolitical stakes of my argument.

▸ The artists, writers, and scholars at the Instituto Superior de Arte in Havana, Cuba; the Centre for Modernist Studies at Sussex University in Brighton, England; the Modernist Studies Group at Harvard University; the English and Comparative Literature Departments at Oklahoma State University; and the Universidad de Antioquia/Museo de Arte Moderno in Medellín, Colombia, who invited me to speak about spirals at various stages of this project.

▸ Research assistants Iemanja Brown and Samuel Gold; editorial assistant Whitney Johnson; copy editor Kerri Cox Sullivan; and senior editor Irene Pavitt and senior designer Lisa Hamm, each of whom attended so assiduously to the words and to the pictures that appear in this book.

▸ Friends and colleagues who read parts of the manuscript and offered editorial suggestions or emotional support, including Betty Bederson, Richard Begam, Sandy Broyard, Meg Cranston, Catherine Dana, Paolo Fasoli, Laura Frost, Chris GoGwilt, Adam Green, Matt Hart, Richard Kaye, Damian Lanigan, Andrew Leitch, Joanne Mariner, Joe O'Neill, Marjorie Perloff, John Paul Riquelme, Hanneline Rogeberg, Victoria Rosner, and Thad Ziolkowski, with special thanks to Emily O. Wittman for her eagle eye and editorial flair, and to Jennifer Wicke, for her unwavering support and invaluable friendship.

▸ The following people/publications that allowed me to republish parts of this manuscript that appear elsewhere: Heesok Chang/Blackwell Publishing, Anthony Uhlmann/*The Journal of Beckett Studies*, and Mariangela Méndez Prencke/Colombian Ministry of Culture.

▸ The editors of the Modernist Latitudes series, Jessica Berman and Paul Saint-Amour, and readers for the press, Jean-Michel Rabaté and Martin Harries, each of whom provided me with superb editorial advice and offered tools for necessary cognitive re-mapping.

▸ Columbia University Press's acquisitions editor, Philip Leventhal, expert shepherd of this project from its incipient stages to its near-completion, whose responsiveness and overall professionalism I cannot praise highly enough.

▸ Steadfast friends Ron Kaye, Matt Hale, and Eric Zucker, and parents, Mickey and Raye Israel, whom I thank for their encouragement, their bewilderment, and their occasionally silly, deflating jokes.

▸ My wife, Bliss Broyard, who has offered her constant love and partnership while providing her own stellar example of writerly patience and persistence.

▸ Finally, and most especially of all, my adored children, Esme and Roman Broyard Israel, who, in the raw material of their youth in all its rawness, have shown me again and again that there are things far more important than the endless fiddling we call writing. This book is for them.

INDEX

Numbers in italics refer to pages on which illustrations appear.